TALIBAN

2 Vols. Set

Volume 1

TALIBAN

2 Vols. Set

Volume 1

N K Verma

MD PUBLICATIONS PVT LTD
NEW DELHI
www.mdppl.com

Published by :

MD Publications Pvt Ltd
"MD House", 11, Darya Ganj,
New Delhi - 110 002
Phone : +91-11-45355555
E-mail : contact@mdppl.com
Website: www.mdppl.com

ISBN: 978-81-7533-270-6 (Set of 2 Vols.)
978-81-7533-271-3 (Vol. 1)

Published and Printed by Mr. Pranav Gupta on behalf of **MD Publications Pvt Ltd** at Times Press, New Delhi.

PREFACE

Talib is an Arabic word, which literally means 'one, who is seeking,' but generally Talib refers to 'someone who is seeking religious knowledge.' Taliban are students of "deeni madrassas" or religious seminaries, which have existed in Afghanistan, the Indian-Subcontinent, and the Central Asia since the arrival of Islam in these areas.

The overwhelming majority of the Taliban movements were ethnic Pashtuns from southern Afghanistan and western Pakistan, along with a smaller number of volunteers from Islamic countries. The Taliban received valuable training, supplies and arms from the Pakistani government, particularly the Inter-Services Intelligence (ISI), and many recruits from madrasahs for Afghan refugees in Pakistan, primarily ones established by the Jamiat Ulema-e-Islam(JUI).

The Taliban movement emerged out of the chaos and uncertainty of the Soviet-Afghan War (1979-1989) and subsequent civil war in Afghanistan. During the 1980s Afghanistan was occupied by the Union of Soviet Socialist Republics (USSR) and ruled by a Soviet-backed government. Afghanistan's long war with the USSR was largely fought by mujahideen (Islamic guerrilla) factions with assistance from the United States; Pakistan also provided places of refuge, military training, and other support. After the Soviets completed their withdrawal in 1989, civil war broke out between the mujahideen factions and the central government and initially enjoyed enormous goodwill from Afghans weary of the corruption, brutality, and the incessant fighting of Mujahideen warlords.

The Taliban's extremely strict and 'anti-modern' ideology has been described as an "innovative form of sharia combining Pashtun tribal codes," or Pashtunwali, with radical Deobandi interpretations of Islam favored by members of the Pakistani fundamentalist Jamiat Ulema-e-Islam (JUI) organization and its splinter groups. However, most of the leaders of the current Taliban regime in Afghanistan have been influenced by the teachings of Islam in Pakistan, where they had migrated with millions of other Afghans after the Soviet invasion. There, they attended religious seminaries or 'madrassas', while many of them also remained active fighting the Soviets in the battlefields. They are the followers of the "Deobandi" school of thought, preached by mullahs (clerics) in Pakistani madrassas.

The initial goals of the Taliban were to disarm the country, end lawlessness and enforce the Islamic law or the Sharia on a united Afghanistan. The Taliban so far have been successful in bringing relative law and order in around 85% of the country that they control. They have done so mainly by disarming and in certain cases by incorporating in their ranks, the previous warring groups. The Taliban ideology was not static and before its capture of Kabul, members of the Taliban talked about stepping aside once a government of "good Muslims" took power and law and order were restored. The decision making process of the Taliban in Kandahar was modeled on the Pashtun tribal council (jirga), together with what was believed to be the early Islamic model. Since 2004, the predominantly Pashtun movement has re-emerged and mounted an effective insurgency against Western forces and the Afghan government. Facing rising international and domestic pressure, Pakistan's military began a campaign against them widely seen as a test of Pakistan's resolve to tackle the insurgency.

I am very grateful to Mr. Pranav Gupta, Director of MD Publications Pvt Ltd, New Delhi, for his kind cooperation and support for this book.

N K Verma

CONTENTS

Vol. 1

Vol. 2

1

The Origins of the Taliban

The Taliban (meaning "students"), also Taleban, is a Sunni Islamist, predominantly Pashtun fundamentalist religious and political movement that governed Afghanistan from 1996 until 2001, when its leaders were removed from power by Northern Alliance and NATO forces. It has regrouped and since 2004 revived as a strong insurgency movement fighting a guerrilla war against the current government of Afghanistan, Pakistan, allied NATO forces participating in Operation Enduring Freedom, and the NATO-led International Security Assistance Force (ISAF). It operates in Afghanistan and the Frontier Tribal Areas of Pakistan. The Taliban movement is headed by Mullah Mohammed Omar.

Mullah Omar's original commanders were "a mixture of former small-unit military commanders and madrasah teachers," and the rank and file made up mostly of Afghan refugees who had studied at Islamic religious schools in Pakistan. The overwhelming majority of the Taliban movement was ethnic Pashtuns from southern Afghanistan and western Pakistan, along with a smaller number of volunteers from Islamic countries or regions in North Africa, the Middle East and the former Soviet Union.

The Taliban received valuable training, supplies and arms from the Pakistani government, particularly the Inter-Services Intelligence (ISI), and many recruits from madrasahs for Afghan refugees in Pakistan, primarily ones established by the

Jamiat Ulema-e-Islam (JUI). Although in control of Afghanistan's capital (Kabul) and much or most of the country for five years, the Taliban regime, which called itself the "Islamic Emirate of Afghanistan", gained diplomatic recognition from only three states: Pakistan, Saudi Arabia, and the United Arab Emirates. The Taliban implemented one of the "strictest interpretations[s] of Sharia law ever seen in the Muslim world".

The word *Taliban* is Pashto, *taliban,* meaning "students", the plural of *talib.* This is a loan word from Arabic *talib,* plus the Indo-Iranian plural ending -an (the Arabic plural being *tullab,* whereas *taliban* is a dual form with the incongruous meaning, to Arabic speakers, of "two students"). Since becoming a loanword in English, *Taliban,* besides a plural noun referring to the group, has also been used as a singular noun referring to an individual. For example, John Walker Lindh has been referred to as "an American Taliban" rather than "an American Talib". In the English language newspapers of Pakistan the word talibans is often used when referring to more than one taliban. The spelling 'Taliban' has come to predominate over 'Taleban' in English.

ORIGIN

The Taliban initially enjoyed enormous good will from Afghans weary of the corruption, brutality, and the incessant fighting of *Mujahideen* warlords. Two contrasting narratives explain the beginnings of the Taliban. One is that the rape and murder of boys and girls from a family traveling to Kandahar or a similar outrage by *Mujahideen* bandits sparked Mullah Omar and his students to vow to rid Afghanistan of these criminals. The other is that the Pakistan-based truck shipping mafia known as the "Afghanistan Transit Trade" and their allies in the Pakistan government, trained, armed, and financed the Taliban to clear the southern road across Afghanistan to the Central Asian Republics of extortionate bandit gangs.

Although there is no evidence that the CIA directly supported the Taliban or Al Qaeda, some basis for military support of the Taliban was provided when, in the early 1980s, the CIA and the ISI (Pakistan's Inter-Services Intelligence agency) provided arms to Afghans resisting the Soviet invasion of Afghanistan, and the ISI assisted the process of gathering radical Muslims from around the world to fight against the Soviets. Osama Bin Laden was one of the key players in organizing training camps for the foreign Muslim volunteers.

The U.S. poured funds and arms into Afghanistan, and "by 1987, 65,000 tons of U.S.-made weapons and ammunition a year were entering the war." The Taliban were based in the Helmand, Kandahar, and Uruzgan regions and were overwhelmingly ethnic Pashtuns and predominantly Durrani Pashtuns. The first major military activity of the Taliban was in October-November 1994 when they marched from Maiwand in southern Afghanistan to capture Kandahar City and the surrounding provinces, losing only a few dozen men.

Starting with the capture of a border crossing and a huge ammunition dump from warlord Gulbuddin Hekmatyar, a few weeks later they freed "a convoy trying to open a trade route from Pakistan to Central Asia" from another group of warlords attempting to extort money. In the next three months this hitherto "unknown force" took control of twelve of Afghanistan's 34 provinces, with *Mujahideen* warlords often surrendering to them without a fight and the "heavily armed population" giving up their weapons. By September 1996 they had captured Afghanistan's capital, Kabul.

TALIBAN IDEOLOGY AND ITS APPLICATION

The Taliban's extremely strict and "anti-modern" ideology has been described as an "innovative form of sharia combining Pashtun tribal codes," or Pashtunwali, with radical Deobandi interpretations of Islam favored by members of the Pakistani fundamentalist Jamiat Ulema-e-Islam (JUI) organization and its splinter groups. Also contributing to the admixture was the Wahhabism of their Saudi financial benefactors, and the jihadism and pan-Islamism of sometime comrade-in-arms Osama bin Laden. Their ideology was a departure from the Islamism of the anti-Soviet *Mujahideen* rulers they replaced who tended to be mystical Sufis, traditionalists, or radical Islamicists inspired by the Ikhwan.

Sharia law was interpreted to ban a wide variety of activities hitherto lawful in Afghanistan. Critics complained that most Afghans were non-Pashtuns who followed a different, less strict and less intrusive interpretation of Islam. Despite their similarity to the Wahhabis, the Taliban did not eschew all traditional popular practices. They did not destroy the graves of *pirs* (holy men) and emphasized dreams as a means of revelation.

Taliban have been described as both anti-nationalist and Pushtun nationalist. According to journalist Ahmed Rashid, at least in the first years of their rule, they followed Deobandi and Islamist anti-nationalist belief and opposed "tribal and feudal structures," eliminating traditional tribal or feudal leaders from "leadership roles." According to Ali A. Jalali and Mr. Lester W. Grau, the Taliban "received extensive support from Pashtuns across the country who thought that the movement might restore their national dominance. Even Pashtun intellectuals in the West, who seriously differ with the Taliban on many issues, expressed support for the movement on purely ethnic grounds."

In any case, the Taliban were very reluctant to share power, and since their ranks were overwhelmingly Pashtun the spread of their rule to non-Pashtun areas of Afghanistan meant Pashtun rule over non-Pashtuns. At the national level, "all senior Tajik, Uzbek and Hazara bureaucrats" were replaced "with Pashtuns, whether qualified or not. As a result of this loss of expertise, the ministries by and large ceased to function." In local units of government like city councils of Kabul or Herat, Taliban loyalists, not locals, dominated, even when the Pashto-speaking Taliban could not communicate with the local Persian-speaking Afghans (roughly half of the population of Afghanistan spoke Dari or other non-Pashtun tongues.) Critics complained this "lack of local representation in urban administration made the Taliban appear as an occupying force."

Like Wahhabi and other Deobandis, the Taliban do not consider Shias to be Muslims. The Taliban also declared the Hazara ethnic group, which totaled almost 10% of Afghanistan's population, "not Muslims." Along with being very strict, the Taliban were averse to debate on doctrine with other Muslims. "The Taliban did not allow even Muslim reporters to question [their] edicts or to discuss interpretations of the Qur'an." As they established their power the Taliban created a new form of Islamic radicalism that spread beyond the borders of Afghanistan, mostly to Pakistan. By 1998-1999 Taliban-style groups in the Pashtun belt, and to an extent in Pakistan-administered Kashmir, "were banning TV and videos and forcing people, particularly women to adapt to the Taliban dress code and way of life."

GOVERNANCE

The Taliban government has been described as "a secret society run by Kandaharis ... mysterious, secretive, and dictatorial." They did not hold elections, as their spokesman explained:

> The Sharia does not allow politics or political parties. That is why we give no salaries to officials or soldiers, just food, clothes, shoes and weapons. We want to live a life like the Prophet lived 1400 years ago and jihad is our right. We want to recreate the time of the Prophet and we are only carrying out what the Afghan people have wanted for the past 14 years.

Instead of an election, their leader's legitimacy came from "Bay'ah" or oath of allegiance in imitation of the Prophet and the first four Caliphs. On 4 April 1996, Mullah Omar had "the Cloak of the Prophet Mohammed," taken from its shrine "for the first time in 60 years." Wrapping himself in the relic, he appeared on the roof of a building in the center of Kandahar while hundreds of Pashtun mullahs below shouted "Amir al-Mu'minin!" (Commander of the Faithful) in a *de facto* pledge of support.

Also in keeping with the governance of early Muslims was a lack of state institutions or "a methodology for command

and control" standard today internationally even among non-Westernized states. The Taliban didn't issue "press releases, policy statements or hold regular press conferences," and of course the outside world and most Afghans didn't even know what they looked like, since photography was banned. Their regular army resembled "a lashkar or traditional tribal militia force" with only 25,000 to 30,000 men, these being added to as the need arose.

Cabinet ministers and deputies were mullahs with a "madrassa education." Several of them, such as the Minister of Health and Governor of the State bank, were primarily military commanders who left their administrative posts to fight when needed. If and when military reverses trapped them behind lines or led to their deaths, this created "even greater chaos" in the national administration. In the Ministry of Finance there was no budget or "qualified economist or banker." Cash to finance Taliban war efforts was collected and dispersed by Mullah Omar without book-keeping.

Business dealings

In 1997, the Taliban and Unocal had meetings in Texas to negotiate arrangements for CentGas to build a gas pipeline from Turkmenistan to Pakistan. Reportedly, a deal was struck but later failed. The cause of the failure was rumored to be competing negotiations with Bridas, an Argentinian company.

Swat's emerald mines 2009

The emerald mines in Pakistan's Swat valley (not a tribal area) have been taken over by the Taliban which has taken control of the once 'Switzerland of Pakistan' a popular tourist area for skiers. While the government of Pakistan did not react to the move, the Taliban has an agreement with the mining labor of the region wherein the Taliban deduct one-third of the miners' yield while the costs are shared equally by both. The Taliban does not take part in the mining operations.

Consistency

The Taliban ideology was not static. Before its capture of Kabul, members of the Taliban talked about stepping aside once a government of "good Muslims" took power and law and order were restored. The decision making process of the Taliban in Kandahar was modeled on the Pashtun tribal council (*jirga*), together with what was believed to be the early Islamic model. Discussion was followed by a building of a consensus by the believers.

However, as the Taliban's power grew, decisions were made by Mullah Omar without consulting the *jirga* and without Omar's visiting other parts of the country. He visited the capital, Kabul, only twice while in power. Taliban spokesman Mullah Wakil explained:

> Decisions are based on the advice of the Amir-ul Momineen. For us consultation is not necessary. We believe that this is in line with the Sharia. We abide by the Amir's view even if he alone takes this view. There will not be a head of state. Instead there will be an Amir al-Mu'minin. Mullah Omar will be the highest authority and the government will not be able to implement any decision to which he does not agree. General elections are incompatible with Sharia and therefore we reject them.

In 1999, Omar issued a decree stating the Buddha statues at Bamyan would be protected because Afghanistan had no Buddhists, implying idolatry would not be a problem. But in March 2001 they were destroyed after the previous decision was reversed with a decree stating that "all the statues around Afghanistan must be destroyed."

CRITICISM OF IDEOLOGY

The Taliban were criticized for their strictness toward those who disobeyed the (Bid'ah) rule. Some Muslims complained that many Taliban prohibitions – such as bans on clapping during sports events; kite flying; beard trimming; or sports for women – had no validity in the Qur'an or sharia. Another source of objection was that the Taliban called their 20% tax on truckloads of opium "zakat," when zakat is limited to 2.5% of the zakat-payers' disposable income.

The bestowing of the title of Amir al-Mu'minin on Muhammad Omar was criticized on the grounds that he lacked scholarly learning, tribal pedigree, or connections to the Prophet's family. Sanction for the title required the support of all of the country's ulema, whereas only some 1200 Pashtun Taliban-supporting Mullahs had declared Omar the Amir. "No Afghan had adopted the title since 1834, when King Dost Mohammed Khan assumed the title before he declared jihad against the Sikh kingdom in Peshawar. But Dost Mohammed was fighting foreigners, while Omar had declared jihad against other Afghans."

Explanation of ideology

Jamiat Ulema-e-Islam (JUI) was important to the Taliban because the "vast majority" of its rank and file and most of the leadership, (though not Mullah Omar), were Qur'anic students who had studied at madrassas set up for Afghan refugees, usually by the JUI. The leader of JUI, Maulana Fazal-ur-Rehman, was a political ally of Benazir Bhutto. After Bhutto became Prime Minister, Rehman "had access to the government, the army and the ISI," whom he influenced to help the Taliban. Journalist Ahmed Rashid suggests that the devastation and hardship of the war against the Soviet Union and the civil war that followed was another factor influencing the ideology of the Taliban.

The young rank and file Taliban were Qur'anic students in Afghan refugee camps whose teachers were often "barely literate," and did not include scholars learned in the finer points of Islamic law and history. The refugee students, brought up in a totally male society, not only had no education in mathematics, science, history or geography, but also had no traditional skills of farming, herding, or neither handicraft-making, nor even knowledge of their tribal and clan lineages.

In such an environment, war meant employment, peace unemployment. Domination of women was an affirmation of manhood. For their leadership rigid fundamentalism was a matter not merely of principle, but of political survival. Taliban leaders "repeatedly told" Rashid "that if they gave women greater freedom or a chance to go to school, they would lose the support of their rank and file."

LIFE UNDER THE TALIBAN REGIME

Sharia law was interpreted to ban a wide variety of activities hitherto lawful in Afghanistan: employment, education and sports for women, movies, television, videos, music, dancing, hanging pictures in homes, clapping during sports events, kite flying, and beard trimming. One Taliban list of prohibitions included: Pork, pig, pig oil, anything made from human hair, satellite dishes, cinematography, and equipment that produces the joy of music, pool tables, chess, masks, alcohol, tapes, computers, VCRs, television, anything that propagates sex and is full of music, wine, lobster, nail polish, firecrackers, statues, sewing catalogs, pictures, Christmas cards.

Men were required to have a beard extending farther than a fist clamped at the base of the chin. On the other hand, they had to wear their head hair short. Men were also required to wear a head covering. Possession was forbidden of depictions of living things, whether drawings, paintings or photographs, stuffed animals, and dolls.

These rules were issued by the Ministry for the Promotion of Virtue and Suppression of Vice (PVSV) and enforced by its "religious police," a concept thought to be borrowed from the Wahhabis. In newly conquered towns hundreds of religious police beat offenders (typically men without beards and women who were not wearing their *burqas* properly) with long sticks. Theft was punished by the amputation of a hand, rape and murder by public execution. Married adulterers were stoned to death. In Kabul, punishments were carried out in front of crowds in the city's former soccer stadium.

TREATMENT OF WOMEN

Women in particular were targets of the Taliban's restrictions. They were prohibited from working; from wearing clothing regarded as "stimulating and attractive," including the "Iranian chador," (viewed as insufficiently complete in its covering); from taking a taxi without a "close male relative" (*mahram*); washing clothes in streams; or having their measurements taken by tailors.

Employment for women was restricted to the medical sector, since male medical personnel were not allowed to examine women. One result of the banning of employment of women by the Taliban was the closing down in places like Kabul of primary schools not only for girls but for boys, because almost all the teachers there were women. Women were also not permitted to attend co-educational schools; in practice, this prevented the vast majority of young women and girls in Afghanistan from receiving even a primary education.

Women were made to wear the *burqa*, a traditional dress covering the entire body except for a small screen to see out of. Taliban restrictions became more severe after they took control of the capital. In February 1998, religious police forced all women off the streets of Kabul and issued new regulations ordering "householders to blacken their windows, so women would not be visible from the outside." Home schools for girls, which had been allowed to continue, were forbidden. In June 1998, the Taliban stopped all women from attending general hospitals, leaving the use of one all-women hospital in Kabul. There were many reports of Muslim women being beaten by the Taliban for violating their version of the Sharia.

While in power in Afghanistan, the Taliban became notorious internationally for their treatment of women. Their stated aim was to create "secure environments where the chasteness and dignity of women may once again be sacrosanct," reportedly based on Pashtunwali beliefs about living in purdah. Women were forced to wear the *burqa* in public, because, according to a Taliban spokesman, "the face of a woman is a source of corruption" for men not related to them.

They were not allowed to work. They were not allowed to be educated after the age of eight, and until then were permitted only to study the Qur'an. Women seeking an education were forced to attend underground schools such as the Golden Needle Sewing School, where they and their teachers risked execution if caught. They were not allowed to be treated by male doctors unless accompanied by a male chaperone, which led to illnesses remaining untreated. They faced public flogging and execution for violations of the Taliban's laws. The Taliban allowed and in some cases encouraged marriage for girls under the age of 16. Amnesty International reported that 80 per cent of Afghan marriages were considered to be by force.

GENDER POLICIES

From the age of eight, women were not allowed to be in direct contact with men, other than a close blood relative, husband, or in-law. Other restrictions were:

- Women should not appear in the streets without a blood relative or without wearing a *Burqa* (also Burkha, Burka or Burqua).
- Women should not wear high-heeled shoes as no man should hear a woman's footsteps lest it excite him.
- Women must not speak loudly in public as no stranger should hear a woman's voice.
- All ground and first floor residential windows should be painted over or screened to prevent women being visible from the street. A Taliban representative explained that "the face of a woman is a source of corruption for men who are not related to them".
- The photographing or filming of women was banned as was displaying pictures of females in newspapers, books, shops or the home.
- The modification of any place names that included the word "women." For example, "women's garden" was renamed "spring garden".
- Women were forbidden to appear on the balconies of their apartments or houses.
- Ban on women's presence on radio, television or at public gatherings of any kind.

DRESS CODE

Before its prescription, the *burqa* was just one of a choice of hijab. Its use generally occurred in urban areas to preserve female modesty and protect them from being coveted by other men. The Taliban decree that the *burqa* must be worn on public outings was unpopular with the more cosmopolitan Afghan women, one of whom described it as "a moving prison...The Taliban want to steal my face, forbid us all our faces." Negotiating and navigating busy urban areas in a *burqa* could be hazardous due to impeded vision and hearing, and the voluminous cloth made the threat of exposing skin if the wearer should stumble a legitimate fear.

The *burqa* also proved impractical for rural women as it interferes with physical work in the fields and care of livestock. Reports state that enforcement varied between districts, as rural, nomadic and even some women in Herat suffered no negative reprisals for simply covering their heads with large scarves and leaving their faces visible. In Kabul enforcement was more stringent and physical punishment was a very real consequence for those who failed to adhere.

Brightly colored clothes were also banned as they were viewed as sexually attracting; a characteristic most unsuitable for women to display. A Taliban decree from 1996 states, 'If women are going outside with fashionable, ornamental, tight and charming clothes to show themselves, they will be cursed by the Islamic Sharia, and should never expect to go to heaven.'

MOBILITY

The Taliban rulings regarding public conduct placed severe restrictions upon a woman's freedom of movement and created difficulties for those who could not afford a *burqa* or didn't have any mahram. These women faced virtual house arrest. A woman who was badly beaten by the Taliban for walking the streets alone stated "my father was killed in battle...I have no husband, no brother, no son. How am I to live if I can't go out alone?"

A field worker for the NGO Terre des hommes witnessed the impact on female mobility at Kabul's largest state-run orphanage, Taskia Maskan. It is recorded that after the female staff were relieved of their duties the approximately 400 girls living at the institution were locked inside for a year without being allowed outside for recreation.

Decrees that affected women's mobility:

- Ban on women riding bicycles or motorcycles, even with their mahrams.
- Women were forbidden from riding in a taxi without a mahram.
- Segregated bus services introduced to prevent males and females traveling on the same bus.

The lives of rural women were less dramatically impacted as they generally lived and worked within secure kin environments. A relative level of freedom was necessary for them to continue with their chores or labor. If women wished to travel to a nearby town the same urban restrictions would have applied.

EMPLOYMENT

The Taliban disagreed with past Afghan statutes that allowed the employment of women in a mixed sex workplace. They claimed this was a breach of purdah and sharia law. On September 30th 1996 the Taliban decreed that all women should be banned from employment. It is estimated that 25 per cent of government employees were female, and when compounded by losses in other sectors, many thousands of women were affected. This had a devastating impact on household incomes, especially on vulnerable or widow headed-households which were common in Afghanistan.

Another loss was for those whom the employed women served. Elementary education of children, not just girls, was shut down in Kabul, where virtually all of the elementary school teachers were women. Thousands of educated families fled Kabul for Pakistan after the Taliban took the city in 1996. A substantial number of the Afghan refugees who fled to Pakistan did so due to the impact of losing female earnings. Although many refugees supported the Taliban, the ban on female employment compounded by the harsh economic climate proved a disincentive for families to return.

Among those who remained in Afghanistan there was an increase in mother and child begging as the loss of vital income reduced many families to the margin of survival. Taliban Supreme Leader Mohammed Omar assured female civil servants and teachers they would still receive wages of around US$5 per month, although this was a short term offering. A Taliban representative stated:

"The Taliban's act of giving monthly salaries to 30,000 job-free women, now sitting comfortably at home, is a whiplash in the face of those who are defaming Taliban with reference to the rights of women. These people through baseless propaganda are trying to incite the women of Kabul against the Taliban".

The Taliban promoted the use of the extended family, or zakat system of charity to ensure women should not need to work. However, years of conflict meant that nuclear families often struggled to support themselves let alone aid additional relatives. Qualification for legislation often rested on men, such as food aid which must be collected by a male relative. The possibility that a woman may not possess any male relatives was dismissed by Mullah Ghaus the acting foreign minister who was surprised at the degree of international attention and concern for such a small percentage of the Afghan population.

For rural women there was generally little change in their circumstance as their lives were dominated by the unpaid domestic, agricultural and reproductive labour necessary for subsistence. Female health professionals were exempted from the employment ban yet they operated in much depleted conditions. The ordeal of physically getting to work due to the segregated bus system and widespread harassment influenced some women to leave their jobs by choice.

Of those who remained, many lived in fear of the regime and chose to reside at the hospital during the working week to minimise exposure to Taliban forces. These women were vital to ensure the continuance of gynaecological, ante-natal and midwifery services, be it on a much compromised level. Under the Rabbani regime there had been around 200 female staff working in Kabul's Mullalai Hospital yet barely 50 remained under the Taliban. NGOs operating in Afghanistan after the fall of the Taliban in 2002 found the shortage of female health professionals to be a significant obstacle to their work.

The other exception to the employment ban allowed a reduced number of humanitarian workers to remain in service. The Taliban segregation codes meant women were invaluable for gaining access to vulnerable women or conducting outreach research. This exception was not sanctioned by the entire Taliban movement so instances of female participation or lack there of, varied with each circumstance.

The town of Herat was particularly affected by Taliban adjustments to the treatment of women, as it had been one of the more cosmopolitan and outward-looking areas of Afghanistan prior to 1995. Women were allowed to work in a limited range of jobs but this was stopped by Taliban authorities. The new governor of Herat, Mullah Razzaq, issued orders for women to be forbidden from passing his office for fear of their distracting nature.

EDUCATION

The Taliban claimed to recognize their Islamic duty to offer education to both boys and girls, yet a decree was passed that banned girls above the age of 8 from receiving instruction. Maulvi Kalamadin insisted it was only a temporary suspension and that females would return to school and work once facilities and street security were adapted to prevent cross-gender contact. The Taliban wished to have total control of Afghanistan before calling upon an Ulema body to determine the content of a new curriculum to replace the Islamic yet unacceptable Mujahadin version.

The Taliban requested time to achieve these ends and criticized the international aid community for its insistence on binding support to the immediate return of women's rights. The Taliban believed in the merit of their actions, and a representative stated in an Iranian interview "no other country has given women the rights we have given them. We have given women the rights that God and His Messenger have instructed, that are to stay in their homes and to gain religious instruction in hijab [seclusion]".

The female employment ban was felt greatly in the education system. Within Kabul alone the ruling affected 106,256 girls, 148,223 boys and 8,000 female university undergraduates. 7,793 female teachers were dismissed, a move that crippled the provision of education and caused 63 schools to close due to a sudden lack of educators. Some women ran clandestine schools within their homes for local children. Both the learners, parents and educators were aware of the consequences should the Taliban discover their activities, but for those who felt trapped under the strict Taliban rule, such actions allowed them a sense of self-determination and hope.

HEALTH CARE

Prior to the Taliban taking power in Afghanistan male doctors had been allowed to treat women in hospitals, however the decree that no male doctor should be allowed to touch the body of a woman under the pretext of consultation was soon introduced. With fewer female health professionals in employment the distances many women had to travel for attention increased while provision of ante-natal clinics declined.

In Kabul some women established informal clinics in their homes to service family and neighbours, yet as medical supplies were hard to obtain their effectiveness was limited. Many women endured prolonged suffering or a premature death due to the lack of treatment. For those families that had the means, inclination, and mahram support, medical attention could be sought in Pakistan.

In October 1996 women were barred from accessing the traditional hammam, public baths, as the opportunities for socialising were prescribed as un-Islamic. This affordable hot water rite had been enjoyed by women and was an important facility in a nation where few possessed running water. It gave cause for the UN to predict a rise in scabies and vaginal infections among women denied methods of hygiene as well as access to health care. Nasrine Gross, an Afghan-American author, stated in 2001 that it has been four years many Afghan women hadn't been able to pray to their God as "Islam prohibits women from praying without a bath after their periods".

In June 1998 the Taliban banned women from attending general hospitals in the capital – whereas before they could attend a women-only ward of general hospitals – leaving only one hospital in Kabul at which they could seek treatment.

Family harmony was badly affected by mental stress, isolation and depression that often accompanied the forced confinement of women. A survey of 160 women concluded that 97% showed signs of serious depression and 71% reported a decline in their physical well being. Latifa, a Kabul resident and author, wrote:

"The apartment resembles a prison or a hospital. Silence weighs heavily on all of us. As none of us do much, we haven't got much to tell each other. Incapable of sharing our emotions, we each enclose ourselves in our own fear and distress. Since everyone is in the same black pit, there isn't much point in repeating time and again that we can't see clearly."

The nutrition of many urban Afghans was negatively affected by poverty, inflated food prices and the restricted mobility to purchase fresh food.

Culture

Taliban restrictions on the cultural presence of women cover several areas. Place names including the word 'women' have been modified so that the word is not used. Women are forbidden from laughing loudly as it is considered improper for a stranger to hear a woman's voice. Women are prohibited from participating in sports or entering a sports club.

The organisation known as RAWA (Revolutionary Association of the Women of Afghanistan) deals specifically with these issues. It was founded by Meena Keshwar Kamal, a woman who amongst other things established a bi-lingual magazine called 'Women's Message' in 1981. She was assassinated in 1987 at the age of 30, but is revered as a heroine among Afghan women.

Punishments

Punishments were often carried out publicly, either as formal spectacles held in sports stadiums or town squares or spontaneous street beatings. Civilians lived in fear of harsh penalties as there was little mercy; women caught breaking decrees were often treated with force.

Examples of punishments:

- In October 1996, a woman had the tip of her thumb cut off for wearing nail varnish.
- In December 1996, Radio Shari'a announced that 225 Kabul women had been seized and punished for violating the sharia code of dress. The sentence was handed down by a tribunal and the women were lashed on their legs and backs for their misdemeanor.
- In May 1997, 5 female CARE International employees with authorisation from the Ministry of the Interior to conduct research for an emergency feeding programme were forced from their vehicle by members of the religious police. The guards used a public address system to insult and harass the women before striking them with a metal and leather whip over 1.5 meters (almost 5 feet) in length.

The mother of seven children had been found guilty of killing her husband while he slept, after allegedly being beaten by him. The footage can be seen here.

- In 1999, a mother of seven was executed in front of 30,000 spectators in Kabul's Ghazi Sport stadium for the murder of her abusive husband. She was imprisoned for 3 years and extensively tortured prior to the execution; yet she refused to plead her innocence in a bid to protect her daughter, reportedly the actual culprit.
- When a Taliban raid discovered a woman running an informal school in her apartment, they beat the children;

threw her down a flight of stairs causing her to break her leg; and then imprisoned her. They threatened to publicly stone her family if she didn't sign a declaration of loyalty to the Taliban and its laws.

Many punishments were carried out by individual militias without the sanction of Taliban authorities as it was against official Taliban policy to punish women in the street. A more official line was the punishment of men for instances of female misconduct; a reflection of a patriarchal society and the belief that men are duty bound to control women. Maulvi Kalamadin stated in 1997, "since we cannot directly punish women, we try to use taxi drivers and shopkeepers as a means to pressurize them" to conform.

Examples of male punishments:

- If a taxi driver picked up a female customer with her face uncovered or unaccompanied by a mahram then he faced a jail sentence and the husband would be punished.
- If a woman was caught washing clothes in a river then she would be escorted home by Islamic authorities where her husband/mahram would be severely punished.
- Tailors found taking female measurements faced imprisonment.

INTERNATIONAL RESPONSE

The international community largely claimed that Afghan women were denied their basic and fundamental human rights, such as freedom to mix with men while at work and the expression and association with men under Taliban rule. Although both the Taliban and aid community claimed to provide women with a dignified and appropriate place in society, they stood poles apart on their preferred methods. After the Taliban takeover of Herat in 1995, the UN hoped the gender policies would become more 'moderate' "as it matured from a popular uprising into a responsible government with linkages to the donor community". The Taliban refused to bow to international pressure and reacted calmly to aid suspensions.

- In November 1995, UNICEF suspended all aid to education in regions under Taliban control, as they argued the ban on mixing males and females in education was a breach of the Convention of the Rights of the Child. In the aftermath of the 1995 Beijing Women's Conference, this action moved to solidify UNICEF's role as a leading agency in matters concerning women and children.
- In 1996 Save the Children (UK) also withdrew support as communication with women, the primary child carers, was most difficult.

The protests of international agencies carried little weight with Taliban authorities, who gave precedence to their interpretation of Islamic law and did not feel bound by UN codes or human rights laws, legislation it viewed as instruments for Western imperialism.

The plight of Afghan women received international exposure, particularly from American media and political figures that publicly condemned Taliban policies as brutal and inhumane.

- UN Secretary General Boutros Boutros Ghali expressed his concern regarding the status of Afghan women.
- In 1999 Secretary of State Madeline Albright publicly stated "We are speaking up on behalf of the women and girls of Afghanistan, who have been victimised...it is criminal and we each have a responsibility to stop it" after the Taliban refused to hand over alleged terrorist Osama bin Laden.

In January 2006 a London conference on Afghanistan led to the creation of an International Compact, which included benchmarks for the treatment of women. The Compact includes the following point, 'Gender:By end-1389 (20 March 2011): the National Action Plan for Women in Afghanistan will be fully implemented; and, in line with Afghanistan's MDGs, female participation in all Afghan governance institutions, including elected and appointed bodies and the civil service, will be strengthened.' However, an Amnesty International report on the 11th June 2008 declared that there needed to be 'no more empty promises' with regard to Afghanistan, citing the treatment of women as one such unfulfilled goal.

PROHIBITIONS ON CULTURE

Movie theaters were closed and music was banned. Hundreds of cultural artifacts that were deemed polytheistic were also destroyed including a major museum and countless private art collections. At the Kabul zoo most animals were killed or left to starve. A sample Taliban edict issued after their capture of Kabul is one decreed in December 1996 by the "General Presidency of Amr Bil Maruf and Nahi Anil Munkar" (or Religious Police) banning a variety of things and activities: music, shaving of beards, keeping of pigeons, flying kites, displaying of pictures or portraits, western hairstyles, music and dancing at weddings, gambling, "sorcery," and not praying at prayer times. In February 2001, Taliban used sledgehammers to destroy representational works of art at the National Museum of Afghanistan.

Local festivities were not exempt from bannings. The Taliban banned the traditional Afghan New Year's celebration of Nowruz as anti-Islamic, and "for a time they also banned Ashura, the Shia Islamic month of mourning and even restricted any show of festivity at Eid." The Afghan people were not allowed to have any cultural celebrations if women were present. If there were only men at the celebration it would be allowed to go forth, so long as it did not go over the curfew time of 9:00 pm.

Taliban official Mullah Mohammed Hassan explained, "of course we realize that people need some entertainment but they can go to the parks and see the flowers, and from this they will learn about Islam." The Education Minister Mullahs Abdul Hanifi told questioners that the Taliban "opposes music because it creates a strain in the mind and hampers study of Islam."

BUDDHAS OF BAMIYAN

In March 2001, the Taliban ordered the demolition of two statues of Buddhas carved into cliffsides at Bamiyan, one 38 metres (125 ft) tall and carved in 507 CE, the other 53 metres (174 ft) tall and carved in 554 CE. The act was condemned by UNESCO and many countries around the world. The intentions of the destruction remain unclear. Mullah Omar initially supported the preservation of Afghanistan's heritage, and Japan linked financial aid to the preservation of the statues. However, after a few years, a decree was issued claiming all representations of humans and idols, including those in museums, must be destroyed in accordance with Islamic law which prohibits any form of idol worship.

The government of Pakistan (itself host to one of the richest and most ancient collections of Buddhist art) implored the Taliban to spare the statues. Saudi Arabia and the United Arab Emirates later denounced the act as savage. Sayed Rahmatullah Hashemi, a senior representative of the Taliban designated as the roving Ambassador visited the US in March, 2001. He represented the Taliban's action not as an act of irrationality, but as an act of rage over UNESCO and some western governments denying the Taliban use of the funds intended for the repairs of the war-damaged statues of the Buddha. He contended that the Taliban intended to use the money for drought relief.

The Buddhas of Bamyan were two monumental statues of standing Buddhas carved into the side of a cliff in the Bamyan valley in the Hazarajat region of central Afghanistan, situated 230 km (143 miles) northwest of Kabul at an altitude of 2500 meters (8,202 ft). Built during the sixth century, the statues represented the classic blended style of Gandhara art. The main bodies were hewn directly from the sandstone cliffs, but details were modeled in mud mixed with straw, coated with stucco. This coating, practically all of which was worn away long ago, was painted to enhance the expressions of the faces, hands and folds of the robes; the larger one was painted carmine red and the smaller one was painted multiple colors.

The lower parts of the statues' arms were constructed from the same mud-straw mix while supported on wooden armatures. It is believed that the upper parts of their faces were made from great wooden masks or casts. The rows of holes were spaces that held wooden pegs which served to stabilize the outer stucco. They were intentionally dynamited and destroyed in 2001 by the Taliban, on orders from leader Mullah Mohammed Omar, after the Taliban government declared that they were "idols" (which are forbidden under Sharia law). International opinion strongly condemned the destruction of the Buddhas, which was viewed as an example of the intolerance of the Taliban and of fundamentalist Islam.

Japan and Switzerland, among others, have pledged support for the rebuilding of the statues. Bamyan lies on the Silk Road, a caravan route linking the markets of China with those of Western Asia. Until the eleventh century AD, Bamyan was part of the kingdom of Gandhara. It was the site of several Buddhist monasteries, and a thriving center for religion, philosophy, and Indian art. It was a Buddhist religious site from the second century up to the time of the Islamic invasion in the ninth century.

Monks at the monasteries lived as hermits in small caves carved into the side of the Bamyan cliffs. Many of these monks embellished their caves with religious statuary and elaborate, brightly-colored frescoes. The two most prominent statues were the giant, standing Buddhas Vairocana and Sakyamuni, identified by the different mudras performed, measuring 55 and 37 metres (180 and 121 feet) high respectively, the largest examples of standing Buddha carvings in the world. They were perhaps the most famous cultural landmarks of the region and the site was listed by UNESCO as a World Heritage Site along with the surrounding cultural landscape and archaeological remains of the Bamyan Valley.

The smaller of the two statues was built in AD 507, the larger in 554. The statues are believed to have been built by the Kushans, with the guidance of local Buddhist monks, at the heyday of their empire. The Chinese Buddhist pilgrim Xuanzang passed through the area around AD 630 and described Bamyan as a flourishing Buddhist center "with more than ten monasteries and more than a thousand monks". He also noted that both Buddha figures were "decorated with gold and fine jewels". Intriguingly, Xuan Zang mentions a third, even larger, reclining statue of the Buddha.

A monumental sitting Buddha similar in style to those at Bamyan still exists in the Bingling Temple caves in China's Gansu province. The destruction of the Bamyan Buddhas became a symbol of oppression and a rallying point for the freedom of religious expression. Despite the fact that most Afghans are Muslim, they too had embraced their past and many were appalled by this destruction.

ELEVENTH TO THE TWENTIETH CENTURY

The enormous Buddhas, the male Salsal and the (smaller) female Shamama, as they were called by the locals, did not fail to fire the imagination of islamic writers in centuries past. The largest statue reappears as the malevolent giant Salsal in medieval Turkish tales. When Mahmud of Ghazni attacked Afghanistan and part of west India in the eleventh century, the destruction of the Buddhas and frescoes were beyond his understanding. Therefore he moved on to looting Buddhist monasteries and other important artifacts. Nader Shah fired cannons at the statues but it was beyond his capabilities as well. Since then, the statues had remained largely untouched.

PREFACE TO 2001, UNDER THE TALIBAN

In July 1999, Mullah Mohammed Omar issued a decree in favor of the preservation of the Bamyan Buddhas. Because Afghanistan's Buddhist population no longer existed, which removed the possibility of the statues being worshipped, he added: "The government considers the Bamyan statues as an example of a potential major source of income for Afghanistan from international visitors. The Taliban states that Bamyan shall not be destroyed but protected."

Afghanistan's radical clerics began a campaign to crack down on "un-Islamic" segments of Afghan society. The Taliban soon banned all forms of imagery, music and sports, including television, in accordance with what they considered a strict interpretation of Islamic law.

Information and Culture Minister Qadratullah Jamal told Associated Press of a decision by 400 religious clerics from across Afghanistan declaring the Buddhist statues against the tenets of Islam. "They came out with a consensus that the statues were against Islam," said Jamal.

According to UNESCO Director-General Koïchiro Matsuura, a meeting of ambassadors from the 54 member states of the Organisation of the Islamic Conference (OIC) was conducted. All OIC states - including Pakistan, Saudi Arabia and the United Arab Emirates, three countries that officially recognised the Taliban government - joined the protest to spare the monuments. A statement issued by the ministry of religious affairs of Taliban regime justified the destruction as being in accordance with Islamic law. Saudi Arabia and the United Arab Emirates later condemned the destruction as "savage".

DYNAMITING AND DESTRUCTION, MARCH 2001

The statues were destroyed by dynamite over several weeks, starting in early March, carried out in different stages. Initially, the statues were fired at for several days using anti-aircraft guns and artillery. This damaged them, but did not obliterate them. Later, the Taliban placed anti-tank mines at the bottom of the niches, so that when fragments of rock broke off from artillery fire, the statues would receive additional destruction from particles that set off the mines. In the end, the Taliban lowered men down the cliff face and placed explosives into holes in the Buddhas.

On 6 March 2001 *The Times* quoted Mullah Mohammed Omar as stating, "Muslims should be proud of smashing idols. It has given praise to God that we have destroyed them." During a 13 March interview for Japan's Mainichi Shimbun, Afghan Foreign Minister Wakil Ahmad Mutawakel stated that the destruction was anything but retaliation against the international community for economic sanctions: "We are destroying the Buddha statues in accordance with Islamic law and it is purely a religious issue".

On 18 March, *The New York Times* reported that a Taliban envoy said the Islamic government made its decision in a rage after a foreign delegation offered money to preserve the ancient works. The report also added, however, that other reports "have said the religious leaders were debating the move for months, and ultimately decided that the statues were idolatrous and should be obliterated."

Then Taliban ambassador-at-large, Sayed Rahmatullah Hashemi, said that the destruction of the statues was carried out by the Head Council of Scholars after a single Swedish monuments expert proposed to restore the statues' heads. Hashimi is reported as saying: "When the Afghani head council asked them to provide the money to feed the children instead of fixing the statues, they refused and said, 'No, the money is just for the statues, not for the children'. Herein, they made the decision to destroy the statues". However, he did not comment on the fact that a foreign museum offered to "buy the Buddhist statues, the money from which could have been used to feed children."

Aftermath of the destruction

The Taliban government decreed that the statues, which had survived for over 1,500 years, were idolatrous and un-Islamic. During the destruction, Taliban Information Minister Qudratullah Jamal lamented that, "this work of destruction is not as simple as people might think. You can't knock down the statues by shelling as both are carved into a cliff; they are firmly attached to the mountain." The two largest Buddhas faced dynamite and tank barrages and were demolished after almost a month of intensive bombardment.

Commitment to rebuild

Though the figures of the two large Buddhas are almost completely destroyed, their outlines and some features are still recognizable within the recesses. It is also still possible for visitors to explore the monks' caves and the passages which connect them. As part of the international effort to rebuild Afghanistan after the Taliban war, the Government of Japan and several other organizations, among them the Afghanistan Institute in Bubendorf, Switzerland, along with the ETH in

Zurich, have committed themselves to rebuilding the two largest Buddhas; anastylosis is one technique being considered.

Developments since 2002

In May 2002, a mountainside sculpture of the Buddha was carved out of a mountain in Sri Lanka. It was designed to closely resemble one of the Buddhas of Bamyan. The Afghan government has commissioned Japanese artist Hiro Yamagata to recreate the Bamyan Buddhas using fourteen laser systems to project the images of the Buddhas onto the cliff where they once stood. The laser systems will be solar and wind-powered. The project, which will cost an estimated $9 million, is currently pending UNESCO approval. If approved, the project is estimated to be completed by June 2012.

In September 2005, Mawlawi Mohammed Islam Mohammadi, Taliban governor of Bamyan province at the time of the destruction and widely seen as responsible for its occurrence, was elected to the Afghan Parliament. On 26 January 2007, he was gunned down in Kabul.

Swiss filmmaker Christian Frei made a 95-minute documentary entitled *The Giant Buddhas* (released in March 2006) on the statues, the international reactions to their destruction, and an overview of the controversy. The movie makes the controversial claim (quoting a local Afghan) that the destruction was ordered by Osama Bin Laden and that initially, Mullah Omar and the Afghans in Bamyan had opposed the destruction.

In the summer of 2006, Afghan officials were deciding the timetable for the re-construction of the statues. The mullahs in the province have stated that the destruction was an "atrocity" and the statues deserve restoration. While they wait for the Afghan government and international community to decide whether to rebuild them, a $1.3 million UNESCO-funded project is sorting out the chunks of clay and plaster - ranging from boulders weighing several tons to fragments the size of tennis balls - and sheltering them from the elements.

The Buddhist remnants at Bamyan were included on the 2008 World Monuments Watch List of the 100 Most Endangered Sites by the World Monuments Fund. It is hoped that the listing will put continued national and international attention on the site in order to ensure its long-term preservation, and to make certain that future restoration efforts maintain the authenticity of the site and that proper preservation practices are followed.

Oil painting discovery

After the destruction of the Buddhas, 50 caves were revealed. In 12 of the caves wall paintings were discovered. In December 2004, Japanese researchers stated the wall paintings at Bamyan were painted between the fifth and the ninth centuries, rather than the sixth to eighth centuries, citing their analysis of radioactive isotopes contained in straw fibers found beneath the paintings. It is believed that the paintings were done by artists travelling on the Silk Road, the trade route between China and the West.

Scientists from the National Research Institute for Cultural Properties in Tokyo (Japan), the Centre of Research and Restoration of the French Museums-CNRS (France), the Getty Conservation Institute (United States) and the ESRF (the European Synchrotron radiation facility) in Grenoble analysed samples from the paintings, typically less than 1 mm across. They discovered that the paint contained pigments such as vermilion (red mercury sulfide) and lead white (lead carbonate). These were mixed with a range of binders, including natural resins, gums (possibly animal skin glue or egg) and oils, probably derived from walnuts or poppies.

Specifically, researchers identified drying oils from murals showing Buddhas in vermilion robes sitting cross-legged amid palm leaves and mythical creatures as being painted in the middle of the 7th century. It is believed that they are the oldest known surviving examples of oil painting, possibly predating oil painting in Europe by as much as six centuries. The discovery may lead to a reassessment of works in ancient ruins in Iran, China, Pakistan, Turkey and India.

Some have cautioned that the oils may in fact be contamination from fingers, as the touching of the painting is encouraged in Buddhist tradition; however, analysis by spectroscopy and chromatography indicates an unambiguous signal for the use of oils rather than any other contaminant. In addition oils were discovered underneath other layers of paint, negating the presence of surface contaminants.

Another giant statue unearthed

On 8 September 2008 archeologists searching for the fabled 300 meter statue at the site of the already dynamited Buddhas announced the discovery of a new 19-meter-long (62 ft) "sleeping Buddha", the pose known to Buddhists as the scene where the Buddha passed into nirvana. This discovery may have confirmed the Chinese pilgrim Xuanzang's mention of a large Buddha in a sleeping posture in this area, which were recorded by Xuanzang one thousand four hundred years ago.

ETHNIC MASSACRES AND PERSECUTION

The worst attack on civilians came in summer of 1998 when the Taliban swept north from Herat to the predominantly Hazara and Uzbek city of Mazar-e-Sharif, the largest city in the north. Entering at 10 am on 8 August 1998, for the next two days the Taliban drove their pickup trucks "up and down the narrow streets of Mazar-e-Sharif shooting to the left and right and killing everything that moved - shop owners, cart pullers, women and children shoppers and even goats and donkeys." More than 8000 noncombatants were reported killed in Mazar-e-Sharif and later in Bamiyan.

Contrary to the injunctions of Islam, which demands immediate burial, the Taliban forbade anyone to bury the corpses for the first six days while they rotted in the summer heat and were eaten by dogs. In addition to this indiscriminate slaughter, the Taliban sought out and massacred members of the Hazara, a mostly Shia ethnic group, while in control of Mazar-e-Sharif. While the slaughter can be attributed to several factors – ethnic difference, suspicion of Hazara loyalty to their co-religionists in Iran, fury at the loss of life suffered in an earlier unsuccessful Taliban takeover of Mazar – the belief by some Sunni Taliban that the Shia Hazaras were guilty of *takfir* (apostasy) may have been the principal motivation. It was expressed by Mullah Niazi, the commander of the attack and governor of Mazar after the attack, in his declaration from Mazar's central mosque:

"Last year you rebelled against us and killed us. From all your homes you shot at us. Now we are here to deal with you. The Hazaras are not Muslims and now we have to kill Hazaras. You either accept to be Muslims or leave Afghanistan. Wherever you go we will catch you. If you go up we will pull you down by your feet; if you hide below, we will pull you up by your hair."

Hazara also suffered a siege by the Taliban of their Hazarajat homeland in central Afghanistan and the refusal by the Taliban to allow the UN to supply food to Hazara in the provinces of Bamiyan, Ghor, Wardak and Ghazni. A month after the Mazar slaughter, Taliban broke through Hazar lines and took over Hazarajat. The number of civilians killed was not as great as in Mazar, but occurred nevertheless. During the years that followed, rapes and massacres of Hazara by Taliban forces were documented by groups such as Human Rights Watch.

ECONOMY

Peace did not bring economic development to Afghanistan. The so-called "transportation mafia" operating out of Pakistan "cut down millions of acres of timber in Afghanistan for the Pakistani market, denuding the countryside as there was no reforestation. They stripped down rusting factories ... even electricity and telephone poles for their steel and sold the scrap to steel mills in Lahore."

OPIUM

Opium poppies have traditionally been grown in Afghanistan and, with the war shattering other sectors of the economy, opium became the number one export of the country. The Taliban have provided an Islamic sanction for farmers ... to grow even more opium, even though the Qur'an forbids Muslims from producing or imbibing intoxicants. Abdul Rashid, the head of the Taliban's anti-drugs control force in Kandahar, spelled out the nature of his unique job. He is authorized to impose a strict ban on the growing of hashish, "because it is consumed by Afghans and Muslims." But, Rashid told me without a hint of sarcasm, "Opium is permissible because it is consumed by kafirs in the West and not by Muslims or Afghans."

But in 2000 the Taliban banned opium production, a first in Afghan history. In 2000, Afghanistan's opium production still accounted for 75% of the world's supply. On 27 July 2000, the Taliban again issued a decree banning opium poppy cultivation. According to opioids.com, by February 2001, production had been reduced from 12,600 acres (51 km) to only 17 acres (7 ha). When the Taliban entered North Waziristan in 2003 they immediately banned poppy cultivation and punished those who sold it. Another source claims opium production was cut back by the Taliban not to prevent its use but to shore up its price, and thus increase the income of poppy farmers and revenue of Afghan tax collectors.

The official verdict of the Taliban however was otherwise. Mullah Amir Mohammed Haqqani, the Taliban's top drug official in Nangarhar, said the ban would remain regardless of whether the Taliban received aid or international recognition. "It is our decree that there will be no poppy cultivation. It is banned forever in this country," he said. "Whether we get assistance or not, poppy growing will never be allowed again in our country."

However, with the 2001 US/Northern Alliance expulsion of the Taliban, opium cultivation has increased in the southern provinces liberated from the Taliban control, and by 2005 production was 87% of the world's opium supply, rising to 90% in 2006. Hashemi also detailed this in his March 2001 lecture in California.

CONSCRIPTION

According to the testimony of Guantanamo captives before their Combatant Status Review Tribunals, the Taliban, in addition to conscripting men to serve as soldiers, also conscripted men to staff its civil service.

Post September 11th, Pre-collapse Taliban conscription

The *Australian Broadcasting Corporation* quotes a young Afghan, who reported:

"They're rounding men up for a fight to the last man."

According the ABC report Ahmed Zia said there had been a large-scale exodus from Kabul. He claimed the Taliban were rounding up young boys for battle. He also claimed the Taliban were forcing people to give blood. The British paper *The Daily Telegraph* reported, on September 29, 2001, that the Taliban's supreme leader, Mullah Omar, had closed all Afghanistan's religious schools, so the students could fight beside the Taliban.

The *Los Angeles Times* reported, on October 13, 2001, an account of a young man who had a lucky encounter with a Taliban conscription patrol reminiscent of the 18th Century Royal Navy press gang:

"Samim, the young man who fled with his family, is an ethnic Tajik. He said he had a lucky escape Thursday night, walking home from the bazaar with his friend, Farid Alsoo.

"They stumbled across a Taliban patrol roughly shoving young men into a minivan. About five or 10 young men were already captive. The Taliban men seized Alsoo and pushed him into the van.

"'They tried to get me, but I ran,' Samim said.They chased me for a few meters, but I got away,' he said, speaking in English. As the family breadwinner, he couldn't afford to be arrested or pressed to fight."

POST-COLLAPSE TALIBAN CONSCRIPTION

Accounts of the Taliban's conscription policies from Guantanamo detainees

On March 3, 2006, after exhausting all it legal appeals, the US Department of Defense was forced to comply with a court order and release information about the identity of the captives held in extrajudicial detention in the Guantanamo Bay detainment camps, in Cuba. The DoD released thousands of pages of documents prepared for, or arising from, the captives' Combatant Status Review Tribunals and Administrative Review Board hearings.

Those thousands of pages of documents revealed that many of the detainees described themselves as conscripts, somethimes enlisted at gunpoint, and imprisoned in their barracks under armed guards, kept on hand for the Taliban to use as "cannon fodder".

Enemy combatant status

Some skeptical commentators have discounted the accounts of Guantanamo detainees whose stories suggested they weren't hardened terrorists. However, there are captives who even the American intelligence analysts acknowledged were reluctant conscripts. Under questioning by US District Court Judge Joyce Hens Green US Government lawyer Brian Boyle confirmed that the definition of "enemy combatant" status was so broad that even a little old lady from Switzerland, who sent money to what she thought was a legitimate charity, could be classified as an "enemy combatant" if workers for that charity clandestinely diverted some of its resources to back projects with ties to terrorism.

Some of the Guantanamo detainees had their classification as "enemy combatants" confirmed because they had a business arrangement to supply al Qaeda, or the Taliban, with mundane items, like firewood. Some of the Guantanamo detainees had their classification as "enemy combatants" confirmed even when they claimed they were enlisted at gunpoint, and housed in their barracks under armed guard.

Some of the Guantanamo detainees had their classification as "enemy combatants" confirmed even when they claimed they were kidnapped, and employed as kitchen helpers, or servants, as virtual slaves. Some of the Guantanamo detainees reported that they were conscripted, not for military duties, but simply to perform civilian duties the Taliban couldn't fill through normal hiring practices.

WAR WITH THE NORTHERN ALLIANCE

Taliban's strict policies and condescending behavior toward their local allied troops caused an uprising in which thousands of the Taliban's best troops were killed. In 1997, Ahmad Shah Massoud devised a plan to utilize guerrilla tactics in the Shamali plains to defeat the Taliban advances. In collaboration with the locals, Massoud had deployed his forces to be stationed at civilian dwellings and other hidden places. Upon the arrival of the Taliban, some locals, who had vowed pacts of peace with the Taliban, as well as Massoud's forces, came out of hiding and in a surprise attack captured the north of Kabul.

Soon after, the Taliban put a major effort into taking control of the Shamali plains, indiscriminately killing young men, uprooting and expelling the population. Kamal Hossein, a special reporter for the UN, had written a full report on these and other war crimes that further insinuated and inflamed the issue of ethnicity. In 8 August 1998 the Taliban again took Mazar-e-Sharif this time avenging their earlier defeat and creating more international controversy with mass killings of thousands of civilians and several Iranian diplomats.

This offensive left the Northern Alliance in control of only a small part of Afghanistan (10–15%) in the north. The Taliban retained control of most of the country until the 2001 9/11 attacks. On 9 September 2001, a suicide bomber, posing as an interviewer and widely thought to be connected to Al-Qaeda, assassinated the Northern Alliance *Mujahideen* military leader Ahmad Shah Massoud. Despite his removal, the Taliban were driven from most of Afghanistan by American bombing and Northern Alliance ground troops a couple of months later in the 2001 War.

2

Taliban and Civil War in Afghanistan

The Civil war in Afghanistan continued after the capture of Kabul by the Taliban, with the formation of the United Islamic Front for the Salvation of Afghanistan (more commonly known as the Northern Alliance), which attempted to oust the Taliban, from 1996 to 2001. It proved largely unsuccessful, as the Taliban continued to make gains and eliminated much of the Alliance's leadership. The Northern Alliance was supported by Russia, Turkey, Iran and India while the Taliban were supported by Saudi Arabia, Pakistan and the United Arab Emirates.

Since 1978, Afghanistan had been in a civil war between different factions. The Mujahedin eventually succeeded in taking control in 1992, only to then descend into chaos as they fractured into different groups all fighting for control of the nation. In 1994 the Taliban was formed and made gains against the other factions, and by 1996 they had taken Kabul and executed the former President of Afghanistan, Mohammad Najibullah, who had been residing there under UN protection since his regime was ousted in 1992.

The Taliban practiced a radical form of Sunni Islam that took strict stances on women and society. Additionally, they were a predominantly Pashtun militia, and so imposed their ethnic customs onto non-Pashtuns. Much of the civil war could be characterized as an ethnic conflict between the Pashtun Taliban, and the non-Pashtun Northern Alliance, since both sides of the conflict espoused fundamentalist Islam, though the Taliban subscribed to a particularly narrow interpretation of Islam.

NORTHERN ALLIANCE FORMED

After the fall of Kabul to the Taliban on September 27, 1996, Uzbek General Dostum joined forces with the Tajik Ahmed Shah Massoud to form the Northern Alliance, a grouping of non-Pashtun militias that aimed to defeat the Pashtun Taliban. Both parties espoused Islamic fundamentalism, and wished to impose Sharia law in the country.

The Northern Alliance began to get funding and arms from Russia and Iran, who both feared the Taliban's growing influence, while the UAE and Saudi Arabia backed the Taliban as ideological allies. Pakistan also backed the Taliban, as they were viewed as the only capable group of bringing peace to Afghanistan - a goal which would allow Pakistan to open trade ties with the Central Asian republics, while at the same time allowing for the return of the some 3 million Afghans who had taken refuge in Pakistan.

Alliance pushes to Kabul

In October 1996, the Taliban began to strike points north of Kabul with jets and artillery while Dostum and Massoud massed forces in preparation for an offensive. On October 19, the alliance pushed forward with tanks, armored personnel carriers, and heavy weapons into the Bagram airbase, which was the first major victory against the Taliban since they lost Kabul. They continued their advance and vowed to retake Kabul, with Massoud's front line commander stating "God willing, we will be in Kabul today or tomorrow." But fighting raged for several days, and the lack of a major breakthrough forced the Alliance to withdraw to northern positions.

Dostum faces uprising

In 1997 the Taliban began an offensive against the territories held by General Dostum that caused some of his forces, led by General Abdul Malik, to rebel and join the Taliban on May 20. This led him to flee Afghanistan, leaving much of his army behind, and seek refuge in Uzbekistan. The newly Taliban-friendly forces handed over the city of Mazari Sharif to the Taliban. Soon, however, their strict stance against Shiite Muslims led to a confrontation between Hazara militias and the Taliban.

In intense fighting in the city of Mazar-e-Sharif, the Taliban were defeated, and 3,000 of their soldiers were captured and executed. The forces of Massoud attempted another push towards the capital. After making gains north of the capital, they once again met heavy resistance in Kabul. The Taliban continued to push into the Alliance's territory, however, and reached Mazar-e-Sharif, taking it again by August 8, 1998. Upon taking it, they began a mass killing of the locals; 4,000 to 5,000 civilians were executed, and many more reported tortured. This offensive by the Taliban left them in control of 90% of the nation.

Iranian crisis

Also among those killed in Mazari Sharif were several Iranian diplomats. Others were kidnapped by the Taliban, touching off a hostage crisis that nearly escalated to a full scale war, with 250,000 Iranian soldiers massed on the Afghan border at one time. It was later admitted that the diplomats were killed by the Taliban, and their bodies were returned to Iran. In September the Taliban claimed that Iran violated its airspace, and later Iran claimed minor clashes occurred between the Taliban and Iran after it led a raid into eastern Iran, though the Taliban denied it led the raid. Eventually with UN mediation, the tensions cooled.

Continued push

The Taliban continued to push north, making gains against the Northern Alliance in 1999. At one time they held roughly 95% of the nation and had pushed the Northern Alliance out of range of Kabul entirely. But Ahmed Shah Massoud once again defended the Panjshir Valley from Taliban advances and brought the war to another stand still.

Massoud assassinated

On September 9, 2001, a suicide bomber, posing as a journalist, blew himself up after gaining access to Ahmed Shah Massoud office. The suicide bomber was killed along with one of Massoud's followers, and the Afghan commander's guards killed the second person posing as a journalist. Massoud was struck in the chest with shrapnel from the bomb, which was either hidden in the camera or concealed around the waist of one of the terrorists. Massoud died shortly after being taken to Tajikistan for emergency care.

It is reported that *Al Qaeda* carried out this attack against Massoud to eliminate the Northern Alliance's most effective military leader. At this time Taliban human rights violations and actions such as the destruction of the Buddhas of Bamiyan, were creating international support for Massoud's group as the legitimate representatives of Afghanistan, while *Al Qaeda* was planning the September 11th, 2001 attacks on America which were sure to provoke serious retaliation and create a need for the Taliban's protection.

The killing was reportedly handled by Ayman Zawahiri and the Egyptian Islamic Jihad wing of al-Qaeda. The attack left the Northern Alliance leaderless, and removed "the last obstacle to the Taliban's total control of the country ..." But did not lead to chaos as some had feared. The Northern Alliance held together and would go on to work with the USA and its coalition in Operation Enduring Freedom. At the time of Massoud's assassination, Northern Alliance strength was estimated at 11,000 troops and the Taliban at 45,000.

INTERNATIONAL RELATIONS

During its time in power, the Taliban regime or "Islamic Emirate of Afghanistan" gained diplomatic recognition from only three states: the United Arab Emirates, Pakistan, and Saudi Arabia all of whom also provided aid. Most states in the world, including Russia, Iran, India, Uzbekistan, Kyrgyzstan, and Tajikistan, and later the USA, opposed the Taliban and aided their enemy the Northern Alliance.

RELATIONS WITH PAKISTAN

For a period of seven years since their origin, Pakistan's government had been the Taliban's main sponsor. It provided military equipment, recruiting assistance, training and tactical advice that enabled the band of village mullahs and their adherents to take control of Afghanistan. Officially Pakistan denied it was supporting the Taliban, but its support was substantial-one year's aid (1997/1998) was an estimated US$30 million in wheat, diesel, petroleum and kerosene fuel, and other supplies.

The Taliban's influence in its neighbour Pakistan was deep. Its "unprecedented access" among Pakistan's lobbies and interest groups enabled it "to play off one lobby against another and extend their influence in Pakistan even further. At times they would defy" even the powerful ISI.

RELATIONS WITH THE UNITED STATES

Foreign powers, including the United States, were at first supportive of the Taliban in hopes it would serve as a force to restore order in Afghanistan after years of division into corrupt, lawless warlord fiefdoms. The U.S. government, for example, made no comment when the Taliban captured Herat in 1995 and expelled thousands of girls from schools. These hopes faded as it began to be engaged in warlord practices of rocketing unarmed civilians, targeting ethnic groups (primarily Hazaras) and restricting the rights of women.

In late 1997, American Secretary of State Madeleine Albright began to distance the U.S. from the Taliban and the next year the American-based Unocal, previously having implicitly supported the Taliban in order to build a pipeline south from Central Asia; the oil company withdrew from a major deal with the Taliban regime concerning an oil pipeline.

In early August 1998 the Taliban's difficulties in relations with foreign groups became much more serious. After attacking the city of Mazar, Taliban forces killed several thousand civilians and 10 Iranian diplomats and intelligence officers in the Iranian consulate. Alleged radio intercepts indicate Mullah Omar personally approved the killings. The Iranian government was incensed and a "full-blown regional crisis" ensued with Iran mobilizing 200,000 regular troops, though war was averted.

A day before the capture of Mazar, affiliates of Taliban guest Osama bin Laden bombed two U.S. embassies in Africa killing 224 and wounding 4500 mostly African victims. The United States responded by launching cruise missiles attacks on suspected terrorists camps in Afghanistan killing over 20 though failing to kill bin Laden or even many al-Qaeda. Mullah Omar condemned the missile attack and American President Bill Clinton. Saudi Arabia expelled the Taliban envoy in Saudi Arabia in protest over the Taliban's refusal to turn over bin Laden and after Mullah Omar allegedly insulted the Saudi royal family. In mid-October the UN Security Council voted unanimously to ban commercial aircraft flights to and from Afghanistan and freeze its bank accounts world wide.

RELATIONS WITH INDIA

India was one of the most outspoken critics of the Taliban-regime in Afghanistan. Ahmad Shah Massoud, who led the operations of the Northern Alliance against Taliban, was particularly noted for his closeness to India. India was concerned about growing Islamic militancy in its neighborhood and refused to recognize the Taliban regime in Afghanistan.

In December 1999, Indian Airlines Flight 814 en route from Kathmandu to Delhi was hijacked and taken to Kandahar, Afghanistan. The Taliban moved its militias near the hijacked aircraft supposedly to prevent Indian Special Forces from storming the aircraft and also stalled the negotiations between India and the hijackers for days. The *New York Times* later reported of credible links between the hijackers and the Taliban.

As a part of the deal between the hijackers and the Indian government, India released three Islamist militants so as to secure the release of all the hostages on-board the Indian Airlines plane. The Taliban gave a safe passage to the hijackers and the three released militants. The links between Osama bin Laden, the hijackers and the militants released was also reported in Indian media.

Following the hijacking, India drastically increased its efforts to help Ahmed Shah Massoud in his operations against the Taliban. An arms depot for the Northern Alliance was setup by India in Dushanbe, Tajikistan. India also provided Northern Alliance a wide range of high-altitude warfare equipment, helicopter technicians, medical services and tactical advice. According to one report, Indian military support to anti-Taliban forces totaled-US$70 million in aid including two Mi-17 helicopters, three additional helicopters in 2000 and US$8 million worth high-altitude equipment in 2001.

RELATIONS WITH THE UNITED NATIONS AND AID AGENCIES

A major issue during the Taliban's reign was its relations with the United Nations (UN) and non-governmental organizations (NGOs). Twenty years of continuous warfare, first with the Soviets and then between *Mujahideen*, had devastated Afghanistan's infrastructure and economy. There was no running water, little electricity, few telephones, motorable roads or regular energy supplies. Basic necessities like water, food and housing and others were in desperately short supply.

In addition, the clan and family structure that provided Afghans with a social/economic safety net was also badly damaged. Afghanistan's infant mortality was the highest in the world. A full quarter of all children died before they reached their fifth birthday, a rate several times higher than most other developing countries. Consequently international charitable and/or development organisations (NGOs) were extremely important to the supply of food, employment, reconstruction, and other services in Afghanistan. With one million plus deaths during the years of war, the number of families headed by widows had reached 98,000 by 1998. Thus Taliban restrictions on women were sometime a matter not only of human rights, but of life and death.

In Kabul, where vast portions of the city had been devastated from rocket attacks, more than half of its 1.2 million people benefited in some way from NGO charity, even for water to drink. The civil war and its refugee-creation processes continued during the entire time the Taliban were in power. During that time, more than three-quarters of a million civilians were displaced by new Taliban offensives in the north around Mazar, on the Herat front, and in the fertile Shomali valley around Kabul. The offensives used "scorched-earth" tactics to prevent civilians from supplying the enemy with aid.

Despite the receipt of UN and NGO aid, the Taliban's attitude toward the UN and NGOs was often one of suspicion, not gratitude or even tolerance. The UN operates on the basis of international law, not Islamic Sharia, and the UN did not recognize the Taliban as the legitimate government of Afghanistan. Additionally, most of the foreign donors and aid workers, who had tried to persuade the Taliban to change its strict policies and allow women more freedom, were non-Muslims.

As the Taliban's Attorney General Maulvi Jalil-ullah Maulvizada expressed it:

Let us state what sort of education the UN wants. This is a big infidel policy which gives such obscene freedom to women which would lead to adultery and herald the destruction of Islam. In any Islamic country where adultery becomes common, that country is destroyed and enters the domination of the infidels because their men become like women and women cannot defend themselves. Anyone who talks to us should do so within Islam's framework. The Holy Qur'an cannot adjust itself to other people's requirements; people should adjust themselves to the requirements of the Holy Qur'an.

Frustrations of aid agencies were numerous. Taliban decision-makers, particularly Mullah Omar, seldom if ever talked directly to non-Muslim foreigners, so aid providers had to deal with intermediaries whose approvals and agreements were often reversed by Taliban higher-ups. In September 1997, the European Commissioner for Humanitarian Affairs, Emma Bonino, and 19 Western journalists and aid workers were arrested and held for three hours by the Taliban religious police in Kabul when photographs were taken of women patients.

Around the same time the heads of three UN agencies in Kandahar were expelled from the country after protesting that a female lawyer for the UN High Commissioner for Refugees (UNHCR) was forced to talk to Taliban officials from behind a curtain so her face would not be visible. When the UN increased the number of Muslim women staff to satisfy Taliban demands for Muslim staff, the Taliban then insisted "all female Muslim UN staff traveling to Afghanistan to be chaperoned by a mahram or a blood relative." In 20 July 1998, the Taliban closed "down all NGO offices by force" after those organization refused to move to a bombed out former Polytechnic College as ordered. One month later the UN offices were also shut down.

As food prices rose and conditions deteriorated, the Taliban Planning Minister Qari Din Mohammed explained the Taliban's indifference to the loss of humanitarian aid:

> We Muslims believe God the Almighty will feed everybody one way or another. If the foreign NGOs leave then it is their decision. We have not expelled them.

RELATIONSHIP WITH OSAMA BIN LADEN

In 1996, Osama bin Laden moved to Afghanistan from Sudan. He came without any invitation from the Taliban, and sometimes irritated Mullah Omar with his declaration of war and fatwa to murder citizens of third-party countries, and follow-up interviews, but relations between the two groups became closer over time, and eventually bonded to the point where Mullah Omar rebuffed its patron Saudi Arabia, insulting Saudi minister Prince Turki and refusing to turn over bin Laden to the Saudis as Omar had reportedly promised to earlier.

Bin Laden was able to forge an alliance between the Taliban and his *Al Qaeda* organization. It is understood that al-Qaeda-trained fighters known as the 055 Brigade were integrated with the Taliban army between 1997 and 2001. Several hundred Arab Afghan fighters sent by bin Laden assisted the Taliban in the slaughter at Mazar-e-Sharif. Taliban-*Al Qaeda* connections, were also strengthened by the reported marriage of one of bin Laden's sons to Omar's daughter. During Osama bin Laden's stay in Afghanistan, he may have helped finance the Taliban.

Perhaps the biggest favor *Al Qaeda* did for the Taliban was the assassination by suicide bombing of the Taliban's most effective military opponent *Mujahideen* commander and Northern Alliance leader Ahmad Shah Massoud shortly before 9 September 2001. This came at a time when Taliban human rights violations and extremism seemed likely to create international support for Massoud's group as the legitimate representatives of Afghanistan. The killing, reportedly handled by Ayman Zawahiri and the Egyptian Islamic Jihad wing of al-Qaeda, left the Northern Alliance leaderless, and removed "the last obstacle to the Taliban's total control of the country."

After the 1998 U.S. embassy bombings in Africa, Osama bin Laden and several *Al Qaeda* members were indicted in U.S. criminal court. The Taliban protected Osama bin Laden from extradition requests by the U.S., variously claiming that bin Laden had "gone missing" in Afghanistan, or that Washington "cannot provide any evidence or any proof" that bin Laden is involved in terrorist activities and that "without any evidence, bin Laden is a man without sin... he is a free man." Evidence against bin Laden included courtroom testimony and satellite phone records. Bin Laden in turn, praised the Taliban as the "only Islamic government" in existence, and lauded Mullah Omar for his destruction of idols like the Buddhas of Bamiyan.

TALIBAN IN PAKISTAN

Closely tied with JUI party in Pakistan, the Taliban received manpower from Madrasahs in Pakistan's border region. After a request for help from Mullah Omar in 1997, Maulana Samiul Haq shut down his 2500+ student madrassa and "sent his entire student" body hundreds of miles away to fight alongside the Taliban. The next year, the same religious leader helped persuade 12 madrassas in Pakistan's North-West Frontier Province to shut down for one month and send 8000 students to provide reinforcements for the Taliban army in Afghanistan.

The Taliban returned the favor, helping spread its ideology to parts of Pakistan. By 1998 some groups "along the Pashtun belt" were banning TV and videos, imposing Sharia punishments "such as stoning and amputation in defiance of the legal system, killing Pakistani Shia and forcing people, particularly women to adapt to the Taliban dress code and way of life." In December 1998 the Tehrik-i-Tuleba or Movement of Taliban in the Orakzai Agency ignored Pakistan's legal process and publicly executed a murderer in front of 2000 spectators Taliban-style. They also promised to implement Taliban-style justice and ban TV, music and videos.

In Quetta, Pashtun pro-Taliban groups "burned down cinema houses, shot video shop owners, smashed satellite dishes and drove women off the streets". In Kashmir Afghan Arabs from Afghanistan attempted to impose a "Wahhabi style dress code" banning jeans and jackets. "On 15 February 1999, they shot and wounded three Kashmiri cable television operators for relaying Western satellite broadcasts."

As of early 2007, Taliban influence in Pakistan continues in conjunction with the Taliban insurgency. Citing a suicide bombing of a restaurant in Peshwar in retaliation for the arrest of a relative of Taliban commander Mullah Dadullah, the *Associated Press* states "... in Pakistan's frontier regions, ... scores of people have been executed over the past two or three years apparently for being too aligned with the Pakistani government or America - allies in the U.S.-led war on terrorism."

The formation of a Pakistan Taliban umbrella group called Tehrik-i-Taliban Pakistan was announced in December 2007. On February 18, 2009, the president of Pakistan Asif Ali Zardari signed a deal with the Taliban to implement Shariah law in some parts of Pakistan banning all the girls from school. On April 13, 2009, Zardari signed into law a peace deal for the nation's Swat Valley, implementing sharia law in the region.

On June 30, 2009, the Taliban withdrew from the peace deal to protest the continuing airstrikes by American drones. Soon after the announcement that the truce was no longer in play, approximately 150 militants attacked a Pakistani military convoy near Miramshah, killing an estimated 30 soldiers. An additional 4 people were killed in southwestern Pakistan by a car bomber who targeted NATO supply trucks. Guerrilla attacks will be launched against the Pakistani military unless drone attacks are stopped and government troops are pulled out of North Waziristan. We will attack forces everywhere in Waziristan unless the government fulfills these two demands.

- Ahmadullah Ahmadi, spokesperson for Pakistani Taliban Faction, New York Times

The Pakistani government is also concerned about these attacks because they could indicate that the Taliban is preparing for a full-on assault. The government was planning to transport supplies through that region, and now is unable to due to the danger of guerilla attacks. The largest worry by far is that the factions may be organizing themselves to attack the Pakistani military on multiple fronts. The leader of the North Waziristan faction, Hafiz Gul Bahadur, has made it known that "attacks on the security forces will continue". Pakistani leaders are concerned that Bahadur is not the only one planning to carry out attacks.

ISLAMIC EMIRATE OF WAZIRISTAN

The Islamic Emirate of Waziristan, also known as the

Islamic Republic of Waziristan, is a rebel organization, in Waziristan, Pakistan that some commentators claim gained *de facto* recognition from the Government of Pakistan when it was named as party to the Waziristan Accord, the agreement reached between Islamabad and local tribesmen to end the undeclared Waziristan War on 5 September 2006.

Description

The Islamic militants in Waziristan are said to have close affiliations with the Taliban. Waziristan is often mentioned as a haven for *Al Qaeda* fighters, who will be required to either leave the area or act peacefully as a condition of the negotiated peace accord. Some of these militants call their organization the "Taliban." "The tribal militants call themselves "Pakistani Taliban," or members of a newly coined and loosely knit entity, the Taliban."

Tribal leaders control the area of the North Waziristan Agency and the South Waziristan Agency of the Federally Administered Tribal Areas (FATA). In practice they have replaced these two agency-level governments as the political body controlling the area, although formal dissolution of the agencies is not part of the truce agreement.

Partisans in North Waziristan declared an "Islamic state" in February 2006. According to anonymous sources, the Pakistan government effectively acknowledged the organization in the Waziristan accord of 5 September 2006 which referred to the organization in the agreement, however the agreement does not recognize the Taliban as an independent state, but only as a security body charged with fulfilling the obligations of the treaty.

There is speculation that Osama bin Laden and other *Al Qaeda* leaders have found refuge in the area controlled by the Emirate, which is a staging ground for militant operations in Afghanistan. A condition of the truce is that no support be given for these operations. Local observers view the truce accord as a prelude to hot pursuit chases of *Mujahideen* into Pakistan by NATO forces in Afghanistan.

LEADERSHIP STRUCTURE

The Taliban in Waziristan is led by Maulavi Jalaluddin Haqqani, a veteran *Mujahideen* commander and member of the Zadran tribe, who aligned himself with the Taliban and rose to be a cabinet member of the Islamic Emirate of Afghanistan (the official name of the former Taliban government of Afghanistan). He has delegated much of the day-to-day field operation to his son, Sirajuddin Haqqani, who is said to be military commander over all the Taliban-aligned militants in the Waziristan tribal regions. Experts estimate the number of Taliban operatives at between 30,000 and 35,000 in this region.

In June 2006, in advance of the Waziristan accord, the elder Haqqani issued a decree that stated that while the fight with the US and Karzai governments will continue "till the last drop of blood", it was no longer Taliban policy to continue to fight with the Pakistan army. The ceasefire edict was circulated only in South Waziristan, however, to keep pressure on the Pakistan government towards reaching a peace accord in the north (ultimately the Waziristan accord).

The Haqqani edict resulted in a partial ceasefire in South Waziristan, although some tribal militias continued to fight on in hopes of winning the release of fellow rebels imprisoned by the government. Ultimately it would be the Waziristan accord that would secure the release of all rebel fighters, both Taliban and non-Taliban. While reporting on the June ceasefire in South Waziristan, the Dawn newspaper in Pakistan also reported that a senior Taliban figure (left unnamed), in consultation with local tribal leaders, had blessed Maulavi Nazir Ahmad as head of the militants of the Ahmadzai Wazir (tribe).

The senior leader also endorsed Baitullah Mehsud to continue as head of the *Mujahideen* of the Mahsud tribe and appointed, Abdullah Mehsud, a renowned fugitive jihadist, to head a shura of *Mujahideen* representing four additional tribes. It is not clear if Maulavi Jalaluddin Haqqani, and thus the entire Pakistan Taliban leadership, identifies himself as a part of a Taliban, or if it is a smaller, and perhaps non-Taliban, group of militants who invoke this name as a rallying cry.

After an initial miscue, the Government of Pakistan has consistently emphasized the Taliban was not party to the accord. However, on 24 September, The Daily Telegraph published an article revealing the previously unnamed "senior leader" to be none other than Mullah Omar, the former leader of the Taliban in Afghanistan. Regarding Mullah Omar's role in the southern ceasefire and the truce in North Waziristan, the Telegraph quotes Lateef Afridi, a tribal elder and former member of the Pakistan national assembly, as saying:

"Had [local tribal militants] been not asked by Mullah Omar, none of them were willing to sign an agreement.... This is no peace agreement, it is accepting Taliban rule in Pakistan's territory."

Though proclaimed by the rebels as a "state" or "emirate", there are questions regarding the region being called as such. Those who support that the region is a state point to the facts that the federal authority is little to nonexistent and that the area is ruled mostly by tribal elders. Moreover, Taliban reportedly control most of the region with its own authoritarian rule including beheadings and other violent punishments which the Pakistan government has been unable to stop. Such brazen show of authority has led one author in the *Wall Street Journal* to remark that Waziristan Agency was a "state within a state."

PAKISTAN'S NEW WAZIRISTAN STRATEGY

On 4 June the National Security Council of Pakistan met to decide the fate of Waziristan and take up a number of political and administrative decisions to control "Talibanization" of the area. The meeting was chaired by President Pervez Musharraf and it was attended by the Chief Ministers and Governors of all 4 provinces. They discussed the deteriorating law and order situation and the threat posed to state security. The government decided to take a number of actions to stop the "Talibanization" and crush the armed militancy in the Tribal regions and the NWFP.

The NSC of Pakistan has decided the following actions will be taken to achieve the goals:

- Deployment of unmanned reconnaissance planes
- Strengthening law-enforcement agencies with advanced equipment
- Deployment of more troops to the region
- Operations against militants on fast-track basis
- Focused operations against militant commanders
- Action against madrasahs preaching militancy
- Appointment of regional coordinators
- Fresh Recruitments of police officers in NWFP

The ministry of interior has played a large part in the information gathering for the operations against militants and their institutions. The Ministry of Interior has prepared a list of militant commanders operating in the region and they have also prepared a list of seminaries for monitoring. The Government is also trying to strengthen the law enforcement in the area by providing the NWFP Police with weapons, bullet-proof jackets and night-vision devices. The paramilitary Frontier Corps will be provided with artillery and APC's. The state agencies are also working on studying ways to block FM frequencies of illegal FM radio channels.

U.S.-LED INVASION AND DISPLACEMENT OF THE TALIBAN

After the 11 September attacks and the PENTTBOM investigation, the USA delivered this ultimatum to the Taliban:

1. Deliver to the US all of the leaders of Al Qaeda;
2. Release all imprisoned foreign nationals;
3. Close immediately every terrorist training camp;
4. Hand over every terrorist and their supporters to appropriate authorities;
5. Give the United States full access to terrorist training camps for inspection.

On 21 September 2001, the Taliban responded that if the United States could bring evidence that bin Laden was guilty, they would hand him over, and stating there was no evidence in their possession linking him to the 11 September attacks.

On 22 September 2001, the United Arab Emirates, and later Saudi Arabia, withdrew recognition of the Taliban as the legal government of Afghanistan, leaving neighboring Pakistan as the only remaining country with diplomatic ties. On 4 October 2001, it is believed that the Taliban covertly offered to turn bin Laden over to Pakistan for trial in an international tribunal that operated according to Islamic Sharia law, but Pakistan refused the offer. On 7 October 2001, before the onset of military operations, the Taliban ambassador to Pakistan offered to "detain bin Laden and try him under Islamic law" if the United States made a formal request and presented the Taliban with evidence. This counter offer was immediately rejected by the U.S. as insufficient.

Coalition attack

Shortly afterward, on 7 October 2001, the United States, aided by the United Kingdom, Canada, and supported by a coalition of other countries including several from the NATO alliance, initiated military actions in Afghanistan, and bombed Taliban and *Al Qaeda* related camps. CIA's elite Special Activities Division (SAD) units were the first US forces to enter Afghanistan. Their efforts organized the Afghan Northern Alliance for the subsequent arrival of US Special Operations forces. SAD, US Army Special Forces and the Northern Alliance combined to overthrow the Taliban in Afghanistan with minimal loss to Americans lives. They did this without the need for US military conventional forces.

The Washington Post stated in an editorial by John Lehman in 2006:

What made the Afghan campaign a landmark in the U.S. Military's history is that it was prosecuted by Special Operations forces from all the services, along with Navy and Air Force tactical power, operations by the Afghan Northern Alliance and the CIA were equally important and fully integrated. No large Army or Marine force was employed.

The stated intent of military operations was to remove the

Taliban from power because of the Taliban's refusal to hand over Osama bin Laden for his alleged involvement in the 11 September attacks, and disrupt the use of Afghanistan as a terrorist base of operations.

On 14 October the Taliban offered to discuss handing over Osama bin Laden to a neutral country if the US halted bombing, but only if the Taliban were given evidence of Bin Laden's involvement in 9/11. The U.S. rejected this offer as an insufficient public relations ploy and continued military operations. The ground war was fought mainly by the Northern Alliance, the remaining elements of the anti-Taliban forces which the Taliban had routed over the previous years but had never been able to entirely destroy.

Mazari Sharif fell to U.S.-Northern Alliance forces on 9 November, leading to a cascade of provinces falling with minimal resistance, and many local forces switching loyalties from the Taliban to the Northern Alliance. On the night of 12 November, the Taliban retreated south from Kabul. On 15 November, they released eight Western aid workers after three months in captivity. By 13 November the Taliban had withdrawn from both Kabul and Jalalabad. Finally, in early December, the Taliban gave up their last city stronghold of Kandahar and dispersed in various directions.

WAR IN AFGHANISTAN (2001–PRESENT)

The War in Afghanistan, which began on October 7, 2001 as the U.S. military operation Operation Enduring Freedom, was launched by the United States with the United Kingdom, and NATO-led, UN authorized ISAF in response to the September 11 attacks. The stated aim of the invasion was to find the whereabouts of Osama bin Laden and other high-ranking *Al Qaeda* members and put them on trial, to destroy the whole organization of al-Qaeda, and to remove the Taliban regime which supported and gave safe harbor to al-Qaeda. The United States' Bush Doctrine stated that, as policy, it would not distinguish between terrorist organisations and nations or governments that harbor them.

Two military operations in Afghanistan are fighting for control over the country. Operation Enduring Freedom (OEF) is a United States combat operation involving some coalition partners and currently operating primarily in the eastern and southern parts of the country along the Pakistan border. Approximately 28,300 U.S. troops are in OEF. The second operation is the International Security Assistance Force (ISAF), which was established by the UN Security Council at the end of December 2001 to secure Kabul and the surrounding areas. NATO assumed control of ISAF in 2003. By January 12, 2009, ISAF had around 55,100 troops from 41 countries, with NATO members providing the core of the force. The United States has approximately 23,300 troops in ISAF.

The U.S. and the UK led the aerial bombing campaign, with ground forces supplied primarily by the Afghan Northern Alliance. In 2002, American, British and Canadian infantry were committed, along with Special Forces from several allied nations including Australia. Later, NATO troops were added. The initial attack removed the Taliban from power, but Taliban forces have since regained some strength. The war has been less successful in achieving the goal of restricting al-Qaeda's movement than anticipated.

Since 2006, Afghanistan has seen threats to its stability from increased Taliban-led insurgent activity, record-high levels of illegal drug production, and a fragile government with limited control outside of Kabul. The war has been unsuccessful in its primary purpose of capturing Osama bin Laden, while tensions have grown between the USA and Pakistan due to incidents of coalition troops crossing the Pakistan border while pursuing Taliban fighters.

Osama Bin Laden had been living in Afghanistan along with other members of Al-Qaeda, operating terrorist training camps having a loose alliance with the Taliban. Following the 1998 U.S. embassy bombings in Africa, the U.S. military launched submarine-based cruise missiles at these camps with limited effect on their overall operations. The UN Security Council had issued Resolutions 1267 and 1333 in 1999 and 2000 directed towards the Taliban which applied financial and military hardware sanctions to encourage them to turn over Bin Laden for trial in the deadly bombings of two U.S. embassies in Africa in August 1998, and close terrorist training camps and also children terrorist training camps.

U.S. PLANS TO REMOVE THE TALIBAN PRIOR TO SEPTEMBER 11, 2001

NBC News reported in May 2002 that a formal National Security Presidential Directive submitted two days before September 11, 2001 had outlined essentially the same war plan that the White House, the CIA and the Pentagon put into action after the Sept. 11 attacks. The plan dealt with all aspects of a war against *Al-Qaeda,* ranging from diplomatic initiatives to military operations in Afghanistan, including outlines to persuade Afghanistan's Taliban government to turn *Al Qaeda* leader Osama bin Laden over to the United States, with provisions to use military force if it refused.

According to a 2004 report by the bipartisan commission of inquiry into 9/11, on the very next day, one day before the September 11, 2001 attacks, the Bush administration agreed on a plan to oust the Taliban regime in Afghanistan by force if it refused to hand over Osama bin Laden. At that September 10 meeting of the Bush administration's top national security officials it was agreed that the Taliban would be presented with a final ultimatum to hand over Bin Laden. Failing that, covert military aid would be channelled by the U.S. to anti-Taliban groups. And, if both those options failed, "the deputies agreed that the United States would seek to overthrow the Taliban regime through more direct action."

However, an article published in March 2001 by *Jane's*, a media outlet serving the military and intelligence communities, suggests that the United States had already been planning and taking just such action against the Taliban six months before September 11, 2001. According to Jane's, Washington was giving the Northern Alliance information and logistics support as part of concerted action with India, Iran, and Russia against Afghanistan's Taliban regime, with Tajikistan and Uzbekistan being used as bases.

The BBC News reported that, according to a Pakistani diplomat, Niaz Naik, a former Pakistani Foreign Secretary, had been told by senior American officials in mid-July 2001 that military action against Afghanistan would proceed by the middle of October at the latest. The message was conveyed during a meeting on Afghanistan between senior U.S., Russian, Iranian, and Pakistani diplomats. The meeting was the third in a series of meetings on Afghanistan, with the previous meeting having been held in March 2001.

During the July 2001 meeting, Mr. Naik was told that Washington would launch its military operation from bases in Tajikistan - where American advisers were already in place - and that the wider objective was to topple the Taliban regime and install another government in place. An article in *The Guardian* on September 26, 2001 also adds evidence that there were already signs in the first half of 2001 that Washington was moving to threaten Afghanistan militarily from the north, via Tajikistan and Uzbekistan.

A U.S. Department of Defense official, Dr. Jeffrey Starr, visited Tajikistan in January 2001 and U.S. General Tommy Franks visited the country in May 2001, conveying a message from the Bush administration that the US considered Tajikistan "a strategically significant country". U.S. Army Rangers were training special troops inside Kyrgyzstan, and there were unconfirmed reports that Tajik and Uzbek special troops were training in Alaska and Montana. Reliable western military sources say a U.S. contingency plan existed on paper by the end of the summer to attack Afghanistan from the north, with U.S. military advisors already in place in Tajikistan and Uzbekistan.

SEPTEMBER 11, 2001 ATTACKS

days after the events of September 11, 2001, U.S. President George W. Bush identified Osama Bin Laden as the 'prime suspect' in the attacks. Osama bin Laden was understood to be in Afghanistan at the time. On September 20, 2001, in an address to a joint session of Congress, President Bush issued an ultimatum demanding that the Taliban government of Afghanistan:

- Deliver *Al Qaeda* leaders located in Afghanistan to the United States authorities.
- Release all imprisoned foreign nationals, including American citizens.
- Protect foreign journalists, diplomats, and aid workers in Afghanistan.
- Close terrorist training camps in Afghanistan and "hand over every terrorist and every person and their support structure to appropriate authorities".
- Give the United States full access to terrorist training camps to verify their closure.

"They will hand over the terrorists or they will share in their fate" said Bush. No specifics were attached to the threat, though there followed a statement suggesting military action: "Our war on terror begins with al Qaeda, but it does not end there." The Taliban government responded through their embassy in Pakistan, asserting that there was no evidence in their possession linking bin Laden to the September 11 attacks. They also stressed that bin Laden was a guest in their country. Pashtun and Taliban codes of behavior require that guests be granted hospitality and asylum.

On September 22, 2001, the United Arab Emirates, and on the following day, Saudi Arabia withdrew their recognition of the Taliban as the legal government of Afghanistan, leaving neighboring Pakistan as the only remaining country with diplomatic ties. On October 7, 2001, before the onset of military hostilities, the Taliban did offer to try bin Laden in Afghanistan in an Islamic court. This offer was rejected by the U.S., and the bombing of targets within Afghanistan by U.S. and British forces commenced the same day.

October 14, 2001, seven days into the U.S./British bombing campaign, the Taliban offered to surrender Osama bin Laden to a third country for trial, if the bombing halted and they were shown evidence of his involvement in the September 11 terrorist attacks. This offer was also rejected by

U.S. President Bush, who declared "There's no need to discuss innocence or guilt. We know he's guilty."

The United Nations Security Council (UNSC) did not authorize the U.S.-led military campaign in Afghanistan (Operation Enduring Freedom). There is some debate as to whether UNSC authorization was required, centered around the question of whether the invasion was an act of collective self-defense provided for under Article 51 of the UN Charter, or an act of aggression. Also, the U.S. Administration did not officially declare war, and labeled Taliban troops and supporting terrorists rather than soldiers, denying them the protections of the Geneva Convention and due process of law.

This position has been successfully challenged in the U.S. Supreme Court and questioned even by military lawyers responsible for prosecuting affected prisoners. On December 20, 2001, the UNSC did authorize the creation of an International Security Assistance Force (ISAF) with authority to take all measures necessary to fulfill its mandate of assisting the Afghan Interim Authority in maintaining security. Command of the ISAF passed to NATO on August 11, 2003.

2001: INITIAL ATTACK

Teams from the Central Intelligence Agency's famed Special Activities Division were the first U.S. forces to enter Afghanistan and begin combat operations. They were soon joined by U.S. Army Special Forces from the 5th Special Forces Group and other units from USSOCOM. These combined forces led the Northern Alliance to overthrow the Taliban in Afghanistan with minimal loss to American lives. They did this without the need for U.S. Military conventional forces.

On October 7, 2001, strikes were reported in the capital, Kabul (where electricity supplies were severed), at the airport and military nerve-center of Kandahar (home of the Taliban's Supreme Leader Mullah Omar), and also in the city of Jalalabad. At 17:00 UTC, President Bush confirmed the strikes on national television and Prime Minister of the United Kingdom Tony Blair also addressed the UK. Bush stated that at the same time as Taliban military and terrorists' training grounds would be targeted, food, medicine, and supplies would be dropped to "the starving and suffering men, women and children of Afghanistan".

CNN released exclusive footage of Kabul being bombed to all the American broadcasters at approximately 5:08 p.m. October 7, 2001. A number of different technologies were employed in the strike. U.S. Air Force general Richard Myers, chairman of the U.S. Joint Chiefs of Staff, stated that approximately 50 Tomahawk cruise missiles, launched by British and U.S. submarines and ships, 25 strike aircraft from U.S. aircraft carriers, USS *Carl Vinson* and USS *Enterprise* and 15 U.S. Air Force bombers, such as B-1 Lancer, B-2 Spirit, B-52 Stratofortress were involved in the first wave, launched from Diego Garcia.

Two C-17 Globemaster transport jets delivered 37,500 daily rations by airdrop to refugees inside Afghanistan on the first day of the attack. A pre-recorded videotape of Osama bin Laden had been released before the attack in which he condemned any attacks against Afghanistan. *Al Jazeera*, the Arabic satellite news channel, reported that these tapes were received shortly before the attack. In this recording bin Laden claimed that the United States would fail in Afghanistan and then collapse, just as the Soviet Union did.

INITIAL AIR CAMPAIGNS

Bombers operating at high altitudes well out of range of anti-aircraft fire bombed the *Al Qaeda* training camps and Taliban air defenses. During the initial build-up preceding the actual attack, there had been speculation in the media that the Taliban might try to use U.S.-built Stinger anti-aircraft missiles that were the bane of Soviet helicopters during the Soviet occupation in the 1980s. If any of these missiles existed at the time of the air campaign, they were never used and the U.S. did not lose any aircraft to enemy fire. U.S. aircraft, including Apache helicopter gunships, operated with impunity throughout the campaign.

The strikes initially focused on the area in and around the cities of Kabul, Jalalabad, and Kandahar. Within a few days, most Taliban training sites were severely damaged and the Taliban's air defenses were destroyed. The campaign then focused on command, control, and communication targets which weakened the ability of the Taliban forces to communicate. However, the line facing the Afghan Northern Alliance held, and no tangible battlefield successes had yet occurred on that front. Two weeks into the campaign, the Northern Alliance demanded the air campaign focus more on the front lines. Meanwhile, thousands of Pashtun militiamen from Pakistan poured into the country, reinforcing the Taliban against the U.S. led forces.

The next stage of the campaign began with carrier based F/A-18 Hornet fighter-bombers hitting Taliban vehicles in pinpoint strikes, while other U.S. planes began cluster bombing Taliban defenses. For the first time in years, Northern Alliance commanders finally began to see the serious results that they had long hoped for on the front lines. The Taliban support structure began to erode under the pressure of the air-strikes. U.S. Army Special Forces then launched an audacious raid deep into the Taliban's heartland of Kandahar, even striking one of Mullah Omar's compounds.

At the beginning of November, the Taliban front lines were bombed with 15,000-pound daisy cutter bombs, and by AC-130 gunships. The Taliban fighters had no previous experience with American firepower, and often even stood on top of bare ridgelines where Special Forces could easily spot them and call in close air support. By November 2, Taliban frontal positions were decimated, and a Northern Alliance march on Kabul seemed possible for the first time. Foreign fighters from *Al Qaeda* took over security in the Afghan cities, demonstrating the instability of the Taliban regime.

Meanwhile, the Northern Alliance and their Central intelligence Agency/Special Forces advisors planned the next stage of their offensive. Northern Alliance troops would seize Mazari Sharif, thereby cutting off Taliban supply lines and enabling the flow of equipment from the countries to the north, followed by an attack on Kabul itself. The *Washington Post* stated in an editorial by the former Madical Seceratary Lamar Hose' Christopherson in 2006:

What made the Afghan campaign a landmark in the U.S. Military's history is that it was prosecuted by Special Operations forces from all the services, along with Navy and Air Force tactical power, operations by the Afghan Northern Alliance and the CIA were equally important and fully integrated. No large Army or Marine force was employed.

AREAS MOST TARGETED

During the early months of the war the U.S. military had a limited presence on the ground. The plan was that Special Forces, and intelligence officers with a military background, would serve as liaisons with Afghan militias opposed to the Taliban, would advance after the cohesiveness of the Taliban forces was disrupted by American air power. The Tora Bora Mountains lie roughly east of Afghanistan's capital Kabul, which is itself close to the border with Pakistan.

American intelligence analysts believed that the Taliban and *Al Qaeda* had dug in behind fortified networks of well-supplied caves and underground bunkers. The area was subjected to a heavy continuous bombardment by B52 bombers. The U.S. forces and the Northern Alliance also began to diverge in their objectives. While the U.S. was continuing the search for Osama bin Laden, the Northern Alliance was pressuring for more support in their efforts to finish off the Taliban and control the country.

Scott Peterson, writing in the *Christian Science Monitor*, quoted a defector he described as the Taliban deputy interior minister, and "highest ranking Taliban defector to date". According to Peterson this defector described the American bombardment as very effective:

- "Kabul city has seen many rockets, but this was a different thing."

- "The American bombing of Taliban trenches, cars, and troops caused us to be defeated. All ways were blocked, so there was no way to carry food or ammunition to the front. All trenches of the Taliban were destroyed, and many people were killed."

LEADUP TO THE GROUND WAR

Mazar- i- Sharif became a primary objective for the U.S. and its allies and its seizure was the result of the first major U.S. backed offensive of the 2001 war in Afghanistan. The decision to launch the first major strike of the war in Northern Afghanistan came following a meeting between U.S. Army General Tommy Franks with Northern Alliance commander Mohammed Fahim in Tajikstan early in October. In the days leading up to the battle, Noıthern Alliance troops advanced on population centers within the Shol Ghar district, 25 kilometers from Mazar-e-Sharif. In addition, phonelines into the city were severed and officials related stories of Northern Alliance forces charging Taliban tanks on horseback while short distance away targets were being engaged by Americans calling in CAS.

Handbills (leaflets) were dropped from airplanes listing the radio frequencies over which Americans would be broadcasting anti-Taliban statements, where weapons can be turned in, who the opposition targets are and where civilian safe havens were. On November 5, General Dostum led the Uzbek faction in an attack on the cities of Keshendeh-bala, Keshendeh-pane and various other strongholds within the Darya Suf Valley south-west of Mazar-e-Sharif, seizing them with U.S. Special Operators and his horse-mounted troops. But, it was in the town of Bai Beche that the tide began to turn with the death of a key Taliban commander, the capture of another and the destruction of 150 troops during a battle that lasted over 12 hours.

General Noor, meanwhile, led 2000 Tajik forces against Ag Kupruk directly south of the city, along with six Special Forces soldiers, and seven others who directed bombing from behind Taliban lines north of the city, and it was seized two days later. On November 7, New York University Director of Studies on International Cooperation Barnett Rubin appeared before the American Committee on International Relations hearing on *The Future of Afghanistan*, and warned that with Mazar-e-Sharif clearly about to fall, there was a responsibility to ensure that there were no reprisal killings of Taliban members by the Northern Alliance; noting that the last two times the city had been overrun, thousands had been killed by Taliban, a sentiment echoed by a the opposition's key Shiite Muslim Commander, Mohammed Mohaqik.

PRECISION TARGETING CAMPAIGN

As Al-Qaeda-backed Harkat-ul-Jihad-al-Islami began moving 4,000 fighters across the countryside towards Mazar-e-Sharif in preparation for battle, American Special Operation Forces launched a precision targeting campaign utilizing J-DAM's from platforms such as B-52 bombers, F/A 18's and F-14's and engaged dug-in Taliban defenders concentrated in the Chesmay-e-Safa gorge that marked the southern entrance to the city. At the Kuh-e Al Borz pass, while being shelled by artillery, an American Air Force Special Operations JTAC called in close air support and destroyed all the targets allowing U.S. and Northern Alliance Forces the ability to push through the choke point on their way towards Mazar-i Sharif.

This pass was the southern most Taliban-controlled entrance to the city. The interlocking bunkers at the pass were manned by over 200 mounted Taliban and *Al Qaeda* personnel with anti-aircraft ZSU 23-2's and a BM21 multiple rocket launch artillery system. Despite their losses, the Taliban stated they were still able to bring 500-8,000 fresh fighters into the city to prepare for the coming battle. In an attempt to shoot down U.S. Aircraft, Taliban forces fired their anti-aircraft guns at the planes, but were unsuccessful.

THE NORTHERN ALLIANCE'S ADVANCES ON MAZAR-E-SHARIF

The battle for Mazar-e-Sharif was considered important,

not only because it is the home of the Shrine of Hazrat Ali or "Blue Mosque", a sacred Muslim site, but also because it is the location of two main airports and a major road that leads into Uzbekistan. On November 9, Northern Alliance forces, under the command of generals Abdul Rashid Dostum and Ustad Atta Mohammed Noor, swept across the Pul-i-Imam Bukhri Bridge, meeting some resistance and seized the city's main military base and airport.

While on horseback, U.S. Special Operation Forces (namely ODA 595 and their Air Force counterparts) utilized Close Air Support platforms to accompany a push into the city of Mazar-e-Sharif in the Balkh Province by the United Islamic Front for the Salvation of Afghanistan ("Northern Alliance") which, resulted in the withdrawal of Taliban forces that had held the city since 1998 and triggered jubilant celebrations among the local citizens. The fall of the city was a "body blow" to the Taliban and *Al Qaeda* and ultimately proved to be a "major shock", since the United States Central Command (CENTCOM) had originally believed that the city would remain in Taliban hands well into the following year, and any potential battle would be "a very slow advance".

After outlying villages fell from precision air strikes on key command and control centers, approximately 5,000-12,000 Taliban and foreign fighters - including Chechen, Pakistan, Arabs, Uzbeks and Chinese Uyghurs, began their withdrawal from the city towards Kunduz, in pickup trucks, SUVs and flat bed trucks fitted with ZSU 23-2's (anti-aircraft guns that were used to engage ground forces), in an effort to regroup.

The "ragtag" non-uniformed Northern Alliance forces entered the city from the Balk Valley on "begged, borrowed and confiscated transportation," and met only light resistance. By sunset, the vast majority of the Taliban forces had retreated to the north and east, in an attempt to mass for a counter-offensive. It was later estimated that 400-600 people had died in the battle. Approximately 1,500 Taliban were captured or defected to the U.S. backed opposition.

A British newspaper, The Times, claimed "The seizure of

Mazar-e-Sharif on Friday [November 9] represented the first substantial victory of the campaign...It made it possible, at last, to draw a cross on a map to show where the Taliban had been pushed back." Upholding the claim by Taliban officials that they would be able to move 500 fresh fighters into the city, as many as 900 Pakistani fighters reached Mazar-e-Sharif in the following days as the majority of the Taliban were evacuating. It was determined later that many of these young fighters were recruited by a Pakistani Mullah, Sufi Mohammed, who used a loudspeaker riveted onto pickup trucks which blared "Those who die fighting for God don't die! Those who go on jihad live forever, in paradise!"

For almost two days as the group, led by a large number of Chechen and Arab hardliners, gathered in the abandoned Sultan Razia Girls' School building up their fighting positions, the town officials and Northern Alliance attempted negotiations for their surrender, but the fighters vehemently refused, ultimately killing two peace envoys, one town mullah and a soldier escort. All the while they constantly fired at anyone that moved within the vicinity of the building, including civilian bystanders. After the murders of the envoys, the Northern Alliance began returning fire on the school with machine guns with little effect. This gun battle went on for hours. Inside the battered school, someone scrawled on the walls the words of their mullah: "Die for Pakistan" and "Never Surrender."

At mid-afternoon, U.S. military advisers approved the building for a bombing run. "We had determined the school was an appropriate target," said Army Col. Rick Thomas of the U.S. Central Command. "Our philosophy has been surrender or die." During the battle, on November 10, 2001, nearly 2 months to the date of the September 11 attacks on the World Trade Center, an American Special Operations JTAC called in the air strike which obliterated the compound and the enemy within. For that Direct Action mission, combined with the numerous engagements and actions throughout Northern Afghanistan, Sgt. Stephen E. Tomat has been credited with over 950 Enemy KIA and was awarded the Silver Star.

Mazar-e-Sharif had significant strategic import, as its capture opened resupply routes and provided a potential airstrip for humanitarian aid via U.S. airlifts as well as deliveries by relief organizations to hungry people in the countryside. This aid alleviated Afghanistan's looming food crisis, which had threatened more than six million people with starvation. A large proportion of those in most urgent need lived in rural areas to the south and west of Mazar-e-Sharif. Despite some European papers hesitancy to label the seizure of the city a military victory, others saw their retreat as the beginning of their demise. It is considered the first major defeat of the Taliban and its allies.

AFTER THE FALL OF MAZAR-E-SHARIF

Following rumors that Mullah Dadullah may be headed to recapture the city with as many as 8,000 Taliban fighters, a thousand American 10th Mountain Soldiers were airlifted into the city, which provided the first solid foothold from which Kabul and Kandahar could be reached. While prior military flights had to be launched from Uzbekistan or Aircraft carriers in the Arabian Sea, now the Americans held their own airport in the country which allowed them to fly more frequent sorties for resupply missions and humanitarian aid.

These missions allowed massive shipments of humanitarian aid to be immediately shipped to hundreds of thousands of Afghans facing starvation on the northern plain. After the U.S. Special Operation Forces departed the city for further operations in and around Konduz, there were later purported reports of summary executions and the kidnapping of civilians by the Northern Alliance. It was also told that the young men who were captured, were often brutally abused by their Northern Alliance captors who demanded a ransom from their families for their return. Some of them may still be incarcerated.

It was also revealed that the airfield had been boobytrapped by the Taliban as they left, with explosives planted around the property, as well as being badly damaged by their own Air Interdiction missions in order to prevent it being used by the enemy. The destroyed runways on the airfield were patched by the U.S. Air Force Red Horse personnel and local Afghans hired to fill bomb craters with asphalt and tar by hand, and the first cargo plane was able to land ten days after the battle. The airbase wasn't declared operational until December 11.

The American-backed forces now controlling the city began immediately broadcasting from *Radio Mazar-e-Sharif*, the former Taliban *Voice of Sharia* channel on 1584 kHz, including an address from former President Burhanuddin Rabbani. Music was also broadcast over Kabul radio for the first time in five years, and the songs were introduced by a female announcer-another major breakthrough for a city where women have been banned from education, work, and many other civil liberties since 1996.

THE FALL OF KABUL

On the night of November 12 Taliban forces fled from the city of Kabul, leaving under cover of darkness. By the time Northern Alliance forces arrived in the afternoon of November 13, only bomb craters, burned foliage, and the burnt out shells of Taliban gun emplacements and positions were there to greet them. A group of about twenty hardline Arab fighters hiding in the city's park were the only remaining defenders. This Taliban group was killed in a brief 15-minute gun battle, being heavily outnumbered and having had little more than a telescope to shield them. After these forces were neutralized Kabul was in the hands of the U.S./NATO forces and the Northern Alliance.

The fall of Kabul marked the beginning of a collapse of Taliban positions across the map. Within 24 hours, all of the Afghan provinces along the Iranian border, including the key city of Herat, had fallen. Local Pashtun commanders and warlords had taken over throughout northeastern Afghanistan, including the key city of Jalalabad. Taliban holdouts in the north, mainly Pakistani volunteers, fell back to the northern city of Kunduz to make a stand. By November 16, the Taliban's last stronghold in northern Afghanistan was besieged by the Northern Alliance. Nearly 10,000 Taliban fighters, led by foreign fighters, refused to surrender and continued to put up resistance. By then, the Taliban had been forced back to their heartland in southeastern Afghanistan around Kandahar.

By November 13, *Al Qaeda* and Taliban forces, with the possible inclusion of Osama bin Laden, had regrouped and were concentrating their forces in the Tora Bora cave complex, on the Pakistan border 50 kilometers (30 mi) southwest of Jalalabad, to prepare for a stand against the Northern Alliance and U.S./NATO forces. Nearly 2,000 *Al Qaeda* and Taliban fighters fortified themselves in positions within bunkers and caves, and by November 16, U.S. bombers began bombing the mountain fortress. Around the same time, CIA and Special Forces operatives were already at work in the area, enlisting and paying local warlords to join the fight and planning an attack on the Tora Bora complex.

DRONE STRIKE AGAINST MOHAMMAD ATEF

Al Qaeda leader Mohammad Atef was killed in an airstrike on November 15, 2001. The Hellfire missile was fired by a MQ-1 Predator outside Gardez. The attack also killed other high ranking *Al Qaeda* personnel.

THE FALL OF KUNDUZ

Just as the bombardment at Tora Bora was stepped up, the siege of Kunduz that began on November 16 was continuing. Finally, after nine days of heavy fighting and American aerial bombardment, Taliban fighters surrendered to Northern Alliance forces on November 25-November 26. Shortly before the surrender, Pakistani aircraft arrived ostensibly to evacuate a few hundred intelligence and military personnel who had been in Afghanistan previous to the U.S. invasion for the purpose of aiding the Taliban's ongoing fight against the Northern Alliance. However, during this airlift, it is alleged that up to five thousand people were evacuated from the region, including Taliban and *Al Qaeda* troops allied to the Pakistanis in Afghanistan.

THE BATTLE OF QALA-I-JANGI

On November 25, the day that Taliban fighters holding out in Kunduz surrendered and were being herded into the Qala-I-Janghi fortress near Mazar-e-Sharif, a few Taliban attacked some Northern Alliance guards, taking their weapons and opening fire. This incident soon triggered a widespread revolt by 300 prisoners, who soon seized the southern half of the complex, once a medieval fortress, including an armory stocked with small arms and crew-served weapons.

One American CIA operative who had been interrogating prisoners, Johnny Micheal Spann, was killed, marking the first American combat death in the war. The revolt was finally put down after seven days of heavy fighting between an SBS unit along with some US Army Special Forces and Northern Alliance, AC-130 gunships and other aircraft took part providing strafing fire on several occasions, as well as a bombing airstrikes. 86 of the Taliban prisoners survived, and around 50 Northern Alliance soldiers were killed. The quashing of the revolt marked the end of the combat in northern Afghanistan, where local Northern Alliance warlords were now firmly in control.

CONSOLIDATION: THE TAKING OF KANDAHAR

By the end of November, Kandahar, the movement's birthplace, was the last remaining Taliban stronghold and was coming under increasing pressure. Nearly 3,000 tribal fighters, led by Hamid Karzai, a westernized and polished loyalist of the former Afghan king, and Gul Agha Sherzai, the governor of Kandahar before the Taliban seized power, put pressure on Taliban forces from the east and cut off the northern Taliban supply lines to Kandahar. The threat of the Northern Alliance loomed in the north and northeast. Meanwhile, the first significant U.S. combat troops had arrived. Nearly 1,000 Marines, ferried in by CH-53E Super Stallion helicopters, set up a Forward Operating Base known as Camp Rhino in the desert south of Kandahar on November 25. This was the coalition's first strategic foothold in Afghanistan, and was the stepping stone to establishing other operating bases.

The first significant combat involving U.S. ground forces occurred a day after Rhino was captured when 15 armored vehicles approached the base and were attacked by helicopter gunships, destroying many of them. Meanwhile, the airstrikes continued to pound Taliban positions inside the city, where Mullah Omar was holed up. Omar, the Taliban leader, remained defiant despite the fact that his movement only controlled 4 out of the 30 Afghan provinces by the end of November and called on his forces to fight to the death.

As the Taliban teetered on the brink of losing their last bastion, the U.S. focus increased on the Tora Bora. Local tribal militias, numbering over 2,000 strong and paid and organized by Special Forces and CIA paramilitaries, continued to mass for an attack as heavy bombing continued of suspected *Al Qaeda* positions. 100-200 civilians were reported killed when 25 bombs struck a village at the foot of the Tora Bora and White Mountains region. On December 2, a group of 20 U.S. commandos was inserted by helicopter to support the operation. On December 5, Afghan militia wrested control of the low ground below the mountain caves from *Al Qaeda* fighters and set up tank positions to blast enemy forces.

The *Al Qaeda* fighters withdrew with mortars, rocket launchers, and assault rifles to higher fortified positions and dug in for the battle. By December 6, Omar finally began to signal that he was ready to surrender Kandahar to tribal forces. His forces broken by heavy U.S. bombing and living constantly on the run within Kandahar to prevent himself from becoming a target, even Mullah Omar's morale lagged. Recognizing that he could not hold on to Kandahar much longer, he began signaling a willingness in negotiations to turn the city over to the tribal leaders, assuming that he and his top men received some protection.

The U.S. government rejected any amnesty for Omar or any Taliban leaders. On December 7, Mullah Mohammad Omar slipped out of the city of Kandahar with a group of his hardcore loyalists and moved northwest into the mountains of Uruzgan Province, reneging on the Taliban's promise to surrender their fighters and their weapons. He was last reported seen driving off with a group of his fighters on a convoy of motorcycles. Other members of the Taliban leadership fled into Pakistan through the remote passes of Paktia and Paktika Provinces. Nevertheless, Kandahar, the last Taliban-controlled city, had fallen, and the majority of the Taliban fighters had disbanded. The border town of Spin Boldak was surrendered on the same day, marking the end of Taliban control in Afghanistan. The Afghan tribal forces under Gul Agha seized the city of Kandahar while the Marines took control of the airport outside and established a U.S. base.

BATTLE OF TORA BORA

Al Qaeda fighters were still holding out in the mountains of Tora Bora, however, while an anti-Taliban tribal militia steadily pushed bin Laden back across the difficult terrain, backed by withering air strikes guided in by U.S. and UK Special Forces. Facing defeat, the *Al Qaeda* forces agreed to a truce to give them time to surrender their weapons. In retrospect, however, many believe that the truce was a ruse to allow important *Al Qaeda* figures, including Osama bin Laden, to escape. On December 12, the fighting flared again, probably initiated by a rear guard buying time for the main force's escape through the White Mountains into the tribal areas of Pakistan.

Once again, tribal forces backed by British and U.S. special operations troops and air support pressed ahead against fortified *Al Qaeda* positions in caves and bunkers scattered throughout the mountainous region. By December 17, the last cave complex had been taken and their defenders overrun. A search of the area by U.S. and UK forces continued into January, but no sign of bin Laden or the *Al Qaeda* leadership emerged. It is almost unanimously believed that they had already slipped away into the tribal areas of Pakistan to the south and east. It is estimated that around 200 of the *Al Qaeda* fighters were killed during the battle, along with an unknown number of anti-Taliban tribal fighters. No U.S. or UK deaths were reported.

DIPLOMATIC EFFORTS

Meetings of various Afghan leaders were organized by the United Nations Security Council and took place in Germany. The Taliban were not included. These meetings produced an interim government and an agreement to allow a United Nations peacekeeping force to enter Afghanistan.

The UN Security Council resolutions of November 14, 2001, included "Condemning the Taliban for allowing Afghanistan to be used as a base for the export of terrorism by the *Al Qaeda* network and other terrorist groups and for providing safe haven to Osama bin Laden, *Al Qaeda* and others associated with them, and in this context supporting the efforts of the Afghan people to replace the Taliban regime"· The UN Security Council resolution of December 20, 2001, "Supporting international efforts to root out terrorism, in keeping with the Charter of the United Nations, and reaffirming also its resolutions 1368 (2001) of September 12, 2001 and 1373 (2001) of September 28, 2001."

HUMANITARIAN EFFORTS

Before the U.S.-led invasion, there were fears that the invasion and resultant disruption of services would cause widespread starvation and refugees. The United Nations World Food Programme temporarily suspended activities within Afghanistan at the beginning of the bombing attacks but resumed them after the fall of the Taliban agricultural programme through grass-roots village organizations in the province that they estimated could produce up to 30,000 tons of cereals annually.

By November 1, U.S. C-17s flying at 30,000 feet (10,000 m) had dropped 1,000,000 food and medicine packets marked with an American flag.

2002: OPERATION ANACONDA

Following Tora Bora, U.S. forces and their Afghan allies consolidated their position in the country. Following a Loya jirga or grand council of major Afghan factions, tribal leaders, and former exiles, an interim Afghan government was established in Kabul under Hamid Karzai. U.S. forces established their main base at Bagram airbase just north of Kabul. Kandahar airport also became an important U.S. base area. Several outposts were established in eastern provinces to hunt for Taliban and *Al Qaeda* fugitives. The number of U.S-led coalition troops operating in the country would eventually grow to over 10,000.

Meanwhile, the Taliban and *Al Qaeda* had not given up. *Al Qaeda* forces began regrouping in the Shahi-Kot Mountains of Paktia province throughout January and February 2002. A Taliban fugitive in Paktia province, Mullah Saifur Rehman, also began reconstituting some of his militia forces in support of the anti-U.S. fighters. They totalled over 1,000 by the beginning of March 2002. The intention of the insurgents was to use the region as a base area for launching guerrilla attacks and possibly a major offensive in the style of the *Mujahideen* who battled Soviet forces during the 1980s.

U.S. allied to Afghan militia intelligence sources soon picked up on this buildup in Paktia province and prepared a massive push to counter it. On March 2, 2002, U.S. and Afghan forces launched an offensive on *Al Qaeda* and Taliban forces entrenched in the mountains of Shahi-Kot southeast of Gardez. The jihadist forces, which used small arms, rocket-propelled grenades, and mortars, were entrenched into caves and bunkers in the hillsides at an altitude that was largely above 10,000 feet (3,000 m). They used "hit and run" tactics, opening fire on the U.S. and Afghan forces and then retreating back into their caves and bunkers to weather the return fire and persistent U.S. bombing raids.

To compound the situation for the coalition troops, U.S. commanders initially underestimated the Taliban and *Al Qaeda* forces as a last isolated pocket numbering fewer than 200. It turned out that the guerrillas numbered between 1,000-5,000 according to some estimates and that they were receiving reinforcements. By March 6, eight Americans and seven Afghan soldiers had been killed and reportedly 400 opposing forces had also been killed in the fighting. The coalition casualties stemmed from a friendly fire incident that killed one soldier, the downing of two helicopters by rocket-propelled grenades and small arms fire that killed seven soldiers, and the pinning down of U.S. forces being inserted into what was coined as "Objective Ginger" that resulted in dozens of wounded.

However, several hundred guerrillas escaped the dragnet heading to the Waziristan tribal areas across the border in Pakistan. During Operation Anaconda and other missions during 2002 and 2003, Special Forces from several western nations were also involved in operations. These included the Australian Special Air Service Regiment, the Canadian Joint Task Force 2, the German KSK, the New Zealand Special Air Service and Norwegian Marinejegerkommandoen.

POST-ANACONDA OPERATIONS

Following the battle at Shahi-Kot, it is believed that the *Al Qaeda* fighters established sanctuaries among tribal protectors in Pakistan, from which they regained their strength and later began launching cross-border raids on U.S. forces by the summer months of 2002. Guerrilla units, numbering between 5 and 25 men, still regularly crossed the border from their sanctuaries in Pakistan to fire rockets at U.S. bases and ambush American convoys and patrols, as well as Afghan National Army troops, Afghan militia forces working with the U.S-led coalition, and non-governmental organizations. The area around the U.S. base at Shkin in Paktika province saw some of the heaviest activity.

Meanwhile, Taliban forces continued to remain in hiding in the rural regions of the four southern provinces that formed their heartland, Kandahar, Zabul, Helmand Province, and Uruzgan. In the wake of Operation Anaconda the Pentagon requested that British Royal Marines who are highly trained in mountain warfare, be deployed. They conducted a number of missions over several weeks with varying results. The Taliban, who during the summer of 2002 numbered in the hundreds, avoided combat with U.S. forces and their Afghan allies as much as possible and melted away into the caves and tunnels of remote Afghan mountain ranges or across the border into Pakistan during operations.

2003-2005: RENEWED TALIBAN INSURGENCY

After managing to evade U.S. forces throughout mid-2002, the remnants of the Taliban gradually began to regain their confidence and started to begin preparations to launch the insurgency that Mullah Muhammad Omar had promised during the Taliban's last days in power. During September, Taliban forces began a recruitment drive in Pashtun areas in both Afghanistan and Pakistan to launch a renewed "jihad" or holy war against the Afghan government and the U.S-led coalition. Pamphlets distributed in secret during the night also began to appear in many villages in the former Taliban heartland in southeastern Afghanistan that called for jihad.

Small mobile training camps were established along the border with Pakistan by *Al Qaeda* and Taliban fugitives to train new recruits in guerrilla warfare and terrorist tactics, according to Afghan sources and a United Nations report. Most of the new recruits were drawn from the madrassas or religious schools of the tribal areas of Pakistan, from which the Taliban had originally arisen. Major bases, a few with as many as 200 men, were created in the mountainous tribal areas of Pakistan by the summer of 2003. The will of the Pakistani paramilitaries stationed at border crossings to prevent such infiltration was called into question, and Pakistani military operations proved of little use.

The Taliban gradually reorganized and reconstituted their forces over the winter, preparing for a summer offensive. They established a new mode of operation: gathered into groups of around 50 to launch attacks on isolated outposts and convoys of Afghan soldiers, police, or militia and then breaking up into groups of 5-10 men to evade subsequent offensives. U.S. forces in the strategy were attacked indirectly, through rocket attacks on bases and improvised explosive devices.

To coordinate the strategy, Mullah Omar named a 10-man leadership council for the resistance, with himself at the head. Five operational zones were created, assigned to various Taliban commanders such as the key Taliban leader Mullah Dadullah, in charge of Zabul province operations. *Al Qaeda* forces in the east had a bolder strategy of concentrating on the Americans and catching them when they could with elaborate ambushes.

The first sign that Taliban forces were regrouping came on January 27, 2003, during Operation Mongoose, when a band of fighters allied with the Taliban and Hezb-i-Islami were discovered and assaulted by U.S. forces at the Adi Ghar cave complex 15 miles (24 km) north of Spin Boldak. 18 rebels were reported killed and no U.S. casualties reported. The site was suspected to be a base to funnel supplies and fighters from Pakistan. The first isolated attacks by relatively large Taliban bands on Afghan targets also appeared around that time.

As the summer continued, the attacks gradually increased in frequency in the "Taliban heartland." Dozens of Afghan government soldiers, non-governmental organization and humanitarian workers, and several U.S. soldiers died in the raids, ambushes, and rocket attacks. In addition to the guerrilla attacks, Taliban fighters began building up their forces in the district of Dai Chopan, a district in Zabul Province that also straddles Kandahar and Uruzgan and is at the very center of the Taliban heartland.

Dai Chopan district is a remote and sparsely populated corner of southeastern Afghanistan composed of towering, Rocky Mountains interspersed with narrow gorges. Taliban fighters decided it would be the perfect area to make a stand against the Afghan government and the coalition forces. Over the course of the summer, perhaps the largest concentration of Taliban militants gathered in the area since the fall of the regime, with up to 1,000 guerrillas regrouping. Over 220 people, including several dozen Afghan police, were killed in August 2003 as Taliban fighters gained strength.

COALITION RESPONSE

As a result, coalition forces began preparing offensives to root out the rebel forces. In late August 2005, Afghan government forces backed by U.S troops and heavy American aerial bombardment advanced upon Taliban positions within the mountain fortress. After a one-week battle, Taliban forces were routed with up to 124 fighters (according to Afghan government estimates) killed. Taliban spokesmen, however, denied the high casualty figure and U.S estimates were somewhat lower.

2006: NATO IN SOUTHERN AFGHANISTAN

From January 2006, a NATO International Security Assistance Force (ISAF) started to replace the U.S. troops of Operation Enduring Freedom in southern Afghanistan. The British 16th Air Assault Brigade (later reinforced by Royal Marines) formed the core of the force in Southern Afghanistan, along with troops and helicopters from Australia, Canada and the Netherlands. The initial force consisted of roughly 3,300 British, 2,300 Canadian, 1,963 from the Netherlands, 290 from Denmark, 300 from Australia, and 150 from Estonia. Air support was provided by U.S., British, Dutch, Norwegian and French combat aircraft and helicopters.

In January 2006, NATO's focus in southern Afghanistan was to form Provincial Reconstruction Teams with the British leading in Helmand Province and the Netherlands and Canada would lead similar deployments in Orûzgan Province and Kandahar Province respectively. Local Taliban figures voiced opposition to the incoming force and pledged to resist it.

Southern Afghanistan faced in 2006 the deadliest spate of violence in the country since the ousting of the Taliban regime by U.S.-led forces in 2001, as the newly deployed NATO troops battled resurgent militants. NATO operations have been led by British, Canadian and Dutch commanders. Operation Mountain Thrust was launched on May 17, 2006 with the purpose of rooting out Taliban forces.

In July, Canadian Forces launched Operation Medusa in an attempt to clear the areas of Taliban fighters once and for all, supported by U.S., British, and Dutch and Danish forces. Further NATO operations included the Battle of Panjwaii, Operation Mountain Fury and Operation Falcon Summit. The fighting for NATO forces was intense throughout the second half of 2006. NATO has been successful in achieving tactical victories over the Taliban and denied areas to them, but the Taliban were not completely defeated, and NATO had to continue operations into 2007.

2007: COALITION OFFENSIVE

In January and February 2007, British Royal Marines mounted Operation Volcano to clear insurgents from firing points in the village of Barikju, north of Kajaki. This was followed by Operation Achilles, a major sweeping offensive that started in March and ended in late May. The UK ministry of defence announced its intention to bring British troop levels in the country up to 7,700 (committed until 2009). Further operations, such as Operation Silver and Operation Silicon, were conducted to keep up the pressure on the Taliban in the hopes of blunting their expected spring offensive.

On March 4, 2007, at least 12 civilians were killed and 33 were injured by U.S. Marines in the Shinwar district of the Nangrahar province of Afghanistan as the Americans reacted to a bomb ambush. The event has become known as the Shinwar Massacre. The 120 member Marine unit responsible for the attack was asked to leave the country because the incident damaged the unit's relations with the local Afghan population.

On May 12, 2007, ISAF forces killed Mullah Dadullah, a Taliban commander in charge of leading operations in the south of the country; eleven other Taliban fighters were killed in the same firefight. Operation Achilles ended on May 30, 2007 and was immediately followed by Operation Lastay Kulang that night. During the summer, NATO forces achieved tactical victories over the Taliban at the Battle of Chora in Orûzgan

Province, where Dutch and Australian ISAF forces are deployed.

On August 28, 2007, at least 100 Taliban fighters and one Afghan National Army soldier were killed in several skirmishes in the Shah Wali Kot district of Kandahar province. On October 28, 2007, about 80 Taliban fighters were killed in a 24 hour battle with forces from the U.S.-led coalition in Afghanistan's Helmand province. During the last days of October, Canadian forces surrounded around 300 militants near Arghandab and killed at least 50 of them. This was said to have stopped a potential Taliban offensive on Kandahar.

The strength of Taliban forces was estimated by Western officials and analysts at about 10,000 fighters fielded at any given time, according to an October 30 report in The New York Times. Of that number, "only 2,000 to 3,000 are highly motivated, full-time insurgents", the *Times* reported. The rest are part-timers, made up of alienated, young Afghan men angry at bombing raids or fighting in order to get money. In 2007, more foreign fighters were showing up in Afghanistan than ever before, according to Afghan and United States officials.

An estimated 100 to 300 full-time combatants are foreigners, usually from Pakistan, Uzbekistan, Chechnya, various Arab countries and perhaps even Turkey and western China. They tend to be more fanatical and violent, and they often bring skills such as the ability to post more sophisticated videos on the Internet or bombmaking expertise.

On November 2, 2007, Afghan security forces killed a top-ranking militant, Mawlawi Abdul Manan, after he was caught trying to cross into Afghanistan from neighboring Pakistan. The Taliban confirmed his death. On November 10, 2007, the Taliban ambushed a patrol in eastern Afghanistan, killing six American and three Afghan soldiers while losing only one insurgent. This attack brought the U.S. death toll for 2007 to 100, making it the deadliest year for Americans in Afghanistan.

Security operations were conducted in the north by ISAF and Afghan forces, including Operation Harekate Yolo I & II.

The exact death toll had not been disclosed at the time, but according to Norwegian news reports "between 20 and 25 insurgents" were killed in action, the German MoD verified further 14 hostile fighters killed in action (Norwegian and German forces taking part in the operation). The operation ended on November 6/7. The Battle of Musa Qala took place in December 2007. Afghan units were the principal fighting force, supported by British forces. Taliban forces were forced to pull out of Musa Qala.

2008

Admiral Mike Mullen, Staff Chairman of the Joint Chiefs of Staff, said that while the situation in Afghanistan is "precarious and urgent," the 10,000 additional troops needed there would be unavailable "in any significant manner" unless withdrawals from Iraq are made. However, Admiral Mullen stated that "my priorities . . . given to me by the commander in chief are: Focus on Iraq first. It's been that way for some time. Focus on Afghanistan second."

The U.S. government suspended, on March 27, 2008, AEY Inc. of Miami, Florida, a company hired by the U.S. military, for violating its contract. The company is accused of supplying ammunition, which was corroded and made in China from 1962 through 1974, to the Afghan National Army and police. United States Army-documents showed that since 2004 the company entered agreements with the U.S. government that totaled about $10 million.

The papers also revealed the company received much larger orders in 2007 with contracts totaling more than $200 million to supply ammunition, assault rifles and other weapons. Army criminal investigators were sent to look at the packages in January 2008. The House Oversight Committee planned to hold a hearing into the matter on April 17, 2008. The 22-year-old international arms dealer Efraim Diveroli and president of AEY Inc will face a congressional inquiry. On April 27, President Karzai escaped another attempt on his life: gunmen opened fire during a military parade celebrating the nation's victory and liberation from the eight year occupation of the Soviet Union. The firefight lasted about a quarter of an hour, with 3 dead and over 10 wounded.

On April 29, 2,300 U.S. Marines assaulted the town of Garmsir in Helmand province, a region of Afghanistan where the Taliban had a stronghold. In the first 5 months of 2008, the number of U.S. troops in Afghanistan increased by over 80% with a surge of 21,643 more troops, bringing the total number of U.S troops in Afghanistan from 26,607 in January to 48,250 in June. In September, 2008, George Bush announced the withdrawal of over 8,000 troops from Iraq in the coming months and a further increase of up to 4,500 U.S. troops in Afghanistan.

In May, Norwegian-led ISAF forces conducted a military operation in Badghis province. In June 2008, British prime minster Gordon Brown announced the number of British troops serving in Afghanistan would increase to 8,030 - a rise of 230 personnel. The same month, the UK lost its 100th serviceman killed in the war since 2001.

On June 13, Taliban fighters demonstrated their ongoing strength, liberating all prisoners in Kandahar jail. The well-planned operation freed 1200 prisoners, 400 of whom were Taliban prisoners-of-war, causing a major embarrassment for NATO in one of its operational centres in the country. On July 13, 2008, a coordinated Taliban attack was launched on a remote NATO base at Wanat in the Kunar province. On August 19, French troops suffered their worst losses in Afghanistan in an ambushý. Later in the month, an airstrike which targeted a Taliban commander in Herat province killed 90 civilians.

Late August saw one of the largest operations by NATO forces in Helmand province, Operation Eagle's Summit, with the aim bringing electricity to the region. On September 3, the war spilled over on to Pakistani territory for the first time when heavily armed commandos, believed to be US Special Forces, landed by helicopter and attacked three houses in a village close to a known Taliban and *Al Qaeda* stronghold. The attack killed between seven and twenty people. According to local residents, most of the dead were civilians. Pakistan responded furiously, condemning the attack. The foreign ministry in Islamabad called the incursion "a gross violation of Pakistan's territory".

On September 6, in an apparent reaction to the recent cross-border attack, the federal government announced disconnection of supply lines to the allied forces stationed in Afghanistan through Pakistan for an indefinite period. On September 11, militants killed two U.S. troops in the eastern part of the country. This brought the total number of US losses to 113, making 2008 the deadliest year for American troops in Afghanistan since the start of the war. The year was also the deadliest for several European countries in Afghanistan.

Total casualties for the year

By January 2009 the Taliban made the extremely exaggerated claim that they had killed 5,220 foreign troops, downed 31 aircraft, destroyed 2,818 NATO and Afghan vehicles and killed 7,552 Afghan soldiers and police in 2008 alone. The Associated Press estimated that a total of 286 foreign military personnel were actually killed in Afghanistan in 2008. Icasualties puts the total amount of coalition soldiers killed in 2008 at 294.

2009

Joint intelligence center

The Khyber Border Coordination Center between the U.S., Pakistan, and Afghanistan, at Torkham on the Afghan side of the Khyber Pass, has been in operation for nine months. But U.S. officials at the Khyber Center say language barriers; border disputes between Pakistani and Afghan field officers, and longstanding mistrust among all three militaries have impeded progress.

Increase in US troops

In January, about 3,000 U.S. soldiers from the 3rd Brigade Combat Team of the 10th Mountain Division, moved into the provinces of Logar and Wardak. The troops were the first wave of an expected surge of reinforcements originally ordered by George W. Bush and increased by Barack Obama.

In mid-February, it was announced that 17,000 additional troops would be deployed to the country in two brigades and additional support troops; the 2nd Marine Expeditionary Brigade of about 3,500 from the 7,000 Marines, and the 5th Brigade, 2nd Infantry Division, a Stryker Brigade with about 4,000 of the 7,000 US Army soldiers. The U.S. commander in Afghanistan, General McKiernan, had called for as many as 30,000 additional troops, effectively doubling the number of troops currently in the country.

OPERATION KHANJAR

On Thursday 25 June, American Officials announced the launch of Operation Khanjar ("strike of the sword"). About 4000 US Marines from the 2nd Marine Expeditionary Brigade and 650 Afghan soldiers are currently involved in Operation Khanjar, which will be staged on the Helmand River. It is the biggest push since the Pentagon moved additional troops into the conflict earlier in 2009. Khanjar follows a British-led operation codenamed Operation Panther's Claw in the same region and is the first big push since US Gen. Stanley McChrystal took over as Allied commander. Officials call it the Marines' largest operation since the 2004 invasion of Fallujah, Iraq.

Initially, Afghan and American soldiers have been moving into towns and villages along the Helmand River to secure the civilian population from the Taliban. The main objective of the operation is to push troops into insurgent strongholds along the river. After America takes and holds captured areas, security responsibilities will be transferred to the Afghan soldiers. A secondary aim is to bring security to the Helmand Valley in time for presidential elections, set to take place on August 20.

The first aggressive phase will last 36 hours, where the secondary aim will be achieved first. Key targets of the assault include the districts of Garmsir and Nawa, which are towards the southern border with Pakistan. Many of the insurgents are said to take refuge in those locations, and are involved in the opium trade funding the Taliban.

SUPPLY LINES TO AFGHANISTAN

TALIBAN ATTACKS ON SUPPLY LINES THROUGH PAKISTAN

In November and December 2008, there were multiple incidents of major theft, robbery, and arson attacks against NATO supply convoys in Pakistan. Transport companies south of Kabul have also been reported to pay protection money to the Taliban. In an attack on November 11, 200 Taliban fighters in Peshawar hijacked a convoy carrying NATO supplies from Karachi to Afghanistan. The militants took two military Humvees and paraded them in front of the media as trophies.

The coalition forces bring 70 per cent of supplies through Pakistan every month, of a total of 2,000 truckloads in all. The area east of the Khyber Pass in Pakistan has seen very frequent attacks. Cargo trucks and Humvees have been set ablaze by Taliban militants. Half-dozen raids on depots with NATO supplies near Peshawar destroyed 300 cargo trucks and Humvees in December 2008. The Taliban destroyed an iron bridge on the highway between Peshawar and the Khyber Pass in February 2009.

On Dec 30, 2008, Pakistani security forces shut down the supply line when they launched an offensive against Taliban militants who dominate the Khyber Pass region. After three days of fighting, they declared the Khyber Pass open. The other supply route through Pakistan, via Chaman, was briefly shut down in early 2009. On Jan 10, tribesmen used vehicles to block the road to protest a raid by Pakistani counter-narcotics forces that left one villager dead. The protesters withdrew on Jan 14 after police promised to take their complaints to provincial authorities.

NORTHERN DISTRIBUTION NETWORK

In response to the increased risk of sending supplies through Pakistan, work began on the establishment of a Northern Distribution Network (NDN) through Russia and several Central Asian republics. Initial permission for the U.S. military to move troop supplies through the region was given on January 20, 2009, after a visit to the region by General Petraeus. The first shipment along the NDN route left on February 20 from Riga, Latvia, then traveled 3,212 miles (5,169 km) to the Uzbekistan town of Termez, on the Afghanistan border. U.S. commanders have stated their hope that 100 containers a day will be shipped along the NDN. By comparison, currently 140 containers a day are shipped through the Khyber Pass.

On May 11, 2009, Uzbekistan president Islam Karimov announced that the airport in Navoi, Uzbekistan was being used to transport non-lethal cargo into Afghanistan. Due to the still unsettled relationship between Uzbekistan and the United States following the 2005 Andijon massacre and subsequent expulsion of U.S. forces from Karshi-Khanabad airbase, U.S. forces were not involved in the shipment of supplies. Instead, South Korea's Korean Air, which is currently involved in overhauling Navoi's airport, officially handles logistics at the site.

Originally only non-lethal resources were allowed on the NDN. In July 2009, however, shortly before a visit by President Obama to Moscow, Russian authorities announced that U.S. troops and weapons could use the country's airspace to reach Afghanistan. Some analyists worry that use of the NDN will come at the cost of increased Russian demands concerning missile defense and NATO enlargement. Additionally, human rights advocates are concerned that the U.S. is again working with the government of Uzbekistan, which is often accused of violating human rights. Nevertheless, U.S. officials have promised increased cooperation with Uzbekistan, including further assistance to turn the Navoi airport into a major regional distribution center for both military and civilian ventures.

SPLIT WITH PAKISTAN

An unnamed senior Pentagon official told the BBC that at some point between July 12 and September 12, 2008, President George W. Bush issued a classified order to authorize U.S. raids against militants in Pakistan. Pakistan however said it would not allow foreign forces onto its territory and that it would vigorously protect its sovereignty. In September, the Pakistan military stated that it had issued orders to "open fire" on American soldiers who crossed the Pakistan border in pursuit of militant forces. On September 25, 2008 Pakistani troops shot towards ISAF helicopters, which belonged to American troops.

This caused confusion and anger in the Pentagon, which asked for a full explanation into the incident, and they denied that American choppers were in Pakistani airspace. Pakistani President Asif Ali Zardari was quick to deny that shots were fired but instead insisted that the Pakistani troops shot flares to warn the Americans that they were in Pakistani airspace. This has added to the doubts that have been expressed by certain Pentagon and Bush Administration officials about the capabilities of the Pakistani Armed Forces to confront the militant threat.

This has all added to the split that occurred when American troops apparently landed on Pakistani soil to carry out an operation against militants in the North-West Frontier Province but 'Pakistan reacted angrily to the action, saying 20 innocent villagers had been killed by US troops'. On October 1, 2008, a suspected U.S. drone fired a missile against militants inside Pakistan's North-West Frontier Province near the Afghan border. It is believed that six people died in the incident.

Attacks of such have drawn a stiff response from Islamabad, accusing the United States of violating their airspace, although Americans have expressed frustration at the lack or failure of action by the Pakistani side against the militants held up on Pakistani soil. On December 30, 2008

Pakistani officials announced closure of the main supply line through Khyber Pass due to military operation against local militiants.

RISK OF A FAILED STATE

In November 2006, the U.N. Security Council warned that Afghanistan may become a failed state due to increased Taliban violence, growing illegal drug production, and fragile State institutions. In 2006, Afghanistan was rated 10th on the failed states index, up from 11th in 2005. From 2005 to 2006, the number of suicide attacks, direct fire attacks, and improvised explosive devices all increased. Intelligence documents declassified in 2006 suggested that Al Qaeda, Taliban, Haqqani Network and Hezb-i-Islami sanctuaries had by then increased fourfold in Afghanistan.

The campaign in Afghanistan successfully unseated the Taliban from power, but has been significantly less successful at achieving the primary policy goal of ensuring that *Al Qaeda* can no longer operate in Afghanistan. BBC News released an article on June 19, 2007 about life in Afghanistan since the U.S. occupation. The article focuses on the life of the villagers of Asad Khyl. What seems to be suggested is that security in Afghanistan seems to have been better, but poverty & corruption is still a very big problem. As of 2008, Afghanistan is ranked 10th on the failed state index.

In a recent interview, former head of U.S. troops in Iraq and now the head of Central Command, General David H. Petraeus, insisted that the Taliban are gaining strength. He cited the recent uptick in attacks in Afghanistan and in neighboring Pakistan. Petraeus also insisted that the challenges faced in Afghanistan are more complicated than the ones that were faced in Iraq during his tour and in order to turn around the recent events this would require removing militant sanctuaries and strongholds, which are widespread inside Afghanistan.

On October 1, 2008, the top American general in Afghanistan, David McKiernan, warned that the situation in

Afghanistan could get a lot worse. The international forces within Afghanistan have not been able to hold territory they have cleared because of the lack of troops. For this reason the general called for an extra three combat brigades (roughly 20,000 troops). Without this urgent rush of troops the Taliban would be able to get back into the communities that were once cleared by international troops.

The general went on to say that things could get a lot worse before they get better. Observers also have argued that the mission in Afghanistan is hampered by a lack of agreement on objectives, a lack of resources, lack of coordination, too much focus on the central government at the expense of local and provincial governments, and too much focus on Afghanistan instead of the region.

POSSIBLE LONG-TERM U.S. MILITARY PRESENCE

Many of the thousands of U.S. troops in Afghanistan are positioned in what experts say are large, permanent bases. In February 2005, U.S. Senator John McCain called for the establishment of permanent U.S. military bases in Afghanistan, saying such bases would be "for the good of the American people, because of the long-term security interests we have in the region".

He made the remarks while visiting Afghan President Hamid Karzai in Kabul as part of a five-member, bi-partisan Senate delegation travelling through the region for talks on security issues. The same delegation also included then-Senator Hillary Clinton, now U.S. Secretary of State.

In mid-March, 2005, U.S. Joint Chiefs of Staff Chairman General Richard Myers told reporters in Kabul that the U.S. Defense Department was studying the feasibility of such permanent military bases. At the end of March, the U.S. military announced that it was spending $83-million on its two main air bases in Afghanistan, Bagram Air Base north of Kabul and Kandahar Air Field in the south of the country.

A few weeks after this series of U.S. statements, in April 2005, during a surprise visit to Kabul by U.S. Defense

Secretary Donald Rumsfeld, Afghan President Hamid Karzai hinted at a possible permanent U.S. military presence in Afghanistan, saying he had also discussed the matter with President Bush. Rumsfeld refused to say whether or not the U.S. wanted permanent American military bases in Afghanistan, saying the final decision would come from the White House.

As of July 2008, hundreds of millions of dollars were being spent on permanent infrastructure for foreign military bases in Afghanistan, including a budget of $780-million to further develop the infrastructure at just the Kandahar Air Field base, described as "a walled, multicultural military city that houses some 13,000 troops from 17 different countries - the kind of place where you can eat at a Dutch chain restaurant alongside soldiers from the Royal Netherlands Army." The Bagram Air Base, run by the U.S. military, was also expanding according to military officials, with the U.S military buying land from Afghan locals in different places for further expansion of the base.

As of January 2009, the U.S. had begun work on $1.6 billion of new, permanent military installations at Kandahar. In February 2009, The Times reported that the U.S. will build two huge new military bases in southern Afghanistan. One will be built in Kandahar province near the Helmand border, at Maiwand-a place famous as the site of the destruction of a British army during the Second Anglo-Afghan War. The other new U.S. military base will be built in Zabul, a province now largely controlled by the Taleban and criminal gangs.

GEO-STRATEGIC MILITARY BUILD-UP

The dramatic build-up of an indefinite Western military presence in Afghanistan has unsettled some regional powers, including Russia. "Is it all to fight a number of Taliban - 10,000, 12,000 Taliban?" Zamir Kabulov, Russia's ambassador to Kabul has questioned. "Maybe this infrastructure, military infrastructure, [is] not only for internal purposes but for regional also."

Russia views the large and indefinite military build-up as a potential threat "because Afghanistan's geographical location is a very strategic one," Kabulov said. "It's very close to three main world basins of hydrocarbons: Persian Gulf, Caspian Sea, and Central Asia."

Other observers have also noted that through a stronger military presence in Afghanistan, the U.S. may be seeking to strengthen its own position in the region to counter increasingly warm relations among India, China and Russia. Along with its proximity to the vast Central Asian and Caspian Sea energy sources and being in the midsts of the regional powers of India, China, and Russia, Afghanistan also holds strategic significance given its border with Iran.

Afghan resistance to permanent U.S. military bases

The idea of permanent U.S. military bases vexes many people in Afghanistan, which has a long history of resisting foreign invaders. In May 2005, riots and protests that had started over a false report in Newsweek of U.S. interrogators desecrating the Qur'an and turned into the biggest anti-U.S. protests in Afghanistan since the 2001 invasion included demands that the Kabul government reject U.S. intentions to create a permanent military presence in Afghanistan.

The International Security Assistance Force

The International Security Assistance Force (ISAF) is an international stabilization force authorized by the United Nations Security Council on December 20, 2001. On July 31, 2006, the NATO-led International Security Assistance Force assumed command of the south of the country, and by October 5, 2006, also of the east Afghanistan.

INTERNATIONAL REACTIONS

PUBLIC OPINION

Although the war was supported by most Americans, the UN Security Council and the NATO, most people in the world, Europeans in particular, oppose the war. In a 47-nation June 2007 survey of global public opinion, the Pew Global Attitudes Project found considerable opposition to U.S. and NATO operations in Afghanistan. Only in just 4 out of the 47 countries surveyed was there a majority that favoured keeping foreign troops: the U.S. (50%), Israel (59%), Ghana (50%), and Kenya (60%).

In 41 of the 47 countries, pluralities want U.S. and NATO troops out of Afghanistan as soon as possible. In 32 out of 47 countries, clear majorities want U.S. and NATO troops out of Afghanistan as soon as possible. Majorities in 7 out of 12 NATO member countries say troops should be withdrawn as soon as possible. A smaller 24-nation Pew Global Attitudes survey in June 2008 similarly found that majorities or pluralities in 21 of 24 countries want the U.S. and NATO to remove their troops from Afghanistan as soon as possible.

Only in 3 out of the 24 countries - the United States (50%), Australia (60%), and Britain (48%) - did public opinion lean more toward keeping troops there until the situation has stabilized. Since that June 2008 global survey, however, public opinion in Australia and Britain has also diverged from that in the U.S., and a majority of Australians and Britons now want their troops to be brought home from Afghanistan. A September 2008 poll found that 56% of Australians oppose the continuation of their country's military involvement in Afghanistan, while 42% support it.

A November 2008 poll found that 68% of Britons want their troops withdrawn within the next 12 months. In the United States, a September 2008 Pew survey found that 61% of Americans wanted U.S. troops to stay until the situation has stabilized, while 33% wanted them removed as soon as possible. Public opinion at the beginning of the war also reflected this dichotomy between the United States and most other countries. When the invasion began in October 2001, polls indicated that about 88% of Americans and about 65% of Britons backed military action in Afghanistan.

On the other hand, a large-scale 37-nation poll of world opinion carried out by Gallup International in late September 2001, found that large majorities in most countries favoured a legal response, in the form of extradition and trial, over a military response to 9/11: Only in just 3 countries out of the 37 surveyed - the United States, Israel, and India - did majorities favour military action in Afghanistan.

In 34 out of the 37 countries surveyed, the survey found many clear and sizeable majorities that did not favour military action: in the United Kingdom (75%), France (67%), Switzerland (87%), Czech Republic (64%), Lithuania (83%), Panama (80%), Mexico (94%), and other countries. However, since the Taliban refused to hand over bin Laden or his followers for trial, extradition was not a viable option by the time the war began. An Ipsos-Reid poll conducted between November and December 2001 showed that majorities in Canada (66%), France (60%), Germany (60%), Italy (58%), and the U.K. (65%) approved of U.S. airstrikes while majorities in Argentina (77%), China (52%), South Korea (50%), Spain (52%), and Turkey (70%) opposed them.

PROTESTS, DEMONSTRATIONS AND RALLIES

The war has repeatedly been the subject of large protests around the world starting with the large-scale demonstrations in the days leading up to the official launch of U.S. Operation Enduring Freedom under George W. Bush in October 2001 and every year since. Protesters consider the bombing and invasion of Afghanistan to be unjustified aggression. The deaths of thousands of Afghan civilians caused directly and indirectly by the U.S. and NATO bombing campaigns is also a major underlying focus of the protests.

THE IMPACT OF ARMED CONFLICT ON CIVILIANS

Very few people in Afghanistan have been unaffected by the armed conflict there. Those with direct personal experience make up 60% of the population, and most others also report suffering a range of serious hardships. In total, almost everyone (96%) has been affected in some way – either personally or due to the wider consequences of armed conflict.

CASUALTIES

In 2008 the number of Coalition deaths in Afghanistan reached 1,000, and is now higher.

Civilian casualties

There are no official and reliable figures available of civilian deaths caused by the invasion. The UN Assistance Mission in Afghanistan (UNAMA) reported that 2,118 Afghan civilians were killed by armed conflict in 2008 (the highest number since the end of the initial 2001 invasion), 55% by insurgents and 39% by international-led military forces.

According to Marc W. Herold's Dossier on Civilian Victims of United States' Aerial Bombing at least 3,700 and probably closer to 5,000 civilians were killed by the end of 2002 as a result of U.S. bombing. Herold's study omitted those killed indirectly, when air strikes cut off their access to hospitals, food or electricity. Also exempt were bomb victims who later died of their injuries. When there were different casualty figures from the same incident, in 90% of cases Professor Herold chose a lower figure.

Some people have disputed Herold's estimates. Self-described neoconservative Joshua Muravchik of the American Enterprise Institute questioned Professor Herold's study in an opinion article published in the neoconservative magazine The Weekly Standard, but did so entirely on the basis of one single incident that involved 25-93 deaths.

In a pair of January 2002 studies, Carl Conetta of the Project on Defense Alternatives estimated that, *at least* 4,200-4,500 civilians were killed by mid-January 2002 as a result of the U.S. war and airstrikes, both directly as casualties of the aerial bombing campaign, and indirectly in the humanitarian crisis that the war and airstrikes contributed to.

A *Los Angeles Times* review of U.S., British and Pakistani newspapers and international wire services found that between 1,067 and 1,201 direct civilian deaths were reported by those news organizations during the five months from October 7, 2001 to February 28, 2002. This review excluded all civilian deaths in Afghanistan that did not get reported by U.S., British, or Pakistani news, excluded 497 deaths that did get reported in U.S., British, and Pakistani news but that were not specifically identified as civilian or military, and excluded 754 civilian deaths that were reported by the Taliban but not independently confirmed.

On March 15, 2009 in an interview with Margaret Warner of *The NewsHour with Jim Lehrer*, General David D. McKiernan, NATO commander in Afghanistan, stated that 80% of civilian casualties in Afghanistan were caused by the Taliban. He added that the by the nature of the Taliban insurgency, "the enemy mixes in on purpose with the civilian population." On March 22, 2009, General Stanley A. McChrystal announced new restrictions on airstrikes in order to reduce civilian casualties.

DRUG TRADE

In 2000, the Taliban had issued a ban on opium production, which led to reductions in Pashtun Mafia opium production by as much as 90%. Soon after the 2001 U.S. led invasion of Afghanistan, however, opium production increased markedly. By 2005, Afghanistan had regained its position as the world's #1 opium producer and was producing 90% of the world's opium, most of which is processed into heroin and sold in Europe and Russia. While U.S. and allied efforts to combat the drug trade have been stepped up, the effort is hampered by the fact that many suspected drug traffickers are now top officials in the Karzai government.

In fact, recent estimates by the United Nations Office on Drugs and Crime (UNODC) estimate that 52% of the nation's GDP, amounting to $2.7 billion annually, is generated by the drug trade. The rise in production has been linked to the deteriorating security situation, as production is markedly lower in areas with stable security. The poppy eradication policy propagated by the international community and in particular the United States, as part of their War on Drugs, has been a failure, exacerbated by the lack of alternative development projects to replace livelihoods lost as a result of poppy eradication.

Rather than stemming poppy cultivation, poppy eradication has succeeded only in adding to the extreme poverty in rural areas and general discontent, especially in the south of Afghanistan. The extermination of the poppy crops is not seen as a viable option, due to the fact that the sale of poppies constitutes the livelihood of Afghanistan's rural farmers. Opium is more profitable than wheat and destroying opium fields could possibly lead to discontent or unrest amongst the indigent population. Several alternatives to poppy eradication have been proposed, including controlled opium licensing for poppy for medicine projects.

HUMAN RIGHTS ABUSES

There have been multiple accounts of human rights violations in Afghanistan. The fallout of the U.S. led invasion, including resurgence in Taliban forces, record-high drug production, and re-armed warlords, has led to a threat to the well-being and rights of hundreds of thousands of innocent Afghan citizens, according to Human Rights Watch.

HISTORY OF HUMAN RIGHTS ABUSES IN AFGHANISTAN

Afghanistan has suffered extensive human rights violations over the last twenty years. The subsequent civil war brought extensive abuses by the armed factions vying for power. The Taliban rose to power in 1998 and ruled Afghanistan for five years until the U.S. attacks in 2001. They were notorious for their human rights abuses against women.

The increase in Taliban power has led to increased human rights violations against women in Afghanistan, according to the U.S. State Department. According to Amnesty International, the Taliban commit war crimes by targeting civilians, including killing teachers, abducting aid workers and burning school buildings. Amnesty International said that up to 756 civilians were killed in 2006 by bombs, mostly on roads or carried by suicide attackers belonging to the Taliban.

FORMER AFGHAN WARLORDS

Former Afghan warlords and political strongmen were responsible for numerous human rights violations in 2003 including kidnapping, rape, robbery, and extortion.

Controversy over Torture

In March 2002, ABC News claimed top officials at the CIA authorized controversial, harsh interrogation techniques. The Bush administration declared that *Al Qaeda* members captured on the battlefield were not subject to the Geneva Conventions as it was not a conventional war, as set by the convention. Amnesty International stated on April 26, 2007, that a new deal to let Canadian officials visit enemy detainees in Afghanistan is aimed more at saving political face than keeping prisoners safe.

The possible interrogation techniques included shaking and slapping, shackling prisoners in a standing position, keeping the prisoner in a cold cell and dousing them with water, and water boarding. The U.S. operated a secret prison in Kabul where these techniques are claimed to have been employed.

Allegations of unethical conduct or war crimes by the Taliban

NATO has alleged that the Taliban have used civilians as human shields. As an example, NATO pointed to the victims of NATO airstrikes in Farah province in May 2009 in which the Afghan government claimed up to 150 civilians was killed. NATO stated that it had evidence that the Taliban forced civilians into buildings likely to be targeted by NATO aircraft involved in the battle. US Lieutenant Colonel Greg Julian, a spokesman for NATO's Afghanistan commander, General David D. McKiernan, said of the Taliban's tactics, "This was a deliberate plan by the Taliban to create a civilian casualty crisis. These were not human shields; these were human sacrifices. We have intelligence that points to this. Patient after patient just kept telling the doctors their story and how they were forced by the Taliban to stay in these locations."

White phosphorous use

White phosphorous has been condemned by human rights organizations as cruel and inhuman because it causes severe burns. There cases have been confirmed of white phosphorous burns on the bodies of civilians wounded in Afghanistan caused by clashes between US and Taliban forces near Bagram. The U.S.A. accuses the Taliban of use of using white phosphorous weapons in 38 of these cases. No independent report has confirmed the use of phosphorous by the Taliban. The only forces known to use phospherous weapons before are NATO members.

RESURGENCE OF THE TALIBAN

As of 2009, the insurgency, in the form of a Taliban guerrilla war, continues. However, the Pashtun tribal group, with over 40 million members, has a long history of resistance to occupation forces in the region so the Taliban themselves may comprise only a part of the insurgency. Most of the post-invasion Taliban fighters are new recruits, drawn again from that region's madrassas. The more traditional village schools are the primary source of the new fighters.

Before the summer 2006 offensive began, indications existed that Canadian soldiers in Afghanistan had lost influence and power to other groups, including potentially the Taliban. The most notable sign was the rioting in May after a street accident in the city of Kabul. The continued support from tribal and other groups in Pakistan, the drug trade and the small number of NATO forces, combined with the long history of resistance and isolation, led to the observation that Taliban forces and leaders are surviving and will have some influence over the future of Afghanistan.

A new introduction is suicide attacks and terrorist methods not used in 2001. Observers have suggested that poppy eradication policies, which destroy the livelihoods of rural Afghans, and civilian deaths caused by the bombing campaigns of international troops, are linked to the resurgence of the Taliban. These observers maintain that counter-insurgency policy should focus on the battle for the hearts and minds of the Afghan people and on the reconstruction of the Afghan economy, which could profit from the licensing of poppies to make medicine rather than their eradication.

In September 2006, the Islamic Emirate of Waziristan, an association of Waziristani chieftains with close ties to the Taliban, were recognized by the Government of Pakistan as the de facto security force in charge of North and South Waziristan. This recognition was part of the agreement to end the Waziristan War which had extracted a heavy toll on the Pakistan Army since early 2004. Some commentators viewed Islamabad's shift from war to diplomacy as implicit recognition of the growing power of the resurgent Taliban relative to American influence, with the US distracted by the threat of looming crises in Iraq, Lebanon, and Iran. Other commentators view Islamabad's shift from war to diplomacy as a means to appease growing discontent in Pakistan. Because of its leadership structure, the assassination of Mullah Dadullah in May 2007 will not significantly affect the Taliban, but it may set-back the incipient relations with Pakistan.

According to Human Rights Watch, bombings and other attacks which have led to civilian casualties are reported to have "sharply escalated in 2006" with "at least 669 Afghan civilians were killed in at least 350 armed attacks, most of which appear to have been intentionally launched at non-combatants." By 2008 the Taliban had increased its attacks using suicide bombers and the targeted killing of unarmed civilian aid workers such as Gayle Williams.

3

Mazar-e-Sharif 1997

Massacre in the North

As the Taliban advances on the Hazara city of Mazar-e-Sharif, in north Afghanistan (in the second year of the Taliban's sweep over the country), the Shiite population resists putting down its weapons to the Taliban's Sunni Pashtun fighters. A squabble turns into a battle. The Taliban, unfamiliar with the city's streets, is overwhelmed by Hazara fighters. Fifteen hours of fighting leaves some 600 Taliban fighters massacred and 1,000 captured. United Nations offices are looted and UN personnel forced to flee. Many captured Taliban men are later found dead in containers.

Losing Mazar-e-Sharif would prove to be the Taliban's worst defeat until it was routed by the Northern Alliance and American Special Forces in the 2001 invasion. However, the Taliban avenged its loss in Mazar through genocidal massacres of its own in August 1998, when they surrounded the Hazara in Mazar.

As Ahmad Rashid writes in *Taliban*, What followed was another brutal massacre, genocidal in its ferocity, as the Taliban took revenge on their losses the previous year. A Taliban commander later said that Mullah Omar had given them permission to kill for two hours, but they had killed for two days. The Taliban went on a killing frenzy, driving their pick-ups up and down the narrow streets of Mazar shooting to the left and right and killing everything that moved - shop owners, cart pullers, women and children shoppers and even goats and donkeys. Contrary to all injunctions of Islam, which demands immediate burial, bodies were left to rot on the streets.

'They were shooting without warning at everybody who happened to be on the street, without discriminating between men, women and children. Soon the streets were covered with dead bodies and blood. No one was allowed to bury the corpses for the first six days. Dogs were eating human flesh and going mad and soon the smell became intolerable,' said a male Tajik who managed to escape the massacre.

MAZARI SHARIF

Mazar-e-Sharif or Mazari Sharif is the fourth largest city of Afghanistan, with population of 300,600 people (2006 estimate). It is the capital of Balkh province and is linked by roads to Kabul in the south-east, Herat to the west and Uzbekistan to the north. Mazari Sharif means "Noble Shrine," a reference to the large, blue-tiled sanctuary and mosque in the center of the city known as the Shrine of Hazrat Ali or the *Blue Mosque*. It is believed by some Muslims that the site of the tomb of Ali ibn Abi Talib, the cousin and son-in-law of Prophet Muhammad, is in Mazari Sharif. Twelver Shi'as however, believes that the real grave of Ali is found within Imam Ali Mosque in Najaf, Iraq, as was disclosed by the Sixth Twelver Shi'a Imam, Ja'far as-Sadiq.

The city is a major tourist attraction because of its fabulous Muslim and Hellenistic archeological sites. In July 2006, the discovery of new Hellenistic remains was announced. The ethnic majority in the city are Tajiks. According to tradition, Mazari Sharif owes its existence to a dream. At the beginning of the 1100s, a local mullah had a dream in which Ali bin Abi Talib, the Muhammad's cousin and son-in-law and one of the four Rightly Guided Caliphs appeared to reveal that he had been secretly buried near the city of Balkh. After investigation, the Seljuk sultan Sanjar ordered a city and shrine to be built on the spot, where it stood until its destruction by Genghis

Khan. Although later rebuilt, Mazar stood in the shadow of its neighbor Balkh, until that city was abandoned in 1866 for health reasons.

During the Soviet invasion of Afghanistan, Mazari Sharif was a strategic base for the Soviet Army, as they used its airport to launch air strikes on Afghan *Mujahideen*. In the early 1990s, after the Soviet Union withdrew from Afghanistan, control of Mazar was contested by the Tajik militias (Jamiat-e Islami of Ahmad Shah Massoud and Burhanuddin Rabbani, and the Uzbek militia Jumbesh-e Melli led by Abdul Rashid Dostum. As a garrison for the communist Afghan army, the city was under the command of Dostum, who mutinied against Najibullah's regime in 1992 and established the autonomous administration of North Afghanistan with the aid of Massoud.

Under Dostum's Uzbek *Jumbesh-e-Melli* militia from the early 1990s to early 1997, Mazar was an oasis of peace during the civil war, and as the rest of the country disintegrated and was slowly taken over by the Taliban, Dostum strengthened political ties with the newly independent central Asian states and Turkey, printed his own currency and established his own airline. This peace was shattered in May 1997, when he was betrayed by one of his generals, Abdul Malik Pahlawan, and he fled Mazar as the Taliban were getting ready to take the city.

Between May and July 1997, the Taliban unsuccessfully attempted to take Mazar, leading to approximately 3,000 Taliban soldiers being massacred by Abdul Malik and his Shia followers. In retaliation for this incident, the Taliban on August 8, 1998, was reported to have returned and led a six-day killing frenzy of Hazaras, a report which was refuted in a report that pointed out that all claims of military deaths were sourced and referenced, but the accounts of civilian massacres were not attributable to any reliable source and were allegedly fabricated by enemies of their rule.

Soon after, the city was occupied and taken over by the Taliban. It was this capture of Mazar, the last major city in Afghanistan to fall to the Taliban that prompted Pakistan's recognition of the Taliban regime. Soon afterward, the UAE, and Saudi Arabia extended official recognition to the regime, while Turkmenistan resumed relations - although the Taliban was not officially recognized by Turkmenbashi as the rulers of Afghanistan.

Following 9/11, Mazar was the first Afghan city to fall to the Northern Alliance (former militias). The Taliban's defeat in Mazar quickly turned into a rout from the rest of the north and west of Afghanistan. On November 9, 2001 the city was recaptured by the Afghan Northern Alliance after the Battle of Mazar e Sharif with help from the United States Special Operations Forces.

Small scale clashes between militias belonging to different commanders persisted throughout 2002, and were the focus of intensive UN peace-brokering and small arms disarmament programme. After some pressure, an office of the Afghan Independent Human Rights Commission opened an office in Mazar in April 2003. There were also reports about northern Pashtun people being ethnic cleansed by the other groups.

Mazari Sharif is currently in full control of the Military of Afghanistan led by president Harnid Karzail, under the new Afghan government that is led by US backed President Hamid Karzai. There are also NATO peacekeeping forces in and around the city providing assistance to the new government. The German lead ISAF Regional Command North is stationed in the Camp Marmal which lies near to the city at an airport. Provincial Reconstruction Team (PRT) in Mazari Sharif is led by Sweden. Norwegian and Latvian forces also operate out of the Norwegian Camp Nidaros, which is part of the German Camp Marmal.

The conditions are being established for a slaughter at Kunduz, in northern Afghanistan. Up to 20,000 Taliban fighters, including several thousand of the Taliban's foreign supporters, are trapped in the city-many of them fled there last week after neighbouring cities such as Mazar-e-Sharif and Taloqan fell to the US-backed Northern Alliance. Apart from the southern city of Kandahar, it is the last significant Taliban stronghold.

According to Pakistani newspapers, Taliban leaders inside Kunduz indicated on Monday their willingness to surrender but not to the Northern Alliance, which has already carried out the summary execution of prisoners elsewhere. Taliban commanders indicated that they were prepared to lay down their arms before a UN observer team or a multinational coalition force and hand over the city in return for safe passage.

The US quickly stepped in to scotch any such plan. US Defence Secretary Donald Rumsfeld said he would do everything he could to prevent a negotiated deal to end the stalemate in Kunduz. Referring to the foreign Taliban fighters, he said: "My hope is that they will either be killed or taken prisoner. They're people who have done terrible things." He left any talks up to the Northern Alliance, saying that the US was not inclined to negotiate surrender.

The UN rapidly followed suit, washing its hand of any involvement in surrender. Special representative to Afghanistan Lakhdar Brahimi acknowledged that the UN had been contacted by Taliban leaders in Kunduz but was not in a position to agree as it had no forces in the area. He told the press that he would ask his deputy Francesc Vendrell to ask the Northern Alliance to "treat this situation with as much humanity as possible".

As a result, the Northern Alliance will decide the fate of thousands of Taliban fighters. General Mohammed Daud, the Northern Alliance commander on the Kunduz front, has already made his attitude clear. He is prepared to negotiate a deal with Afghan Taliban leaders but has ruled out any talks with "foreign terrorists". He declared last week: "We will not deal with them, they are killers... The foreigners are living between life and death."

Another Northern Alliance commander Pir Muhammad was even more explicit: "These foreigners have killed thousands of civilians. Their hands are covered with the blood of our people. We will avenge this." He said the Northern Alliance would have no trouble picking out the "terrorists" and foreigners among the thousands of other troops in

Kunduz. "We know who the criminals are," he said. Daud has issued an ultimatum to the Taliban to surrender by Friday or face the consequences. Negotiations are still underway but only with Afghani representatives of the Taliban.

Sketchy details from refugees fleeing Kunduz, which had a population of around 100,000, paint a picture of chaos. The US is continuing to heavily bomb the city on a daily basis. A number of civilians have been killed and injured, including three children who were playing when a bomb hit a nearby house. One refugee, who made clear she did not support the Taliban, said: "People are not happy with the bombing... They say the Americans should bomb the front lines [rather than the city] because our children are being killed."

The international media have highlighted reports that foreign Taliban supporters in Kunduz are preparing to fight to the death and have executed hundreds of Afghani deserters. The press routinely identifies all foreigners with Osama bin Laden, the alleged perpetrator of the September 11 attacks, and his *Al Qaeda* network. Within Afghanistan, US propaganda transmitted in local languages by radio from US planes reinforces the same message, exhorting Afghanis to drive the "foreign terrorists" out of the country.

The majority of "foreigners" fighting alongside the Taliban, have not, however, been recruited by bin Laden. Many are supporters of Islamic fundamentalist parties in Pakistan. Some are not even trained fighters but raw recruits who joined in recent weeks after being incensed by the US attacks on Afghanistan. Mahsood Ali, 22, held prisoner by the Northern Alliance in a squalid jail in Taloqan is one such "foreign terrorist". He came to Afghanistan from Peshawar three weeks ago with three of his friends. They are all dead and, clearly fearing for his own life, he told a *Time* reporter: "I think I made a mistake coming to Afghanistan."

The exact composition of Taliban forces in Kunduz is unclear. Even General Daud, however, who claims that there are more than 10,000 foreign fighters in the city, says that only 1,000 are connected to *Al Qaeda* network. According to him, at least two-fifths are Pakistanis and the remainders are from Central Asia and the Middle East. The purpose of branding all foreign Taliban as "terrorists" is obvious: it is to justify in advance any slaughter that takes place in Kunduz and elsewhere.

MASSACRE AT MAZAR-E-SHARIF

The fate being prepared for the "foreign terrorists" is evident in neighbouring Mazar-e-Sharif, just 200 kilometres to the west of Kunduz. The entry of the Northern Alliance into Mazar-e-Sharif on November 9 was the start of the rapid collapse of Taliban across the country. Reports soon began to emerge that the Northern Alliance had murdered Taliban fighters. On November 14, UN spokeswoman Stephanie Bunker, speaking in Islamabad, confirmed reports that 100 Taliban had been killed by Northern Alliance troops. "I don't know whether we can say they're out of control and running amok," she said.

The Northern Alliance denied the accusation, claiming that the Taliban had not surrendered but were killed in the course of fighting. More details have now begun to emerge. A *Time* journalist who entered Mazar-e-Sharif last week pieced together the story from local Northern Alliance commanders, their fighters and civilian eyewitnesses. According to this account, some 900 Pakistanis were left behind by the Taliban as they fled the city. Northern Alliance troops found them holed up in former girls schools, which they used as their garrison. Fighting broke out when they refused to surrender.

The following day, two US fighter bombers were called in and, guided by "spotters," scored two direct hits on the front of the school, killing scores of those inside. A crowd of onlookers gathered outside the school. Some called on the Pakistanis to give themselves up, others chanted "Kill the tourists"-a contemptuous reference not only to their recent arrival but also their fighting skills.

The bitterness stems from a legacy of atrocities in Mazar-e-Sharif. The Taliban first took the city in 1997 but provoked a local uprising with the imposition of their rule, particularly among the ethnic Hazaras whose adherence to the Shiite sect is treated by the Taliban as heresy. The local militia-now part of the Northern Alliance-brutally murdered at least 1,000 Taliban prisoners. The Taliban captured the city the following year, taking their revenge by butchering thousands of Hazaras-men, women and children.

According to the *Time* report, the Pakistanis decided to surrender following the US attack on the school. The Pakistanis could hear the chants of the crowd. "But they shouted back that they were coming out to be arrested. Alliance soldiers waited until more than 100 had emerged, eyewitnesses say, then opened fire. Most of the Taliban soldiers were cut down as they walked. A handful fought back, scaled the walls and escaped into the city. The Alliance troops gave chase, shooting them as they ran through the streets and pursuing them into nearby houses. The Taliban took several families hostage; eyewitnesses said an unknown number died in the crossfire."

The standoff continued for several days. On November 12, a number of local mullahs approached the school calling on the troops to surrender. Suspecting another trap, the Pakistanis shot them. The Northern Alliance then attacked the building and set fire to it. Some of the Taliban were taken prisoner when they ran out and immediately put down their weapons. Others were shot in cold blood. The siege finally ended the following day when Northern Alliance troops stormed the building. Of the 900 fighters, only 325 were taken prisoner. Red Cross officials have recovered 400 bodies and 200 remain unaccounted for.

One question remains. What was the US involvement in this atrocity? For weeks now, hundreds of US Special Forces troops, military advisers and CIA operatives have been active in Afghanistan. While there is a virtual media blackout on their activities, it has been reported that they have been operating closely with the Northern Alliance and were involved in preparing and planning the offensive against Mazar-e-Sharif. Special Forces troops have been engaged in identifying targets and guiding the attacks of US warplanes.

If the cloak of secrecy is ever lifted from this dirty affair, there are some obvious questions. How closely were US advisers involved in planning the Northern Alliance offensive against Mazar-e-Sharif and what were the orders in relation to Taliban prisoners? Did US military personnel accompany Northern Alliance troops in the capture of the city and in what capacities? Who were the "spotters" that brought in the air strikes against the Taliban-held school on November 10?

Whatever the direct US involvement, US spokesmen have made no strong protest against this massacre or the summary execution of Taliban prisoners elsewhere by Northern Alliance troops. This tacit approval gives the green light to the US-allied warlords to carry out further atrocities. Human Rights Watch today warned that the Taliban's current military offensive in the Hazarajat region of central Afghanistan could result in the torture and deaths of many more ethnic Hazaras, a Shi'ite minority whom the Taliban has targeted in the past. Aid workers in Pakistan say that thousands of Hazaras were killed when the Taliban took the northern city of Mazar-e-Sharif last month.

Human Rights Watch called on the United Nations Security Council, which has already expressed deep concern about the human rights situation in Afghanistan, to launch a formal investigation into the killings in Mazar-e Sharif, with the aim of setting up a tribunal if appropriate. "The outside world has for too long ignored the crisis in Afghanistan," said Patricia Gossman, senior researcher at Human Rights Watch. "Meanwhile, Afghanistan's neighbors have kept the war going. Intervention by the U.N. now might help insure that one day the victims obtain justice and the cycle of violence is slowed, if not stopped."

The U.N. should also initiate urgent talks with the Taliban to post human rights observers on the ground in Hazarajat, Gossman said. She noted that since the U.S. airstrikes in Afghanistan last month, all foreign aid workers have been evacuated, leaving no witnesses to the war. Human Rights Watch further called on the United States and the European Union to urge the International Monetary Fund to bear in mind

Pakistan's role in providing military support to the Taliban as the agency considers a planned economic rescue package for Pakistan. Pakistan should also condemn the killings and investigate the role Pakistani fighters may have played in the massacres, Gossman said.

Western diplomats, UN officials, and Western aid workers say thousands of Hazaras, mostly males, were killed in front of their families in Mazar-e-Sharif, the capital of the anti-Taliban alliance in northern Afghanistan, when the Taliban captured the city last month. According to aid workers, young men over 16 had their throats slit, while younger boys and women had both hands chopped off at the wrist. These attacks on the Hazaras have the potential of igniting a wider war. Iran has long backed the Hazara militia, Hezb-e Wahdat, while Pakistan has supported the Taliban.

A senior Taliban official has confirmed that nine of the eleven Iranian diplomats nationals missing since the city of Mazar-e-Sharif fell to Taliban forces last month were killed. A number of Pakistanis, including members of the extremist Sunni organization Sipah-i-Sahaba, reportedly fought with the Taliban in Mazar-e Sharif. The Taliban is now poised to move further into the central enclave of Hazarajat, a region populated almost exclusively by Hazaras, and home now to many displaced Hazaras who fled Mazar-e-Sharif during the Taliban offensive. According to press reports, the Taliban are closing in on the region from three sides and have already taken several towns.

The region's capital city, Bamiyan, is surrounded on all four sides by the Taliban. Since 1997 the Taliban have enforced a blockade on the Hazarajat region, preventing food and other humanitarian assistance from reaching there from the south, while anarchical conditions in the north blocked access from the other direction. The blockade was only lifted temporarily in May of this year. The Hazaras, a Shi'ite Muslim minority which has suffered a history of discrimination in Afghanistan, have been targeted by the Taliban since the militia began its military campaign four years ago. With few exceptions, the

Taliban come from the Pashtun ethnic group that dominates the predominantly rural areas of southeastern Afghanistan and western Pakistan. The Hazaras' Shia faith is anathema to the Taliban, which is seeking to impose its version of a Sunni Muslim theocracy in Afghanistan.

The Taliban has jailed Hazara refugees returning from Iran. Among those fleeing the current fighting, Hazaras have been stopped and taken away for questioning. The enmity also has its roots in the cycles of revenge killings that have marked Afghanistan's civil war: The Hazara militia Hezb-I Wahdat was responsible for atrocities against Pashtuns before the Taliban took Kabul, and may have been involved in the massacre of some 2000 Taliban soldiers during a failed attempt by the Taliban to take Mazar-e-Sharif in May 1997.

The U.N. promised to investigate the massacre but failed to do so. If a tribunal is established, those killings should also come under its purview. The Taliban has denied responsibility for the killings but has refused to allow aid workers, the UN, or foreign journalists to return to Mazar-e Sharif.

4

Human Rights and Taliban

There was no functioning central government, until December 22, 2001 when the Afghan Interim Administration (AIA) took office. During most of the year, the Taliban, a Pashtun-dominated ultra-conservative Islamic movement, controlled approximately 90 per cent of the country, including the capital of Kabul, and all major urban areas, except Faizabad. In 1997 the Taliban issued an edict renaming the country the Islamic Emirate of Afghanistan, and named its leader, Mullah Omar, Head of State and Commander of the Faithful, granting him ultimate authority.

Omar headed the inner Shura (Council), located in the southern city of Kandahar. The Taliban's power structure reportedly narrowed during the year, and its principal consultative bodies, the Shuras, reportedly no longer functioned. Until October 7, a rival regime, the Islamic State of Afghanistan (generally known as the Northern Alliance or United Front), which nominally was headed by former Afghanistan President Burhanuddin Rabbani, an ethnic Tajik, controlled about 10 per cent of the country. Rabbani and his chief military commander, Ahmed Shah Masood, for most of the year, controlled the majority Tajik areas in the country's extreme northeast.

The Rabbani regime controlled most of the country's embassies and retained Afghanistan's U.N. seat after the U.N. General Assembly again deferred a decision on Afghanistan's credentials. A number of provincial administrations maintained limited functions, but civil institutions were rudimentary. There was no countrywide recognized constitution, rule of law, or independent judiciary. In 1999 the Taliban claimed that it was drafting a constitution based on Islamic law but there were no further announcements regarding a constitution during the year.

Hostilities between the Taliban and the Northern Alliance continued throughout the year. Before October 7, attempts to achieve a peaceful resolution to the conflict continued. The U.N. Secretary General's Personal Representative to Afghanistan, Francesco Vendrell, was engaged in extensive discussions with various Afghan parties and interested nations, but made no progress in ending the conflict. A process to convene a Loya Jirga, or Grand Assembly of traditional leaders, which focused on installing Rome-based former King Zahir Shah, continued to gather support but achieved no resolution.

On October 7, Operation Enduring Freedom (OEF), a U.S.-led coalition, began a military action aimed at toppling the Taliban regime and eliminating the *Al Qaeda* terrorist network in Afghanistan. U.S. forces worked in concert with anti-Taliban forces of the Northern Alliance as well as others in southern Afghanistan. By mid-November the Taliban had been removed from power and had retreated from Kabul to southwestern Afghanistan. Taliban leader Mullah Omar and *Al Qaeda* leader Usama bin Ladin remained fugitives at year's end, and U.S. military operations continued in an effort to capture and detain remaining Taliban and *Al Qaeda* fighters.

On December 5, a U.N.-sponsored Afghan peace conference in Bonn, Germany approved a broad agreement for the establishment of a 6-month interim authority (AIA) to govern the country. The AIA Chairman, Hamid Karzai, and his cabinet took office December 22. During most of the year, the Taliban remained the country's primary military force. Its militia and the religious police, part of the Ministry for the Promotion of Virtue and Suppression of Vice (PVSV), were responsible for internal security in areas under Taliban control. The Taliban and members of other warring Afghan factions committed numerous serious human rights abuses in areas they occupied.

The dislocations associated with more than 20 years of fighting, together with years of severe drought, have reduced the country's economy to a bare subsistence level. A U.N.-sponsored health survey in northern Afghanistan in January found alarming levels of malnutrition, especially among women and children, and officials warned that the situation could worsen dramatically. Most of the population of approximately 25.8 million was engaged in agriculture and animal husbandry. In previous years, opium poppy cultivation was the mainstay of the economy and largely financed the military operations of various factions. In 1999 and 2000, the country was the world's largest opium producer.

In 2000 the Taliban banned cultivation of the opium poppy but failed to destroy the existing stockpile, reportedly the worlds largest. During the year, the Taliban reportedly announced that poppy cultivation could be resumed. Planting is believed to have begun. The severe drought affected over half of the population and severely affected approximately 5 to 6 million persons. The drought increased internal displacement and caused massive loss of livestock and other means of earning a living. Livestock losses were reported at about 50 per cent. The country's grain production fell by about 50 per cent in the past 2 years and met less than half of the country's requirements. Crop loss in many areas averaged 75 per cent.

Additionally, a lack of resources and the prolonged civil war impeded reconstruction of irrigation systems, repair of market roads, and replanting of orchards. The presence of millions of landmines and unexploded ordnance throughout the country restricted areas available for cultivation and slowed the return of refugees needed to rebuild the economy. Trade consisted mainly of opium, fruits, minerals, gems, and carpets, as well as the smuggling of goods to Pakistan. Both factions printed highly inflated rival currencies.

Formal economic activity remained minimal in most of the country, especially rural areas, and was inhibited by recurrent fighting. The country was dependent on international assistance, and large portions of the population required food aid to survive. Per capita income, based on World Bank figures, was about $280 per year. Only minimal reconstruction continued in Herat, Kandahar, and Ghazni, areas that had been under firm Taliban control for several years. Areas outside of Taliban control suffered from brigandage. The overall human rights situation remained extremely poor, and the Taliban committed numerous serious and systemic abuses.

The reported informal easing of restrictions in 2000 reversed during the year; before November, the Taliban attempted to increase its control by increasing the authority of the PVSV religious police, by increasing restrictions, and by committing a greater number of abuses. Citizens remained unable to change their government or choose their leaders peacefully. The Taliban carried out summary justice in the areas that it controlled, and reportedly was responsible for political and other extrajudicial killings, including targeted killings, summary executions, and deaths in custody. In September alleged foreign agents of *Al Qaeda* killed Northern Alliance commander Ahmed Shah Masood.

In November Taliban forces captured and executed opposition leader Abdul Haq and two associates. The Taliban took reprisals against civilian populations, such as the summary executions in January of an estimated 300 men and teenage boys of the Hazara ethnic minority in Bamiyan's Yakawlang district. There were allegations that Taliban forces were responsible for disappearances. The Taliban imposed strict and oppressive order by means of stiff punishments for crimes in the areas that it controlled.

The Taliban's religious police and Islamic courts enforced the Taliban's ultra-conservative interpretation of Islamic law, carrying out punishments such as stoning, flogging, amputations for theft, and public executions for adultery and murder. For lesser infractions, Taliban militiamen often judged accused offenders and meted out punishments, such as beatings, on the spot. Prison conditions were poor. The Taliban arbitrarily arrested and detained persons and infringed on citizens' privacy rights. Taliban military tactics forced tens of thousands of civilians to flee their homes. The Taliban also indiscriminately bombarded civilian areas and harassed, detained, and even killed members of relief organizations.

Civil war conditions and the actions of competing factions effectively limited the freedoms of speech, press, assembly, and association. Freedom of religion was restricted severely; conversion from Islam to Christianity or Judaism was punishable by death. In March in Bamiyan the Taliban completely destroyed two giant statutes of the Buddha that dated from pre-Islamic times and called for destruction of images in the collection at the Kabul Museum. Freedom of movement also was limited. Years of conflict have left more than 1.2 million citizens internally displaced, while more than 3.5 million of the country's population live outside the country as refugees. Continued fighting and related security concerns, as well as the drought, discouraged many refugees from returning to their country, and caused many more to leave.

Although all factions harassed domestic and international NGO's, the Taliban in particular increased its activities in this regard during the year. Such harassment forced many NGO's to curtail their activities and, together with the intensified military activity late in the year, forced most international assistance workers to leave the country. The human rights situation for women was extremely poor for most of the year, with widespread and widely accepted societal discrimination throughout the country. Violence against women remained a serious problem. Women and girls were subjected to rape, kidnaping, and forced marriage.

Taliban restrictions against women and girls remained widespread, institutionally sanctioned, and systematic throughout most of the year. The Taliban increased enforcement of strict dress codes and maintained the prohibition against women working outside the home except in strictly limited circumstances in the health care field and in some humanitarian assistance projects. The Taliban appeared to reverse a 2-year trend of relaxing enforcement of restrictions on women and girls and increasingly restricted female education and participation in the labor force. Although girls were prohibited formally from attending school, some organizations clandestinely operated elementary schools and home schools with girls in attendance. The Taliban detained persons because of their ethnic origins.

Worker rights were not defined. Reports from refugees and others indicate there was widespread disregard for and abuse of internationally recognized worker rights. Child labor persisted. The human rights situation in areas outside of Taliban control also remained extremely poor, and Northern Alliance members reportedly committed numerous, serious abuses. Opposition forces continued sporadic rocket attacks against Kabul and bombarded civilians indiscriminately.

In November Northern Alliance forces reportedly killed 100 to 300 Taliban fighters in Mazar-e-Sharif; there were conflicting reports as to whether some of the Taliban forces attempted to surrender before they were shelled. On November 25, Northern Alliance forces reportedly killed at least 120 prisoners in Mazar-e-Sharif, allegedly during the suppression of a riot. Various factions infringed on citizens' privacy rights. Armed units of the Northern Alliance, local commanders, and rogue individuals were responsible for political killing, abduction, kidnaping for ransom, torture, rape, arbitrary detention, and looting.

RESPECT FOR HUMAN RIGHTS

SECTION 1 RESPECT FOR THE INTEGRITY OF THE PERSON, INCLUDING FREEDOM FROM:

a. Arbitrary or Unlawful Deprivation of Life

Taliban forces committed a large number of political and other extrajudicial killings, both within the country and in the refugee community in Pakistan during the year.

In September agents believed to be associated with Usama bin Laden's *Al Qaeda* organization and working with the Taliban killed Northern Alliance Defense Minister and key military leader Ahmed Shah Masood. The agents disguised themselves as journalists to gain access to Masood and concealed explosives in their camera equipment, which they detonated in Masood's presence. The perpetrators also were killed in the explosion.

On October 25, Taliban forces captured opposition leader Abdul Haq and two associates. The three were accused of spying and attempting to bribe tribesmen. Haq and his two associates were executed the next day. According to Haq's family, he had been travelling unarmed with companions. In June 2000, Amnesty International reported that over the previous 2 years, more than a dozen prominent citizens advocating an end to the war and establishment of a government representing all ethnic groups had been arrested and killed by the Taliban.

Much of the political and extrajudicial killing in Afghanistan during the year occurred in connection with the renewed conflict between the Taliban and the Northern Alliance that began in mid- summer and intensified late in the year. The conflict was characterized by sporadic, indiscriminate shelling and bombing, as well as mass killings. There were reliable reports that Taliban forces fighting to recapture Yakawlang in early January were under instructions from the Taliban leadership to kill prisoners as well as civilian males. Reports indicate that the Taliban summarily executed approximately 300 Hazara men and boys.

Many were shot by firing squads in public view. Those killed reportedly included aid workers and an Afghan member of a U.N. organization. According to Human Rights Watch, the killings apparently were intended as collective punishment for local residents, whom the Taliban suspected of cooperating with the Northern Alliance, and to deter such cooperation in the future. The Taliban denied responsibility but barred journalists from the area. Some sources reported that foreign Taliban volunteers were responsible for the killings. During the attack on Yakawlang, eyewitnesses reported that both sides violated the neutrality of medical facilities and failed to treat civilians as noncombatants.

Also in January, Taliban forces reportedly executed at least 31 ethnic Uzbek civilians while the Taliban retreated from Takhar province. In October there were credible reports that Taliban troops fired rockets into the middle of a crowded bazaar killing 2 civilians and injuring 16. There were unconfirmed reports in November that foreign Taliban soldiers killed approximately 400 Afghan Taliban soldiers attempting to defect to the Northern Alliance in the city of Kunduz.

From August 9, 2000, through September 5, 2000, when the Taliban captured it, there was intense fighting around and in the town of Taloqan. During the offensive to capture Taloqan, Taliban aircraft bombed the city many times. No statistics are available regarding civilian casualties in Taloqan, but 60,000 to 75,000 persons left their homes in Taloqan and other areas in the northern part of the country to flee the fighting. Amnesty International reported that during the fighting in Taloqan, the Taliban bombarded a village, burned all of the houses there, and killed some of the villagers. It was also reported that the Taliban cut the throat of one man in front of his relatives.

In February 2000, indiscriminate bombing by the Taliban in the Panjshir valley killed eight civilians. In mid-June 2000, the Taliban began offensives in the Shomali and Kunduz areas, using aircraft to support ground troops. On July 1, 2000, the Taliban launched large-scale attacks near the towns of Baghram and Charikar, approximately 30 miles north of Kabul. Civilians continued to be the primary victims of the fighting. On July 1-2, 2000, the Taliban conducted air raids on the towns of Charikar and Jabal-as Saraf, reportedly taking civilian lives.

In mid-July 2000, there were reports—denied by the Taliban—of summary executions of prisoners by the Taliban forces in the conflict areas. On July 23, 2000, Taliban aircraft bombed several towns and villages in northern Afghanistan, reportedly killing three and wounding seven civilians. On July

30, 2000, the Taliban used heavy artillery and aircraft to bomb the town of Nahreen before capturing it. When the Taliban recaptured Bamiyan in 1999, there were reports that Taliban forces carried out summary executions upon entering the city. Amnesty International reported that hundreds of men, and in a few instances women and children, were separated from their families, taken away, and killed.

There was no investigation by the Taliban of these widely publicized allegations. The Taliban also took no action and conducted no investigation into allegations by Amnesty International that dozens of noncombatants were killed systematically by Taliban forces when they captured most of the Shomali valley in late July 1999. In 1998 the Taliban reportedly executed as many as 189 prisoners it captured during fighting near Mazar-e-Sharif in order to avoid exchanging them with the Northern Alliance. The Taliban denied these allegations; by year's end, there had been no investigation into these alleged killings.

The Taliban employed swift summary trials and implemented strict punishments in accordance with Islamic law. Executions, whippings, and amputations at times took place before crowds of up to 30,000 persons. Amnesty International has reported that from 1998 to 2000, dozens of Afghan leaders and intellectuals living in Pakistan had received death threats, and several had been killed. Many believe that these political killings occurred at the direction of the Taliban. A number of moderate activists left Pakistan for other countries, partly in reaction to these killings.

In June 2000, a hooded gunman shot and wounded Mohammad Enam Wak, an Afghan author, at his home in Peshawar. By year's end, no action had been taken in the case. The shooting may have been in response to a book Wak had published examining the idea of an Afghan federation on the basis of ethnic groups. Opposition forces also reportedly committed extrajudicial killings during the year, according to press reports. In November Northern Alliance forces killed approximately 100 to 300 Taliban fighters in the city of Mazar-e-Sharif, when it shelled a former girls' school that was being used as a military barracks by the Taliban. There were conflicting reports as to whether some of the Taliban forces had attempted to surrender before the shelling.

On November 25, Northern Alliance forces reportedly killed at least 120 Taliban prisoners in Mazar-e-Sharif, allegedly during the suppression of a riot. Opposition forces fired rockets into Kabul on a number of occasions. In many of these attacks, civilians were killed or injured. Taliban soldiers reportedly were killed and injured by landmines laid by the Northern Alliance as they advanced in the Shomali plains.

In other areas, combatants sought to kill rival commanders and their sympathizers. The perpetrators of these killings and their motives often were difficult to identify, as political motives often are entwined with family and tribal feuds, battles over the drug trade, and personal vendettas. On December 4, 2000, United Front Commander Abdullah Jan Wahidi reportedly was killed in an ambush. Northern Alliance military leader Ahmed Masood's forces executed the individuals allegedly responsible for the ambush on December 6, 40 hours after their arrest, and denied charges by Amnesty International and the individuals' relatives that the accused had been tortured. The Northern Alliance also claimed that a civilian rather than a military court tried the accused.

On August 5, 2000, seven deminers working for the U.N.-funded Organization for Mine Clearance and Rehabilitation were ambushed, killed, and burned in Badghis Province; one of the deminers may have been alive at the time he was burned. It is not clear who was responsible, but the group that attacked the deminers reportedly was large, well organized, and well armed. In 1998 the U.N. found several mass graves connected with the massacre of Taliban soldiers near Mazar-e-Sharif in 1997, which contained evidence consistent with mass executions. Independent investigations of these and other killings, including killings by the Taliban, were hindered by the continuing warfare and the unwillingness of local commanders to allow investigators to visit the areas in question. The Taliban leadership had indicated in several of these cases that investigations were underway or that investigations would be permitted. However, according to neutral observers, no real progress was made by the Taliban in facilitating investigations, and mass and other killings from 1997 and 1998 have not been investigated fully.

There has been no investigation into the 1998 killing of Lieutenant Colonel Carmine Calo, an Italian serving with the U.N. Special Mission. In November during the capture of Kabul by the Northern Alliance, there were unconfirmed reports of civilians killing fleeing Taliban. An estimated 400,000 Afghans have been killed or wounded by landmines. Casualties caused by landmines and unexploded ordnance are estimated at 10 to 12 per day.

b. Disappearance

The strict security enforced by the Taliban in areas under its control had resulted in a decrease in abductions, kidnapings, and hostages taken for ransom. However, there are credible allegations that Taliban forces were responsible for disappearances, abductions, kidnapings, and hostage-takings, and that the Taliban maintained private prisons to settle personal vendettas in areas it controlled. Amnesty International reported that hundreds of persons were separated from their families in the Taloqan area during the Taliban's 2000 summer offensive, and that these persons were taken away and are believed to have been killed.

There were unconfirmed reports that some Taliban soldiers (often reported to be foreigners) abducted girls and women from villages in the Taloqan area during fighting from June through October 2000. There also were reports of the abduction of women by the Taliban in August 1999 when the Taliban retook the Shomali plains; women reportedly were taken in trucks from the area of fighting and were trafficked to Pakistan and to the Arab Gulf states. In 1998 there were credible reports that the Taliban detained hundreds of persons, mostly ethnic Hazaras, after the takeover of Mazar-e-Sharif; the whereabouts of many such persons remained unknown at year's end. There were unconfirmed reports that some Taliban soldiers abducted girls and women from Hazara neighborhoods in Mazar-e-Sharif in 1998; the whereabouts of some of these women also were unknown at year's end.

Since 1998 persons who have disappeared include: General Abdul Rahman, General Farooq, Moulvi Shabuddin, Waliullah Dagarwal, General Syed Agha Rayees, Engineer Nabi Shah, and Wolaswal Ismail. There were credible reports of some instances in which Taliban soldiers arrested individuals, often from minority ethnic groups, to extract ransoms. Abductions, kidnapings, and hostage-taking for ransom or for political reasons also occurred in non-Taliban areas, but specific information regarding such acts was unavailable. According to the U.N., in northern areas women were at risk of being raped and kidnapped. There have been unconfirmed reports that forces on both sides kidnaped young women. Some of the women reportedly then were forced to marry their kidnapers; others remained missing.

To avoid this danger, some families reportedly sent their daughters to Pakistan or to Iran. Groups in Russia listed nearly 300 Soviet soldiers formerly serving in Afghanistan as missing in action or prisoners of war (POW's). Most were thought to be dead or to have assimilated voluntarily into Afghan society, although some are alleged to be held against their will. A number of persons from the former Soviet Union missing since the period of the Soviet occupation are presumed dead.

c. Torture and Other Cruel, Inhuman, or Degrading Treatment or Punishment

The Taliban reportedly tortured opponents and beat some persons detained for political reasons. In July 2000, the U.N. Special Rapporteur on Human Rights in Afghanistan met in Iran with a former governor of Herat, General Ismail Khan, and two of his colleagues. The three stated that they were detained in a Kandahar prison on political grounds for 3 years prior to their escape in March 2000. They were kept in windowless cells and shackled the entire time. The General's colleagues reported that they were tortured by the prison authorities, and all three reported the torture of other prisoners, including beatings administered with cables to prisoners who were hung upside down by their legs.

During the year, there were credible reports that the Taliban detained and tortured persons who they believed were being helpful to Western journalists. In July 2000, a Western journalist observed his Afghan associate being beaten severely. The associate subsequently was detained and beaten routinely until he was able to escape from prison. All Afghan factions were believed to have used torture against opponents and POW's, although specific information generally was lacking. Torture did not appear to be a routine practice in all cases. Some of military leader Ahmed Masood's commanders in the north reportedly used torture routinely to extract information from and break the will of prisoners and political opponents.

In December 2000, following the ambush of United Front commander Abdullah Jan Wahidi, Masood's forces arrested six persons. According to Amnesty International, at least one of the prisoners reportedly was tortured severely prior to being executed; the family of Hemayatollah Hamed Akhundzada claimed that, at his burial, they saw that his nails had been pulled out and that there were signs of abuse on the rest of his body. The Taliban ruled strictly in areas that it controlled, establishing ad hoc and rudimentary judicial systems, based on its understanding of Islamic justice. Taliban courts imposed their extreme interpretation of Islamic law and punishments followed swift summary trials.

Murderers were subjected to public executions, a punishment that at times was inflicted by the victims' families. Thieves were subjected to public amputations of one hand, one foot, or both. Adulterers were stoned to death or publicly given 100 lashes. For example, in September 2000, a man convicted of adultery was stoned publicly in Maymana in Fariab province. The woman with whom he was convicted of engaging in adultery was sentenced to 100 lashes, but the sentence was postponed because she was pregnant. A second woman, who was convicted of arranging the adultery, was sentenced to 39 lashes. The stipulated punishment for those found guilty of homosexual acts was to have walls toppled on them. Although there were no known instances of such punishment during the year, this punishment was carried out on at least one occasion in 1999, and seven times in 1998 (resulting in five deaths).

There was documentary evidence that Taliban forces, particularly religious police, threatened and beat women for what they considered immodest dress, including failure to wear a full body covering. Religious police also assaulted men for immodest dress, incorrect beard length, and long hair. In one incident in 2000, a visiting Pakistani soccer team playing in Kandahar had their heads forcibly shaved in the middle of a match by Taliban authorities.

Prison conditions were poor. Prisoners held by some factions were not provided food; this generally was the responsibility of prisoners' relatives, who were allowed to visit to provide them with food once or twice a week. Prisoners with no relatives had to petition the local council or rely on other inmates. Prisoners lived in overcrowded, unsanitary conditions in collective cells.

There have been credible reports that torture occurred in prisons under the control of both the Taliban and the Northern Alliance. Local authorities maintained prisons in territories under their control and reportedly established torture cells in some of them. The Taliban operated prisons in Kandahar, Herat, Kabul, Jalalabad, Mazar-e-Sharif, Pul-i-Khumri, Shibarghan, Qala-e-Zaini, and Maimana. The Northern Alliance maintained prisons in Panjshir and Faizabad. According to one credible report, prison authorities in Badakhshan Province routinely used rubber and plastic bound cables in beatings.

According to Amnesty International, there were reports that the Taliban forced prisoners to build a new story for the Kandahar prison building, and that some Taliban prisoners held by Masood's forces were forced to work in life-threatening conditions, such as digging trenches in mined areas. The

International Committee of the Red Cross (ICRC) continued to visit detainees throughout the year; however, intensified fighting and poor security for foreign personnel limited the ability of the ICRC to monitor prison conditions. There were reports that an Afghan human rights organization visited a Taliban prison in Mazar-e-Sharif in February 1999.

d. Arbitrary Arrest, Detention, or Exile

In the absence of formal legal and law enforcement institutions, justice was not administered according to formal legal codes, and persons were subject to arbitrary detention. There are credible reports that both Taliban and Northern Alliance militia extorted bribes from civilians in return for their release from prison or to avoid arrest. Judicial and police procedures varied from locality to locality. Little is known about the procedures for taking persons into custody and bringing them to justice. In both Taliban and non-Taliban areas, the practices varied depending on the locality, the local commanders, and other authorities. Some areas have a more formal judicial structure than others.

The Taliban reportedly detained approximately 60 civilians when it reoccupied Bamiyan's Yakawlang district in June; their whereabouts remained unknown at year's end. In August the Taliban jailed eight foreign workers associated with Shelter Now International, a German NGO, on charges of proselytizing. They also arrested 48 Afghan employees of the organization on unspecified charges, reportedly including apostasy, which is a capital crime. The foreign volunteers initially were denied consular access and not permitted to see their relatives or consult with an attorney. In addition, they were not informed of the specific charges against them or of the legal procedures under which they would be tried.

On November 15, following the fall of Kabul, the eight workers were freed by opposing forces. In November the Taliban detained 25 followers of tribal leader Hamid Karzai following an attack on Karzai's camp in Uruzgan province. The status of those detained was unknown at year's end. Taliban arrests and detentions of journalists increased during the intensified military conflict late in the year. The Taliban also harassed and detained NGO workers throughout the year.

On July 9, 2000, the Taliban's PVSV jailed for several days a foreign aid worker who had lived and worked in Afghanistan for several years, as well as a number of her Afghan associates. The aid worker and her associates promoted home-based work for women and home schools for girls. She was expelled from the country shortly after her release on July 12, 2000. She returned to Kabul in late September 2000, but again was ordered to leave the country; she departed on October 6, 2000. No reason was given by the Taliban for her arrest and deportation. In July 2000 in Kabul, the Taliban arrested 40 members of a local group advocating a peaceful settlement of the conflict on charges of attempting to destabilize the country.

There were reports that another member of this group was arrested by Pakistani authorities in Peshawar, Pakistan. No further information was available at year's end. Amnesty International reported that the Taliban had taken children hostage in an effort to compel their fathers to surrender; the fathers of such children generally were reported to be political opponents of the Taliban. The families of these children have been told that the children would be released when their fathers surrendered to the Taliban. A Dr. Ayub, a respected physician who headed the Shuhada Hospital in Jaghoray, was taken into custody during the Bamiyan military action in 1999 and remained in Taliban custody without charges. There was no information available on his status at year's end.

The U.N. Special Rapporteur on Human Rights in Afghanistan met in July 2000 in Iran with a former governor of Herat, General Ismail Khan, and two of his colleagues. The three claimed that they were detained in a Kandahar prison on political grounds for three years prior to their escape on March 26, 2000. They were kept in windowless cells and shackled for the entire time. The General's colleagues reported their own torture by the prison authorities, and all three reported the torture of other prisoners, including being hung upside down by the legs while being beaten with cables.

A number of persons arrested by the Taliban in 1998 for political reasons were believed still to be in detention until the fall of the Taliban late in the year. The status of such detainees was uncertain at year's end. All factions most likely held political detainees, but no firm numbers are available. Both the Taliban and the Northern Alliance held thousands of combatants. The Northern Alliance reportedly held a number of Pakistanis and other third country nationals, along with several hundred Taliban soldiers, as POW's. In June 2000, the Taliban and the Northern Alliance sent delegations to inspect each other's prisoners in advance of an exchange of prisoners; however, the prisoner exchange initiative ended when fighting resumed in the summer of 2000. There was no information available regarding forced exile.

e. Denial of Fair Public Trial

With no functioning nationwide judicial system, many municipal and provincial authorities relied on some interpretation of Islamic law and traditional tribal codes of justice. The Bonn Agreement called for the establishment of a Judicial Commission to rebuild the domestic justice system in accordance with Islamic principles, international standards, the rule of law, and Afghan legal traditions. However, by year's end, the Commission members had not been announced and there was no independent judiciary.

The Taliban used Islamic courts in areas under their control to judge criminal cases and resolve disputes. According to the U.N., the Taliban asserted that there was a lower court and a higher court in every province, and a Supreme Court in Kabul. According to press reports, in 1999 Mullah Omar promulgated a decree ordering the Supreme Court and military courts not to interfere with one another. The courts reportedly dealt with all complaints, relying on the Taliban's extreme interpretation of Islamic law and punishments, as well as on traditional tribal customs.

Punishments handed down by the courts included execution and amputation. In cases involving murder and rape, convicted prisoners generally were ordered executed, although relatives of the victim could instead choose to accept other restitution or could enforce the verdict themselves. Decisions of the courts were reportedly final. The courts reportedly heard cases in sessions that lasted only a few minutes. According to Amnesty International, some judges in these courts were untrained in law and at times based their judgments on a combination of their personal understanding of Islamic law and a tribal code of honor prevalent in Pashtun areas.

Defendants did not have the right to an attorney, although they were permitted attorneys in some instances. In August eight foreign aid workers were arrested on charges of promoting Christianity. Their trial began, but immediately was adjourned. The U.N. warned the Taliban that it was violating international norms by refusing to let the detained foreign aid workers consult with representatives of their governments or lawyers. The aid workers eventually were freed by opposition forces on November 15.

Little is known about the administration of justice in the areas that were controlled by the Northern Alliance. The administration and implementation of justice varied from area to area and depended on the inclinations of local commanders or other authorities, who summarily executed, tortured, and meted out punishments, including executions, without reference to any other authority. Following the ambush of a Northern Alliance commander in December 2000, six prisoners were arrested and executed within 40 hours of their arrest. Spokespersons for military leader Ahmed Masood claimed that the prisoners were tried before a civilian court before they were executed; however, it provided no information regarding the nature of their trial.

All factions most likely held political prisoners, but there were no reliable estimates of the numbers involved.

f. Arbitrary Interference With Privacy, Family, Home, or Correspondence

Continued fighting often resulted in the homes and businesses of civilians being invaded and looted by forces on all sides. Some armed gunmen reportedly acted with impunity, due to the absence of a responsive police force or legal protection for victims. It was unclear what authority controlled the actions of the Taliban militiamen who patrolled the streets of cities and towns. A number of incidents were reported in which Taliban soldiers, persons masquerading as Taliban, or foreign volunteers fighting alongside the Taliban, entered private homes without prior notification or informed consent. In Kabul soldiers allegedly searched homes for evidence of cooperation with the former authorities or for violations of Taliban decrees, including the ban on the possession of depictions of living things, including photographs, stuffed animals, and dolls.

At various times, the Taliban also banned certain traditional recreational activities, such as flying kites and playing chess. Members of the PVSV, the Taliban's religious police, arrested or assaulted individuals on the streets for infractions of Taliban rules concerning dress, hair length, and facial hair, as well as for the violation of the prohibition on women being in the company of men who were unrelated to them. The Taliban required women to wear a *burqa*, a tent-like outer garment that covers a woman from head to toe, when in public. Men were required to wear their beards a certain length or longer, not to trim their beards, and to wear head coverings.

Men whose beards did not conform to the guidelines on beard length set out by the Taliban were subject to imprisonment for 10 days and mandatory Islamic instruction. According to Amnesty International, Taliban members took children hostage in an effort to compel their fathers to surrender. The Taliban reportedly also required parents to give their children "Islamic" names. Many of these restrictions were eased by year's end following the removal of the Taliban and the establishment of the AIA on December 22. On July 12, the Taliban banned use of the Internet, although it was unclear whether the ban applied to humanitarian agencies.

On July 19, the Taliban banned the import of 30 items it claimed were "un-Islamic," including musical instruments, cassettes, and computer discs. In 1998 the Taliban had banned televisions, satellite dishes, videocassette recorders, and video and audio cassettes. Nonetheless, televisions reportedly were sold widely. There were also reports that the Taliban forcibly conscripted or attempted forcibly to conscript persons, and that in several instances such attempts were resisted. Resistance to forced conscription resulted in an increased Taliban dependence on foreign volunteers.

There were reports that some prisoners of the Taliban, including the sons of families that had opposed Taliban social restrictions, were drafted forcibly and sent to the front. The Taliban reportedly followed a longstanding practice of forcibly expelling ethnic Hazara and Tajiks from areas controlled by the Taliban, and otherwise harassing these minorities. In October 2000, the Northern Alliance alleged that the Taliban forced the residents of Humber Koh and Hazrab villages near Taloqan to leave their homes before burning the dwellings.

g. Use of Excessive Force and Violations of Humanitarian Law in Internal Conflicts

The Taliban posed serious obstacles to the efforts of international aid organizations to deliver food aid and other humanitarian assistance. U.N.-led negotiations to obtain Taliban permission for delivery of food and nonfood aid across the front lines into the Panjshir Valley and the Dara-i-Suf area remained at an impasse during the period that the Taliban controlled these areas. The Taliban imposed severe restrictions on international assistance activities, severely hampering personnel and limiting their effectiveness.

It also restricted the ability of women to take advantage of the limited aid available by restricting their movement, and at times banned or limited deliveries into areas inhabited by non-Pashtun groups. Such restrictions and actions against humanitarian organizations by the Taliban increased during the intensified fighting late in the year. After the fall of the Taliban, looting by armed groups and individuals, general insecurity, and harsh weather conditions at times hampered humanitarian assistance efforts.

In October Taliban soldiers seized food warehouses of the U.N. World Food Program (WFP) in Kabul and Kandahar, seizing approximately 7,000 tons of food. According to a WFP spokesperson, the WFP regained control of the warehouse shortly following the takeover. In October Medecins sans Frontieres closed its medical relief programs in two Afghan cities after armed gangs looted them of medicine, equipment, and vehicles.

On October 16, Taliban members reportedly intermittently looted the offices of the Swedish Committee for Afghanistan over a period of 2 days in five separate Afghan cities—Mazar-e-Sharif, Pul-e-Khumri, Kunduz, Taloqan, and Ghazni. According to the organization's director, Afghan staff of the committee were beaten and forced to flee, fuel reserves were set on fire, and nearly half of the committee's 80 vehicles, as well as computers, printers, photocopying machines, telephones, and furniture, were removed.

According to Human Rights Watch, on October 7 armed Taliban soldiers entered the compound of a demining NGO in Kabul. The soldiers beat staff members and broke some of the locks on vehicles. There also were credible reports that in Kandahar at least 15 to 20 vehicles also were confiscated, mostly from the U.N. Mine Action Program. On October 8, armed Taliban forces entered the compound of the U.N. Coordinator for Humanitarian Affairs (UNCHA) in Mazar-e-Sharif and looted communications equipment. The forces destroyed the windows of nine U.N. vehicles on the compound. On October 8, armed Taliban soldiers entered the compound of a demining NGO in Kandahar and demanded vehicles.

Staff that resisted were beaten and ordered to leave the compound. The soldiers left with seven ambulances, seven pick-up trucks, and six cargo trucks. Another demining organization working in Kandahar reported to Human Rights Watch that Taliban forces confiscated 1 vehicle on September 26, 3 ambulances on October 3, 9 pick-up trucks on October 11, and 22 additional vehicles on October 15. The forces also looted the office of the organization, taking spare parts, generators, radios, and the personal property of organization personnel. Soldiers reportedly beat staff members who resisted. None of the vehicles had been returned by year's end. On October 15, armed men entered the Mazar-e-Sharif offices of a demining organization.

Officials of the agency reported to Human Rights Watch that the men beat the organization's guards and looted the office. On October 15, armed men entered the compound of the International Organization for Migration (IOM), beat two guards, and looted the office. The same men reportedly returned on October 16 and removed three vehicles from the compound. Various other forces also reportedly harassed or otherwise interfered with the operation of humanitarian relief organizations. On October 13, a group of approximately 20 armed men entered the Kandahar offices of the Islamic Relief Organization, demanding vehicles at gunpoint. Taliban security forces intervened, and a clash ensued.

One vehicle was taken from the compound by the unidentified armed men. On November 9, Northern Alliance forces reportedly seized a 10-truck, 200-metric-ton UNICEF supply convoy, which was carrying 300 water pumps and 150 family tents with heaters. There were reports in 1999 that some individual Northern Alliance commanders in the northeast were "taxing" humanitarian assistance entering Afghanistan from Tajikistan, harassing NGO workers, obstructing aid convoys, and otherwise hindering the movement of humanitarian aid.

By year's end, the international community was working closely with AIA officials in the delivery of humanitarian assistance. The Taliban's rapid fall from power averted a much-feared large-scale humanitarian disaster. The primary limitations for the delivery of assistance by the end of the year were logistical and centered on the difficulties in moving relief goods overland to Afghanistan's geographically remote areas. According to refugees who fled Kabul, Taliban forces took cover among the civilian population and hid their military equipment in mosques and schools to avoid U.S. air strikes.

In November following the capture of Kabul by the Northern Alliance, there were credible reports that as Taliban members fled the city, they ransacked offices, stole vehicles, looted the museum, and stole an estimated $1.5 million in the currency exchange district. During most of the year, continued internal conflict resulted in many instances of the use of excessive force. The Taliban frequently bombed cities held by the Northern Alliance resulting in the deaths of civilians, property damage, and the displacement of residents. The Taliban reoccupied Bamiyan's Yakawlang district in June and, according to Human Rights Watch, destroyed public, residential, and commercial buildings and detained approximately 60 civilians, whose whereabouts remained unknown at year's end.

As many as 50,000 residents were displaced. The Taliban units involved in the action reportedly included a large number of foreign volunteers, who were responsible for a disproportionate percentage of abuses committed by Taliban forces. The conflict leading up to the fall of Taloqan in September 2000 displaced 60,000 to 75,000 persons, but many families quickly returned once it became clear that the Taliban was not following its scorched earth policy of previous years.

During the May 1999 recapture of Bamiyan by the Taliban, there were reports of systematic killings and summary executions by Taliban forces, as well as reports of hundreds of persons being taken away in Taliban trucks. Taliban forces reportedly also took hundreds of persons after the capture of Yakawlang the same month and in the late summer of 1999, refugees from the Taliban offensive in the Shomali plain reported summary executions of non-combatants. The number of those killed or detained in fighting by the Taliban in 1999 is unknown. In August 1998, the Taliban captured Mazar-e-Sharif and reportedly massacred as many as 5,000 persons, mostly ethnic Hazara civilians.

In general independent investigations of alleged killings were hindered by continuing warfare and the unwillingness of local commanders to allow investigators to visit the areas in question. While it was in control, the Taliban denied charges that its forces massacred or committed abuses against civilians and claimed that civilian deaths, if any, resulted from combat. The Taliban claimed that the Northern Alliance bombed Shekhar Darra and Gol Darra in the summer of 2000, killing an unspecified number of civilians.

Afghanistan is the most heavily mined country in the world, according to U.N. mine-clearing experts. The U.N. estimates that there are 5 to 7 million landmines and over 750,000 pieces of unexploded ordnance throughout the country, planted mainly during the Soviet occupation. However, some NGO's estimate that there may be fewer than 1 million mines. There have been claims that 162 of 356 districts are mine-affected. The most heavily mined areas are the provinces bordering Iran and Pakistan.

The landmines and unexploded ordnance caused deaths and injuries, restricted areas available for cultivation, and slowed the return of refugees. In 1999 the NGO Halo Trust estimated that mines covered more than 420 square miles, including over 285 square miles of grazing land, over 100 square miles of agricultural land, almost 25 square miles of roads, approximately 7.5 square miles of residential area, and over 2 square miles of irrigation systems and canals. From 1995 to 1997, new mines were believed to have been laid over 90 square miles of land, reportedly mostly by the Northern Alliance in the western provinces of Badghis and Faryab.

Additional newly mined areas were reported but not confirmed in 2000 and during the year in the conflict areas north of Kabul. The Northern Alliance reportedly laid these mines in response to the Taliban's summer 2000 offensive. Taliban leader Mullah Omar reportedly banned the use, production, trade, and stockpiling of mines in 1998. Despite the general prohibition on the depiction of living things, the Taliban reportedly once allowed the visual depiction of persons in demining educational materials. An estimated 400,000 Afghans have been killed or wounded by landmines. Casualties caused by landmines and unexploded ordnance are estimated at 10 to 12 per day. In some parts of the country, including Herat and Kandahar, the presence of landmines causing bodily harm and restricting travel affected almost 90 per cent of households.

An estimated 96 per cent of civilian mine and unexploded ordnance casualties are male. Approximately 53 per cent of mine and unexploded ordnance casualties occur in the 18 to 40 age group, while 34 per cent of the casualties involve children, according to the U.N. Mine Action Center. Landmines and unexploded ordnance resulted in death in approximately 30 per cent of cases and in serious injuries and disability, including amputation and blindness, in approximately 20 per cent of cases. With funding from international donors, the U.N. has organized and trained mine detection and clearance teams, which operate throughout the country and nearly all areas that have been cleared are in productive use, and approximately 1.5 million refugees and internally displaced persons (IDPs) have returned to areas cleared of mines and unexploded ordnance. Nonetheless, the mines are expected to pose a threat for many years.

Clearance rates and safety have increased for clearance teams assisted by dogs. U.N. agencies and NGO's had instituted a number of educational programs and mine awareness campaigns for women and children in various parts of the country. Many were curtailed as a result of Taliban restrictions on women and girls, but have been reinvigorated since the fall of the Taliban. Continued warfare, as well as prolonged and severe drought, also resulted in massive forced displacement of civilians. Over the course of the year, it is estimated that up to 500,000 Afghans were displaced (300,000 internally displaced persons and 200,000 refugees) due to internal fighting, drought, and the military activities beginning in October.

SECTION- 2 RESPECT FOR CIVIL LIBERTIES, INCLUDING

a. Freedom of Speech and Press

There were no laws that effectively provide for freedom of speech and of the press, and senior officials of various warring factions attempted to intimidate journalists and influence their reporting. There were fewer than 10 regular publications in the country. All other newspapers were published only sporadically, and for the most part were affiliated with different factions. Various factions maintained their own communications facilities. The Taliban selectively banned the entry of foreign newspapers into their territory. Many foreign books were prohibited. The Taliban radio station, the Voice of Shariat, broadcast religious programming and Taliban pronouncements.

As anti-Taliban forces began liberating areas of Afghanistan formerly under Taliban control in November and December, facilities began broadcasting a wider variety of programming, including music programs. All factions attempted to pressure foreign journalists who reported on the conflict. The Taliban initially cooperated with members of the international press who arrived in Kabul, but later imposed restrictions on them. The Taliban banned all foreign journalists from filming or photographing persons or animals and required them to be accompanied at all times by a Taliban escort to ensure that such restrictions were enforced. Foreign male journalists were not permitted to interview women.

In August 2000, the Taliban introduced additional strict regulations governing the work of foreign journalists in the country. A list of 21 points "to be respected" was provided to foreign journalists upon arrival. The list included an item requiring journalists "not to offend the people's feelings." Journalists were required to inform the Taliban authorities when they traveled outside of Kabul and to stay out of prohibited areas. Journalists could work only with approved interpreters and local assistants, were required to renew their work permits every year, and were required to register all of their professional equipment. The Taliban also required most journalists to stay at the Intercontinental Hotel in Kabul, allegedly for security and economic reasons.

The Taliban had arrested an estimated 34 journalists since it took control of Kabul in September 1996. In March the Taliban authorities expelled a BBC journalist for what it considered biased reporting on the destruction of the statues of the Buddha in Bamiyan. Taliban arrests of and restrictions against journalists increased during the intensified military conflict late in the year. Beginning in September, the Taliban banned foreign media from areas under their control, and stated that they would not issue visas.

In September the Taliban arrested British journalist Yvonne Ridley, along with two Pakistani guides, Gul Muhmand and Jan Ali. Ridley was held for 10 days on charges of spying. She was released on October 8. Muhmand and Ali were released on November 13. On October 9, the Taliban arrested French journalist Michel Peyrard, who illegally had entered the country disguised in a *burqa,* and a Pakistani reporter, Mukkaram Khan, and a Pakistani guide, Mohammad Irfan. The three were charged with spying. Peyrard was released on November 3, Irfan was released on November 10 and escorted to the Pakistani border, and Khan was released on November 12 and returned to Pakistan. On October 22, the Taliban arrested a Japanese journalist, Daigen Yanagida, in Asadabad. Yanagida was imprisoned until November 16, and then released.

After meeting in Pakistan with Canadian diplomats and Pakistani authorities, the Taliban on December 1 released Ken Hechtman, a Canadian journalist, who had been held captive in Spin Boldak by approximately 11 armed Taliban members. In July 2000, a Western journalist, while being detained, observed his Afghan associate being beaten severely. The journalist subsequently was expelled from the country, and his associate was detained and beaten routinely until he escaped from prison. In August 2000, the PVSV arrested three foreign journalists, allegedly for photographing a soccer match in Kabul.

The journalists were interrogated for 2 hours, after which their film was confiscated. PVSV officials stated that taking pictures of living things was forbidden. A number of journalists were killed during the intensified fighting late in the year. On November 11, Taliban forces fired on a Northern

Alliance military convoy, killing three journalists—Pierre Billaud, Volker Hankloik, and Johannes Sutton—who were riding with the Northern Alliance soldiers in an armored personnel carrier. The convoy was advancing toward Taliban positions near the city of Taloqan.

On November 19 in Mnangarhar Province, armed men forced four journalists, Harry Burton, Maria Grazia Cutuli, Julio Fuentes, and Azizullah Haidari, out of their convoy of vehicles and executed them. On November 26, in an apparent attempted robbery, armed gunmen broke into a home in Taloqan in northeast Afghanistan in which Swedish journalists were sleeping. The gunmen killed journalist Ulf Stromberg. The intruders demanded money and stole equipment, including cameras, computers, and a satellite phone.

There have been numerous threats to Afghan journalists working in exile in Pakistan; the United Nations High Commission for Refugees (UNHCR) has assisted approximately 10 Afghan journalists in relocating to Western countries from Pakistan. Many believe that Taliban authorities made these threats in response to critical reporting. For example, in July 2000, Inayat-ul-Haq Yasinin, a journalist in Peshawar, received death threats for publishing the results of an opinion poll on Afghan refugees living in Peshawar.

The Taliban prohibited music, movies, and television on religious grounds. In August 1998, television sets, videocassettes, videocassette recorders, audiocassettes, and satellite dishes were outlawed in order to enforce the prohibition. The ban continued during most of the year, although televisions reportedly were sold widely, and their use generally was ignored unless reported by a neighbor. By year's end after the AIA took office, televisions, radios and other electronic goods were sold freely, and music was played widely. In July the Taliban banned use of the Internet. The Taliban severely restricted academic freedom, particularly education for girls.

b. Freedom of Peaceful Assembly and Association

War, tenuous security, and likely opposition from local authorities seriously inhibited freedom of assembly and association during most of the year, particularly in areas that were under Taliban control. In the past, the Taliban has used excessive force against demonstrators, but there were no such reports during the year.

It is unknown whether laws existed that governed the formation of associations. Many domestic NGO's operated in the country, and many international NGO's also operated during most of the year. All factions continued to harass and interfere with the operations of domestic and international NGO's, including aid organizations. The Taliban interfered consistently with the operations of the U.N. and NGO's. The Taliban reportedly required NGO's to undergo burdensome registration procedures to obtain permission to operate and attempted to exert control over NGO staffing and office locations, especially in Kabul. Other Taliban restrictions on freedom of association included threatening to impound vehicles of NGO's that did not work on projects approved by the Taliban and forcing organizations to employ Taliban supervisors or workers.

In September the Taliban occupied the offices of many NGO's throughout the country, including the WFP, restricting communications to foreign headquarters but generally allowing local staff to operate the organizations. Almost all foreign personnel of NGO's in the country had left areas under Taliban control when the U.S.-led coalition military operations began in October, either on their own or after being expelled by the Taliban. Foreign personnel had begun returning to Kabul and other major cities where security conditions permitted their return by year's end.

In May religious police raided an Italian-funded hospital in Kabul, assaulted staff members, and forced the hospital to suspend operations because male and female staff allegedly mixed in the dining rooms and operating wards. The Taliban detained the director of one NGO and impounded all of the NGO's equipment in an effort to increase Taliban control of the organization. In August the Taliban arrested 8 foreign aid workers and an estimated 48 Afghan employees of the NGO on charges of proselytizing; they were freed by opposing forces on November 15.

The Taliban announced in March 1998 that foreign Muslim women, including U.N. workers, would be allowed to perform their jobs only if accompanied by a male relative, a decision that continued to hamper NGO and relief operations during the year. The U.N. withdrew its personnel from southern Afghanistan in late March 1998 to protest the assault on a U.N. worker by the Taliban governor of Kandahar Province and the interference with its work by the Taliban. After reaching agreements with local officials, the U.N. returned to Kandahar in May 1999.

On June 15, 1999, members of the Taliban detained and beat staff members of an international NGO in Bamiyan Province. After the incident, Mullah Omar issued an edict stating that any person causing annoyance to a foreign worker could face punishment of up to 5 years in prison. However, in November 1999, U.N. properties were targeted in organized demonstrations in several cities when U.N. sanctions related to terrorism were imposed on the country. Certain key issues, including the mobility of international female Muslim staff and access by Afghan women and girls to programs, remained unresolved at year's end.

There were reports in 1999 that military leader Ahmed Masood's commanders in the northeast were "taxing" humanitarian assistance entering Afghanistan from Tajikistan, harassing NGO workers, obstructing aid convoys, and otherwise hindering the movement of humanitarian aid. At year's end, NGO's and international organizations continued to report that local commanders were charging them for the relief supplies they were bringing into the country.

c. Freedom of Religion

Freedom of religion was restricted severely. Due to the absence of a constitution and the ongoing civil war, religious freedom is determined primarily by the unofficial, unwritten, and evolving policies of the warring factions. For most of the year in most parts of the country, the Taliban vigorously enforced its extreme interpretation of Islamic law. Sunni Islam of the Hanafi School of jurisprudence traditionally has been the dominant religion, and the Taliban also nominally adhered to the Hanafi School. The Taliban claimed in mid-1999 that it was drafting a new constitution based on the sources of Islamic religious (Shari'a) law (the Qur'an, the Sunna, and Hanafi jurisprudence.)

A Taliban spokesman stated that the new constitution would ensure the rights of all Muslims and of religious minorities; however, a constitution never was adopted. Custom and law required affiliation with some religion, and atheism was considered apostasy and was punishable by death. Licensing and registration of religious groups do not appear to be required by the authorities in any part of the country. The small number of non-Muslim residents remaining in the country may practice their faith but may not proselytize.

The country's official name, according to the Taliban, was the Islamic Emirate of Afghanistan; according to the Northern Alliance, it was the Islamic State of Afghanistan. These names reflected the desire of both factions to promote Islam as the state religion. Taliban leader Mullah Omar carried the title of Commander of the Faithful.

The Taliban ruled strictly in areas that it controlled, establishing ad hoc and rudimentary judicial systems. The Taliban established Islamic courts to judge criminal cases and resolve disputes. Taliban courts imposed their extreme interpretation of Islamic law and punishments following swift summary trials.

The Taliban sought to institute its extreme interpretation of Islamic observance in areas under its control and declared that all Muslims in areas under Taliban control must abide by the Taliban's interpretation of Islamic law. The Taliban announced its proclamations and edicts through broadcasts on the Taliban's Radio Shariat and relied on a religious police force under the control of the PVSV to enforce rules regarding appearance, dress, employment, access to medical care, religious practice, expression, and other behavior. Members of the PVSV, which was raised to the status of a Ministry in May 1998, regularly monitored persons on the street to ensure that individuals were conforming to Taliban edicts. Persons found to be in violation of the edicts were subject to punishment meted out on the spot, including beatings and detention. In practice the rigid policies adopted both by the Taliban and by certain opposition groups had a chilling effect on adherents of other forms of Islam and on other faiths.

Enforcement of Taliban social strictures was erratic; Taliban edicts generally were enforced in the cities, especially in Kabul, but enforced less consistently in rural areas, in which more discretion was permitted based on local custom. Reliable sources estimate that 85 per cent of the populations are Sunni Muslim and most of the remaining 15 per cent are Shi'a. Shi'a, including the predominately Shi'a Hazara ethnic group, are among the most economically disadvantaged persons in the country. The Shi'a minority seeks a national government that would give them equal rights as citizens.

There also are small numbers of Ismailis living in the central and northern parts of the country. Ismailis are Shi'a, but consider the Aga Khan their spiritual leader. In the past, small communities of Hindus, Sikhs, Jews, and Christians lived in the country, but most members of these communities have left. Almost all members of the country's small Hindu and Sikh populations, which once numbered about 50,000 persons, have emigrated or taken refuge abroad.

In March the Taliban, acting on what it claimed to be religious grounds, completely destroyed two giant statues of the Buddha dating from pre-Islamic times, which were carved into the cliffs near Bamiyan. The statues had been damaged in the past, but the Taliban claimed that the damage was unauthorized vandalism committed by a soldier, and that they would protect the statutes from further damage. The destruction of the statues received worldwide criticism, including from numerous Islamic authorities.

On February 26, Mullah Omar had ordered the destruction of all statues in the country. The Taliban also claimed to have destroyed statues and images in the collections of the Kabul Museum and elsewhere dating from the pre-Islamic period.

There reportedly are no practicing Buddhists in the country; however, the Bamiyan statues and the collection of pre-Islamic images, most dating from the classic Gandhara period, are widely considered to be important cultural artifacts and religious symbols.

On May 23, the Taliban decreed that Hindus and Sikhs would be required to wear a piece of yellow cloth attached to their clothing to identify their religious affiliation. The Taliban purportedly imposed this system of identification to spare non-Muslims from the enforcement of rules mandatory for Muslims and from harassment by agents of the PVSV. The requirement later was suspended, and an identity card was to be issued instead. On July 3, the Taliban announced that Hindus would be consulted before ordering them to wear any distinctive mark to differentiate themselves from Muslims.

According to Human Rights Watch, in September 1999, the Taliban issued decrees barring non-Muslims from building places of worship but allowing them to worship at existing holy sites; forbidding non-Muslims from criticizing Muslims; ordering non-Muslims to identify their houses by placing a yellow cloth on their rooftops; banning non-Muslims from living in the same residence as Muslims; and requiring that non-Muslim women wear a yellow dress with a special mark so that Muslims could keep their distance.

In Taliban-controlled areas, the Taliban had decreed that all Muslims were required to take part in five daily prayers. Those who were observed not praying at appointed times or who were late attending prayer were subject to punishment, including severe beatings. Friday noon prayers at mosques reportedly were compulsory for all Muslim men; women and girls reportedly were forbidden to enter mosques and thus were forced to pray at home.

During most of the year, publishing and distribution of literature of any kind, including religious material, was rare. On January 7, the Taliban issued a decree calling for capital punishment for any Afghan who converted from Islam. Decree 14, which was issued in June and related to foreigners in

Afghanistan, stated that those preaching other religions to Afghan Muslims would be deported after being imprisoned for 3 to 10 days. Taliban officials subsequently stated that the initial decree was only a guideline. A small number of foreign Christian groups were allowed in the country to provide humanitarian assistance; however, they were forbidden to proselytize. Conversion from Islam was considered apostasy and was punishable by death. There was no information available regarding converts and no information available concerning restrictions on the training of clergy.

In August the Taliban arrested eight foreign aid workers affiliated with an NGO on charges of proselytizing. An estimated 48 Afghan employees of the NGO also were arrested and reportedly also charged with apostasy. All those arrested reportedly were freed by opposition forces on November 15, following the fall of Kabul. The Taliban reportedly stated that 59 children who had been taught by the arrested workers were sent to a correctional facility, where they would remain until all Christian influences were removed. In August the Taliban expelled two other religion-based NGO's with longtime presences in the country on unspecified grounds, ordering their foreign personnel to depart the country within 72 hours.

The Taliban reportedly had a long history committing numerous human rights violations against the mostly Shi'a Hazaras, including summary executions, massacres, and mass arrests. There were reliable reports that the Taliban summarily executed approximately 300 Hazara men and boys after recapturing Yakawlang in early January. There were reports of mass arrests by the Taliban in Hazara neighborhoods of Kabul in January 1998. There also were credible reports of the massacre of thousands of civilians and prisoners by the Taliban during and after the capture of Mazar-e-Sharif in August 1998; this massacre reportedly was aimed at ethnic Hazaras. In September 1998, approximately 500 persons were killed when the Taliban took control of the city of Bamiyan.

The Hazaras regained control of Bamiyan in April 1999 following prolonged guerrilla-style warfare; however, the

Taliban recaptured Bamiyan in May 1999 and reportedly killed a number of Shi'a residents. There were reports during 1999 and 2000 that there were forced expulsions of ethnic Hazaras and Tajiks from areas controlled or conquered by the Taliban, as well as harassment of these minorities throughout Taliban controlled areas. The Ismaili community fought for the Northern Alliance against the Taliban and suffered when the Taliban occupied territories once held by Ismaili forces. There were reports of mistreatment of Ismailis at the hands of the Taliban and destruction of some of their cultural monuments.

The Taliban, following its extreme interpretation of Shari'a, required women when in public to wear a head-to-toe garment known as the *burqa,* which has only a mesh screen for vision. The requirement to wear the *burqa* represented a significant change in practice. According to a decree announced by the religious police in 1997, women found outside the home who were not covered properly would be punished severely, along with their family elders. In Kabul and elsewhere, women found in public not wearing the *burqa,* or whose *burqa*s did not cover their ankles, were beaten by Taliban militiamen.

According to Taliban regulations, men's beards were required to extend farther than a fist clamped at the base of the chin. Men also were required to wear head coverings and to wear their hair short. A man who had shaved or cut his beard was subject to imprisonment for 10 days and required to undergo Islamic instruction. All students at Kabul University reportedly were required to have beards in order to study there (no female students were allowed). There also were credible reports that Taliban members gave forced haircuts to males in Kabul. In January the Taliban reportedly arrested 28 barbers in Kabul for giving customers a haircut styled after that of actor Leonardo DiCaprio in the film "Titanic."

In March religious police reportedly ordered all students across the country to wear turbans in class. Students from grades one to six reportedly were required to wear black turbans and students in higher grades to wear white turbans. Students who did not follow the instructions were turned away from their classrooms. At various times, the Taliban banned certain traditional recreational activities, such as flying kites and playing chess. Dolls, stuffed animals, and photographs were prohibited under the Taliban's interpretation of religious injunctions against representations of living beings; in search of these objects, Taliban soldiers or persons masquerading as Taliban members reportedly entered private homes without prior notification or informed consent. The Taliban reportedly had required parents to give their children Islamic names.

The Taliban continued to prohibit music, movies, and television on religious grounds in Taliban-controlled areas. In 1998 television sets, videocassette recorders, videocassettes, audiocassettes, and satellite dishes were outlawed in order to enforce the prohibition. However, subsequent reports indicated that many persons in urban areas around the country owned such electronic devices despite the ban. While some Taliban leaders claimed tolerance of religious minorities, the Taliban reportedly imposed some restrictions on Shi'a Muslims in Taliban-controlled territory, although not uniformly. For example, the Taliban allegedly ordered Shi'a to confine their Ashura commemorations during the month of Muharram to their mosques and to avoid the public processions that are an integral part of Ashura in other countries with Shi'a populations. There are unconfirmed reports that the Taliban occupied and "cleaned" Shi'a mosques for use by Sunnis, including a Shi'a mosque in Mazar-e-Sharif in 1998.

d. Freedom of Movement Within the Country, Foreign Travel, Emigration, and Repatriation

Although in principle male citizens have the right to travel freely both inside and outside the country, their ability to travel within the country was hampered by warfare, brigandage, landmines, a road network in a state of disrepair, and limited domestic air service, complicated by factional threats to air traffic. Some Afghans reported difficulty in receiving necessary permits to leave the country for tourism or business purposes, while others reported no such difficulty. The Taliban's restrictions on women further curtailed freedom of movement.

Despite these obstacles, many persons continued to travel relatively freely, with buses using routes in most parts of the country. However, due to intensified fighting, international aid agencies often found that their ability to travel, work, and distribute assistance was hampered severely. International travel continued to be difficult as both the Taliban and the Northern Alliance threatened to shoot down any planes that flew without their permission over areas of the country that they controlled. U.N. Security Council sanctions imposed because of the Taliban's links to international terrorism eliminated landing rights for the Afghan airline Ariana at non-Afghan airports and urged member states to restrict the entry into their territories of senior Taliban officials.

Commercial trade was impeded in certain non-Taliban areas, as local commanders and criminals continued to demonstrate their control over the roads by demanding road tolls and at times closing roads. Afghans continued to form one of the world's largest refugee populations, and the number of refugees increased as a result of the intensified military actions late in the year. According to the UNHCR, at year's end more than 3.5 million Afghans remained outside the country as registered refugees: Over 2 million in Pakistan; more than 1.5 million in Iran; and some in Russia, India, and Central Asia. Women and children constituted 75 per cent of the refugee population. In addition there were a reported 1.1 million IDP's following years of fighting and drought, even before the events of the latter part of the year.

Since October an estimated 300,000 more have left their homes. Many more are believed to be too poor to afford transportation or too weak to move. A total of 4,069,000 Afghan refugees have been repatriated since 1988, with over 1.5 million returning to the country in the peak year of 1992. An estimated 70,000 Afghan refugees returned to their home communities from Pakistan and Iran between November and year's end. Late in the year, all six countries neighboring Afghanistan

(Pakistan, Iran, Tajikistan, Turkmenistan, Uzbekistan, and China) officially closed their borders to refugees, citing both security reasons and an inability to absorb more refugees.

According to the UNHCR, during the first 6 months of the year, the Government of Iran deported an estimated 82,000 Afghans, and on July 15, announced that it would deport any Afghan who lacked documentation or who had failed to register. In addition, on September 25, Iranian newspapers reported that 248 Afghans who had fled from Afghanistan because of fears of a U.S.-led military action on the country were arrested and returned to Afghanistan. In 2000`133,600 refugees were repatriated voluntarily from Iran under a UNHCR-Iran program, and another 50,000 are estimated to have returned outside the program. Despite the Government of Pakistan's official closed border policy, Afghans in Pakistan are known to cross and recross the border routinely.

In October the Government of Iran set up two camps for Afghan IDP's who were attempting to flee to Iran from territory that was then controlled by the Taliban. The camps sheltered more than 10,000 refugees at year's end. According to a November UNHCR report, Northern Alliance forces surrounded a Taliban-occupied camp for displaced persons in southwestern Afghanistan, apparently trapping 6,000 Afghan civilians inside the camp. There was no available information on policies regarding refugees, asylum, provision of first asylum, or the forced return of refugees.

SECTION 3- RESPECT FOR POLITICAL RIGHTS: THE RIGHT OF CITIZENS TO CHANGE THEIR GOVERNMENT

There was no functioning central government in the country. The continuing struggle for political power among the major armed groups prevented citizens from changing their government or choosing their leaders peacefully. Most political changes came about through shifting military fortunes. No faction held elections or respected citizens' right to change their government peacefully. The Taliban movement's authority had emanated from its leader, Mullah Omar, who carried the title Commander of the Faithful, and from the Taliban's military occupation of most of the country. Governmental functions reportedly were exercised through the key Taliban governing body, the Inner Shura, which was based in Kandahar, as well as by ministries based in Kabul.

Nominal president Burhanuddin Rabbani headed the Northern Alliance. Rabbani's support was based primarily in his Tajik ethnic group, with military support provided by the forces once commanded by the late Ahmed Shah Masood. Rabbani received nominal support from General Rashid Dostam and a faction of the Shi'a Hazara Hezb-i-Wahdat. Another faction of the Hezb-i-Wahdat nominally allied itself with the Taliban early in 1999. Northern Alliance forces controlled the northeastern, largely Tajik, portion of the country, including the strategic Panjshir valley north of Kabul, until the events late in the year.

On October 7, Operation Enduring Freedom (OEF), a U.S.-led coalition, began a military action aimed at toppling the Taliban regime and eliminating the *Al Qaeda* terrorist network in Afghanistan. U.S. forces worked in concert with anti-Taliban forces of the Northern Alliance as well as with others in southern Afghanistan. By mid-November the Taliban had been removed from power, and forces had retreated from Kabul to southwestern Afghanistan. Taliban leader Mullah Omar and *Al Qaeda* leader Usama bin Ladin remained fugitives at year's end, and U.S. military operations continued in an effort to capture and detain remaining Taliban and *Al Qaeda* fighters.

On December 5, Afghan representatives of the Northern Alliance and of groups formerly in exile—the Rome Group, the Cyprus Group, and the Peshawar Group—met in Bonn, Germany under U.N. auspices and signed the Bonn Agreement, a broad framework document for political transition in Afghanistan leading to a permanent government. The Bonn Agreement also outlined the establishment of other provisional institutions and bodies to assist in the formation of a broad-based multi-ethnic and representative government.

Finally, the Bonn Agreement proposed an international security force for the country until the Afghan authorities are prepared to assume responsibility and called on the international community to assist in the formation of a national army and police force.

The first provisional governing body for Afghanistan, the AIA, was named in the Bonn Agreement. The AIA was sworn in on December 22 in Kabul, led by Chairman Hamid Karzai, assisted by five Vice-Chairmen and 24 Cabinet members. The 30-member AIA is representative of Afghanistan's diverse geographic and ethnic makeup, and includes expatriates and two women. Until the Taliban's fall from power, discontent with the Taliban's strictures and its rural southern Pashtun values was strong in Kabul and in non-Pashtun cities in the north. The Taliban's previous military successes did not encourage the group's leaders to engage in meaningful political dialog with opponents.

SECTION 4 - GOVERNMENTAL ATTITUDE REGARDING INTERNATIONAL AND NON-GOVERNMENTAL INVESTIGATION OF ALLEGED VIOLATIONS OF HUMAN RIGHTS

There are many NGO's, both domestic and international, in the country. Some of these are based in neighboring countries, mostly Pakistan, with branches inside the country; others are based in Afghan cities and rural areas. The focus of their activities is primarily humanitarian assistance, rehabilitation, health, education, and agriculture. Several domestic human rights NGO's also operated in the country; however, war and lack of security continued to make it difficult for human rights organizations to monitor adequately the situation inside the country. The Afghan League of Human Rights, which operates both in Afghanistan and Pakistan, produced an annual report. The Cooperation Center for Afghanistan (CCA) is an Afghan NGO that operates in both Pakistan and Afghanistan.

The CCA maintains an office in Peshawar, where it

produces a monthly newsletter on the Afghan human rights situation. It also monitored and documented the human rights situation from several offices in both Taliban-controlled and Northern Alliance-controlled cities. The National Commission on Human Rights in Afghanistan began operations during 1998 in Pakistan, conducting seminars on human rights issues, issuing press statements criticizing specific instances of human rights abuses, and placing articles in Pashtu and Dari newspapers. The Afghanistan Commission for Human Rights, founded in 1997 after discussions with Taliban authorities on Islamic aspects of human rights, also began activities in Pakistan in 1998, focused on the plight of Afghan prisoners in Pakistani prisons and on children's rights.

In 2000 the Taliban issued an edict banning women's employment (except in the health care sector) by U.N. agencies and NGO's. In March the Taliban granted a visa to the U.N. Special Rapporteur on Human Rights to visit Afghanistan, but restricted her to Kabul. In September 2000 and in January, the Taliban refused to issue her a visa. During the year, the Taliban continued to pose serious obstacles to the international aid community's efforts to deliver food aid and other humanitarian assistance to citizens.

The Taliban continued to harass domestic and international NGO's, as well as U.N. agencies, and continued to interfere with their operations. Tactics used included detaining NGO members, threatening to impound the vehicles of NGO's that did not work on projects preferred by the Taliban, and threatening to close projects that do not include Taliban supervisors or workers. In August the Taliban arrested 8 foreign aid workers and an estimated 48 Afghan employees of the NGO on charges of proselytizing; they were freed by opposing forces on November 15. The Taliban detained the director of a local NGO and impounded all of the NGO's equipment in an effort to increase Taliban control of the organization.

The Taliban announced in March 1998 that foreign Muslim women, including U.N. workers, would be allowed to perform their jobs only if accompanied by a male relative, a directive that continued to hamper NGO and relief operations during most of the year. In 1999 staff members of an international NGO were detained and beaten by members of the Taliban in Bamiyan Province. After the incident, Mullah Omar issued an edict stating that any person causing annoyance to a foreign worker could face punishment of up to 5 years in prison. However, in November 1999, U.N. properties were targeted in organized demonstrations in several cities when U.N. sanctions related to terrorism were imposed on the country.

Certain key issues, including the mobility of international female Muslim staff and access by Afghan women and girls to programs, remained to be addressed at year's end. There were reports in 1999 that military leader Ahmed Masood's commanders in the northeast were "taxing" humanitarian assistance entering Afghanistan from Tajikistan, harassing NGO workers, obstructing aid convoys, and otherwise hindering the movement of humanitarian aid. There were similar reports during the year.

SECTION 5- DISCRIMINATION BASED ON RACE, SEX, RELIGION, DISABILITY, LANGUAGE, OR SOCIAL STATUS

For much of the year, there was no functioning constitution or legal provisions prohibiting or protecting against discrimination based on race, sex, religion, disability, language, or social status. However, the December 5 Bonn Agreement stated that the 1964 Constitution of Afghanistan would apply on an interim basis until the adoption of a new constitution. Those provisions of the 1964 Constitution relating to the monarchy and to the executive and legislative bodies would not apply; however, provisions prohibiting discrimination based on race, sex, and religion would be in effect.

Despite the legal primacy of the 1964 Constitution at year's end, local custom and practices generally prevailed. Discrimination against women remained prevalent throughout the country. Its severity varied from area to area, depending on the local leadership's attitude toward education for girls and employment for women and on local attitudes. Historically the minority Shi'a faced discrimination from the majority Sunni population. There was greater acceptance of persons with disabilities as the number of persons maimed by landmines and warfare increased, and as the presence of persons with disabilities became more widespread. In 1998 and 1999, the Taliban on several occasions sought to execute homosexuals by toppling walls on them; this is not known to have occurred during the year.

Women

As lawlessness and interfactional fighting continued in some areas, violence against women occurred frequently, including beatings, rapes, forced marriages, disappearances, kidnapings, and killings. Such incidents generally went unreported, and most information was anecdotal. It was difficult to document rapes, in particular, in view of the social stigma that surrounds rape. Although the stability brought to much of the country by Taliban rule generally may have reduced violence against women, particularly rapes and kidnapings, Taliban members threatened or beat women to enforce the Taliban's dress code for women, and the Taliban imposed wide-ranging and even life-threatening restrictions on women's mobility and their ability to obtain gainful employment.

There were unconfirmed reports that the Taliban, or foreign "volunteers" fighting alongside the Taliban, abducted women during the military offensive on Taloqan and elsewhere in 2000. There also were unconfirmed reports that Taliban soldiers or foreign volunteers abducted women in the offensive in the Shomali plains in 1999 and that they raped and abducted women from Hazara neighborhoods in Mazar-e-Sharif in August 1998. The whereabouts of some of these women was unknown at year's end. The enforced seclusion of women within the home greatly limited the information available on domestic violence and marital rape. In a climate of secrecy and impunity, it was likely that domestic violence against women remained a serious problem.

Women accused of adultery also were subjected to violence. Adultery was punishable by death through stoning. In 2000 at least one accused adulteress was sentenced to 100 lashes; a female accomplice was sentenced to 30 lashes. Overall, the situation of women and girls remained mostly unchanged under Taliban rule, as the Taliban generally continued to apply its ultra-conservative interpretation of Islamic law. Following the Taliban's fall from power and the signing of the Bonn Agreement and easing of restrictions on women, some Afghan women made tentative steps towards resumption of public life. However, lack of education and unavailability of jobs remained significant problems for many women seeking greater opportunity despite the removal of the Taliban.

Discrimination against women in areas under Taliban control was particularly harsh. The Taliban initially excluded women from all employment outside the home, apart from the traditional work of women in agriculture; women were forbidden to leave the home except in the company of a male relative. In urban areas, and particularly after the Taliban took Kabul in 1996, the Taliban forced almost all female professionals and clerical workers, including teachers, doctors, nurses, bank tellers, and aid workers, to quit their jobs. In a few cases, the Taliban permitted women to work in health care occupations under restricted circumstances.

In July 2000, the Taliban issued a decree banning women's employment (except in the health care sector) by U.N. agencies and NGO's. Implementation remained erratic, but the U.N. and NGO's nonetheless required their female staff to remain at home to avoid open confrontation with the Taliban. The prohibition on women working outside of the home was especially difficult for the large numbers of widows left by 20 years of civil war; there were an estimated 30,000 widows in Kabul alone. Many women reportedly were reduced to selling all of their possessions and to begging to feed their families. On August 6, 2000, the Taliban issued an order closing down the 25 widows' bakeries operated by the WFP, which provided food to the neediest citizens, including many war widows and other female-headed households. The Taliban reversed its decision the next day, apparently accepting the WFP's explanation that female staff of the bakeries was not direct hire WFP employees and therefore not subject to the July 6 order.

Girls formally were prohibited from attending school, apart from instruction provided in mosques, which was mainly religious in content. Some girls were educated in formal, community-based or home schools operated in country by international NGO's; however, their activities were restricted severely during the year. Some home schools also existed, but were forced to operate clandestinely. Students, teachers, and their families were subject to punishment if discovered. By year's end, some girls were returning to schools; however, the lack of teachers and materials remained deterrents to girls' education.

Most citizens lack any access to adequate medical facilities, and the provision of health care under Taliban rule remained poor. Such conditions particularly affected women. Life expectancy was estimated at 45.1 years for women and 46.6 years for men. In most regions, there was less than 1 physician per 10,000 persons. Health services reached only 29 per cent of the population and only 17 per cent of the rural population. Clean water reached only about 12 per cent of the population. Health care for both men and women was hampered by the Taliban's ban on images of humans, which caused the destruction of public education posters and made the provision and dissemination of health information in a society with high levels of illiteracy more difficult. Tuberculosis rates for women and maternal mortality rates were extremely high. Taliban actions significantly reduced women's access to health care.

In practice women were excluded from treatment by male physicians in most hospitals. These rules made obtaining treatment extremely difficult for most women, and especially for widows in Kabul, many of whom have lost all male family members, who would be needed to escort them to any visit to a male doctor. In addition, even when a woman was permitted to be treated by a male doctor, the doctor was prohibited from examining her except if she were fully clothed in Taliban-approved garb, as well as from touching her, thus limiting the possibility of meaningful diagnosis and treatment. Participants in a 1998 survey of 160 Afghan women reported little or no access to health care in Kabul.

Most of the participants also reported a decline in their mental health. There were credible reports that the restrictions on women's health care were not applied in practice and that there were some improvements in access to health care for women in 1999 and 2000. By the end of 1999, all Kabul hospitals apart from the military hospital reportedly treated women. Rabia Balkhi Women's Hospital in Kabul provided a full range of health services to women, although there was only one maternity hospital in the country. However, the trend of improved access to health care appeared to slow during the year. The Taliban decreed what women could wear in public. Women in public spaces were required to wear a *burqa*, a loose, head-to-toe garment that has a small cloth screen for vision.

While in many, particularly rural, areas of the country, the *burqa* was the customary women's outer garment, the requirement for all women to wear the *burqa* represented a significant change in practice for many women, particularly in urban areas. According to a decree of the religious police in 1997, women found outside the home who were not covered properly would be punished severely, along with their family elders. In Kabul and elsewhere women found in public who were not wearing the *burqa*, or whose *burqa*s did not cover their ankles, were beaten by Taliban militiamen. Some women could not afford the cost of a *burqa*, and thus had to remain at home or risk beatings if they left their houses uncovered.

During 1999 there were reports of differences in the enforcement of the requirement for women to wear the *burqa*. Enforcement reportedly was relatively lax in rural and non-Pashtun areas, and there were reports that some women in Herat and in rural areas cover their heads with large scarves that leave the face uncovered without reprisal. However, there were credible reports that the Taliban increased enforcement of the dress code during the year. The Taliban's dress code for women apparently was not enforced strictly upon the nomad population of several hundred thousand or upon the few female foreigners, who nonetheless had to cover their hair, arms, and legs. Women in their homes could not be visible from the street; the Taliban required that homes with female occupants have their windows painted over.

Women were expected to leave their homes only while escorted by a male relative, further curtailing the appearance and movement of women in public even when wearing approved clothing and women appearing in public without male relative risked beatings by members of the Taliban. Some observers reported observing fewer and fewer women on the streets in Taliban-controlled areas. Under the Taliban, women were not permitted to drive, and taxi drivers reportedly were beaten for taking unescorted women as passengers. On June 21, religious police arrested four female Afghan WFP employees in a taxi outside the WFP office because they were not accompanied by a male relative.

The women were detained for 2 days. In October 2000, taxi drivers were warned by the PVSV not to pick up unaccompanied female passengers at risk of having their driving privileges revoked. Women could ride only on buses designated as women's buses; reportedly there were not enough such buses to meet the demand, and the wait for women's buses could be long. In December 1998, the Taliban ordered that bus drivers who took female passengers must encase the bus in curtains and put up a curtain so that the female passengers cannot see or be seen by the driver. Bus drivers also were required to employ boys under the age of 15 to collect fares from female passengers; neither the drivers nor the fare collectors were to mingle with the passengers.

Amnesty International reported that the Taliban ordered the closure of women's public baths. Women were also forbidden from entering mosques or other places of worship unless the mosque had separate sections for men and women.

Most women prayed at home alone or with other family members. Women also reportedly were prohibited from appearing on the streets for certain periods during the month of Ramadan. The Taliban's restrictions regarding the social behavior of men and women were communicated by edicts and enforced mainly by the PVSV. The U.N. and numerous other sources noted that the edicts were enforced with varying degrees of rigor throughout the country.

The restrictions were enforced most strictly in urban areas, where women had enjoyed wider access to educational and employment opportunities before the Taliban gained control. Even with the fall of the Taliban by year's end, Afghanistan's poverty and lack of employment opportunities remained deterrents for women seeking to return to work. After her 1999 visit, the U.N. Special Rapporteur on Violence Against Women noted some improvements in the status of women, including the existence of home schools as well as limited primary educational institutions for girls run by the Religious Ministry in Kabul, increased access of women to health care, and the permission for widows to work.

The Special Rapporteur also noted continuing violations of the physical security of women and the practice of lashings and public beatings, violations of the rights to education, health, employment, freedom of movement, and freedom of association, and of family rights, including the existence of polygyny and forced marriage. She also noted that minority women sometimes were subject to forced displacement and that there were some cases of trafficking in women and children.

Children

Local administrative bodies and international assistance organizations undertook to ensure children's welfare to the extent possible; however, the situation of children was very poor. Approximately 45 per cent of the populations were made up of children age 14 or under. The infant mortality rate was 250 out of 1,000 births; Medecins Sans Frontieres reported in

2000 that 250,000 children per year die of malnutrition. One-quarter of children die before the age of 5. These figures most likely have increased due to another year of drought, intensified fighting, and massive displacement. The Taliban's restrictions on male-female medical treatment, and on the movement of women and girls in areas under its control, hampered the ability of U.N. agencies and NGO's to implement effective health and education programs and had a detrimental effect on children.

Physicians for Human Rights reported that children at times were denied medical care when the authorities did not let male doctors visit children's wards, which in some instances are located within the women's ward of a hospital, or did not allow male doctors to treat children accompanied only by their mothers. An UNICEF study reported that the majority of children is highly traumatized and expect to die before reaching adulthood. According to the study, some 90 per cent have nightmares and suffer from acute anxiety, while 70 per cent have seen acts of violence, including the killing of parents or relatives.

According to a report of the Gender Advisor to the U.N. system in Afghanistan, the educational sector suffered from: Limited human and financial resources; the absence of a national educational policy and curriculum; the inability of authorities to rehabilitate destroyed facilities; and discriminatory policies banning the access of females to all levels of education. Female literacy is approximately 4 per cent, compared with 30 per cent for males. There were reports that the ban on women working outside the home hampered the education of boys, since a large percentage of the country's teachers were women prior the advent of Taliban rule.

The Taliban's implementation of educational policy was inconsistent and varied from region to region, as well as over time. The Taliban had eliminated most of the formal opportunities for girls' education that existed in areas it had taken over; however, some girls' schools still operated in rural areas and some towns. Some girls received an education in informal home schools, which were tolerated to varying degrees by the Taliban around the country. During 2000 there were reports that the number of children reached by these home schools was increasing as was the attendance of girls in various educational settings, including formal schools; however, during the year the authorities increasingly restricted the activities of home schools.

In September 1999, the U.N. Special Rapporteur on Violence Against Women noted the existence of home schools and also of limited primary educational institutions for girls run by the Religious Ministry in Kabul. The Taliban told the Special Rapporteur in 1999 that primary education was available to girls between the ages of 6 and 10 and that such education was provided in mosque schools under the Ministry of Religious Affairs. Approximately three-fourths of the curricula in the Ministry of Religious Affairs schools reportedly dealt with religious and moral subjects. Taliban-sponsored public schools, at both the elementary and secondary levels, provided education only to boys and also emphasized religious studies. However, schools run by NGO's and international donors mostly were open to both boys and girls.

In 2000 UNESCO reported that as few as 3 per cent of Afghan girls were receiving primary education as opposed to up to 39 per cent of boys. However, the Taliban's increasingly anti-education policies further reduced educational opportunities, even for males. Credible sources reported that during the year Taliban elements pressured a Turkish NGO, which had long been present in the country, to close its six secondary schools for boys, most of which operated in Turkic speaking areas. The Taliban reportedly also barred Afghan students from traveling abroad, even to Islamic countries, to complete their education, although this restriction reportedly was not always enforced in practice, and a number of children, including many females related to the Taliban leadership, were able to obtain a foreign education.

Prior to the Taliban takeover in 1996, more than 100,000 girls reportedly attended public school in Kabul in grades kindergarten through 12, according to a U.N. survey. During 1999 approximately 300,000 to 350,000 school-age children attended schools run or funded by various assistance agencies and NGO's. In 1999 the Swedish Committee for Afghanistan reported that it served 170,000 students in 567 schools; most of these were formal schools, although 39 were home schools. In a few areas, over 50 per cent of students reportedly were girls. The SCA reported that 20 per cent of the students in its formal schools, which mostly were located in rural areas, were girls. In March the SCA signed a protocol with the Taliban that was to benefit the SCA's primary schools.

Many boys also were being educated in home schools because of administrative problems in the Taliban-run schools, including problems in the payment of teachers' salaries. In 1999 in areas that had been newly captured by the Taliban, some communities successfully petitioned Taliban representatives to reopen the schools? In Herat, which was captured by the Taliban in 1995, girls' schools remained closed, except in the refugee camps maintained by international NGO's. Nonetheless, approximately 5 per cent of girls were enrolled in school in Kandahar and approximately 20 per cent of girls were enrolled in Herat.

Reports that a relatively high proportion of the students in territory controlled by the Northern Alliance were girls were unconfirmed. There were credible reports that both the Taliban and the Northern Alliance used child soldiers. Northern Alliance officials publicly have stated that their soldiers must be at least 18 years of age, but press sources reported that preteen soldiers were used in Northern Alliance forces. There also were reports that the Taliban conscripted boys, and looted and burned the homes of persons whose children avoided forced conscription.

In the past, there have been some cases of trafficking in children. The Taliban had banned certain recreational activities, such as flying kites and playing chess. In October 2000, the Taliban banned youths from playing soccer in Kabul on Fridays. Dolls and stuffed animals were prohibited by the

Taliban as a result of its interpretation of religious injunctions against representations of living beings. The AIA authorities had lifted these restrictions by year's end.

Persons with Disabilities

No measures had been taken to protect the rights of persons with mental and physical disabilities, or to mandate accessibility for them. Victims of landmines continued to be a major focus of international humanitarian relief organizations, which devoted resources to providing prostheses, medical treatment, and rehabilitation therapy to amputees. There reportedly has been increased public acceptance of persons with disabilities because of their increasing prevalence due to landmines or other war-related injuries.

There are reports that women, who needed prostheses or other aids to walk, virtually were homebound because they were unable to wear the *burqa* over the prosthesis or other aid. An estimated 3 to 4 per cent of the population suffered from disabilities requiring at least some form of assistance. Although community-based health and rehabilitation committees provided services to approximately 100,000 persons, their activities were restricted to 60 out of 330 districts, and they were able to assist only a small number of those in need.

National/Racial/Ethnic Minorities

The Taliban was Pashtun-dominated and showed little tolerance for accommodation with ethnic minorities. There were reliable reports that the Taliban summarily executed approximately 300 Hazara men and boys after recapturing Yakawlang in early January. There also were reports of harassment, extortion, and forced expulsion from their homes of ethnic Hazaras and Tajiks by Taliban soldiers. It is estimated that the Taliban may have killed thousands of members of the ethnic Hazara minority in 1998.

In the past, there were reliable reports that individuals were detained by both the Taliban and Northern Alliance because of their ethnic origins and suspected sympathy with opponents. Ethnic Hazara, who are overwhelmingly Shi'a, reportedly were targeted in ethnically motivated attacks, in particular by the overwhelmingly Sunni and ethnic Pashtun Taliban forces.

SECTION 6- WORKER RIGHTS

a. The Right of Association

Little is known about labor laws and practices. Labor rights were not defined, and in the context of the breakdown of governmental authority there was no effective central authority to enforce them. Many of Kabul's industrial workers were unemployed due to the destruction or abandonment of the city's minuscule manufacturing base. An insignificant fraction of the work force has ever labored in an industrial setting. The only large employers in Kabul were the governmental structure of minimally functioning ministries and local and international NGO's.

Workers in government ministries reportedly have been fired because they received part of their education abroad or because of contacts with the previous regimes, although certain officials in previous administrations were employed under the Taliban. Others reportedly have been fired for violating Taliban regulations concerning beard length. There were no reports of labor rallies or strikes.

b. The Right to Organize and Bargain Collectively

The country lacks a tradition of genuine labor-management bargaining. There were no known labor courts or other mechanisms for resolving labor disputes. Wages were determined by market forces, or, in the case of government workers, dictate. There were no export processing zones.

c. Prohibition of Forced or Compulsory Labor

Little information was available regarding forced or compulsory labor, including forced and bonded labor by children. There have been reports that the Taliban forced prisoners to perform construction work at Kandahar prison and that the Taliban used forced labor after its takeover of the Shomali plains area in the summer of 1999. There were credible reports that Masood forced Taliban prisoners to work on road and airstrip construction projects under life-threatening conditions (such as requiring them to dig in mined areas). There reportedly have been cases of trafficking in women and children.

d. Status of Child Labor Practices and Minimum Age for Employment

There was no evidence that authorities in any part of the country enforced labor laws, if such laws indeed existed, relating to the employment of children. Children from the age of 6 often worked to help support their families by herding animals in rural areas and by collecting paper and firewood, shining shoes, begging, or collecting scrap metal among street debris in the cities. Some of these practices exposed children to the danger of landmines. It is not known whether the law prohibited forced and bonded labor by children, or whether such practices occurred.

e. Acceptable Conditions of Work

There was no available information regarding a statutory minimum wage or maximum workweek, or the enforcement of safe labor practices. Many workers apparently were allotted time off regularly for prayers and observance of religious holidays. Most persons worked in the informal sector.

f. Trafficking in Persons

There was no available information regarding legislation prohibiting trafficking in persons. The U.N. Special Rapporteur on Violence against Women reported in 1999 that there had been some cases of trafficking in women and children. There were reports that some Taliban soldiers (often reported to be foreigners) abducted girls and women from villages in the Shomali plains during fighting in August 1999. Women were taken in trucks from the area of fighting in the Shomali plains and elsewhere and reportedly trafficked to Pakistan and to the Arab Gulf states. There were unconfirmed reports that some Taliban soldiers abducted girls and women from villages in the Taloqan area during fighting from June through October 2000.

5

The Rise of the Taliban

Since their rise in 1994, the Taliban have been a source of conflicting opinions. Their opponents have accused them of being created by Pakistan with the support of Saudi Arabia and the US oil company, UNOCAL, to secure trade routes to the Central Asia. Their supporters, on the other hand, hold that the Taliban are a religious and moral force that arose on their own from villages to save Afghans from the terror, lawlessness and corruption of *Mujahideen* era and to re-unite Afghanistan. The reality, however, seems somewhere in the middle.

It is true that the immediate cause of the rise of Taliban was the fighting among *Mujahideen* groups that had virtually divided Afghanistan in separate fiefdoms resulting in carpet destruction of Kabul, killings of thousands of civilians, and general lawlessness. It is also true that once the Taliban entered the military and political stage, they received support from foreign sources to continue their military march. In this brief introduction, we will try to answer who the Taliban are by discussing the historical context of their rise. Second, we will discuss their goals, policies, and practices. We will also provide links to more detailed study of the Taliban on our web site.

Talib is an Arabic word, which literally means "one who is seeking," but generally Talib refers to "someone who is seeking religious knowledge." Taliban are students of "deeni madrassas" or religious seminaries, which have existed in Afghanistan, the Indian-Subcontinent, and the Central Asia since the arrival of Islam in these areas. Both religious schools and taliban existed long before the modern system of schools and educations were introduced to Afghanistan close to a century ago. Many taliban also used to go to different religious scholars or local mullahs to acquire religious knowledge.

Although taliban have never been, until recent times, at the pinnacle of military and political power, they are not new to Afghanistan. They have been a component of the religious establishment and have always lived in the shadow of other military, political, and economic groups. Mullah Shor Bazar, an Afghan fighter known for inflicting heavy losses on the British during the Third Anglo-Afghan war of 1919, was also a talib, as were Mirwais Khan Hotaki, and Mullah Mushki Alam, who fought against the British occupation of Afghanistan.

During the national struggle against the Soviet invaders, taliban fought alongside the *Mujahideen* mainly under the leadership of Mohammad Nabi, one of the seven sanctioned *Mujahideen* leaders in Pakistan (also known as "Peshawar Tanzeem" Leaders). However, most of the leaders of the current Taliban regime in Afghanistan have been influenced by the teachings of Islam in Pakistan, where they had migrated with millions of other Afghans after the Soviet invasion. There, they attended religious seminaries or "madrassas", while many of them also remained active fighting the Soviets in the battlefields. They are the followers of the "Deobandi" school of thought, preached by mullahs (clerics) in Pakistani madrassas.

The Deobandi School emerged as a reform movement in British India with the aim of rejuvenating Islamic society in a colonial state. The Pakistani version of the Deobandi schools in Afghan refugee camps were, however, often run by inexperienced and semi-literate mullahs, associated with Pakistan's Jami'at-e 'Ulema-e Islam (JUI) political party. Saudi funds and scholarships, during the Afghan struggle against the Soviets, in combination with a lack of appreciation on the part of the mullahs of the reformist Deobandi agenda, brought the schools and its curricula closer to ultraconservative Wahabism, which claims to teach strict adherence to the practices of the Prophet Mohammad (PBUH) and the Four Rightful Caliphs.

But it must be pointed out that the majority of Taliban foot soldiers are the products of Afghani Masjids, may they be inside Afghanistan or within Refugee camps. The Taliban's close ties with the Deobandi schools and in turn their association with JUI and its links with the religious, military, and political establishments of Pakistan and Saudi Arabia have been prime sources of political, financial and military aid for the group. Their opponents charge that even Pakistani military personnel have taken part in their military operations. While hard evidence to substantiate this charge has not surfaced yet, it is well known that the Pakistani madrassas in Afghan refugee camps have continued to supply the Taliban with fresh military recruits.

As a military and political force, the Taliban surfaced in Qandahar in 1994 when Afghanistan was plagued by a vicious civil war. The main military struggle at that time was taking place in Kabul between the forces of Burhanuddin Rabbani and his military commander Ahmad Shah Masood and their allies on one side and the forces of Gulbuddin Hekmatyar and his allies on the other side. As a result, about two thirds of Kabul was razed to the ground resembling "an archeological site" with a UN estimated deaths of 50,000 civilians. The rest of the country was taken by warlords and petty chieftains who ruled their areas with a free-for-all attitude.

The Amnesty International 1995 annual report about Afghanistan begins with these terrifying accounts:

Thousands of civilians were killed and thousands more were wounded in artillery attacks deliberately aimed at residential areas by all factions in the civil war. Hundreds of men, women and children were deliberately and arbitrarily killed by members of the main armed groups during the raids on civilian homes. Torture, including rape of women and children, was reportedly widespread. People were unlawfully imprisoned in private detention centers because of their political opinions, religion, ethnic origin, or as hostages. Journalists covering the war were detained or imprisoned by the warring factions. Hundreds of people "disappeared."

Warlords appointed themselves as so called Islamic judges and ordered punishments including executions.

Not receiving regular pay from their leaders in Kabul, *Mujahideen* fighters in the rest of the country turned on the people by establishing check points on highways forcing truck drivers and passengers to pay their way. According to one report, there were 71 such checkpoints between Herat, a western city in Afghanistan, and Chaman, a border city between Afghanistan and Pakistan. Even in the capital, Kabul, the city was divided among seven armed factions, with several checkpoints between Shahr-e Naw and Karte-Char, covering a distance of just five miles.

The worst effected areas were around Qandahar where lawlessness had spread to such an extent that shopkeepers reportedly could not keep their goods in shops during the night. Afghan women lived in especially bleak conditions during the lawlessness of *Mujahideen* era. Local commanders also abducted, forcefully married and raped women. In Afghanistan: International Responsibility for Human Rights, the Amnesty International described the women's conditions in 1995 as follows:

"Women and girls all over Afghanistan live in constant fear of being raped by armed guards. For years, armed guards have been allowed to torture them in this way without fear of reprimand from their leaders. In fact, rape is apparently condoned by most leaders as a means of terrorizing conquered populations and or rewarding soldiers."

Perhaps the lasting legacy of the fighting among factions of the *Mujahideen* is the deepening ethnic division of Afghanistan. During their struggle to defeat their rivals, Gulbuddin Hekmatyar tried to win over Pashtuns, while Burhanuddin Rabbani and Ahmad Shah Masood appealed to Tajiks. Similarly, Hazara and Uzbek strengthened their militias and fully participated in the fighting, which was deliberately projected as an ethnic crusade. Unfortunately because of the blatant ethnic killings of the *Mujahideen* era and its continued practice during the Taliban era, the "ethnicization" of Afghan politics has cut deep rifts among Afghans in Afghanistan and abroad.

The cycle of violence, destruction, and chaos of the *Mujahideen* era created the condition for the rise of the puritanical Taliban. There are several versions of how a small group of taliban, led by Mullah Muhammad Omar took control of areas around Qandahar in 1994. According to the most widely circulated account amongst the residents of Qandahar, a group of "madrasee" (belonging or originating from a Madrasa) taliban, headed by Mullah Mohammad Omar arrived in Afghanistan with the intent to re-establish law and order and to re-organize themselves.

They took residence in a school near Dand in Qandahar. On September 20, 1994, an Afghan family on its way to Herat from Qandahar, was looted, its male members molested, and its female members were raped by gangs manning one of the so-called "check points" along the route. One of the victims escapes and reaches the newly established Taliban compound. The story goes that Mullah Omar and his followers rushed to the scene, capturing the perpetrators, executing them on the spot and then collecting and burying the bodies of the victims. It is this faithful incident, the Taliban claim that marked the beginning of their campaign in Afghanistan. The Taliban then moved in and disarmed other groups in the area.

They began consolidating their position and procuring weapons by winning the allegiance of several local military commanders. Among the groups who surrendered to the Taliban (through a peaceful arrangement) was that of Mullah Naqib, who along with a group of other warlords, had divided up the province amongst themselves. One of these warlords was Lalai, a former thief and "Sarbaz" (communist militia) who had defected to the Mojahedin during the Jihad era and had now become a post Jihad era warlord of a sector of Qandahar. While there is no a consensus about the triggering events that would mark the rise of the Taliban, it is clear that the initial popularity of the Taliban was due to the complete collapse of law and order under the so called *Mujahideen* era, which had officially begun in 1992.

The Taliban came in international limelight in November 1994 when they rescued a convoy of Pakistani trucks, which were on their way to the newly independent states of the Central Asia as a symbolic gesture of trade between Pakistan and those states. There are many versions to this story but it is widely believed that Commander Lalai, who by then had realized that the Taliban were fast becoming a threat to his interests is made aware of the convoy's schedule and its path, through Chaman-Qandahar highway, which was then controlled by two factions: the son of Haji Magash (a local smuggler turned warlord), and Lalai himself.

It is now known that Lalai then joins forces with the son of Haji Magash and attacks the convoy, taking it hostage. While it is not clear whether Lalai's intentions were immediate economic gains, there are reports that he was trying to use the convoy as a bargaining chip to persuade the Pakistanis to force the Taliban to retreat from Qandahar. Regardless of Lalai's real intentions, the Taliban were able to rush and overrun his positions. Both Lalai and his allies then flee the scene, abandoning their respective fiefdoms. The caravan is freed and Qandahar falls into the hands of Taliban.

Pakistan had hoped that a peaceful travel of the convoy would make the route more attractive to foreign investors and signal the start of new trading routes. In fact, while the arrangement for the convoy was being finalized on October 20, 1994, General Babar, Interior Minister of Pakistan, took Western ambassadors to Herat, which was at the time ruled by General Ismael Khan (a well-known commander of Prof. Rabbani's Jamiat-i Islami organization).

Babar's goal was to showcase Afghanistan as a safe trade route between Pakistan and the Central Asia. The ambassadors were from such countries as the USA, China, Japan, Spain, France, and Germany. The entourage included Prof. Burhanudin Rabbani's Ambassador to Islamabad. Taliban's rescue of the convoy and their subsequent establishment of law and order in the areas under their control demonstrated that they would be the guardians of this new trading route, a role for which they are believed to have received extensive military support from Pakistan.

THE GOALS, POLICIES, AND PRACTICES OF THE TALIBAN

The initial goals of the Taliban were to disarm the country, end lawlessness and enforce the Islamic law or the Sharia on a united Afghanistan. The Taliban so far have been successful in bringing relative law and order in around 85% of the country that they control. They have done so mainly by disarming and in certain cases by incorporating in their ranks, the previous warring groups. However, aside from the restoration of peace and security, the Taliban have failed so far to put forth a concrete plan dealing with Afghanistan's monumental problems at the national and international levels.

After seizing power in Kabul in September of 1996, the Taliban's internal policy has been centered on wresting all of Afghanistan from the control of their opponents, namely, the United Front headed by Prof. Rabbani and made up of a group of fleeting alliances and counter-alliances. In order to achieve their military goal the Taliban have taken on the offensive against their foes, often with devastating casualties on both sides as well as on the innocent civilians caught in the crossfire.

The Taliban and their allies have even engaged, especially after suffering military defeats, in carrying out their own massacres, forced eviction of civilians from their villages, imprisonment and terrorizing suspected enemy collaborators. Only last summer after their initial defeat in Mazar, Bamyan and the Shamali Plains, the Taliban were accused by the UN, International Human Rights groups and the Amnesty International of carrying out the afore-mentioned crimes in areas such as Mazar-e Sharif, Bamyan and the Shamali Plains.

Taliban's strict social policies and their anomalous interpretation of Islam have had detrimental effects on Afghans and have alienated them from the rest of the world.

The Taliban initially banned all girls' schools, although more recently they have opened a handful of schools for girls under the age of 12. They have prevented women from working, except in health care centers; if they leave their houses they have to be covered from head to foot with a veil or a "chadaree". Besides being veiled, women are usually required to be accompanied by a male relative when they go out on the streets.

Taxi drivers have been admonished not to give ride to women unless they are covered fully. And women caught violating these rules have been beaten. Because of these policies, they have been accused of engaging in "gender apartheid." The Taliban argue, however, that these restrictions are solely for the "protection" of women's dignity. They further claim that the 20 years of war have depleted the country's resources to the point where a separate education system for girls is beyond their reach (Prior to Taliban, only high schools for boys and girls were separate.)

In reality the restriction is an extension of rural social value system supercharged with a puritanical religious conditioning. Depending upon their background and the degree of exposure to the more extreme religious interpretations, even the unbending Taliban have moderates (in a very relative way) on the issue of women. In addition to their restrictions on women, men are required to grow untrimmed beards (considered to be Sunnah, something practiced and thus imitated from the Prophet Mohammad (PBUH)) and pray five times a day (one of the five pillars of Islam). They have also cut the hands of thieves and stoned to death those who are convicted for adultery (as outlined, they maintain, by Islamic law).

They have also banned kite flying, chicken fights, keeping pigeons and gambling (since they believe that this will lead to moral corruption). Celebration of new years (since they believe it to be a pagan ritual) and playing or listening to music (yet, according to them, another avenue of moral corruption) is also not allowed. The Taliban continue to justify their policies by stressing that they continue to face a costly war and the country's infrastructure is totally destroyed to accommodate the needs of all. However, critics of the Taliban's strict policies point out that even in cities where the Taliban have brought relative peace and security for the past 4 years there has been little loosening of these harsh and strict measures, making the lives of ordinary Afghans harder in what are already hard times for the population.

These rules are felt more harshly in the urban centers of the country. The Taliban, however, maintain that ordinary people's conditions have improved since the *Mujahideen* era. In reality, the traditional way of life in villages has changed little by Taliban's rule. The situation of Afghans in the countryside controlled by the Taliban has improved because of increased peace and security, giving them the opportunity to rebuild after two decades of war. But this security comes at a cost. Forced recruitment of young men to fight the ever bloody war of attrition against the Northern alliance has depleted the man-power from these rural centers.

In the cities and urban centers, the more modern and liberal way of life conflicts sharply with that of the Taliban's social and religious values and in addition the Taliban have shown little understanding in accommodating and appreciating the basic needs of an urban population. In the development and rebuilding front, Taliban have failed to take any significant and meaningful steps in order to revive the country's shattered economy. But it must be emphasized that the de-evaluation of the Afghan currently is not necessarily a Taliban legacy. Afghan currency was printed by the billions by their predecessors in a check book campaign to buy off their opposition commanders.

However, under Taliban the Economic hardships in cities have increased because of lack of jobs and business opportunities, which are generally the main sources of income in the cities. The standard of living has not improved and in many cases has down spiraled; unemployment is rampant; hunger, mal-nutrition, and diseases are the common traits of the Afghan society at present. A significant portion of the Afghan population, especially those living in cities, relies on assistance and donations provided by the UN and other Humanitarian Organizations. More than two thirds of Kabul residents receive some type of aid from these international organizations.

Some of the Taliban's strict policies and their unyielding position on issues such as, handing over the alleged terrorist Osama Bin Laden to the United States or to another country where he could be tried, have also isolated them internationally, resulting in non-recognition of their regime by the United Nations and imposition of international sanctions, thus denying Afghanistan much needed international aid and investment to rebuild. So far, they have also failed to put forth any comprehensive plan to revive the shattered economy, educational system, and infrastructure of the country. Without substantial international aid and the participation of educated and skilled Afghans, the Taliban do not seem prepared for such challenges in the future, since most of them lack administrative and technical skills.

TALIBAN'S FOREIGN POLICY

In the area of foreign policy, the Taliban have many enemies, but very few friends, evidenced by their unprecedented international isolation. This seems so partly because of their lack of experience, sophistication and in-depth knowledge of the world affairs, and partly because, except Pakistan, Afghanistan's neighboring countries, the West and Russia view the Taliban as a threat to their national interests and have tried to isolate it. The Taliban's lack of appreciation of foreign policy is evidenced by their strict social policies, especially those targeting the women, which is a reversal of the international trend towards greater personal liberty and gender equality.

The Taliban's policy regarding women have resulted in several open confrontation with the UN aid agencies and have hampered their efforts to provide aid to needy Afghans. The Taliban argue that by ending much of the infighting prevalent during the *Mujahideen* era, Afghan women are generally safer today, but the Taliban fail to recognize that the international community is outraged more by the imposition of strict policies on women as a matter of law than by risks of indignities caused by general lawlessness, as evidenced by the difference in degree of the responses of the international community to the situation of women during *Mujahideen* era and the Taliban.

More significantly perhaps, the Taliban's unyielding position on Osama bin Laden, whom the U.S. considers its enemy number one, has put them on crash course with the world's only super power. Although Russia was never a friend of the Taliban, The Taliban's decision to recognize the government of independent Chechnya, a government that exists only in name, has further increased Russia's animosity with them. Showing moral support to the people of Chechnya was certainly called for in the face of their virtual slaughter and destruction by the Russian army, but the Taliban's recognition of an unviable government does not seem sound foreign policy as no other government has recognized the government of Chechnya and the action has infuriated Russia to increase its military, political and economic support for forces of Ahmad Shah Mas'ud.

In addition, Iran came close to attacking western Afghanistan in 1997 by amassing more than 200,000 troops along the Afghan border after the Taliban admitted that their "renegade" soldiers had killed nine Iranian consulate workers and one Iranian journalist during their seizure of Mazar-e-Sharif. Similarly, the Taliban are accused by India of aiding Muslim militants fighting its rule in Kashmir, a conflict that does not directly affect interests of Afghanistan. The Taliban's successes in foreign policy are limited to their recognition by Pakistan, United Arab Emirate and Saudi Arabia and the international praise that they won for their facilitation between the Indian government, which does not recognize the Taliban, and the highjackers of the Indian Airliner, which resulted in freeing of the hostages.

Although the Taliban lack of experience in foreign policy has been an important factor in their international isolation, countries such as Iran, Russia, India, Uzbekistan, and

Tajikistan have also tried very hard to isolate and weaken the Taliban. These countries reportedly have and continue to provide military, economic and political support to Taliban's opponents. In 1998, the government of Kyrgystan confiscated 700 tons of Iranian military hardware, which was bound for Ahmed Shah Mas'ud. Before the Taliban took over Kabul, their jets forced down a Russian transport plane filled with weapons in Kandahar which was also bound for the Prof. Rabbani's regime in Kabul.

Further, there are reliable reports that the Russian and Tajik authorities routinely provide military hardware to Ahmad Shah Mas'ud through Kulyab airport in Tajikistan. The provision of large quantity of weapons to their opponents, and the non-recognition of the Taliban government by other countries, despite their rule over almost 90% of Afghanistan finds parallel in history only perhaps in the experience of communist China which was not recognized by the West for close to two decades even though it ruled over almost all of China.

In any case, the government of Taliban has so far attained recognition only from governments of Pakistan, Saudi Arabia and the United Arab Emirates. Even the Saudis and the UAE have in the past year cooled their relations with the Taliban government, allegedly over the Osama issue. The UN still recognizes the previous regime of Prof. Rabbani. Unfortunately for Afghanistan, the further isolation of the Taliban by the U.S. and thus the U.N. through sanctions have led them closer to militant movements in Pakistan, as evidenced by the recent hijacking of the Indian airliner by Pakistani militants.

Ever since their appearance on the Afghan political scene the Taliban have attracted much attention, often times poorly understood by the world, while at the same time itself has demonstrated a remarkably poor understanding of the world and its realities and contradictions. They have managed to achieve an end to the chaos of the *Mujahideen* era, successfully dis-armed warlords and patched together most parts of Afghanistan under a unitary military, economic and political authority. However, they have failed to end the war and their strict policies at home and abroad have resulted in poverty and difficulties to ordinary Afghans and to international isolation of Afghanistan.

The Afghan ship, thus, still sails in uncertain waters and Afghans tragedies continue to unfold. The Taliban are typically associated with Afghanistan. Too little attention has been given to their larger, expansionist goals, even as they continue to fight for power in their native country. Events in neighboring Pakistan involving Taliban incursions therefore have received only limited attention in the Western press until recently. In recent weeks, the Taliban's activities in Pakistan have been moving rapidly towards an explosive outcome that will be heard around the world.

Because the situation continues to deteriorate rapidly, this analysis can only capture what has happened to date, and will be followed by subsequent updates as the situation evolves. What can be said at the outset is that the situation is extremely fluid and dangerous, not only for Pakistan, but for India, its neighbor to the southeast, and for the rest of the world. Companies with facilities and personnel in India must be particularly alert and well-informed, because the situation may change quite suddenly, and the result may be catastrophic for Western interests.

Taliban Expansion since American forces began their offensive against *Al Qaeda* and the Taliban in Afghanistan after 9/11, the Taliban have been systematically moving fighters across their eastern border into Pakistan, where they have taken over the rugged mountainous region of the Northwest Frontier Province (NWFP). This has accomplished two things: 1) it has protected them from US attacks since they were hiding out within the territory of an American ally, and 2) it has enabled them to build a new power base, separate from Afghanistan. Over the last three years, they patiently established their support and intelligence network throughout the NWFP in preparation for a much bolder incursion.

The movement of the Taliban from the protection of the mountains in the NWFP into the Swat District (click on map for a larger view), and from there into the Buner district, was among the most significant events in Pakistan since the assassination of Benazir Bhutto in December 2007. Their heavily armed incursion into Buner demonstrated their ability to move through the country at will, and served as a serious provocation against the Pakistani government. Although it was later reported that they had withdrawn their troops from Buner, they left behind local members to begin the process of instituting sharia law in the region. Residents also reported that many fighters were still present in the hills surrounding the region.

In Mingora, Swat's main town, the Taliban are already imposing their domination. Residents live in fear of armed groups of Taliban campaigning against the government. In one incident, four local men had their heads and mustaches shaved by Taliban members for the crime of listening to music in their car, according to AFP. Despite the presence of thousands of Pakistani troops, the Taliban remain firmly in control of Swat. On March 12, 2009, sharia courts were officially open for business. In a region formerly known as a popular ski resort that catered to international tourism, policemen and residents have been beheaded in the streets, and men have been publicly lashed since the Taliban gained control.

Some 400 private schools enrolling 40,000 girls have been shut and many destroyed, since education for girls is prohibited by the Taliban. Over the last two years, government buildings have been blown up in the districts of Swat, Bajaur and Mohmand, as the Taliban began to impose shariah law and challenge the authority of the local government. Posters were put up throughout the town, ordering women not to go shopping, but to stay at home. The Taliban consider it 'obscene' for women to leave their homes, and forbid women from venturing out in public without being completely covered from head to toe, and in the company of an immediate male family member.

The posters also warn shopkeepers that they will be dealt with severely if they are caught dealing with women shoppers. In the town of Kohat, in the NWFP, the Taliban demolished 11 houses of the Sikh community after they refused to pay jizya, the tax demanded of non-Muslims for the right to continue living in a Muslim region. In a program of local coercion and intimidation, the Taliban have spread terror and harassed the local population through dedicated FM channels, which they used to broadcast propaganda against the security forces and the government.

Their programming generates fear and lowers the morale of the local residents. When the government seized and destroyed many of the stations that had been put in local houses, the Taliban began using mobile stations to threaten tribesmen. They promised dire consequences against anyone who helped the government forces against the Taliban. Although the Pakistani government says it will jam the stations which they cannot find to destroy, the Taliban have proven to be flexible, resilient, and resourceful. This particular cat and mouse contest has yet to be won.

The steady erosion of Pakistani control in the regions that the Taliban have taken over is ominous. As they move closer to Peshawar and Islamabad, the threat to the secular Pakistani government becomes more ominous. While the Pakistani Army may be hoping to crush the Taliban in theNWFP, the absence of political will on the part of the government may lead to its ultimate failure. A fragile (and now failed) 'peace' agreement between the government and the Taliban is a prime example of how the government is either unable or unwilling to understand or cope with the dimensions of the current conflict.

In a recent example of blatant disregard for the will of the people, and in an effort to halt the fighting in Swat, the government agreed to abolish all laws against sharia and allow Islamic law in the region. In exchange, the Taliban fighters 'agreed' to lay down their arms. The agreement, the Nizam-i-Adl regulation, effectively ceded judicial control of a part of

Pakistan to a band of terrorists who have been waging a savage war against the state and the local population. To appease an uncompromising enemy, this was done despite the fact that under Pakistani law, it is unconstitutional to cede national territory as the government has done.

Within days, the agreement broke down when a soldier was killed in an ambush, two local officials were beheaded, and armed Taliban fighters began patrolling Mingora, Swat's main town. It should come as no shock that terrorists are not likely to keep agreements with governments they intend to overthrow. But the Pakistani government was unprepared for the outcome. On May 5th, Pakistani news source reported that "eleven people, including two security personnel, a police sub-inspector, and eight civilians were killed and several others injured as bullets rattled through parts of district headquarters Mingora . . . . Residents said hundreds of militants have taken positions on rooftops and were patrolling streets and laying mines in Mingora city. They have surrounded scores of security personnel and government functionaries in the government buildings."

There is also evidence that the local police have actually been complicit in the successful arrival of the Taliban into Pakistani villages. According to one report filed with the Pakistani newspaper, The International News, and in contradiction to many other reports, the majority of Taliban who have been responsible for the attacks are Afghan, not Pakistani.

A Pakistani resident of Buner, who had escaped the approaching Taliban by foot over the mountains during the Taliban incursion into his village in late April, was interviewed for the newspaper. He said, ""For God sake, why don't you people listen to our cries as we have been invaded by the Afghan Tajiks! . . . I can swear on Holy Quran that those who have captured our village are Afghan nationals. You people sitting in Islamabad cannot imagine what sort of hell they have unleashed on us after advancing from Swat to our areas," he said, sobbing.

He told the interviewer that the invaders had wantonly destroyed homes and businesses as they advanced. When the people of Buner heard about the approach of the Taliban from Swat, they had formed a resistance group to fight the invaders, but, according to the man, "the local police and law enforcement agencies facilitated them to capture the area." While the government has not given up the fight, and now prepares a well-publicized military offensive against the Taliban in the Swat valley, they are arguably ill-equipped to fight these asymmetrical battles.

The willingness of the Taliban to die in combat and their legendary cruelty to those they view as their enemies generates fear and lowers the Pakistani military morale. In the northernmost section of the NWFP, in the town of Kalam, the entire police force recently abandoned their station. They felt that they are ill-equipped to handle a large scale attack by the Taliban, so they left the population defenseless against it. On Monday, May 4, the Taliban killed five security officials in a suicide attack in Khyber and one policeman in a shooting in Hangu.

Five soldiers and 10 Taliban fighters were killed during clashes in Buner, and one soldier was killed in Shangla. The Taliban vowed to fight to the death and claimed that the attacks were in retaliation for military operations in the region. The western provinces are under siege and the central government seems to be unable to deal effectively with the current situation.

THE IMPLICATIONS OF THE TALIBAN INCURSIONS

Humanitarian Concerns International humanitarian and Pakistani officials have stated that up to one million people have already been displaced in northwestern Pakistan, and as many as 500,000 people may still evacuate the area. As the Taliban persists in pushing into Pakistan and imposing sharia law against the will of the people, Pakistanis will continue to flee from the northern region of Swat. As of this writing, the

Pakistani army is preparing a military operation against the Taliban, and thousands of residents were reported fleeing the region.

Moreover, a large portion of the community - the female population - is marginalized in areas under Taliban control. The huge culture shock and accompanying demoralization of the people will result in further deterioration of humanitarian conditions. Partnering in Terror Today, the Taliban, supported by al Qaeda, is at the forefront of anti-Pakistan attacks.

They are also supported by several other *Al Qaeda* feeder groups: Lashkar-e-Jhangvi (an *Al Qaeda* ally and militant wing of the anti-Shia Sipah-e-Sahaba Pakistan (SSP), which serves as a Trojan Horse for *Al Qaeda* to carry out operations in areas where *Al Qaeda* faces difficulty in operating directly; this was a role formerly played by Laskar-e-Taiba (LET), which trained the terrorists who carried out the Mumbai massacre; and Jais-e-Mohammad, allied to Tehrik-i-Taliban Pakistan (Students' Movement of Pakistan), the primary Taliban umbrella group in Pakistan.

These forces have been responsible for attacks against Pakistan in Lahore, Islamabad, Chakwal, Multan, and Karachi. According to our sources, both the LET and the LEJ are members of Osama bin Laden's International Islamic Front (IIF) for Jihad against the Crusaders (Christians) and the Jewish People. Nuclear Concerns While the West does not know for certain the location of all of Pakistan's nuclear facilities, several sites are known to be near Islamabad.

Among these is the Kahuta facility, east of Islamabad, which is the hub of Pakistan's nuclear weapons program. While the Pakistan government continues to assure the world that their nuclear arsenal is safe, a $100 million security initiative, begun under President George W Bush, was never completed. If the Taliban are able to compromise existing nuclear security and gain possession of a nuclear capability, then the world will face a challenge unlike anything it has faced before. US National Security Advisor James Jones told the BBC that the Pakistan's nuclear weapons in Taliban hands represented "the very, very worst case scenario."

ANALYSIS

In 2007, a Gerard Group colleague long familiar with the region suggested that the US pay attention to what was happening in Dir, a large district which lies along Pakistan's northwest border with Afghanistan. Our suggestions to people in high places bore little fruit. But it was here the Taliban built their powerful hub, from which their attacks against Pakistan were launched. Once the heavily armed Taliban units began moving from Dir into the heart of the province, on the road to Islamabad, it became clear that our colleague's conclusions were correct.

The Taliban had built a powerful base in DIR, from which, because it shares a large border with Afghanistan, Taliban units can now move about freely within the NWFP and across the borders into Afghanistan and even certain areas in the Russian Islamic Republics. Since first learning about the Taliban presence in Dir, we have been watching with growing alarm how the Taliban has been strengthening itself and spreading its influence throughout the Northwest Frontier Province. Little by little, they have been positioning themselves to spread across the rest of Pakistan, imposing a radical Islamist agenda on the people of Pakistan.

Today, the Taliban already commands areas beyond the MWFP and are poised to move south to Peshawar and Islamabad, Pakistan's capital, in a bid to take over the civilian-led government, and create a new Islamic state, based on sharia law. The current regime is politically and militarily weak, putting the government and its military forces at a great disadvantage. The military continues to fight an unconventional war with conventional tactics, and without the necessary training for asymmetrical warfare. They allow themselves to be intimidated by Taliban threats, at times stopping and even retreating in the face of Taliban resistance.

It is clear that the Taliban must be stopped before it progresses further. But that will take ingenuity, courage, and stamina - and the will to win on the battlefield. It is not clear that the government has any of those qualifications any more. If the Taliban can successfully take over Islamabad, they are then likely to spread their campaign south, taking over the Kahuta nuclear facility, and moving on to Lahore and across the border into India. They will no doubt receive support from Iran, who, despite religious differences (Iran is Shia while the Taliban are Sunni) may well choose to use them as another front against the West and in support of their expansionist goals throughout the region.

Iran has a nuclear appetite of its own, so support for this initiative could be easily justified. The fear of compromising Pakistan's nuclear security should not be underestimated. Pakistan is close to becoming a failed state. Any miscalculation will cost the free world dearly. As President Obama prepares to meet with Pakistan's President Asif Ali Zardari later this week, the stakes could not be higher.

6

The Military Rise of the Taliban

It's not so clear that the fundamentalist Talaban militias can quickly bring the Afghan population to heel. Four weeks after the Taliban took Kabul, they were on the defensive, having suffered a series of setbacks which could jeopardize their control over the capital. In any event, while the Taliban may currently control two-thirds of the country, their lightning offensive of the last few months definitely seems to have been stopped, while the open civil war which has been covering the country in blood for the past seventeen years is still going on, with renewed intensity, and with no end in sight.

THE REIGN OF THE WARLORDS

When the Soviet Union invaded Afghanistan in December 1979, its aim was to prevent political instability from developing on its borders; at the same time, it wanted to contain the rise of Islamic fundamentalism which was threatening the neighboring Soviet republics. Not only did this intervention fail to contain or prevent anything, it galvanized opposition to the regime and drove the population into the arms of the Islamic fundamentalists. They were able to present themselves as liberators in contrast to the brutality of the occupying troops.

And American imperialism supplied them with the weapons they needed. Ten years later, the last Russian troops withdrew, defeated, at the end of a war which had led to more than a million deaths. The departure of Soviet troops, however, did not put an end to the civil war. The rival warlords, who had each carved out their own territory over the previous decade, continued their effort to drive out the regime the Soviet troops had left in power. At the same time, they also began to struggle between themselves for power. When the regime fell, or more exactly disintegrated, in April 1992, this struggle intensified.

From February 13, 1989, when the last Russian troops departed, to September 27, 1990, Afghanistan was the scene of a confused and bloody conflict between the four main factions included in the so-called coalition government set up under the authority of the United Nations. Rather than being well-defined clans, these factions were more like unstable conglomerates of local and regional chiefs who had become "commanders" thanks to the stock of weapons they had accumulated; they were linked by clientele-type relations which were often short-lived, and they were prone to changing their alliances.

The most important of these factions was that of the Jamiat-i-Islami, a Tadzhik-dominated fundamentalist party, the main leaders of which were the self-proclaimed president of the republic, Rabbani, and his defense minister, Massoud, the warlord of the Panjshir Valley to the north of the capital. Then there was the Pushtun fundamentalist party Hezb-i-Islami, whose leader, Hekmatyar, although nominally prime minister on several occasions spent more time bombing the troops of the regime from the heights near Kabul than occupying his seat as a minister.

There was also the Shiite fundamentalist Hezb-i-Wahdat front, dominated by the Hazaras, mainly present in the suburbs of Kabul and in the center of the country. Finally there was the faction of the Uzbek warlord Dostam, who had privately set up a fully-fledged independent state in the north-west of the country. For seven years, each of these factions fought the other three under cover of all possible and imaginable combinations of alliances aimed at extending their own influence. That is, until the victorious offensive of this latest faction, the Taliban forced them to set up a united front, since the Taliban themselves refuse to make concessions or consider any alliances.

THE INEXORABLE MARCH OF THE TALIBAN

The capture of Kabul focussed international attention on this deadly and interminable civil war which had almost been forgotten. The most shocking thing about it was the way the Taliban immediately set the clocks back a thousand years for Afghan society. Western TV channels showed ritual burnings of films, cassette players and videos, all symbols of modern culture. The Taliban began to apply the Law of the Qur'an in all its medieval barbarity: with the revolting slavery it imposed on women; the public beatings or even mutilations it prescribed as punishment; prayers five time a day – in short, a whole catalogue of humiliations and ordeals inflicted on the population.

Brutality alone does not explain the Taliban's lightning ascension to power. A year after their first appearance in 1994, they already controlled half the country; today, another year later, they control two thirds of the country, including the capital. They were able to do this in the face of opponents who outnumbered them and who were already well established in power. No doubt the Taliban took advantage of the continuing disintegration of the state apparatus, which enabled them to take whole towns without a fight. The local warlords and allies of the Rabbani and Massoud clan preferred to join the Taliban, or flee from them, rather than having to give battle.

Yet in a country where everyone has weapons and where the whole population has been hardened by so many years of war, the Taliban, relatively weak numerically since they apparently have only 25,000 fighters, could not have established their control over entire regions against the will of a hostile population. We can assume that the way they presented themselves had something to do with their ability to take control. They posed as champions of the fight against corruption and against all the rivalries between warlords which were undermining the country; they cultivated an austere image as selfless fighters. Thus, they were initially able to obtain, if not the active sympathy, at least the resigned consent of an exhausted population which clung to the hope that the Taliban would put an end to the civil war.

Did this mean giving up the most elementary freedoms? In fact, this surrender of freedom was not very significant; the Law of the Qur'an had already been the official law of the country since 1992; women's rights had already been reduced almost to zero, except no doubt for a section of the urban petty bourgeoisie. And the Taliban's barbaric punishments may not have appeared much more terrifying than the exactions demanded by the feudal lords and local chiefs who had previously represented the Kabul government.

This was particularly true in rural areas. Even so, the Taliban could not have obtained popular consent so quickly without having some credibility. That is, they had to provide proof that they could end the war; they had to win an initial battle, then a second one, etc. But to do this, they needed weapons, material means and money. They needed not only to recruit troops but also to arm them, feed them and provide them with the countless Japanese jeeps whose mobility contributed to their success. These material means were provided by Pakistan.

IMPERIALIST ORDER AND REGIONAL RIVALRIES

Pakistan had long intervened in Afghan affairs. Facing regional competition with Iran and rivalry with India, Pakistan sought ways to influence affairs in Afghanistan. From 1947 to 1979, India and Afghanistan maintained privileged relations with the Soviet Union, while Pakistan served as a regional lever for American imperialism against Soviet influence. Throughout this period, the Pakistani government encouraged the emergence of a Pushtun religious opposition in Afghanistan. Split in two by the Pakistani-Afghan border, as early as 1973 the Pushtun found a rear base in Pakistan. They were the first Afghani fundamentalist guerrillas.

With the Russian intervention in Afghanistan, American imperialism turned more openly to Pakistan. In their turn, the Pakistani leaders looked for ways to help set up an Afghan power closer to Pakistan than to India and Iran. The U.S. provided millions of dollars to Pakistan, with the goal of arming the Afghan resistance. The Pakistani political police, the ISI, set about recruiting, arming and training volunteers in the Afghan refugee camps in the border zone. Eventually, the ISI handed over this role to the rising star of Pushtun fundamentalism, Hekmatyar, the leader of the Hezb-i-Islami.

The withdrawal of Soviet troops may have changed the problem for the U.S. - at least slightly - but it did not change Pakistan's ambitions. Facing attempts by the Iranian regime to obtain the good graces of different warlords fighting for power, Pakistan continued to keep Hekmatyar as the instrument of its own regional policy. On the other hand, the collapse of the Soviet Union, with the former Soviet republics of Central Asia gaining independence, completely transformed the regional situation. The potential sphere of regional influence for both Pakistan and Iran was suddenly enlarged by five new states - Turkmenistan, Uzbekistan, Tadzhikistan, Kirghistan and Kazakhstan - three of which shared not only a border, but also common ethnic groups with Afghanistan. Washington, which had practically discarded Pakistan for awhile, suddenly began to look in its direction again.

Once again, American and Pakistani interests coincided. Washington feared that the Afghan civil war would extend to the former Soviet republics, thereby creating a focus of political instability far more dangerous than Afghanistan had previously been. At the same time, the United States still was concerned about containing Iranian influence. Pakistan, for its part, wanted an end to the Afghan civil war, with a regime established in Kabul which could serve as Pakistan's gateway to the republics of Central Asia. Hekmatyar had become an inconvenient ally. Not only did he seem to be the main destabilizing factor in every new turn in the civil war, he was ready to ally himself with the Hezb-i-Wahdat Shiite front, an instrument of Iranian policy in Afghanistan.

No longer subsidized as much by Pakistan, Hekmatyar turned to fundamentalist opposition forces in the Gulf States. Thus, he attracted not only Saudi Arabia's hostility, but also Washington's. Thus, the Pakistani regime decided to abandon Hekmatyar once and for all, thereby causing a few top level heads to roll in its political police. But the Pakistani political police, and the American secret police agencies to which they were linked, did not abandon their objectives. In 1993, students belonging to a radical faction of the Pakistani fundamentalist party Jamiat-ul-Ulema-i-Islam began to work in the Qur'an schools which the Jamiat had created in Afghan refugee camps inside Pakistan.

It was from these schools that the initial core of the Taliban movement emerged the following year. In the summer of 1994, the first guerrilla groups were formed, composed of former participants of the Qur'an schools, organized in part by Pakistani militants. Weapons were graciously supplied by Saudi Arabia, i.e. probably by the American secret police agencies or, at any rate, with their consent. It comes as no surprise that the person who today serves as an intermediary for all attempted negotiations between the Taliban and the other Afghan clans is the Pakistani Minister of the Interior, Naseerulla Babar. This man is simultaneously the direct head of the Pakistani political police, the strong man of Baluchistan and the unofficial spokesman of Jamiat-ul-Ulema-i-Islam within the Pakistani government.

It seems likely, as the opposition in Pakistan has charged that Babar is orchestrating the Taliban operation. Apparently, the only goal of this operation was to create a force in Afghanistan, disciplined enough not to give in to the generalized corruption and capable of seeming like a "new" force to the population. This operation, in order to capitalize on the population's desire to end the civil war, had to create a consensus in support of what is, in reality, nothing more than another reactionary armed band in a country where there are already more than enough.

Behind the strategic concerns of American imperialism and its regional representatives, there are other, much more down-to-earth interests at stake. The day after the Taliban captured Kabul; the American press reported that Chris Taggart, vice-president of Unocal Corporation, a powerful energy and oil consortium based in California, expressed his satisfaction with the way the war was going.

This gentleman stated, among other things: *"I understand Pakistan has already recognized the Taliban government. If the United States follows, it will lead the way to international lending agencies coming in. If the Taliban's victory leads to stability and international recognition, then it's positive."*

The fact is that Unocal, in collaboration with the Saudi company Delta Oil, has been looking into investing in Afghanistan. Concretely, the two companies are proposing to construct a gas pipeline designed to carry natural gas from Turkmenistan to Pakistani thermal power stations, and a crude oil pipeline capable of carrying a million barrels of crude per day also from Turkmenistan to an oil terminal located on the Pakistani coast. But, in both cases, the pipelines have to pass through virtually the whole Afghan territory. Obviously, the two companies are not about to risk the five billion dollars involved in the middle of a civil war.

That's what dictatorships are for: to ensure the safety of capital. Unocal Corporation has some experience in this kind of situation. In alliance with the French group Total, it is currently building a pipeline in Burma, aided by the military junta which polices a vast territory occupied by ethnic minorities in order to protect the project. There are other projects waiting to emerge. The republics of Central Asia have considerable mining resources. Turkmenistan is not the only source for oil. Kazakhstan is reputed to have a quarter of the world's oil resources along with the accompanying natural gas (the American trust Chevron, the Italian company AGIP and British Gas are already on the scene).

Uzbekistan has the biggest gold mine in the world; Tadzhikistan has the biggest known deposit of silver. At the moment there are only two possible ways of getting this mineral wealth out - railways and trans-Iranian pipelines or the route through Russia. These are two routes which American imperialism would like to avoid: the first for political reasons, the second for reasons of cost as much as economic competition, because the Russian bureaucrats take their share of everything which passes through their territory. The only other possibility, therefore, is the route to the sea which is the quickest, the route through Afghanistan.

Road transport through Afghanistan, which would make it possible to exploit the limited but still important consumer goods markets in the republics of Central Asia, is held back not so much by the civil war itself as by the exorbitant transit and protection taxes extorted by each of the warlords, not to mention their regional underlings. In any event, imperialism and its auxiliaries have every reason, both economic and political, to want a quick end to the Afghan conflict which they themselves largely helped to fan.

For the imperialist order and for its profits, it doesn't matter that this haste is likely to impose on the Afghan population one of the most reactionary regimes ever seen in the Third World. Throwing a sop to American public opinion, the American government will make declarations and pass resolutions about human rights in Afghanistan - - which everyone will promptly forget, just as has been the case with so many other dictatorships which the U.S. set up or protected.

It may even apply more or less symbolic economic sanctions, as it has toward Iraq today, sanctions for which only the poor population really pays any price. But it will not relieve the oppression of the population of Afghanistan. The oppression of populations is as inseparable from the imperialist order as is the race for profit.

With the collapse of Stalinism in the former-USSR, and the removal of the threat of Soviet-backed regimes coming to power in the colonial and ex-colonial world, Islamic fundamentalism has replaced 'communism' in the demonology of imperialism. The imperialist powers are terrified at the prospect of potentially hostile fundamentalist regimes coming to power in the Middle East or North Africa which may be forced by the pressure of the working class and poor peasantry to take action against their economic interests.

Islamic fundamentalism is a growing trend throughout this key strategic and economic region for the advanced capitalist countries. From the challenge of the Islamic Salvation Front (FIS) in Algeria and the bombing campaign of Gama'a al-Islamiya in Egypt, to the increasing support for militant Islamic groups in Lebanon and the Israeli-occupied territories, imperialism and the governments of the area are facing a rising tide of opposition expressed in the language of Islam.

The US decision to intervene in Somalia was partly motivated by the fear that, as the country disintegrated; Islamic fundamentalism could provide a rallying point for the population. Situated opposite the Arabian peninsular, an Islamic regime in Somalia could pose a direct threat to the interests of imperialism. Ironically, the intervention of the US and the UN has served to strengthen the fundamentalists. General Aidid, whose standing has been greatly enhanced by the UN attacks on him, is increasingly using Islamic rhetoric to bolster his position. Rallies in south Mogadishu have become radically Islamic, with imams from the fundamentalist Ittihad movement urging jihad, or holy war, against the US.

A similar effect can be seen in Lebanon. The barrage of missiles fired by Israel in July on the Shi'a Muslim south, forcing 400,000 refugees to flee, will drive many recruits into the ranks of Hezbollah. It is not surprising that the radical anti-imperialist rhetoric of the Islamic preachers finds receptive ears, whether in the Palestinian camps or in the slums of Cairo. The idea that the US, and the West in general, is at war with Islam is confirmed in their eyes by the Gulf war and the continued sanctions against Iraq. They compare the recent bombing of Baghdad with the reluctance to defend Muslims in Bosnia.

They see the massive aid given to Israel and the fact that after twenty months of peace talks there is still no sign of an Israeli withdrawal from Gaza or the West Bank. The rulers of the Arab countries are condemned for their capitulation to imperialism. Rulers like Mubarak of Egypt are rightly seen as pliant tools in the hands of US imperialism. Egypt receives $2bn per year in aid from the US - only Israel receives more - ensuring its complicity in imperialist aggression like the Gulf war.

The rise of Islamic fundamentalism is a consequence of the horrendous living conditions facing the overwhelming mass of the populations, due to the exploitation by imperialism and the inability of the weak national rulers to develop the economy, combined with the absence at the moment of any alternative movements which appear capable of leading a struggle for change. The 1980s economic boom in the advanced capitalist countries was in large part due to their intensified exploitation of the colonial and ex-colonial world. Through their domination of world trade the imperialist powers forced down the price of raw materials exported by these countries, including the price of oil, thus depriving them of essential revenue.

When these countries turned to the IMF and the World Bank, loans were only granted on the basis of severe austerity measures. The economic recession at the end of the 1980s exacerbated the problems for the colonial countries, as imperialism tightened its squeeze. The collapse of Stalinism has given much freer rein to imperialism, removing any limited room for diplomatic and economic maneuver which the colonial countries had before. The collapse of the planned economy has also had an affect on the consciousness of the masses in the region. While the fundamental strength of the working class internationally remains intact, the apparent failure of 'socialism' has served to confuse many workers and youth and led them to look for other solutions.

Any attempt to seek an explanation for the growing support for the various forms of Islamic fundamentalism in the religion of Islam itself would be futile. Such an explanation will only be found in the social and economic conditions of the area. It reflects the desperate searching on the part of the oppressed masses for a way out of the seemingly eternal hell of poverty, hunger, unemployment and disease.

Marx described religion as "the sigh of the oppressed". Lenin explained that "the deepest root of religion today is the socially downtrodden condition of the working masses and their apparently complete helplessness in the face of the blind forces of capitalism". In the absence of any worldly salvation many seek solace in religion. When the religious leaders include in their sermons attacks on the ruling elites and urge a struggle against them, even when this is couched in religious phraseology, it seems to echo the thoughts of the oppressed masses themselves.

The Teachings of Islam Can Be Interpereted in Different Ways According to Class Interests. In calling for a return to the pure 'fundamentals' of Islam they argue for a purging of all Western, alien or non-Islamic influences which have corrupted the culture and led society astray. Thus, their religious fundamentalism is mixed up with a radical anti-imperialism, to which the oppressed masses bring their own interpretation. Common to all the fundamentalist organizations is the aim of establishing a completely Islamic theocracy or religious state in which the Sharia, or Islamic law, would be enforced.

As in Iran this would include the enforced Islamic dress code such as the wearing of the veil for women, and the segregation of the sexes in education and other institutions. Marxists are completely opposed to any attempts to subject people to religious laws against their wishes. While defending the right of everyone to practice the religion of their choice Marxists stand for the complete separation of church and state. Islam itself is not intrinsically any more radical or reactionary than other religions. The social content and outlook of any religion will be determined and altered by the changing conditions of society. Like all religions the teachings of Islam can be interpreted in different ways according to the class interests of those who seek to utilize it.

While the development of Islam and its teachings, and the split into the different branches of Sunni, Shi'a and others, is not completely irrelevant to an explanation of Islamic fundamentalism, these factors are subordinate to the wider class struggles within society and of necessity must reflect them, albeit in a distorted fashion. In Saudi Arabia, where Islamic law is enforced, both the dictatorship of the Saudi royal family and the developing opposition's arguments for democratic reforms are justified in terms of the Qur'an.

The fundamentalist leaders of the different groups represent sections of the bourgeois or petty bourgeois. The Muslim Brotherhood opposed the secular Arab nationalism of Nasser, the Egyptian leader from 1954-70, and the land reforms and nationalizations he implemented. In Syria they consistently opposed the reforms of the Baath government based on its abolition of the private ownership of industry and land reform, calling for jihad against the Assad regime. Like all the other fundamentalist leaders they condemn atheistic communism and are virulently anti-socialist. Consequently, although for much of their history they have been suppressed by the Egyptian government, they have also been encouraged as a counterweight to the secular left and Communist Party.

In Afghanistan various Muslim guerrilla organizations fought a counter-revolutionary war, financed and trained by the CIA, to defeat the former Stalinist Najibullah regime. These forces represented the reactionary landlord class which opposed the reforms carried out by the regime. The fundamentalist state of Saudi Arabia is one of the USA's most loyal client states in the Middle East. However, Islamic fundamentalism is not a homogeneous phenomenon.

When it develops as a movement basing itself upon the poor and oppressed, and begins to reflect their desire for change, it becomes a strange hybrid combining contradictory and opposed class interests. On the one hand are the interests of the reactionary leaders, who base themselves on the continuation of capitalist, and in some cases feudal, property relations. On the other hand is a revolutionary desire to change society on the part of the oppressed which can only be satisfied by sweeping away all vestiges of capitalism and feudalism.

The Islamic fundamentalist groups, whose basic aim of the establishment of an Islamic state is thoroughly reactionary, can appear as a radical force only in the absence of a mass socialist movement. This is especially because of the demise of the region's Communist Parties following the collapse of Stalinism but also due to their past failure to lead the masses to power.

Throughout the region there have been many occasions when the working class, despite its relatively small size, has had the opportunity to overthrow capitalism. But under the direction of Moscow, which did not want socialist revolutions to take place, the Communist Parties of the Middle East were led to support bourgeois nationalist movements and so derailed many revolutionary situations. In Iraq in 1958, when the bourgeois democrat Kassem took power, the CP emerged from the underground with a mass following. In 1959 they led a May Day demonstration of half a million workers in Baghdad. Instead of leading a struggle for power they gave their support to Kassem and when he was toppled by a military coup in 1963, over 5,000 communists and their supporters were slaughtered.

In Sudan in 1969 the CP backed a military takeover led by General Numeiri. Despite having a million members out of a population of only 14 million, in 1971 the CP and trade union leaders were arrested and executed. The Numeiri dictatorship increasingly relied on Islamic rhetoric to maintain some support, introducing the Sharia in 1983. Numeiri was overthrown by a revolutionary uprising in 1985, but once again no organization was capable of giving a lead. In 1989 another coup brought the present Islamic military regime to power.

Arab nationalism, which under Nasser won mass support, also proved ultimately incapable of standing up to the power of imperialism. Because Nasser was not prepared to completely break the power of the capitalists and landlords, Egypt remained subservient to the interests of imperialism. With the failure of secular Arab nationalist movements and the betrayal of the Communist Parties, sections of the working class and peasantry have looked to the various Islamic organizations as a vehicle for change. In this sense the rise of Islamic fundamentalism is an expression of the impasse of capitalism in the region and the need for the oppressed masses to find a way out.

Were Islamic fundamentalism to come to power in any of the countries where it is now developing as a force, the most likely case being Algeria, it would not solve any of the economic and social problems facing the masses. With no coherent economic or political program to change society, the Islamic fundamentalist leaders in power would inevitably try to attack the democratic rights and living standards of the workers and peasants who helped to bring them to power.

However, it is not pre-ordained that the reactionary class elements in the leadership of the Islamic fundamentalist movement would triumph in the course of a revolutionary process. In such situation Islamic fundamentalist movements combine both revolution and counter-revolution and the question of which predominates and is finally successful depends upon the balance of class forces within society. A key factor will be whether there is a Marxist organization with a clear program, capable of developing into a mass force, and able to lead the working class and poor peasantry to power.

Where such a party does not exist, or fags to utilize the revolutionary developments to win the mass of the working class to its banner, then the basis would be laid for the counter-revolutionary element within Islamic fundamentalism, based on the middle classes and landlords, to secure victory for reaction. This is what happened in Iran where the revolution of 1979 brought the mullahs to power. Even here, the ultimate triumph of the counter-revolution was not easily achieved and was only possible due to the abject failure of the Communist Party, known as the Tudeh, and other left forces.

The Tudeh party had in the past developed a mass following. In 1946, having led massive strikes, the CP were brought into government, compromised and then thrown out. On the basis of revolutionary events in 1951, the Tudeh party regained mass support. But it failed to utilize this, instead backing the bourgeois democrat Mossadeq, and by 1953 the Shah had been reinstated by a CIA-backed coup. In the revolution [in 1979] which toppled the Shah, the working class, especially the oil workers, played the decisive part. The Shah of Iran was a client of US imperialism, presiding over a repressive regime in which opposition was prohibited.

From October 1977, throughout the whole of 1978, there was an escalating wave of demonstrations and strikes culminating in an insurrectionary movement in February 1979. Given the repression of the Shah's regime one of the few places where dissent could be expressed was in the mosque. Albeit in a distorted and inchoate manner, the mullahs reflected the discontent of the masses. Their radical sermons were interpreted by the masses in their own way.

The mullahs themselves were opposed to the Shah because of the confiscation of church land, and due to their link with the bazaar merchants who opposed the foreign domination of industry and trade. In the absence of any alternative leadership, the mullahs were able to assume a key position in the fight against the Shah and ride to power upon the backs of the working class.

In the Revolution Which Toppled the Shah, the Working Class Played the Decisive Part. Had the working class been conscious of the power it had in its hands and organized itself to defend that power, the beginnings of a socialist workers' republic could have been established. An international appeal to the workers and poor peasants throughout the Gulf region, the Middle East and beyond, appealing also for support from the working class in the advanced capitalist countries would have won an enthusiastic response and ensured the success of the revolution. Unfortunately, due to the absence of a genuine Marxist organization, the workers' movement at the critical moments remained rudderless.

The Tudeh played little role in the events of 1979, simply tail-ending the actions of the Islamic clerics around Khomeini. At no time did the Tudeh put forward the need for soviets, or workers' councils, to be set up to organize the revolution and to defend its gains. Instead they declared that "the political programme of Ayatollah Khomeini... (was) in accordance with the position it had itself adopted". In this way the Tudeh reinforced the position of Khomeini rather than explain the reactionary nature of his program and the interests which he represented.

Once in power there was an immediate conflict of interests, reflected within the clergy itself. The Islamic Republican Party established by the clerics of the newly-formed Revolutionary Council was connected to the old petit bourgeois and the bazaar merchants, who stood for the protection of private property and a government based on their interests. While aiming to represent the economic outlook of these conservative strata, the clerics had to take account of the popular resentment of the masses to the merchants and landlords and their demands for change.

Khomeini immediately tried to restrain the working class and contain their aspirations to overthrow the economic system. However, in the initial period, faced with the enormous strength of the workers' movement, the new regime was forced to go much further than it wanted. Within four months, banks, insurance companies and major sections of industry were nationalized with no resistance from their owners. Strikes and factory occupations developed despite the pleas for restraint from Khomeini. Where the bosses fled the workers started up production on their own and demanded that the government nationalize the plants, which it was obliged to do.

The newly established Islamic government had to tread very cautiously so as not to provoke the working class into opposition. In March 1979, thousands demonstrated against proposed laws enforcing women to wear the veil and the regime backed down. The class character of the new regime was clear from the beginning. On the day the insurance companies were nationalized a bill was published setting up courts with the power to impose ten-year prison sentences for "disruptive tactics in factories or worker agitation". Gradually the regime was able to consolidate itself. The Islamic Republican Guard was used to suppress the left organizations.

Clerics were appointed to run the factories taken over by the workers. By May 1983 the Tudeh, which had been the only

'Marxist' party to be officially legalized by the revolutionary council, was banned and its leaders arrested. The regime relied heavily on anti-imperialist rhetoric to win support, especially utilizing the American hostages in November 1979. When Iraq invaded Iran in 1980 the masses rallied to defend the revolution. The regime, given room for maneuver, was able to go onto the offensive against the opposition. The veil was enforced in 1981. By August 1982 all secular law was null and void and the Sharia was implemented. By 1982 40,000 teachers had been purged. Thousands of working class oppositionists were murdered.

THE OPPOSITION TO THE REGIME IS BECOMING MORE OPEN

The Iranian regime under Khomeini and then Rafsanjani being unable to provide any solution to the economic problems of capitalism, entered crisis. Splits emerged within the regime between those such as Rafsanjani, who wanted to turn more towards the western capitalist powers for trade and economic assistance, and those who reflected more the revolutionary traditions of the mass of the population. The regime has to walk a fine tightrope between trying to arrive at an understanding with imperialism and using anti- imperialist rhetoric to keep the support of the masses.

This attempt to face both ways at once is encapsulated at the luxury Hotel Azadi in Teheran. In the lobby there is a sign saying 'Down with the USA', but at the reception desk guests are told that bills can only be settled in US dollars. The continuing anti-imperialist fervor of the masses was shown by the demonstration of one million in Teheran at the outbreak of the Gulf war, demanding joint action alongside Iraq against the US. This was despite the eight-year long war with Iraq in which 400,000 Iranians died. If the regime does not take this attitude into account it could unleash a movement which would cause it to fall.

This is all the more the case given the growing discontent. While 20% of the population own 49% of the country's wealth there are up to 15 million unemployed out of a population of

60 million. Youth in particular are hostile to the regime with its strict moral code in addition to the economic catastrophe: 60% of the population is under 20 years old. These youth have no recollection of life under the Shah and see only the miserable conditions that the present regime brings, placing the blame on 'the turbanned ones'. The mullahs have been warned by Ayatollah Mi Khamenei to abandon their expensive homes and BMWs or risk facing the wrath of the people. They have become the nomenclature of a religious dictatorship.

While the habit of referring to the lavatory as 'dafar-e-imam', or "the immam's seat", may reflect a subtle form of subversion, the opposition to the regime is becoming more open. Strikes have taken place, including strikes of the oil workers in early 1992, and riots broken out in a number of cities. In an attempt to clamp down on the growing unrest the regime has reconstituted the 'baseej', its irregular shock troops. The dissatisfaction with the regime extends even into the police and the conventional security forces. On occasions the police have intervened to prevent the Revolutionary Guard detaining women for infringing the dress code.

Given the developing unrest and discontent with the regime it is only a matter of time before the working class regroups and asserts itself more determinedly. With the absence of an organized opposition it is possible that a new movement of the working class will manifest itself initially under the banner of a wing of Islam, couching its demands in Islamic terms. The Iranian revolution, with the overthrow of a powerful pro-western monarch and its seeming ability to stand up to imperialism over the last fourteen years, has attracted many in the Middle East to the banner of fundamentalism.

As the opposition to the Islamic dictatorship in Iran develops, the real nature of the regime will be seen not only within Iran but elsewhere in the region and its power of attraction will diminish. In Algeria, the FIS was originally formed in 1981 as a religious organization, sanctioned by the FLN government as an outlet for religious sentiment to counter left-wing opposition and maintain stability. During food riots in October 1988 the FIS acted as a restraining influence. But in 1990, when the ban on political parties was lifted, the FIS transformed itself into a party, attacking government corruption.

In the local elections of June 1990 the FIS won 54% of the vote, taking control of 32 of the 48 regional authorities. In the first round of the general election, held in December 1991, the FIS won 47% of the vote, gaining 188 of the 231 seats in which there was an overall winner, compared with only 23% and 15 seats for the ruling FLN. Faced with the prospect of a fundamentalist victory, the military intervened to annul the election in January 1992 and, in March, banned the FIS. The FIS has since developed a guerrilla organization capable of taking on the government forces in two-day gun battles, with between 10,000 and 15,000 armed activists. It has made inroads into the military itself.

If the FIS Came to Power, it would Act as a Catalyst throughout the Region. If the FIS were to come to power in Algeria it would act as a catalyst for fundamentalist movements throughout the region, threatening the regimes in Egypt, Morocco, Tunisia and as far away as Jordan. Support for the FIS comes not only from those drawn by its fundamentalist religious appeal but even from sections of the secular urban population, where its support rests more on its reputation for incorruptibility and out of hatred for the country's FLN rulers.

The FLN has squandered the revolutionary authority it had previously earned. In an eight-year long war they united the Algerian masses in a revolutionary struggle for national independence against French imperialism, which was eventually forced to withdraw in 1962. There was widespread support for the idea of socialism which was proclaimed in the constitution. However, the failure to defend the living standards of the population, the brutal repression of any opposition, and the rotten corruption of the government served to discredit 'socialism' and created fertile ground for fundamentalism to flourish.

The economy is in absolute crisis with 70% of foreign exchange earnings serving its $27bn foreign debt. Unemployment is over 30%. Food subsidies were cut in 1992, putting basic needs beyond the reach of many. There are undoubtedly many who fear and oppose the establishment of a fundamentalist state. On 2 January 1992, after the landslide vote for the FIS, the Socialist Forces Front (FF8), based mainly in the Berber-speaking Kabylie area, organized an anti-fundamentalist demonstration in Algiers of over 100,000. Although the FFS had won only 7% of the vote it gained 25 seats, more than the FLN, sweeping the board in the Berber-speaking area and winning some seats in Algiers.

The demonstration drew in participants from all over Algeria - Arabs and Berbers, workers and sections of the middle class, school students and the unemployed. There were a large number of women and some of the FLN and UGTA, the main trade union federation, took part. They chanted, 'No to fundamentalism! No to dictatorship!' The FFS was well-placed to transform itself from a party based on the Berbers into a national alternative both to the FLN and the FIS. Had it been capable of explaining a program for the socialist transformation of society it could have won support from the discontented masses who had turned in desperation to the FIS, as well as those who feared what the advent of the FIS to power would mean for Algeria's secular traditions?

Unfortunately the FFS posed no clear alternative, even trying to silence the more radical elements on the march. Although the FFS denounced the suspension of the elections it has not called demonstrations or protests since. The Communist party, called the Party of Socialist Vanguard (PAGS), welcomed the coup! In March 1993, around 100,000 marched in the center of Algiers. Chanting neither Teheran nor Khartoum', they protested at the growing wave of terrorism carried out by the FIS-backed guerrillas. Although the demonstration was organized with government help, with state companies closed and thousands of employees given transport to Algiers, many demonstrators also chanted antigovernment slogans, showing that they supported neither the government nor the fundamentalists.

The experience of Islamic fundamentalism in power in Iran demonstrates its ultimately reactionary character. If it comes to power elsewhere the working class and poor peasantry will learn from bitter experience the need to search for new means of struggle, just as the Iranian workers now have to do. Islamic fundamentalism in power under conditions of international recession would be extremely unstable and would very quickly begin to succumb to the antagonistic class pressures within society and start to split.

The only way of ending the horrific conditions faced by the masses, whether in Iran or Algeria, is not through the false demagogy of the Islamic clergy but through the program of revolutionary Marxism. The freeing of these countries from imperialist exploitation cannot be carried out by the Islamic fundamentalists. This task rests with the working class, drawing behind it the poor peasantry and leading the struggle for the socialist revolution.

Even where the working class constitutes only a small proportion of the population it plays the decisive role by virtue of its role in production. Throughout this region there exists a powerful working class with a revolutionary history. The Egyptian working class, with 23 unions affiliated to the Egyptian Trade Union Federation, has 5 million organized workers. In Algeria in March 1991, although affiliated to the ruling FLN, the UGTA organized a two-day general strike, the first since independence in 1962, in protest at price rises. (The FIS boycotted the strike claiming it was simply a struggle between wings of the FLN).

It will be through strikes and demonstrations, general strikes and insurrections that the working class will strive to change society. It is necessary to build strong Marxist organizations in all of these countries so that revolutionary opportunities are not lost as in the past. The revolutionary socialist transformation of society in north Africa and the Middle East can only be carried out by the conscious action of the working class armed with the program of Marxism based on an international perspective. Marxists have to find a way to reach the predominantly young working class, including the ranks of the unemployed and the peasantry, in all the countries of the region.

The Rise of Fundamentalism is a Complicating Factor in the Struggle to Change Society. By raising the clear program of Marxism it would be possible to build the basis for mass Marxist organizations. A fight for democratic demands - the right to vote, to organize, to strike, to freedom of religion - together with such demands as a shorter working week and a sliding scale of wages linked to prices, would win widespread support. By linking these demands to the call for a revolutionary constituent assembly and the establishment of a workers' government, based on the expropriation of the land and industry from the big landowners and capitalists and the introduction of a plan for organizing and developing the economy, mass revolutionary organizations could be created.

The rise of fundamentalism is a complicating factor for the working class in its struggle to transform society. But with this program, and by exposing the inadequacies of the policies of the fundamentalist leaders, the masses that at this stage are looking towards them could be won away and form part of a mass force for socialism. The working class of Algeria, Egypt, Iran and the other countries of the region will rediscover their revolutionary traditions and move to overthrow their corrupt governments and the domination of the imperialist powers.

SOUTH WAZIRISTAN

The Taliban in South Waziristan have overrun a fort manned by the Frontier Corps in the town of Sararogha. During a massed assault, the Taliban launched a coordinated attack on the military post manned by 42 paramilitary soldiers of the Frontier Corps. The military claimed seven soldiers and up to 50 Taliban were killed. Reports indicate 20 paramilitaries may have been captured by the Taliban.

The Pakistani military confirmed the assault. "Around midnight 400 miscreants attacked the Frontier Corps at Sararogha," military spokesman Major General Athar Abbas told *AFP*. "The fort was captured by militants; we are taking stock of the situation." There are reports of 40 to 50 dead miscreants, while seven personnel embraced martyrdom." Fifteen of the paramilitaries are said to have escaped, but the "exact location of rest of the FC [Frontier Corps] men in the fort [totaling 20] ... is not known," said Abbas. An unconfirmed report from Xinhua stated 30 troops were killed and up to 100 were killed during the fighting.

The Taliban conducted a well-planned military operation. Reports indicate a force sized from 400 to 1,000 Taliban fighters, indicating a battalion- to brigade-sized assault force. Organizing such a large assault force for a night operation requires planning and training. The Taliban breached the wall of the Sararogha fort using explosives, then rushed through the breach to capture the fort. The Sararogha region, which abuts the Afghan border, is a stronghold of Baitullah Mehsud.

Baitullah's fighters captured a company-sized military convoy in South Waziristan during a complex military operation in early September 2007. The Taliban and *Al Qaeda* operate 29 training camps in North and South Waziristan, and the Taliban have been organizing along the lines of military formations. A senior US intelligence official familiar with the Taliban resurgence in Pakistan who wishes to remain anonymous stated the Taliban have organized militarily at the brigade level, if not higher.

Baitullah is the leader of the newly created Tehrik-i-Taliban Pakistan, or Movement of the Taliban in Pakistan. Baitullah was appointed leader of the orgnaization after a gathering of local Taliban leaders throughout the tribal areas and the Northwest Frontier Province in mid-December. Pakistani intelligence intercepted a communication where Baitullah took credit for Benazir Bhutto's assassination and stated he was in the town near an Afghan border.

On Jan. 1, 2008, Maulvi Omar, the spokesman for the Movement of the Taliban in Pakistan said the Taliban would "expand its actions from Waziristan to Kohistan and [the] settled districts" unless military operations were halted in Swat. Baitullah has been feuding with pro-*Al Qaeda* and Taliban warlord Mullah Nazir, a rival in South Waziristan.

7

Pakistan and the Taliban

Two months after reaching a peace deal with the local Taliban in Pakistan's Swat Valley, the army is back on the offensive, attempting to keep the Taliban from moving closer to the capital Islamabad, while the government, enjoying its first consensus against extremism, seeks to regain a modicum of control. For months, Swat has been the epicenter of militancy in the Malakand Division and the militants there led by pro-Taliban cleric Maulana Fazlullah. The peace deal brokered by his father-in-law, Sufi Mohammad, with the liberal-minded provincial government is faltering and the Taliban cannot resist spreading their writ to the adjoining areas of Malakand region.

The peace deal, which allowed the imposition of Sharia law in the area, has failed to yield any clear results, with the Taliban attempting to expand their influence to bordering cities and towns not covered under the agreement. The law introducing Sharia courts in the troubled Malakand division, comprising six northwestern districts including Swat, is viewed by the Taliban as revival of the traditional justice system under which the area was run decades ago. The new law authorized the appointment of judges who would "seek guidance" from the Quran, Sunnah and Ijma for the purpose of trying cases in accordance with Sharia.

Barrister Zulfiqar Maluka, an expert in Sharia law, told ISN Security Watch he feared not only the creation of a parallel judicial system in Pakistan, but also a domino effect as other conservative areas may seek to impose Sharia law, thereby increasing the Taliban's writ in neighboring regions. Taliban spokesman Muslim Khan denied that the group was installing a parallel judicial system under the new deal.

On 19 April, Maulana Sufi Mohammad, responsible for brokering the peace deal, told his followers that the country's superior courts were set up on un-Islamic foundations and follow western laws and legal authorities. He called for reforming the superior court along Islamic lines while refusing any right of appeal against the Taliban courts in Malakand Division. Meanwhile, life in Swat Valley has undergone massive changes.

Though markets and offices have reopened, however briefly, and an estimated 100,000 female students have returned to school, the Valley's once flourishing tourism industry remains at a standstill, as most of the hotels are either in Taliban-controlled areas or their owners are too scared to resume business. Life in the Sharia territory has become impossible for women, with strict restrictions on dress and even public flogging for appearing at the market with any men aside from their husbands.

"Today, new rules forbid music, painting, sculpting, singing, dancing, theater and it is not peace and security that beckon but the fear of punishment that looms large [...]. There is no concept of a peaceful life as a free citizen in areas dominated by the Taliban," Dr Tariq Rahman, a noted professor from Quad-i-Azam University in Islamabad, told ISN Security Watch. Most critics see the advance of the Taliban in Swat and adjoining region as an attempt to control the resources and wealth of the region.

The majority of wealthy landlords and influential politicians have been targeted, with their homes raided and Taliban representatives forcing them to leave the area and abandon their possessions to the renegade militia. Like their mentors in Afghanistan, the local Taliban make most of their money from logging, mining and the collection of toll taxes on vehicles. Marble factories, gem stores and hotels are increasingly falling under Taliban control in the six districts of Malakand division, according to a Peshawar-based senior provincial government official who spoke to ISN Security Watch on condition of anonymity.

Dr Farzana Bari, a civil society activist in Islamabad, criticized what he perceives as the Taliban's hypocrisy as it seeks to take control of the areas wealth, saying it was ironic that "the same group of radicals is desperately seeking Sharia courts for speedy dispensation of justice."

SUCCUMBING TO THE TALIBAN

The government is under growing pressure from domestic and international forces for succumbing to Taliban firepower and blackmail. Shaheen Sehbai, an editor with Pakistan's daily The News, in a recent editorial examined the military's apparent decision to remain on the sidelines, saying that the Pakistani army had in principle decided to follow the civilian leadership and let it take both the credit and blame for the developments resulting from its policies.

Various developments suggest that the military may be waiting to take advantage of the government's failure to deal effectively with the Taliban. The worsening situation is likely to change public perception about the Taliban to the military's benefit. As such, the military may find increasing support for its short and effective military campaigns against the Taliban.

Such was the case with the Pakistani army's most recent campaign, on Tuesday, in which it killed over 80 militants to gain control of a key town in Buner district in the northwest, less than 100 kilometers from Islamabad. The militants had reportedly taken over police stations and kidnapped more than 50 security forces in an apparent response to a US missile attack that killed at least five alleged militants in South Waziristan, near the border with Afghanistan.

NEW CONSENSUS AGAINST EXTREMISM

While the Sharia peace deal in Swat has exposed the Taliban's true designs for Pakistan and its penchant for further expanding its powers, it has also worked to create a consensus within the political leadership against extremism.

The government is now enjoying more political support than it has since its inception. All the political parties - including the Pan-Islamist Jama'at-i-Islami - have voiced opposition to the imposition of Sharia law. Pakistani political analyst Ershad Mahmud told ISN Security Watch that this support would give the new government much-needed confidence to deal with the Taliban threat.

"For the first time since 9/11, the Pakistani nation has understood the nature and intensity of the threat posed to the country by extremism [...]. It is a time for a quick and effective military operation to eradicate these handful clergymen," analyst Ershad Mahmud, a writer for the Times, told ISN Security Watch.

Certain high-ranking officials, however, caution against allowing western allies to call the shots and warn that the government could pay the price politically if it is seen to be toeing Washington's line. "Each drone attack by NATO forces in Afghanistan-bordering tribal areas questions Pakistan's unrelenting support in the war against the Taliban and makes it more difficult for the politicians to defend their position," politician Imran Khan told ISN Security Watch.

When Barack Obama unveiled his new policy on Pakistan and Afghanistan in March, he gave a warning that al-Qaeda, the Taliban and other jihadist gangs were "killing Pakistan from within". The generals who guard Pakistan's national security had shown only "mixed results" in combating the threat, he said. They would no longer enjoy a "blank cheque"; they must show that they are fighting in good faith.

On April 26th, Pakistan gave a glimpse of this: by launching an attack on the Pakistan Taliban in parts of North-West Frontier Province (NWFP) recently overrun by the militants. It began with an assault in Lower Dir, near the border with Afghanistan, in which the army claims to have killed 70 militants and lost ten soldiers, and which displaced some

30,000 people. On April 28th the army launched a bigger offensive in the scenic Buner valley, just 100km (62 miles) from Islamabad, Pakistan's capital. As helicopter gunships and jets strafed their positions, the Taliban took around 70 policemen and soldiers hostage.

But showing more resolve than it had previously, the army said airborne troops had been dropped behind Taliban lines and freed 18 of the captives. Major-General Athar Abbas, a military spokesman, said 50 militants had been killed in the first two days of fighting. He said it would take a week to drive the Taliban out of Buner. This sudden violence seems to have been provoked, in part, by embarrassing media reports of the Taliban's capture of Buner. Many of the bearded fighters had come from the neighbouring district of Swat, a Taliban stronghold, where NWFP's government, at the army's urging, had brokered a ceasefire with the militants in February.

Under the terms of this pact, the government promised to institute Islamic law, *sharia*, throughout the Malakand division (whose seven districts, including Swat and Buner, make up about a third of NWFP's area). In return, the local Taliban, led by a zealot called Mullah Fazalullah, were to lay down their arms. The Taliban's advance into Buner, which had resisted Talibanisation, was a violation of the deal, but at first neither the government nor the army seemed concerned. America, which had opposed the Swat deal from the start, was furious.

On April 22nd Hillary Clinton, the secretary of state, said Pakistan was becoming a "mortal threat" to the world; its government and people needed to "speak out forcefully against a policy that is ceding more and more territory to the insurgents". On April 25th she expressed concern for the safety of Pakistan's nuclear arsenal if the Taliban were to "topple the government". Some Western diplomats considered this scaremongering. The Taliban are near Islamabad because the capital, a 1960s new town, was built close to the rugged border area where these Pushtun tribesmen live. But there is no chance of their seizing Islamabad.

If, unthinkably, the disparate warlords who make up the Pakistan Taliban were to mass together for a frontal attack, Pakistan's army, which is 620,000-strong and well-drilled for conventional warfare, could crush them. Indeed, many pundits reckon that an Islamist takeover in Pakistan would be possible only with the army's support. The Taliban, almost exclusively Pushtun, are not popular in Pakistan. Though often anti-American, and bothered by a growing extremist fringe, most Pakistanis are moderate. Unlike some Taliban leaders, Mullah Fazalullah is not known to have links to al-Qaeda.

Yet Mrs Clinton's warning points to an uncomfortable fact: since 2001, despite lavish American sponsorship, including over $10 billion in military aid, Pakistan has only become more turbulent and violent. Even the country's president, Asif Zardari, has conceded that the Taliban hold "huge amounts of land". The army deserves much of the blame. During a seven-year campaign in NWFP and the Pushtun tribal areas adjoining it, where 120,000 troops are currently deployed, it has oscillated between fighting militants and making deals that, typically, give militants the run of their areas in return for a promise (rarely kept) of good behaviour.

The Taliban in Pakistan are linked by ideology and Pushtun tribal kinship to those fighting in Afghanistan. In South and North Waziristan, two ever-hostile tribal areas, the local commanders, including Baitullah Mehsud, leader of the Pakistani Taliban, are widely believed to play host to al-Qaeda's core leadership. They also send their long-haired gunmen across the border to fight Western and Afghan forces. For America, Britain and other Western countries there is a direct connection between militancy along the lawless "Af-Pak" borderlands and jihadist bombings in Western cities. Yet Pakistan is the biggest victim of the militant tide.

Around half a million people are estimated to have been displaced by fighting in the north-west. From their havens there, many jihadist terrorist groups have launched attacks on the state. Pakistan has suffered over 60 suicide-bombings in each of the past two years, on hotels, restaurants and mosques in Peshawar, Lahore and Islamabad, and on army facilities. Benazir Bhutto, Mr Zardari's wife, a two-time former prime minister and leader of the Pakistan People's Party (PPP) who was murdered in December 2007, was one high-profile victim. Foreigners are also at risk.

In Peshawar, NWFP's increasingly nervy capital, two Afghan diplomats and one Iranian have been kidnapped. America's consul last year had her (bulletproof) car sprayed with bullets. Even if the Taliban cannot conquer Islamabad, they might soon grab some lesser strategic place-just imaginably, Peshawar; or they could close down the motorway linking it to Islamabad. Mr Obama's new policy, which treats Pakistan as the main threat to regional stability, is intended to arrest this slide.

It will come with a lot more money, including $1.5 billion a year in non-military aid over the next five years. At a conference in Tokyo on April 17th America, Britain, Japan, Saudi Arabia, South Korea and other "friends of Pakistan" also pledged $5.3 billion in budget support and other aid. Pakistan will be expected to provide better accounting for how it spends this money; for years its squandering of America's war-on-terror cash has been an open joke.

THE MESS IN MALAKAND

Like a spectre, the Malakand ceasefire had been waiting to test America's renewed commitment to securing Pakistan. It was agreed between NWFP's provincial government and a veteran Swati Islamist, Sufi Muhammad, who is Mullah Fazalullah's father-in-law, shortly before the inaugural visit to Islamabad of Richard Holbrooke, Mr Obama's "Af-Pak" envoy. America considered the pact yet another abdication to the Taliban by an army that has sometimes inexplicably underperformed. By one Western estimate, it has lost 70% of its battles against the Taliban. It has also lost over 1,500 soldiers.

Another cause for alarm is that Swat is not like the tribal areas, which have always been largely beyond the writ of

Pakistan. Swat, by contrast, is a thickly populated former tourist destination, famous for honeymooning couples and Pakistan's only ski-lift. The Taliban's capture of Swat therefore contained a promise of further militant expansion, even into Punjab, Pakistan's richest and most populous province. Nor, judged on the failure of earlier deals, did the ceasefire ever seem likely to weaken the militants, as the government hoped it would.

When it was eventually approved on April 13th by Mr Zardari after much anxious foot-dragging, an American spokesman said it violated the principles of democracy and human rights. But most Pakistanis seemed to welcome the deal, believing it would end recent carnage in Swat. Since mid-2007, when Mullah Fazalullah and his followers took up arms in protest at an army raid on a jihadist citadel in Islamabad, the Red Mosque, they have blown up 200 non-Islamic schools in the district, beheaded scores of government workers and alleged spies, and periodically kidnapped companies of soldiers sent to fight them.

Preaching class warfare, as well as *jihad*, they have seized hundreds of houses and landholdings, including many of Swat's prized orchards. Half of the district's police officers and many administrators have fled, as have most landowners. Around 800 people have been killed, most during a heavy-handed army action that began last October, and displaced at least 100,000 people. The Taliban behaved repellently during that offensive. Residents of Mingora, Swat's biggest town, awoke daily to find still-dripping corpses littering its central plaza, or dangling from lamp-posts there.

They dubbed it *Khooni Chowk*, or "Bloody Square". Yet almost all agree the army killed more civilians than did the militants. "The army was aiming its shells at ordinary people. Or else, did they hit our houses every day by mistake?" asks Fazal Rahman Nono, a local resident. If few Swatis have much love for the Taliban, practically none say they want a military operation to dislodge them; nor do the army and NWFP's government. General Abbas says that if the army had continued with its last offensive in Swat, "the whole valley would have been flattened".

He also defends the ceasefire deal; he says it has isolated the radical Mullah Fazalullah by bolstering Mr Muhammad, who was until recently in prison and disgrace, having led an army of Swatis to be slaughtered by American bombers in Afghanistan in 2001. But far from muzzling his son-in-law's jihadist invective-which Mullah Fazalullah once broadcast regularly, earning him the moniker "Mullah Radio"-Mr Muhammad has echoed it. Ahead of a rally on April 19th to celebrate Mr Zardari's signing of the ceasefire accord, Mr Muhammad was allegedly primed by the provincial government to tell the Taliban to disarm. Instead, addressing a crowd of 40,000 in Mingora, he denounced Pakistan's constitution and said democracy was for infidels.

Similarly, Mullah Fazalullah's commanders say the deal is a first step to imposing *sharia* throughout Pakistan. They clearly have no intention of ceding Swat to the government. Instead, the ceasefire has enabled them to tighten their grip on it. Last week they occupied the office of Médecins Sans Frontières, an NGO, in Saidu Sharif. In early April, they occupied the northern Swati town of Bahrain, and on April 28th shot and injured one policeman there and kidnapped another. Speaking by phone, a local resident says: "Ours is a life of fear and death." Yet the government could probably have lived with this, if the Taliban had not embarrassed it by taking Buner.

On April 24th, four days before the army launched its offensive, the Taliban leader in Buner, Commander Khalil, welcomed your correspondent to his requisitioned house in the village of Sultanwas. He claimed to have been sent to the district by Mullah Fazalullah to check that *sharia* was being followed, in accordance, he said, with the terms of ceasefire agreement. Yet he and his men had proceeded to chase away the district police and a few local resisters, killing eight. They then looted every government and NGO office and well-to-do house or business they could find.

Pointing to a large trove of stolen computers, American-donated food aid and jerry-cans of petrol, he said: "We'll give them to the poor, who really need them. These houses also belonged to rich people, who ran away when we arrived because they were scared to face our justice."

America is delighted by the army's subsequent assault in Buner; a Pentagon spokesman called it "exactly the appropriate response". Some American officials believe the army will even resume its offensive in Swat; and this time crush Mullah Fazalullah. Such optimism might seem justified by a modest improvement in Pakistan's fortunes on other fronts. Courtesy of an IMF loan of $7.6 billion, the offerings of its friends, and some penny-pinching economic management, it is no longer at risk of insolvency, as it was late last year. And in March, skilful diplomacy by the army and America averted a political crisis sparked by Mr Zardari's efforts to have his more-popular rival, Nawaz Sharif, rendered ineligible for election.

If Pakistan now has a window of relative political and economic stability, could Malakand prove to be a turning-point in Pakistan's flagging war with extremism? Probably not. The government has made no effort to use the ceasefire to extend its writ in Swat. Nor has it announced any plan to abrogate the deal. And the army shows little sign of wanting to resume the fighting in Swat. If this suggests Pakistan's top brass may, under pressure from America, be doing no more than the minimum (or slightly less than that) demanded of them, it would not be for the first time. One of the tricks used by the former president, Pervez Musharraf, was to arrest a few of the former jihadist assets of the army's Inter-Services Intelligence (ISI) agency; then later release them.

America has endured many such false hopes in Pakistan. Another was in early 2007 when the ISI backed a Taliban commander in South Waziristan, called Muhammad Nazir to expel some Uzbek militants who had found refuge there. The army suggested that foreign militants would no longer be welcome in the tribal area. But Mr Nazir did not evict his Arab terrorist guests, and in February he declared a new alliance with South Waziristan's main Taliban commander, Mr Mehsud, the alleged mastermind of Ms Bhutto's murder.

In a more recent setback, Abdul Aziz, head of Islamabad's Red Mosque, was released from jail on April 16th. He had survived the army's assault on the mosque (though over a hundred, and perhaps many more, of his followers did not) by fleeing dressed in a black *burqa*. Within hours of his release Mr Aziz was back in the pulpit, claiming credit for the introduction of *sharia* to Swat, and predicting the same for all Pakistan.

Another act of Pakistani slipperiness, the government's failure to dismantle the latest incarnation of the Lashkar-e-Taiba (LET) terrorist group that is alleged to have carried out a murderous commando-style attack in Mumbai last November, may be most troubling. In response to strong American, British and, naturally, Indian pressure, it arrested half a dozen mostly mid-level LET members, and vowed to try them for this crime but there is little prospect that the group's senior leaders, currently under house arrest, will face justice.

And the government has already failed in its obligation to take over LET's assets, which include schools, dispensaries and hospitals. In Punjab, which is home to LET (a group formerly trained by the ISI to fight in Indian-held Kashmir), the government has taken over 20 LET schools and five hospitals. Yet the group is estimated to retain control over an estimated 50-70 other properties, which it holds in other names. Pakistan's failure to suppress LET invites the thought that the army has not entirely abandoned its old proxy. And it still considers India, against whom it has fought three full-scale wars, to be its main enemy.

To some extent, this obsession with India illuminates the army's troubles in the north-west. By maintaining its readiness for a conventional war on Punjab's plains, it has been slow to acquire the necessary counter-insurgency skills; hence its brutish reliance on artillery fire in Swat. Worse, the army stands accused of protecting some of its former militant allies in the tribal areas, to preserve them for future (or perhaps current) use in Afghanistan and Indian-held Kashmir.

This allegation is often cited to explain the army's failures. But there is rarely evidence for it. Increasingly, though, senior American officials decry Pakistan's obsession with India. General David Petraeus, chief of America's Central Command, argues that Pakistan faces greater danger from home-grown extremism. With a smile, General Abbas suggests he doesn't think much of this: "When people come here and tell us about our neighbour, how good or bad he is, allow us to take it with a pinch of salt."

Rigid, deceitful and, it seems, convinced that Islamist militancy poses a much lesser threat to Pakistan than America reckons, the army will always be an awkward ally along the north-west frontier. Then again America is a difficult friend for Pakistan. Its pressing objective is to stanch the flow of Taliban into Afghanistan and to crush al-Qaeda's leadership; these are not priorities for many Pakistanis. And if the Pakistani army's efforts against the Taliban have not been successful, it reasonably counters that the cross-border insurgency has been inflamed by America's own blunders in Afghanistan and its missile strikes into Pakistan.

The army considers that it takes a longer-term view of what is required for its troubled north-west. In Swat, for example, it seems to think it would be fruitless to pulverise the Taliban, and in the process kill many civilians, while Pakistan's civil institutions are too weak to fill the vacuum that would be created. This is not entirely unreasonable. Local dissatisfaction with Pakistan's slothful and corrupt justice system-so much worse, Swatis say, than the traditional system of modified *sharia* that it replaced in 1969-has helped fuel Mullah Fazalullah's insurgency.

Many also seem to believe that, once *sharia* is instituted, the brutal militants will fade away. Inam-ur-Rahman, head of the Swat peace committee, a group that speaks to both the army and Taliban, says: "For God's sake, let's implement the deal. It will bring peace." Alas, that sounds naive. But even a government determined to crush the Taliban will struggle without the support of the local population. "Even if you take a Pushtun person to paradise by force, he will not go," adds Mr Rahman. "He will go with you only by friendly means."

THE TALIBAN AND THE JAMIAT-E ULMA-I ISLAM

It is sad but true that movements launched by various organisations in the name of championing the cause of Indian Muslims have in fact not only kept them in a closed society but also have caused tremendous harm to them. Ever since the eclipse of Mughal Empire in India, the Muslim elite in general and radical Islamists in particular grew apprehensive of the decline of Islamic hegemony in administration. They viewed the British rule in India as alien to Islamic culture and tradition and also fought against it jointly with Hindus but establishment of a secular democratic polity for India was not their dream.

They even fought the first war of Independence of 1857 jointly with Hindus by projecting the last Mughal Emperor Bahadur Shah Zaffar as their ruler. Their historical role behind the origin and development of Muslim separatism is so deeply imprinted in the mind of their co-religionists that it is now more or less impossible to create a unity of mind between the two major religious communities for an integrated Indian society.

Historically, Muslim invaders in India belonged to "the turbulent community of slaves and adventurers from a near primitive social milieu in which family ties or even human values in general had no relevance" (India 1000 to 2000 - Express Publication, Madurai). In fact these marauders used the name of Islam only for their greed of power and to legitimize their mass massacre, plunder and rape. Against this historical background, when Britishers captured the power, the Muslim elite tried to naturalize themselves in Indian society, but did not make any effort to integrate with it.

They rather launched a parallel movement for Muslim separatism, though they fought against the Britishers jointly with Hindus. They joined hands with Congress to overthrow the British Government because the latter was a non-Islamic government (Darul Harab). Shah Waliullah of Delhi sowed the seeds of Muslim separatism in eighteenth century, which gradually grew to a large tree with the help of a number of Islamic organisations/institutions. Prominent among them like Indo Oriental Muslim school (1870), which was upgraded to Anglo Muhammadan Oriental College in 1881 and to Aligarh Muslim University in 1920, Indian Union Muslim League(1906), Tabliq-e-Jamaat (1911), Jamaat-e-Ulma-e-Hind (1919), Jamaat-e-Islami (1941) and All India Muslim Majlish-e-Mushawarat(1964) have all along been in fore front in keeping the movement of Muslim separatism alive at the cost of the social and emotional integration of the two major religious communities in this country.

Most of the Islamic organizations though, accepted the reality of post-colonial Indian polity as a tactical compromise, their movement continues to remain in the domain of Muslim polity. Carrying forward the legacy of communal politics initiated by the Muslim elite since the second half of nineteenth century, Islamic organisations in India are still not ready to reform their movement in this scientific era of democracy and secularism. Their reaction against modernity and aversion to non-Islamic polity are the root causes behind many of the problems we see in the country.

Had the Muslim organisations taken positive steps to consolidate Muslim brotherhood for the overall social, cultural, and economic development of Indian society, there would not have been any scope for communal confrontation. Mahatma Gandhi tried his best to absorb the Muslims in the national mainstream of Indian politics. He accepted separate electorates for Muslims and was instrumental for congress' participation in Khilafat movement. But the radical Islamists never accepted him as a leader of united Indian society. They rather treated him as a leader of Hindus and kept the Muslim masses separated from the latter.

Mopla disturbances in 1924, support for two nation theory, direct action in 1946 and finally the partition of the country in 1947 are the permanent records of history that justify this view. Just after Independence, the Islamic organisations in India were lying low for some time but taking advantage of Indian constitution, which provides equal rights to all its citizens with some special privilege to minorities, they started raising their head by exploiting the vote bank politics of political parties in the country.

Except Indian Union Muslim League (IUML) none of the above mentioned organisations ever participated in any election in India. In 1952 some of the leaders of Jamaat-e-Islami Hind (JEIH) were arrested due to their anti -constitutional stand against nationalism, democracy and secularism. Thus, with a view to guard against any legal action by the government, JEIH made a tactical shift from its political objective of Huqumat-e-Ilahia (Kingdom of God) to Iqamat-e-Deen (Establishment of Islamic form of society).

To achieve this objective it also changed its strategy from Jehad (Holy war) to Saleh Inqilab (virtuous revolution). Despite the known designs of Islamic organisations in post colonial India, the political leadership ignored the movement for their own vested political interests. Their repeated errors of judgement on Pakistan front, which is deeply linked with Hindu-Muslim relation, and also on Muslim front aggravated the situation from bad to worse. Shahbano case of mid eighties is a glaring example of such error.

Noted writer Khuswant Singh has rightly reminded the political leaders of this country that had Prithviraj beheaded Mohammad Ghori in the first battle of Tarain, the course of events in Indian History would have been different (Hindustan Times Dated November 9, 2002). Committing mistakes after mistakes for their vote bank politics and helped by some political parties they allowed the gap of mistrust between Hindus and Muslims widening. Even today, their silence on Muslim fundamentalism and aggressive voice against Hindu fundamentalism has become the main thrust of discussion in parliament.

In the absence of a balanced stand against religious fundamentalism, they encouraged the radical Islamists to accelerate the process of their movement for isolating the Muslin society from the mainstream of Indian society. Hamid Dalwai in his book entitled 'Muslim Politics in India' exposed the communal politics of Islamic fundamentalists and said, "Unless Muslim communalism is eliminated, Hindu communalism will not disappear.

An objective study of Islamic organisations/institutions in India may help us to understand as to how religious sentiment of the Muslim masses was exploited by them to accelerate their movement for Muslim separatism. Unless we discuss the respective roles of various radical Islamist groups in India one by one, we may not do justice to our understanding of the Muslim psyche.. We may therefore like to confine our discussion in this chapter on the protracted movement for Muslim separatism launched by JEIH, which has been on an overdrive for its cherished goal to establish the 'Kingdom of God'.

Maulana Abul Ala Maududi, the founder of JEI was one of the prominent Muslim thinkers of twentieth century, who was also responsible for the growing misunderstanding among the non- Muslims about the Muslims in India. Starting his career as editor of Al - Jamaat, Maududi also remained associated with Mohammad Iqbal for some time. He however, had strong reservations against his contemporary Muslim thinkers on issues like democracy, nationalism, patriotism, Aligarh movement and Muslims' participation in freedom struggle.

The collapse of Ottoman Empire, failure of Khilafat movement and growing assertiveness of Hindus in freedom movement were viewed by Maududi as a threat to Islam and to the Muslim community. By late thirties he established himself as one of the most fundamentalist leaders believing in the concept of Pan- Islam. Critical exposition of Maududi's views by some of the Muslim writers like Safia Amir (Muslim Nationhood), Hamid Dalwai (Muslim Politics in India),

H.E.Hasnain (Indian Muslims-JEI Xrayed), Inayatullah (The real face of JEI), and Munir Commission Report-Lahore 1964) proved that his movement was basically for return of Muslims to the spell of medieval faith.

With the political objective of establishing Hukumat-e-Ilahia, Maududi negated the concept of secular and democratic polity. He was strongly opposed to Western concept of democracy, which according to him would de-Islamise the Muslims. For him democracy and Islam cannot co-exist in India, as it would not have the dominance of Muslims. He held that Muslims in India could not expect justice from Indian nationalists, who would follow the British pattern of governance and democracy would create slavish mentality among them.

The cultural ideals of British imply de-Islamisation of Muslims - Maududi felt. "Musims will be subjugated by the Hindus due to their population ratio". "Muslims of a future free India would be as helplessly in power as of the British at present". He even suggested the establishment of autonomous Muslim states within India in order to preserve the distinct identity and "national life" of the Muslims.

Maududi rejected the concept of nationalism on the plea that it was against the concept of humanity and separates a man of one country from other. For him Indian nationalism was synonymous to Hinduism. He "felt that the ways of the two communities (Hindus and Muslims) were parallel, and although they could cross occasionally, could never unite completely". He urged the Muslims to maintain their distinct dress, language and script and also to abstain from any imitation for preservation of their separate identity. He held that "Muslims were not a nation but an international revolutionary party".

On Aligarh Muslim University "Maududi felt in 1936 that whereas the Aligarh movement had to a certain extent improved the worldly life of Muslims, it had injured their religion more turning them into 'Anglo Muhammadans'. It had sold them to Europe's materialistic culture for a price of a few posts and titles for those calling themselves Muslims". Maududi's attitude towards freedom movement was ambiguous, but indirectly he was opposed to Muslims' participation in it.

He was of the view that Muslims could fight against the British provided it empowers Islam in India and make it 'Darul Islam'. He was not in favour of Indian nationalists to oust the alien government and establish any form of polity, which is not based on Islamic principles. He rather appealed to the Muslims to fight for the freedom but "remain prepared for a war unto death in order to turn the direction of the freedom movement from the government of 'Kufre' to that of truth".

In August 1941 Maududi founded JEI in an assembly of 75 of his supporters at Lahore. He launched it as a movement for return to Islam and its revitalization both as a religion and political force. His political objective was to create a truly Islamic society, which would ultimately overthrow all the Godless system and establish Hukumat-e-Ilahia (Kingdom of God) and Muslim dominance in Indian sub-continent. He did not believe in any form of government except the government prescribed by Islam.

Establishment of Islamic theocracy all over the world in general and dominance of Muslims in the Indian subcontinent in particular were the core objectives of the JEI. A scholar of Persian, Arabic and Urdu, he had strong reservation against the modern and scientific education. He was greatly influenced by his grandfather, who had recalled his son (father of Maududi) from Aligarh school, when he came to know through a friend that his son was seen playing with sticks like English people.

The hotly debated issue of Muslim identity during the freedom struggle culminated into partition of the country but the issue remained unresolved even in Independent India. After partition, the JEI was split into Jamaat-e-Islami Hind (India) and Jamaa-e-Islami Pakistan. Subseqently, JEI Kashmir was also formed separately, as JEIH has reservation in accepting Kashmir as a territory of Indian Union. Maududi settled in Pakistan and continued his movement till his death in 1979. The command of JEIH was left with Maulana Abu Lias Islahi, who subsequently became its president in 1948.

Headquarter of JEIH was set up at Maliabad (Lucknow), which was subsequently shifted to Rampur in 1951, Hyderabad in 1954 and finally to Delhi in 1960. Sirajur Hasan of Karnataka and Mohammad Zaffar from Bihar are the present Amir and Secretary General of the JEIH respectively. The JEI with its three-tier organisational set-up of Marqazi Nizam, the supreme central body, Halqa-e-Nizam as Zonal unit and Moqami Nizam as local unit has been championing for the cause of Muslim separatism for the last sixty years.

In this process it has created total mistrust and misunderstanding among the Hindus about the Muslim community. Though, it has not been able to command its influence over more than 2% of Indian Muslims, it has succeeded in working as a line of defense for those Muslims, who want to live in a closed society. For JEIH any deviation from the era of Prophet Muhammad is a danger to Islam. JEI is very choosy in recruitment of its members. It started with 75 in 1941 and reached to 647 at the time of partition. Before recruitment, a member (ruqun) has to pass through various stages to prove his loyalty to the organisation.

For propagation of its ideology, JEI had a three pronged approach that is - approach towards children up to 12 years, approach towards adults and propaganda through press. With hundreds of Deeni Talimi Madrasas in different parts of the country, the children are indoctrinated to the ideological philosophy of Maududi. It has floated a number of front organisations like Anjuman- e-Khudame Millat, Mujahideen Millat, Stdent Islamic Organisation, and Student Islamic Movement in India, Halqa Talba Islami and Halq1-e-Khawatrren to inculcate its ideology in the minds of adults.

Its number of publications in different languages like Radiance (English weekly), Noor (Urdu weekly), Kanti(Hindi), Aldawa (Arabic), Shahin (Marathi), Nizam (Bengali), and Prabodhani (Malayalam) and hundreds of reading rooms and libraries spread all over the country shows its financial muscle.

Sale of literature, donation from its sympathizers and collection of animal skins during Idul Zoha festival are claimed to be the known sources of JEIH's fund.

However, its foreign links with Islamic organisations all over the world like Motmaz-e-Alam-e-Islami (World Conference of Muslims) formed in Mecca in 1926, Rabita-e-Alam-e-Islami (World League of Muslims) formed in Saudi Arabia in 1962, International Islamic Federation of Students Organisation (IIFSO), World Assembly of Muslim Youths both formed in Saudi Arabia, Muslim Brotherhood formed in Geneva in 1927 and JEI Pakistan shows that such wide range of net work may not be possible within the claimed sources of its funding.

Taking advantage of the democratic rights given to all the Indian citizens, the JEIH along with its front organisations and huge financial resources is working relentlessly for its Islamic mission. Though it does not participate in election, its role in narrow, separatists and aggressive projection of religion in politics has caused much damage to Hindu-Muslim relations in the country. JEIH was never found showing its fraternity with the government at the time of any national crisis.

Its stand on Chinese aggression as appeared in an article in Novemver 1963 issue of its organ 'Irshad' exposed the medieval mindset of its leaders. Khalilullah, the writer of the article felt, "this defeat has proved that our present rulers have no capacity to rule! The only alternative this nation has (is) to hand over all powers to those, who ruled this country for one thousand years. Similarly on Shahbano case JEIH had aggressively mobilised the Muslim masses against the verdict of Supreme Court and compelled the then Congress Government to amend the constitution to nullify the verdict.

JEIH never condemned ultra Islamists like Taliban, Osama bin Laden or Al-Qaeda, which is a net work of net works of Islamic terrorism. Its strong reservation against government stand in tackling the problem of Kashmir, opposition to family planning and issues relating to Hindu-Muslim relation provide an opportunity to the liberal Hindu society to think in terms of Hindu fundamentalism.

India has faced and continues to face communal problems that have gone on for centuries. Unless our political class, social scientists and intellectuals irrespective of their religious affinity discuss the issue in totality and initiate effective steps to stop the movement for separatism, possibility of social integration in Indian society may remain a dream. Banning of certain organisations and lifting it subsequently is no answer to the problem.

THE TALIBAN AND THE ISI

Just hours after they seized Kandahar on November 4, 1994, the Taliban were accused of being mere surrogates of Pakistan's Inter-Services Intelligence Directorate (ISI). Other Afghan warlords, regional countries, Western wire services and the PakistaniPress suggested strongly that the Taliban had been created, launched and armed by Pakistan in order to fulfill the government's 'manifest destiny' of opening up trade routes to Central Asia via Afghanistan.

However, the truth was and remains far more complicated than that. The Taliban have never been anyone's puppets and their strings are certainly not pulled in Islamabad. Yet their links to Pakistan are all-encompassing, forged through nearly two decades of war devastation and life as refugees. The fact that the Taliban leadership is entirely indigenous to Afghanistan and fiercely independent does not detract from their social, economic and political links to Pakistan's own tribal milieu on the Pakistani-Afghanistan border. The shared Pushtun culture of this border region has never been better reflected than in the phenomenon of the Taliban.

Since 1994 Pakistan has rarely defined its Afghan policy - a reflection of the confusion, conflicting interests and rivalries of the various factions in government - but in a speech at the United Nations in November 1996, Foreign Secretary Najmuddin Sheikh spelt out the government's analysis of the Taliban's success. The Taliban phenomenon was a reaction to the state of anarchy in Afghanistan.

It was neither the ideology the Taliban propounded, nor the religious fervour of the people that accounted for their subsequent success. Rather it was the war weariness of the populace which stood ready to welcome any force that promised the disarming of the local brigands, the restoration of peace, and the semblance of an honest administration, no matter how rough and ready its system of justice. Most of the Taliban are the children of the Jehad against the Soviet Union. Many were born in Pakistani refugee camps, educated in Pakistani madrassas and learnt their fighting skills from Afghan *Mujahideen* parties based in Pakistan.

Their families continued to live in Pakistan as refugees even after the fall of Kabul to the *Mujahideen* in 1992. While all Taliban speak their mother tongue Pushto, for many their second language is not Persian, the lingua franca of Afghanistan, but Urdu, the language of Pakistan. Many Taliban carry Pakistani identity cards, as they spent years in refugee camps in Pakistan, and thousands voted in the 1997 elections in Balochistan for their favourite Pakistani party - the Jamiat-e-Ulema-i-Islam (JUI).

Moreover the Taliban recruited hundreds of Pakistani Islamic fundamentalist students to fight for their cause and were closely linked to Pakistan's fundamentalist Islamic parties such as the JUI led by Maulana Fazlur Rahman. None of these links made them Pakistani; instead they contributed to the Taliban's unique interpretation of being Afghan. Nevertheless, the rootlessness of the Taliban and the ease with which they cross two cultures could become a troubling factor for Pakistan in the future. As children of the Jehad their emergence stemmed from their deep disillusionment with the factionalism and criminal activities of the once Islamically-pure *Mujahideen*.

They saw themselves as the cleansers and purifiers of a social system gone wrong. Their social history also allowed them to be extremely well connected to many Pakistani state institutions, political parties and business groups in what was already an extremely fragmented Pakistani power structure.

Thus the Taliban were never beholden to one exclusive Pakistani lobby. Whereas in the 1980s Gulbadin Hekmatyar and other Afghan *Mujahideen* leaders had exclusive relationships with the ISI and the Jama'at-e-Islami (JI), they had few linkages with other powerful political, economic or social groups in Pakistan.

The Taliban's unprecedented depth of contacts and support in Pakistan enabled them at times to defy the ISI, by enlisting the help of government ministers or the transport mafia. At other times the Taliban could defy the federal government by enlisting the support of the provincial governments in Balochistan and the North West Frontier Province (NWFP). Thus the Taliban's main advantage was that they never depended upon an exclusive relationship with just one Pakistani lobby. They had access to more influential lobbies and groups in the border regions than most Pakistanis.

The Taliban's linkages with these groups are what constitute the nature of their 'support' from Pakistan. Many of today's Taliban warriors were too young to fight against the Soviet occupation of their country. Instead they grew up in Afghan refugee camps in Balochistan and Several Taliban leaders, such as Muhammad Omar, fought in the latter stages of the war against the regime of President Najibullah. But after Kabul fell to the *Mujahideen* in April 1992, these warriors expected the war to be over and went back to their families who were living in refugees' camps in Balochistan, or to the southern Afghan provinces of Kandahar, Helmand and Uruzgan.

Remaining in Balochistan after 1992 had an added attraction. Dozens of madrassas run by the JUI offered young Afghans the chance of a free education, studying the Holy Quran and Islamic Law. Thus for thousands of young Afghans, home became Pakistan rather than Afghanistan. It was here that their families lived, their children were educated, and they received international refugee assistance or worked as day labourers. Moreover, many had leased land in Balochistan to grow fodder for their flocks and herds.

In this Pakistani tribal milieu there were several major influences on the Taliban. The primary religious and ideological influence was the JUI, even though during the previous decade of Jehad the JUI had played virtually no role. In the 1980s Pakistan's Afghan policy was conducted with the help of the JI, the main rival of the JUI inside Pakistan, and the Afghan Hezb-e-Islami, led by Gulbadin Hikmatyar. For a decade the ISI's connection with JI and Hezb were the government's main instruments of policy, which for example ensured that armaments from the US and Arab countries went largely to the Ghilzai Pushtun warlords, who lived in central and north eastern Afghanistan.

In comparison, the Durrani Pushtuns, who dominated the south and Kandahar and who generally backed the return of the former Afghan monarch Zahir Shah, were largely ignored by the ISI and the American CIA. After 1992, Pakistan continued to back Hekmatyar, first in his refusal to legitimise the Kabul regime and then his strategic alliance with General Rashid Dostum in 1993 that led to the bloody two-year-long assault on Kabul which virtually destroyed the city.

However by 1994 it was self-evident that Hekmatyar had failed not only to conquer the capital but also to unite the Ghilzai Pushtuns against the Tajik dominated regime of President Burhanuddin Rabbani. The majority of Pushtuns loathed Hikmatyar as much as they disliked Rabbani. Thus for much of 1994, Pakistan's Afghan policy was stranded like a beached whale, directionless and without powerful surrogates in Afghanistan. Throughout the war in the 1980s the JUI had quietly built up a support base amongst the Durrani Pushtuns living in Balochistan and the NWFP, opening up madrassas and carrying out relief work in the refugee camps.

In contrast the JI had little leverage in Balochistan. The Pushtuns that belong to the JUI have a great deal in common with the Taliban. Both come from the Durrani tribes that straddle the porous border between Afghanistan and Balochistan. The activists of the JUI are Deobandis, followers of a fundamentalist reformist sect which interprets Islam, particular its injunctions against women, extremely strictly. The Deobandi tradition is also opposed to the tribal and feudal structures of Pakistani society and there is a strong belief in egalitarianism.

Moreover, there is a deep-seated Deobandi antipathy to Shiite Muslims, who are viewed as unbelievers, and consequently to Iran. The Taliban, with their limited exposure to the world and arriving in the JUI madrassas with only the imparted knowledge of the narrow-minded village mullahs at home, were soon turned into ardent Deobandis. Thus the Taliban's interpretation of Islam, tempered as it was with Pushtunwali - the tribal code of the Pushtuns - was primitive in the extreme.

While the JUI forbade any political role for women, the Taliban were to ban women from both education and work. And whereas the JUI was to rail against Iran and Shias, the Taliban were to kill Abdul Ali Mazari, the principal Shiite leader in Afghanistan, and in June 1997 close down the Iranian embassy in Kabul. In the late 1980s the JUI's influence over the southern Durrani Pushtuns was ignored by the ISI. Kandahar remained a backwater for Pakistani policy-makers, allowing for the mushrooming of dozens of petty Afghan warlords in the region. Moreover, the JUI was politically isolated at home, remaining in opposition to the first Benazir Bhutto government (1988-90) and the first Nawaz Sharif government (1990-93).

But in 1993 a new political situation arose for the JUI. For the first time the party allied itself with the winning Pakistan People's Party (PPP) led by Benazir Bhutto, so becoming a part of the ruling coalition. The JUI's newfound access to the corridors of power allowed it to establish close links with the army, the ISI and the Interior Ministry under retired General Naseerullah Babar. Thus the JUI could influence the central government's attitudes towards the Durranis and the Taliban. Meanwhile Bhutto had gained a useful 'Islamic' ally in combating the JI and the Muslim League (ML), which were now in Opposition.

Maulana Fazlur Rahman was made Chairman of the National Assembly's Standing Committee for Foreign Affairs - a position that enabled him to influence foreign policy. After 1994, Maulana Rahman visited Washington and European capitals to lobby for support for the Taliban. More importantly he went often to Saudi Arabia and the Gulf states to enlist their financial and military help for the Taliban, which was forthcoming. After Prince Turki al-Faisal Saud, head of the Saudi General Intelligence Agency, visited Pakistan secretly in July 1996, Saudi Arabia was to become the principal financial backer of the Taliban.

Fazlur Rahman organised the first bustard hunting trips for Gulf Arab princes to Kandahar in January and February 1996, thereby creating the first contacts between the Taliban and Arab rulers. The Arab hunting parties flew into Kandahar on huge transport planes bringing dozens of luxury jeeps, many of which they left behind for their Taliban hosts. The JUI remained the most vocal advocate for the Taliban even after the fall of the Bhutto government in November 1996 and continued to exert pressure on Prime Minister Nawaz Sharif to recognise the Taliban as the legitimate government of Afghanistan.

The JUI also benefited from the Taliban. Camps used for military training of non-Afghan *Mujahideen* inside Afghanistan (particularly Arab radicals) and which were run by either Pakistan's JI or Hikmatyar, were taken over by the Taliban and handed over to JUI fringe groups. Thus Harakatul Ansar, led by Fazlur Rahman Khalil, a JUI ally and a key Pakistani Islamic militant group sending recruits to Kashmir, Chechnya and Yugoslavia was given Camp Badr near Khost on the Pakistan-Afghanistan border.

Another major Pakistani influence on the Taliban was the truck transport smuggling mafia based in Quetta and Chaman in Balochistan. Made up largely of Pakistani but some Afghan Pushtuns, drawn from the same tribes as the Taliban leadership and closely knitted to them through business interests and intermarriage, this mafia had become frustrated by the warring warlords around Kandahar, who prevented the expansion of their traditional smuggling between Pakistan and Afghanistan further afield into Iran and Central Asia. By contrast, the transport mafia based in Peshawar had been relatively successful in being able to trade between Pakistan, northern Afghanistan and Uzbekistan, despite the continuing war around Kabul.

The Quetta-Chaman mafia funded the Taliban handsomely. Initially the mafia gave the Taliban a monthly retainer, but as the Taliban expanded westwards they demanded more and more funds - and received them. In March 1995, witnesses said the Taliban collected Rs 6 million (US $150,000) from transporters in Chaman in a single day and twice that amount the next day in Quetta as they prepared for an attack on Herat. Meanwhile the one-time, all-inclusive customs duty the Taliban charged trucks crossing into Afghanistan from Pakistan became the Taliban's major source of official income.

The cross-border smuggling trade has a long history, but never has it played such an important strategic role as under the Taliban. In 1950, Pakistan gave landlocked Afghanistan permission to import duty free goods through the port of Karachi under an Afghan Transit Trade (ATT) agreement. For decades Afghan truckers would drive their sealed goods up to Jalalabad or Kandahar and then turn around some of the goods to re-enter Pakistan, where they were sold in smugglers' markets.

However, after the fall of Kabul in 1992, the smuggling of foodstuffs, fuel, building materials and other goods into Afghanistan began to cripple Pakistan's own economy as Afghanistan became virtually a fifth province for Pakistan in economic terms. In Pushtun tribal terms this form of commerce is legitimate 'trade and business', even though it is completely out of any government's jurisdiction. The Central Board of Revenue estimated that Pakistan lost Rs 3.5 billion (US $87.5 million) in customs revenue in the financial year 1992-93, Rs 11 billion (US $275 million) during 1993-94 and Rs 20 billion (US $500 million) during 1994-95 - a staggering increase.

However, these figures appear to be only the tip of the iceberg. In a 1995 study the Pakistan Institute of Development Economics estimated that the smuggling trade had an annual turnover of Rs 100 billion (US $2.5 billion) or almost one third of Pakistan's estimated black economy of Rs 350 billion (US $8.75 billion). A 1995 UN study estimated that Afghanistan-Pakistan's total illicit drugs exports, which use the same routes and carriers as the ATT, were worth another Rs 50 billion (US $1.25 billion) per annum.

Within a few weeks of the Taliban takeover of Kandahar, not only had the volume of smuggling expanded dramatically but also the area. From Quetta, truck convoys were travelling to Kandahar and then southwards to Iran, westwards to Turkmenistan and from there onwards to other Central Asian republics and even Russia. Within a few months the Quetta transporters were urging the Taliban to capture Herat in order to take full control of the road to Turkmenistan. Ismail Khan, the warlord who controlled Herat and was allied to the Kabul regime was charging exorbitant customs fees, having raised his customs duty from Rs 5,000 (US $125) to Rs 10,000 (US $250) per truck for onward movement to Turkmenistan.

The ISI advised the Taliban not to attack Herat, because Pakistan had developed close relations with Ismail Khan and hoped that he might soon rebel against the Kabul government. Moreover, the ISI's own assessment was that the Taliban were unprepared militarily to meet the trained forces of Ismail Khan. Nevertheless, the Taliban rejected the ISI's advice and under the influence of the JUI and the transport mafia launched a major attack on Herat in May 1995. The attack turned into a rout. It was the Taliban's first military defeat and they were pushed back all the way to Kandahar with over 3,000 casualties.

Despite this setback, as business opportunities grew for the Taliban families, so did the clout of the transport mafia that now expanded in Spin Boldak, Kandahar and Herat. Many Taliban bought trucks themselves or had a relative who was directly involved in trucking. Moreover, by 1996 influential heroin smugglers also began willingly to pay a 'zakat' tax of 10 per cent to the Taliban exchequer for permission to transport heroin out of the region.

The heroin trade was officially condoned by the Taliban in contrast to the hashish trade, which they banned. With heroin traders now contributing substantially to the Taliban via the transport mafia, the influence of the Pakistan-based transport mafia became enormous. Ever since the Soviet invasion of Afghanistan, Pakistan's natural allies inside Afghanistan had been the Pushtuns who made up 40-45 per cent of the population, rather than the non-Pushtun minorities.

This was largely because of their ethnic affinity with their own Pushtuns, the influence of Pushtuns in the upper echelons of the Pakistan Army and bureaucracy, and General Ziaul Haq's conviction that the JI would eliminate the appeal of a 'Greater Pushtunistan' advocated by traditional Pushtun nationalists such as Wali Khan. But after the collapse of the Soviet Union in 1992, successive Pakistani governments were desperately keen to open up direct land links for trade and business with the five Central Asian republics of Kazakhstan, Uzbekistan, Kyrghyzestan, Turkmenistan and Tajikistan. The only hindrance to this was the continuing civil war in Afghanistan.

Pakistan's policy-makers were thus faced with a strategic dilemma. Either Pakistan could carry on backing one or the other Pushtun Afghan factions in its continued strategy of trying to bring to power in Kabul a Pushtun group which would be pro-Pakistan. Or Pakistan could radically alter its former policies and pursue a power-sharing agreement between all the Afghan factions at whatever the price for the Pushtuns, so that relative stability would allow the opening of the northern land route to Tashkent via Peshawar, Kabul and Mazar-e-Sharif.

This stark and simple strategic choice - in effect a policy reversal to sacrifice a pure Pushtun government in Kabul in favour of a broad based government that would allow greater trade and goodwill in Central Asia - did not appear attractive enough for the Pakistani military in 1992, which first backed Hekmatyar in his bid to capture Kabul and later the Taliban. As an alternative, and well before the advent of the Taliban, Pushtun elements in the Bhutto government and the military mooted the idea of securing a southern trade route to Central Asia via Quetta, Kandahar and Herat.

Later the Taliban would become the guarantors of this route along which Pakistan planned to build oil and gas pipelines and a railway line to Central Asia. In October 1994, one month before the Taliban captured Kandahar; Bhutto's Interior Minister Naseerullah Babar took a party of six Western ambassadors to Kandahar and Herat. The delegation included senior officials of the Departments of Railways, Highways, Telephones and Electricity. Babar said he wanted to raise US $300 million from international agencies to rebuild the highway from Quetta to Herat and another US $800 million for a railway track and satellite phone system linking 100 towns.

Ismail Khan assured the delegation that work could start as soon as there was peace and security. However, in Kandahar, where nearly a dozen petty warlords competed for influence, the situation was much more complex and difficult. Warlord Amir Lalai, who on November 2, 1994, would lead the gang that stopped a Pakistani truck convoy outside Kandahar, issued a blunt warning to Babar. 'Pakistan is offering to reconstruct our roads, but I do not think that by fixing our roads, peace would automatically follow.

As long as neighbouring countries continue to interfere in our internal affairs, we should not expect peace,' said Lalai. Nevertheless Babar urged Bhutto to push ahead. On October 28, Bhutto met with both Ismail Khan and General Rashid Dostum in Ashgabat, Turkmenistan. Along with President Saparmurad Niyazov, she urged them to come to a settlement so that Pakistan could implement these projects.

By then Pakistan, determined to bulldoze its policy through, was already planning to send a 30 truck convoy of goods through Kandahar to Turkmenistan. The story of that convoy is now a critical part of both the legend and history that surrounds the origins of the Taliban. The advance of the Taliban from Spin Boldak to Takht-e Pul outside Kandahar, where the Pakistani convoy had been halted by Amir Lalai, its subsequent release by the Taliban and the Taliban's capture of Kandahar were to change the political map of Afghanistan.

Just before he was hanged by the Taliban, Amir Lalai told people that JUI students were behind the attack on the city. The Taliban were prompted to move at that moment by Pakistan. A small group of Taliban led by Mullah Muhammad Omar was already preparing to attack the Kandahar warlords because of the breakdown of law and order in the province. The fact that the Taliban would not just free the convoy but then capture Kandahar within 24 hours was beyond any Pakistani or even Afghan expectation. Subsequently the Taliban leaders have expressed surprise at their own initial success, which was achieved with so little bloodshed.

Within days the Taliban demonstrated their independence from Pakistan, as well as their willingness to deal with the Rabbani regime in Kabul. A Taliban founder member and later Foreign Minister, Mullah Muhammad Ghaus, said on November 16 that Pakistan should not bypass the governments in either Kabul or Kandahar by trying to send convoys in future and should not cut deals with individual warlords. He also warned that the Taliban would not allow goods bound for Afghanistan to be carried by Pakistani trucks.

Nevertheless, the Taliban capture of Kandahar was wildly celebrated by the JUI and the Bhutto government, but created uproar amongst other political parties who felt directly threatened. Mehmood Khan Achakzai, head of the Pushtoonkhwa Milli Awami Party in Balochistan, publicly warned Bhutto and the ISI not to interfere in Afghanistan by trying to promote the JUI. Other Baloch and Pushtun politicians issued similar warnings. Qazi Hussain Ahmed, leader of the JI, suggested an imperialist plot was underway as the US and Britain were backing the Taliban.

But the Taliban were now unstoppable. By December 7, just four weeks after taking Kandahar, they had captured the provinces of Helmand and Uruzgan and were advancing on Farah in the west and Zabul and Ghazni to the north. In Helmand they pushed out drug-traffickers and for a few weeks declared opium growing to be illegal - a declaration that led to a flurry of activity and excitement at the US Embassy in Islamabad, followed by clear signals that US diplomats were supportive of the Taliban.

Meanwhile thousands of young Pushtun Afghans studying in madrassas in Balochistan and the NWFP rushed to Kandahar in trucks and coaches to join up with the Taliban. They were soon followed by Pakistani volunteers from madrassas in all four provinces. By early January 1995, some 12,000 madrassa-educated Afghan and Pakistani students had joined the Taliban in Kandahar. Trade now flourished.

In December the first regular Pakistani convoy of 50 trucks carrying raw cotton from Turkmenistan arrived in Quetta, after paying the Taliban over Rs 200,000 (US $5,000) in customs duties. Pakistan had helped the Taliban decisively by allowing them to capture a crucial arms dump outside Spin Boldak. The dump previously belonged to Hikmatyar, but was guarded by troops of Pakistan's Frontier Corps who were under the command of the Interior Ministry rather than the regular army.

These soldiers were ordered to walk away when the Taliban arrived. The Taliban took control of some 18,000 Kalashnikov rifles and 120 artillery pieces as well as large quantities of ammunition. As international and domestic pressure mounted on Pakistan to explain its position, Ms Bhutto issued the first formal denial of any Pakistani backing for the Taliban in February 1995. 'We have no favourites in Afghanistan and we do not interfere in Afghanistan,' she said while visiting Manila.

Later she said Pakistan could not stop new recruits from crossing the border to join the Taliban. 'I cannot fight Mr Rabbani's war for him. If Afghans want to cross the border, I do not stop them. I can stop them from re-entering but most of them have families here,' she said. 'We can't just shut down the schools (madrassas) and allow these people to spread all across the country. We would rather they be confined. Because of the Afghan war, people were taught that to be a Muslim means to spread Islam by armed struggle,' she added.

Pakistan then tried for several months to broker an agreement between the Taliban and General Dostum. After the Taliban finally captured Herat in September 1995, General Dostum sent down Uzbek technicians to help the Taliban repair the ten MiG aircraft and helicopters they had captured. But these efforts never led to an agreement. Pakistan was still trying in February 1996 when Islamabad hosted a meeting between Hikmatyar, General Dostum and the Taliban in Islamabad in order to try to forge an alliance.

At the same time Foreign, Minister Sardar Aseff Ali was in Washington trying to persude the United States to put its weight behind the Taliban. Pakistan failed to persuade the Taliban that if they linked up with Dostum, their credibility would be much higher in Western capitals; even at this stage the Taliban refused to share power with their rivals.

By now it was clear to everyone except the Pakistan government that the Taliban movement as a whole would not be consistently manipulated or guided by Pakistan. Thus when the Taliban captured a seven-man Russian aircrew in August 1995, they refused to release them despite considerable pressure from Islamabad. After Kabul fell to the Taliban in September 1996, Pakistan's attempts at shuttle diplomacy to persuade the Taliban to link up with Dostum also failed.

THE TALIBAN AND PAKISTAN'S PROVINCIAL GOVERNMENTS

During the 1980s, Pakistan's military regime had widened the scope of an already well-established system of patronage for the Pushtun tribal chiefs, politicians and mullahs living on the Pakistan side of the border in Balochistan and the North West Frontier Province. It was prompted to ensure the loyalty of the Pushtun tribes straddling the border, because there were similar overtures of money, weapons and bribes coming from the Kabul regime and the Soviet occupation forces in Afghanistan.

The British Raj began the system of paying stipends to the tribal chief or Maliks along the border to keep their loyalty. Pakistan had continued this practice after 1947. But under General Ziaul Haq the system became much more extensive. Maliks received payments and weapons from the ISI, the provincial governments and *Mujahideen* parties for granting permission to *Mujahideen* fighters to cross their territory to carry supplies for those fighting inside Afghanistan. The Maliks also received payment for hiring out their pack animals, guides and manpower.

The North West Frontier Province and Balochistan provincial governments received a windfall as they were authorised to issue permits to the Maliks to buy foodstuffs on the Pakistani market and then supply the *Mujahideen* inside Afghanistan. With the end of the war against the Soviets in 1989, these sources of income dried up for the Maliks, but the permit system boomed as Afghan cities were liberated, tens of thousands of refugees returned to Afghanistan and the need for food supplies increased dramatically.

In 1994 the Pakistan People's Party government in the North West Frontier Province, established under Chief Minister Aftab Sherpao, remained politically fragile. Sherpao used the permit system as a major source of patronage to retain the loyalty of MPs, politicians and tribal chiefs, Moreover Sherpao was often in competition with the Governor of the North West Frontier Province who had the power to issue his own permits to Maliks in the Federal Administered Tribal Areas - the no man's land of Pushtun tribes that straddle the border.

Those around the Governor and the Chief Minister made a bonanza in the permit business and they were often supplying goods to rival warlords or in opposition to the declared policy emanating from Islamabad. Thus Sherpao continued to issue permits for the supply of food to the

Rabbani regime, even though Pakistan was trying to isolate it internationally.

In Balochistan the provincial government under Chief Minister Zulfiqar Ali Magsi was a complex coalition of political parties, which was largely in opposition to the federal Pakistan People's Party government. Here there was a constant tussle over who benefited from permits. This infighting allowed the Taliban to gain the maximum advantage from the permit system, by playing off one Pakistani faction against another. The Taliban were part of this lucrative system of patronage.

With their own deep links with the border tribes, the Jamiat Ulema-i-Islam, the Maliks, refugee camp officials and the transport mafia, the Taliban had an enormous advantage over other Afghan factions. Their ties with the provincial governments were closer than those of any Afghan faction that preceded them. And the Taliban soon developed close relations with several businessmen close to Asif Ali Zardari, the husband of Benazir Bhutto, who in turn were given the highly lucrative permits to export fuel to Afghanistan.

As the Taliban's war machine expanded, permits for fuel supplies from Pakistan became a major money earner for Pakistani politicians and the Taliban, and a key element in the Taliban's military successes. The permit system thus created a stratum of Pakistani politicians and middlemen who had a vested interest in backing the Taliban and ensuring that the Taliban were able to conquer other cities and as the Taliban expanded, the greater the demand for Pakistani food and fuel in Afghanistan.

The role of Provincial governments only further fragmented Pakistan's policy debate on Afghanistan. The permit issue also created periodic shortages of key foodstuffs in Pakistan and contributed to the rise in inflation. In February 1997, the Nawaz Sharif government faced a crisis over wheat shortages, because of excessive wheat smuggling to the Taliban. Provincial governments thus played a major role in actually blocking the peace process and influencing the Bhutto government and the military to back the Taliban. 'There is a vested interest now amongst the leaders of the two provinces to maintain the present status quo and block the peace process in Afghanistan because there is so much money to be made,' said the former Afghan Minister of State for Foreign Affairs Dr Najibullah Lafraie in 1996.

Before the Taliban's capture of Kandahar in 1994, Pakistan and in particular the ISI's Afghan policy were facing serious problems. The ISI's main proteges, Hikmatyar and Dostum, had failed to capture Kabul and unlimited support for them was proving to be too expensive. Rabbani could not be ousted from Kabul, but he could not be trusted by Islamabad either as he expanded his links with Iran, Russia and India. Moreover, since the end of the Cold War, the ISI, due to the severe economic crisis in Pakistan, had been stripped of the substantial funds to which it had access in the 1980s.

Most significantly, the ISI's resources were directed towards another war of attrition - this one against India for the hearts and minds of the Kashmiris. After 1992 the ISI Chief Lieutenant-General Javed Nasir, appointed by Nawaz Sharif and an advocate of jehad, had continued the agency's backing of Hikmatyar while trying to micro-manage other warlords. The agency's operatives in Afghanistan were Pushtun and Islamic fundamentalist officers - a leftover from the military regime of General Ziaul Haq.

After Sharif's dismissal by President Ghulam Ishaq Khan in 1993, the army under considerable American pressure cleaned up the ISI. General Nasir was retired and dozens of Zia era officers were removed from the agency in July 1993. The ISI's new Chief Lieutenant-General Javed Ashraf Qazi was more cautious than his predecessors. For much of 1994 the ISI had retreated into a shell as far as Afghanistan was concerned. The military stalemate inside Afghanistan explains the ISI's reluctance to start any new policy initiatives.

When the Taliban captured Kandahar, the ISI were initially more sceptical than the government about their chances of further success. While General Babar and the Jamiat Ulema-i-Islam pushed for support to the Taliban, the ISI took a back seat, preferring to watch developments rather than act prematurely in giving the Taliban military backing. Thus Babar had a free hand in 'civilianising' the initial support to the Taliban. He created an Afghan Trade Development Cell in the Interior Ministry, which ostensibly had the task of coordinating ministries to facilitate a trade route to Central Asia.

The principal spinoff was considerable logistical and infrastructure support for the Taliban. Thus Pakistan telecom set up a microwave telephone network for the Taliban in Kandahar, which became part of the Pakistan telephone grid. Kandahar could be dialled from Pakistan as a local call using the prefix 081 - the same prefix as that for Quetta. Civilian engineers from the Public Works Department and the Water and Power Development Authority carried out feasibility studies for road repairs and electricity supply in Kandahar city.

The paramilitary Frontier Corps were used to help the Taliban set up an internal wireless network for their commanders in the field. Pakistan International Airlines (PIA) and the Air Force sent in technicians to repair Kandahar Airport and the MiG fighter jets and helicopters the Taliban had captured. After the capture of Herat, Pakistani efforts intensified. In January 1996, a ten-man team led by the Director-General of the Afghan Trade Development Cell travelled by road from Quetta to Turkmenistan.

Those who accompanied him included officials from Civil Aviation, Pakistan Telecom, PIA, Pakistan Railways, Radio Pakistan and the National Bank of Pakistan. These ministries and government corporations were encouraged to help the Taliban from their own ministerial budgets. After Kabul fell to the Taliban in 1996, Pakistan said it would start building the first 100 kilometres of the Chaman-Kandahar road at a cost of US$2.5 million. Pakistan estimated the total cost of a new road to Torgundi, on the Turkmenistan border, at US$10 million. Pakistan's infrastructural support to the Taliban was farmed out to various government departments.

During 1995 the ISI continued to debate the issue of greater support for the Taliban. The debate centered around those largely Pushtun officers involved in covert operations on the ground, who wanted greater support for the Taliban, and other officers who were involved in longer-term intelligence gathering and strategic planning, who wished to keep Pakistan's support to the minimum so as not to worsen tensions with Central Asia and Iran. The Pushtun grid in the army high command eventually played a major role in determining the military and ISI's decision to give greater support to the Taliban. Both the Army Chief General Abdul Waheed and the head of Military Intelligence Lieutenant-General Ali Kuli Khan were Pushtuns, as were all operational ISI field officers involved with the Taliban.

The military appear to have decided by the summer of 1995 that the Taliban were the only possible alternative for Pakistan's own strategic interests in Afghanistan, especially as President Rabbani appeared to be getting too close to Pakistan's rivals - Russia, Iran and India. Another major factor was the ISI's reluctance to trust Rabbani's commander Ahmad Shah Massood, who had a running battle with the ISI since the 1980s. When the Taliban launched their second attack on Herat, the ISI weighed in with a limited amount of military support.

This included providing ammunition for large-calibre machine guns and artillery shells, of which the Taliban were short; extending their military wireless network; and helping the fledgling Taliban air force, which doubled in size after the capture of Herat. But the ISI's ability to provide sustained military support was severely hampered by serious financial and logistical restraints and a continuing debate within the ISI and between the army and the ISI as to the benefits of long-term support to the Taliban.

The ISI also helped the Taliban by providing them with hundreds of ex-Afghan army officers and technicians who had sought shelter in Pakistan after 1992. Many of these officers were linked to General Shahnawaz Tanai, the former second-in-command of President Najibullah's armed forces, who led an abortive coup attempt against him in March 1990. Tanai's coup was backed by Gulbadeen Hikmatyar and the ISI, but its failure forced Tanai and his men to flee to Pakistan where they were given refuge.

Tanai belonged to the Khalq faction of the People's Democratic Party of Afghanistan. Khalq was predominantly Pushtun and many of its officers were ardent Pushtun nationalists. These officers saw Taliban as a possible vehicle for Pushtun resurgence in Afghanistan and thus were willing to join up with the students, even though they had little else in common with them. By the time the Taliban captured Kabul, their entire air force and a large section of their armour and heavy artillery were being manned by former Khalqis. By then Hikmatyar had fallen out with Tanai and in a bitter rebuttal of his former ally, Hikmatyar claimed that over 1,600 Khalqis were now working for the Taliban.

In Islamabad the involvement of several ministries, corporations, provincial governments and the ISI effectively sidelined the Pakistan Foreign Ministry, which had less and less to do with policy formulation towards the Taliban. The competition within the government only further fragmented Pakistan's decision-making on Afghanistan. The Foreign Ministry's ineffectiveness reduced Pakistan's ability to counter the hostile criticism from neighbouring countries of Islamabad's support for the Taliban.

After the capture of Herat by the Taliban, Iran, Russia and the Central Asian Republics became openly hostile to Pakistan. And after Kabul fell to the Taliban in 1996 all the regional states again made it clear to Pakistan how they opposed the Taliban's expansionist aims. The ISI played a leading role in helping the Taliban's capture of Jalalabad and Kabul, by first helping subvert the Jalalabad Shura and offering its members sanctuary in Pakistan and then allowing the Taliban to reinforce their assault on Kabul by fresh troops drawn from Afghan refugee camps on the border.

Pakistani diplomats and ISI officials arrived in Kabul promising all-out support to the Taliban and the Jamiat Ulema-e-Islam sent a delegation to help the Taliban write a new Afghan Constitution. The ISI had became deeply concerned that an unholy alliance had sprung up between the regional states that would soon include India. But efforts to defuse the tension, such as the secret visit to Moscow in November by ISI Chief Lieutenant-General Naseem Rana and the Prime Minister's Special Envoy Ijlal Zaidi's visits to Iran and Central Asia, did little to defuse regional tensions.

The more Pakistan demonstrated its support to the Taliban, the greater the anger and frustration amongst the regional states. By May 1997, when the Taliban launched their abortive bid to take over Mazar-e-Sharif, the military and the ISI had calculated that a recognised Taliban government which controlled the entire country would be easier to deal with than a Taliban movement. Moreover the ISI estimated that all the regional states would then have to deal with the Taliban reality and these states would look to Islamabad to demonstrate leverage over the Taliban and improve their own relationships with them.

It was a gamble that seriously misfired when the Taliban were pushed back from Mazar-e-Sharif after suffering thousands of casualties. For many experts in and out of government, especially for Pakistan's frustrated diplomatic corps, it was another classic example of Pakistan's overreaching foreign policy aims and ambitions, which were set in the Zia era when the country could at least claim lavish support from the USA, China and Saudi Arabia. But in the post-Cold War era, Pakistan had neither the resources, nor the domestic economic and political stability, to sustain such an ambitious foreign policy.

Yet the fact remains that with the constant infighting and overlap on Afghan policy within the Pakistani establishment and the lack of any serious attempt to create a high-level decision-making body that could make and implement policy, Pakistan's strategy towards the Taliban was characterised as much by drift as by determination. Islamabad's policy was as much driven by corruption, infighting and inefficiency as it was a concerted attempt to push forward a Pushtoon agenda in Afghanistan.

And the Taliban had become masters at using these differences within the Pakistani establishment to their advantage, extracting the maximum benefits from Pakistan without giving any political concessions in return. Thus instead of using its clout with the Taliban to exert leverage on them for key political and social issues, Pakistan appeared to fritter away its authority and respect amongst many Afghans-a respect that had been built up over two decades of support for the Afghan *Mujahideen* and the Afghan nation.

The Taliban movement has extremely serious political implications for Pakistan, which the military and the political elite in the country first ignored and only began to grasp after the battle for Mazar-e Sharif. The Taliban's close links with Pakistani society, their uncompromising stance on their version of Islamic values and the fact that they represent a new form of Islamic radicalism which is admired by a younger generation of Pakistani madrassa students, give them far more clout inside Pakistan than other Afghan *Mujahideen* groups. For many Pakistanis the Taliban are an inspiration.

Moreover, after the battle for Mazar, the Taliban had virtually won over all those more traditional Islamic parties in Pakistan such as the Jama'at-e-Islami, who at first viewed them with suspicion. As Nawaz Sharif's government slipped into inertia six months after being voted into power in February 1997, most major Islamic parties publicly declared that they had lost faith in parliamentary politics and aimed to mobilise a mass movement for an Islamic revolution by the end of the year.

Any such movement will almost certainly be joined by thousands of Pakistani madrassa students who have fought alongside the Taliban in Afghanistan. Armed, trained and motivated, these students would be a formidable force for any state apparatus to encounter. With Pakistan's civil state machinery eaten away by corruption and ineffectiveness and growing public disillusionment with the political system, the law and order agencies would be unable to cope with an Islamic movement which would be violent and self-sacrificing.

Almost immediately, such a movement would come up against the army. But the middle and lower echelons of the army's officer corps are themselves now full of fervent fundamentalist officers, many of them having graduated from a madarassa-style education rather than the public schools of the ruling elite. In any future prolonged confrontation with Qur'an-waving Islamic youths, the army's more secular high command would be hard-pressed to order their troops to open fire. The threat of an Islamic revolution in Pakistan has never been greater.

SWAT, PAKISTAN

By January 2003, there was a notable increase in violence as militant groups in the Swat valley, led by radical cleric Maulana Fazlullah, began attacking and killing civilians as well as police checkposts in Swat. In 59 villages, the militants set up a "parallel government" with Islamic courts imposing sharia law. The region was largely under effective militant control as of January 2009 despite the presence of 20,000 Pakistani troops. Local opponents of the militants have been harshly critical of Pakistani civil society for its lack of concern for their plight as well as critical of the military and provincial government for their ineffective measures for controlling the tide of militancy.

LATE 2007

After a four-month truce ended in late September 2007, fighting resumed. The paramilitary Frontier Constabulary was deployed to the area, but initially was reported to be ineffective. On November 16, 2007 Militants were reported to have captured Alpuri district headquarters in neighbouring Shangla. The local police fled without resisting the advancing militant force which, in addition to local militants, also included Uzbek, Tajik and Chechen volunteers.

In late November 2007, Pakistani regular forces threw out Tehreek-e-Nafaz-e-Shariat-e-Mohammadi militants from its stronghold in the Kabal District of north-western Swat. About

250 militants died in two weeks of fighting according to Pakistani authorities and the militants retreated into the mountains. By December 2007, the militants were on the run, with the valley "largely cleared". Pakistani officials stated at that time that it would take four months to re-establish functioning institutions in the area, in the wake of Islamist ruin.

KILLING OF MALAK BAKHT BAIDAR

On January 13, 2007, Malak Bakht Baidar, vice-president of Awami National Party, District Swat, and well-known businessman, was kidnapped from his village home and killed by around 80 masked and armed militants. Bakht Baidar belonged to a noble and wealthy family and was one of the younger sons of Ferdost Malak, resided in Mamdherai.

Bakht Baidar was known for his nobility and progressive political work in district Swat. He had been resisting Maulvi Fazlullah's agenda from the outset. He was also known to have attended meetings with security forces during their operation in the valley. Bakht Baidar was buried in his ancestral graveyard in Mamdherai, Swat.

KIDNAPPING OF ISRAR MUHAMMAD

The militants have also kidnapped Professor Israr Muhammad of Swat Govt College, who strongly opposed them, trying to enlighten people about their actions. His two sons, Zubair Ahmad and Younas Muhammad, were also supporting his father against militants. But on 21 August 2008, Israr and Zubair were kidnapped by militants.

His other son, Younas, is out of Swat, and the militants are searching for him. The Taliban claim they are non-Muslims because they are against Tehreek-e-Taliban Pakistan (TTP). Trying to find Younas, the Taliban are searching in Peshawar and Mardan, and have delivered brochures stating that Younas is wanted by Sharia Court in Swat.

TARGETING AFZAL KHAN LALA

Abdul Jabbar Khan was wounded during an attack on ANP leaders by gunmen on 21 September 2007. The attacker killed two people and wounded three members of the ANP, including Mohammad Afzal Khan Lala, ex-federal minister and central leader of the ANP. On 24 January 2008, Zakir Khan, the Naib Nazim of Matta Tehsil, was killed in an attack by gunmen along with his brother, Shakir Khan, and friends. Zakir Khan was a nephew of Tehsil Matta's Nazim, Abdul Jabbar Khan, and grandson of Mohammad Afzal Khan Lala, a senior member of ANP and former federal minister.

CHARBAGH TEHSIL SUICIDE BOMBING

On August 23, 2008 a suicide bomber rammed an explosive-laden car into a police station in Charbagh Tehsil of Swat valley, killing 20 people. The Tehrik-e-Taleban organization claimed responsibility. Swat's situation is worsening further and the Taliban now control most of the valley.

DEVELOPMENTS IN 2009

A January 21, 2009 issue of the Pakistan daily newspaper *The News*, reports Taliban enforcement of a complete ban on female education in the Swat district. Some 400 private schools enrolling 40,000 girls have been shut down. At least 10 girls' schools that tried to open after the January 15, 2009 deadline by the Taliban were blown up by the militants in the town of Mingora, the headquarters of the Swat district. "More than 170 schools have been bombed or torched, along with other government-owned buildings."

In a stated attempt at bringing peace to this region, the Pakistani Government on 16 February 2009, signed a peace accord with the Taliban and agreed to the imposition of Sharia law in Swat and suspension of military offensives against the Taliban.

This agreement invoked mixed reactions from the locals: some are relieved on the prospect of relative peace, while others are more skeptical about the *Talibanisation* of this scenic paradise and the push that this accord would give to the spread of Taliban's movement in Pakistan. International concern primarily stems from the rigidity with which the Taliban is seen to be imposing *Sharia*. Others point to the impact such an accord will have in empowering radical Islamists and the jihadi movement in Pakistan and elsewhere.

FEBRUARY 2009 CEASEFIRE

The Pakistani government announced on February 16, 2009 that it would allow Sharia law in the Malakand region. In return, Fazlullah's followers agreed to observe a ceasefire negotiated by Sufi Muhammad.

Reactions to Ceasefire:

- NATO feared that the agreement would only serve to allow militants to regroup and to create a safe haven for cross-border attacks into Afghanistan.
- Amnesty International expressed concern that the agreement would legitimize human rights abuses in the region.
- The people of Swat have welcomed this peace-agreement as welcome respite from the fighting that had brought their lives to a standstill. However, reports from the area suggest that this agreement has been accepted by them out of fear of continuous fighting that has destroyed the once scenic tourist haven. With the imposition of Nizam-e-Adl, some colleges and schools, including those for women, have reopened. However, women have to conceal themselves from head to toe as per the Islamic law or Shariah. Furthermore, Pakistanis are now scared that this deal may only serve to embolden militants to spread their influence into more settled parts of Pakistan.

Despite the reported ceasefire, the Taliban have refused to lay down their arms. Various international political and security analysts are opining that this deal and refusal to lay down arms may have devastating effects on the stability of Pakistan.

APRIL-MAY 2009 PAKISTANI OFFENSIVE

Through a media broadcast, the Pakistani government announced in late April that it would fight the Taliban in the

Swat Valley. This led to a humanitarian crisis. The United Nations Commissioner for Refugees announced that between 150,000 to 200,000 civilians had fled the war zone. The Pakistani military took back multiple Taliban strongholds, such as Rama Kandhao ridge in Matta and a Taliban headquarters in Loenamal.

On the 8th of May, the Pakistani military announced that around 80 Taliban fighters had been killed and two Pakistani soldiers had been injured. Air strikes, artillery bombardment and rocket attacks by helicopter gunships are being undertaken extensively. As of 11th May, the military spokesperson of the ISPR report that as many as 200 militants had been killed in the fighting with Pakistan Army troops, also those Pakistan helibourne commandos had been inserted in the area which is the main stronghold of these militants. By early June 2009, most of Swat was freed from Taliban and Mingora, the main town of Swat, was in complete government control.

Bibliography

Ahmed Rashid. *TALIBAN: Militant Islam, Oil and Fundamentalism in Central Asia*, Yale, 2001.

Antonio Giustozzi. *War, Politics and Society in Afghanistan, 1978-1992*, Georgetown University Press, 2000.

Arthur Bonner. *Among the Afghans*, Duke University Press, 1987.

Abu Khalil, As'ad. *Bin Laden, Islam, and America's New 'War on Terrorism'*. Open Media Pamphlet Series. New York: Seven Stories Press, 2002.

Abraham, A. J. *Islamic Fundamentalism and the Doctrine of Jihad*. Lima, OH: Wyndham Hall Press, 2002.

Brigitte L. Nacos.*Terrorism & the Media: From the Iran Hostage Crisis to the World Trade Center Bombing*, Columbia University Press, 1994 .

Bar, Shmuel. *Warrant for Terror: Fatwas of Radical Islam and the Duty of Jihad*. Hoover Studies in Politics, Economics, and Society. Lanham, MD: Rowman & Littlefield, 2006.

Catholic Institute for International Relations, *Guatemala, Never Again*. Maryknoll, NY: Orbis Books, 1999.

David B. Edwards. *Heroes of the Age: Moral Fault Lines on the Afghan Frontier*, University of California Press, 1996 .

Davies, Barry. *Terrorism: Inside a World Phenomenon*. London: Virgin Books, 2003.

Eric S. Margolis. *War at the Top of the World: The Struggle for Afghanistan, Kashmir, and Tibet*, Routledge, 2001.

Esposito, John L. *Islam: The Straight Path.* 3rd edition. New York: Oxford University Press, 1998.

Esposito, John L. *The Islamic Threat: Myth or Reality?* New York: Oxford University Press, 1992.

Hasan Kakar. Afghanistan: *The Soviet Invasion and the Afghan Response, 1979-1982,* University of California Press, 1995.

Henry S. Bradsher. *Afghan Communism and Soviet Intervention,* Oxford University Press, 1999 .

Huband, Mark. *Warriors of the Prophet: the Struggle for Islam.* Boulder, CO: Westview Press, 1999.

Ian O. Lesser, Bruce Hoffman, John Arquilla, David F. Ronfeldt, Michele Zanini, Brian Michael Jenkins. *Countering,* RAND, 1999.

Jason Elliot. *An Unexpected Light: Travels in Afghanistan,* St.Martin's, 2001.

Jeffrey D. Simon. *Terrorist Trap,* Indiana University Press, 2001.

Jessica Stern. *The Ultimate Terrorists,* Harvard, 2000.

John Arquilla and David Ronfeldt. *Networks and Netwars: The Future of Terror, Crime and Militancy,* RAND, 2001.

Kamal Matinuddin.*The Taliban Phenomenon, Afghanistan 1994-1997,* Oxford University Press. 2000.

Larry P. Goodson. *Afghanistan's Endless War: State Failure, Regional Politics, and the Rise of the Taliban,* University of Washington Press, 2001.

M.J. Gohari.*Taliban: Ascent to Power,* Oxford University Press, 2001.

Marc Miller and Jason File.*Terrorism Factbook: Our Nation at War,* White Wolf Publishing Inc. 2001.

Mark Juergensmeyer. *Terror in the Mind of God: The Global Rise of Religious Violence,* University of California, 2001.

Martha Crenshaw.*Terrorism in Context,* Penn State

University Press, 1995 .

Omar Malik. *Enough of the Definition of Terrorism*, Brookings Institution Press, 2001.

O'Ballance, Edgar. *Islamic Fundamentalist Terrorism: 1979-95*. Basingstoke: Macmillan, 1997.

Ojeda, Auriana. *Islamic Fundamentalism*. San Diego, CA: Greenhaven Press, 2003.

Paul R. Pillar.*Terrorism and U.S. Foreign Policy*, Brookings Institution Press, 2001.

Philip B. Heymann. *Terrorism and America: A Commonsense Strategy for a Democratic Society*, MIT Press, 1998.

Sarah E. Mendelson. *Changing Course: Ideas, Politics, and the Soviet Withdrawal from Afghanistan*, Princeton University Press, 1998.

Walter Laquer.*The New Terrorism: Fanaticism and the Arms of Mass Destruction*, Oxford University Press, 1999 .

William Maley. *Fundamentalism Reborn? Afghanistan and the Taliban*, New York University Press, 1998.

Yossef Bodansky. Bin Laden: *The Man who Declared War on America*: Prima, 2001.

Index

TALIBAN

2 Vols. Set

Volume 2

TALIBAN

2 Vols. Set

Volume 2

N K Verma

MD PUBLICATIONS PVT LTD

NEW DELHI

www.mdppl.com

Published by :

MD Publications Pvt Ltd
"MD House", 11, Darya Ganj,
New Delhi - 110 002
Phone : +91-11-45355555
E-mail : contact@mdppl.com
Website: www.mdppl.com

ISBN: 978-81-7533-270-6 (Set of 2 Vols.)
978-81-7533-272-0 (Vol. 2)

Published and Printed by Mr. Pranav Gupta on behalf of **MD Publications Pvt Ltd** at Times Press, New Delhi.

Preface

Talib is an Arabic word, which literally means 'one, who is seeking,' but generally Talib refers to 'someone who is seeking religious knowledge.' Taliban are students of "deeni madrassas" or religious seminaries, which have existed in Afghanistan, the Indian-Subcontinent, and the Central Asia since the arrival of Islam in these areas.

The overwhelming majority of the Taliban movements were ethnic Pashtuns from southern Afghanistan and western Pakistan, along with a smaller number of volunteers from Islamic countries. The Taliban received valuable training, supplies and arms from the Pakistani government, particularly the Inter-Services Intelligence (ISI), and many recruits from madrasahs for Afghan refugees in Pakistan, primarily ones established by the Jamiat Ulema-e-Islam(JUI).

The Taliban movement emerged out of the chaos and uncertainty of the Soviet-Afghan War (1979-1989) and subsequent civil war in Afghanistan. During the 1980s Afghanistan was occupied by the Union of Soviet Socialist Republics (USSR) and ruled by a Soviet-backed government. Afghanistan's long war with the USSR was largely fought by mujahideen (Islamic guerrilla) factions with assistance from the United States; Pakistan also provided places of refuge, military training, and other support. After the Soviets completed their withdrawal in 1989, civil war broke out between the mujahideen factions and the central government and initially enjoyed enormous goodwill from Afghans weary of the corruption, brutality, and the incessant fighting of Mujahideen warlords.

The Taliban's extremely strict and 'anti-modern' ideology has been described as an "innovative form of sharia combining Pashtun tribal codes," or Pashtunwali, with radical Deobandi interpretations of Islam favored by members of the Pakistani fundamentalist Jamiat Ulema-e-Islam (JUI) organization and its splinter groups. However, most of the leaders of the current Taliban regime in Afghanistan have been influenced by the teachings of Islam in Pakistan, where they had migrated with millions of other Afghans after the Soviet invasion. There, they attended religious seminaries or 'madrassas', while many of them also remained active fighting the Soviets in the battlefields. They are the followers of the "Deobandi" school of thought, preached by mullahs (clerics) in Pakistani madrassas.

The initial goals of the Taliban were to disarm the country, end lawlessness and enforce the Islamic law or the Sharia on a united Afghanistan. The Taliban so far have been successful in bringing relative law and order in around 85% of the country that they control. They have done so mainly by disarming and in certain cases by incorporating in their ranks, the previous warring groups. The Taliban ideology was not static and before its capture of Kabul, members of the Taliban talked about stepping aside once a government of "good Muslims" took power and law and order were restored. The decision making process of the Taliban in Kandahar was modeled on the Pashtun tribal council (jirga), together with what was believed to be the early Islamic model. Since 2004, the predominantly Pashtun movement has re-emerged and mounted an effective insurgency against Western forces and the Afghan government. Facing rising international and domestic pressure, Pakistan's military began a campaign against them widely seen as a test of Pakistan's resolve to tackle the insurgency.

I am very grateful to Mr. Pranav Gupta, Director of MD Publications Pvt Ltd, New Delhi, for his kind cooperation and support for this book.

N K Verma

CONTENTS

Vol. 2

Vol. 1

8

The Taliban and the World

Adding to their unpopularity, the Taliban decided in May to force Hindus living in Afghanistan to wear a distinctive sign on their clothing. The recent UN Security Council embargo has increased the regime's isolation, but its full force is being felt by the Afghan people who are also suffering from an unprecedented drought. To make matters worse, the Taliban have responded to the sanctions by suspending talks with the opposition. Ahmad Shah Massoud, one of its most prominent leaders, received expressions of support in Europe in April. Yet western policy towards Afghanistan remains deeply ambiguous.

Despite all the high-sounding words about human rights and a negotiated solution, western policy towards Afghanistan, led by Washington, has two contradictory themes: let the Taliban win and punish Afghanistan by isolating it. The Soviet withdrawal in 1989 and that of the Kabul regime in 1992 greatly reduced Afghanistan's importance on the world stage. Between 1992 and 1996 the main external players in the civil war were regional powers: Pakistan, Iran and Russia. In consequence, in 1994, the conflict resulted in the emergence of the Taliban, an extreme fundamentalist movement originating in the south of the country. Significant military aid from Pakistan and a degree of popular support enabled them to take all the towns and cities, not least Kabul in September 1996.

The regime's countless human rights violations have provoked international outcry, especially against the treatment of women and the destruction of the giant statues of Buddha at Bamiyan. The United States was, however, initially favourable to the Taliban, and Robin Rafael, then US under-secretary of state, welcomed their taking of Kabul in September 1996 as a "positive step". But contrary to popular belief, US support was not directly related to US oil company Unocal's plans to build a gas pipeline across Afghanistan, linking Pakistan and Turkmenistan.

The usual alignment of Washington's Afghan policy with that of Pakistan and a desire to back the country's reunification seem more convincing hypotheses. Support for the Taliban ceased because of the presence in Afghanistan of Osama bin Laden, an Islamic billionaire from Saudi Arabia, accused of several attacks against US interests. The Kabul regime's human rights violations played only a marginal role in the policy reversal. The bombing of the Islamists' training camps in Afghanistan in reprisal for the attacks on US embassies in east Africa in August 1998 marked the start of this change in direction.

Paradoxically, that operation was the reason why bin Laden was not extradited, for it made him a popular symbol of resistance against American imperialism, especially in Pakistan and the Gulf. But for all that, the US has not given aid of any significance to the opposition dominated by Ahmad Shah Massoud. And the only strategy that might have been effective, putting pressure on Pakistan, was ruled out. The western countries allowed Islamabad to continue its direct intervention and the Taliban prevailed over Massoud.

Last summer several thousand soldiers of the Pakistani regular army were sent to the front; their presence proved decisive in the taking of Taloqan, a small town that Massoud had controlled since 1986 and whose loss is a direct threat to his supply lines between Panjshir and Tadjikistan. The western countries failed to condemn this known and proven presence - for example, before the United Nations Security Council -

even though the opposition is still recognised as the legitimate government in Afghanistan. Why was this? Probably because the West was reluctant to further destabilise a nuclear state that was already experiencing chronic unrest.

An implicit agreement may have been reached after the Kargil crisis to give Pakistan a free hand in Afghanistan in return for a degree of moderation in Kashmir. In addition the US is losing interest in the situation, seeking only to eliminate bin Laden. Here we see the perverse nature of the western position: the more the Taliban gain ground, the less they are included in the political game. The country has been isolated, by sanctions in particular, in the same way as Iraq. After the Taliban took control of Kabul, international recognition was made conditional on progress in three areas: human rights, eradication of drugs and the fight against terrorism.

The Taliban made progress on the least contentious of these, opium production, where they had remarkable success. The two others have, however, remained a dead letter. The Taliban have, in fact, refused to extradite bin Laden, suggesting instead that he appear before an Islamic court. They understand human rights as deriving from the sharia (Islamic law) of which they have a very rigid interpretation. They reject western pressure as illegitimate and politically motivated for, after all, the West recognises the Saudi regime.

The first sanctions were imposed, at US instigation, in November 1999 after the Taliban refused to hand over bin Laden. The measures were designed primarily to ban the national airline Ariana from making international flights, freeze Taliban assets abroad and prohibit investments. They failed to have the desired effect, but their economic and psychological impact on the population was appreciable. Then new sanctions came into force at the start of this year. Acting in the US national interest alone, the Security Council has taken no account of the global context of the crisis or of the drought afflicting the country.

The consequence (or is it the purpose?) of the sanctions is therefore to punish the Afghan population. Sanctions make life even more difficult for civilians, discredit those Afghans who want to modernise the country (they are deemed to be foreign agents), and reinforce the xenophobic and fundamentalist currents that have grown strong since the start of the war. But the question is not so much whether the Taliban are guilty of human rights violations - there is consensus on that point - but how to respond. Sanctions and the regime's growing isolation are incapable of bringing about positive change; instead they make it ever more radical.

REJECTING THE INTERNATIONAL COMMUNITY

The Taliban are, in fact, convinced that they will not gain international recognition. The closure of their representation in New York showed that the US was no longer interested in talking to them. Moreover, the fact that sanctions were proposed by Washington and Moscow was seen as a provocation. The western countries' feeble response to UN requests for aid for the million people displaced by the drought is increasing their physical and psychological isolation. In this context, the destruction of the Bamiyan statues was not a religious act but a sign of political radicalisation. The Taliban used this media coup to express their rejection of the international community.

The first consequence of this policy of isolation has been the de facto abandonment of a negotiated solution. That would involve finding a political compromise which, to be acceptable, would have to reflect the balance of forces on the ground. That in turn would mean accepting that the Taliban are the dominant political player, with Massoud becoming a minority partner in a united government. But the US has ruled this out. The Vendrell mission was therefore doomed to failure before it even began. And in the absence of talks, Massoud's trip to Europe in April this year and the military aid he is receiving from France will achieve little more than to further harden the Taliban's attitude against the western countries, with a real risk of reprisals against the French non-governmental organisations (NGOs) working on the ground.

Many experts have justified this strategy of non-negotiation by maintaining that the Taliban were merely a transient, tribal phenomenon outside of society or that civil society was capable of providing an alternative political solution. Following the UN dogma that "there is no military solution", most thought that time was on Massoud's side. Taliban advances and their level of organisation were systematically under-estimated while the opposition's military capacity and political backing were overrated. The Taliban will not collapse spontaneously because they do, in fact, enjoy support within the country and they are sufficiently well organised to maintain control of a country deeply disrupted by 20 years of civil war. Further, Massoud's disparate coalition ceased to be a political alternative several years ago.

In the absence of a negotiated solution, there are two possible scenarios. Greater military and diplomatic support for Massoud together with pressure on Pakistan could prolong the war almost indefinitely. Massoud would remain locked in the mountains of the northwest, while the Taliban controlled most of the rest of the country. A hypothetical reconquest of the north by Massoud would only complicate matters because the coalition of commanders and parties making up the opposition is too divided to survive even limited success. The alternative outcome is that the Taliban will ultimately take the Panjshir valley. They will consider themselves to have beaten the western powers and the Russians, which will not dispose them to compromise with the international community.

If the country closes up even further, the NGOs - the only foreign presence in Afghan society and the main source of eyewitness accounts - could be forced to withdraw. US strategy has therefore helped further to destabilise and radicalise the crisis. Can Europe offer a different policy? The lifting of sanctions combined with strong diplomatic pressure on Pakistan could halt the Taliban advance and get the two sides talking again. The other aspect to the strategy would be massive investment, through the NGOs in particular, to try and meet certain social needs - education in particular - thus in the medium term encouraging the emergence of new elites.

After suffering a series of post-9/11 attacks by U.S.-led NATO forces, the Taliban's reign of terror and brutality in Afghanistan seemed inactive. But since then, the Taliban has not only re-emerged as a bigger challenge for NATO forces, it has also extended its sphere of influence in Pakistan. Tehrik-i-Taliban, the main Taliban group in Pakistan, is not just a militant organization, it is an ideological movement. Supporting the Taliban does not require that people have rocket launchers strapped to their shoulders or Kalashnikovs in their hands. Taliban ideologues are not only fighters; they work white-collar jobs all over Pakistan.

Former President General Parvez Musharraf addressed this when he suspended the Chief Justice of the Supreme Court, Iftikhar Choudhary. General Musharraf stated that the Supreme Court was creating hurdles in the implementation of government decisions-decisions that were necessary to contain terrorism in Pakistan. It was Musharraf who carried out "Operation Sunrise" in 2007 at Lal Masjid (Red Mosque), a complex used to spread Taliban ideology. During that operation the entire world witnessed a confrontation between the security forces of Pakistan and people in religious costumes armed with modern weapons. On paper, Lal Masjid functioned as a *madrassa* and a charitable organization, but in fact it had become a shelter for terrorists.

In the same operation, people also saw the chief of the mosque, Abdul Aziz, try to escape security forces by veiling himself alongside a group of women. Security forces held Aziz, while his brother was killed during the same operation. Now Pakistan has a civilian government. In March, former Prime Minister Nawaz Sharif tried to hit multiple targets with one arrow by organizing the Long March. He demonstrated his political might to President Asif Ali Zardari, built his image in the judiciary of Pakistan, and got Justice Iftikhar Choudhary reinstated along with other judges who were suspended during the Musharraf regime.

After this reinstatement, among the judicial verdicts, which are coming out now, was the quashing of the disqualification of Sharif brothers for contesting elections. Another was the release of Abdul Aziz, the chief of Lal Masjid. One might ask how a common, secular person's view of the judiciary might be affected by this decision. The Pakistan army is now fighting the Taliban on the Afghan border, but the protests in many cities of Pakistan against this operation reveal something else. After three decades, the leaderships of both Pakistan and the United States have admitted that the C.I.A. and the I.S.I. (Pakistan's intelligence agency) had a role, albeit indirect, in the creation and strengthening of Taliban.

This is evidence in itself that Taliban is not specific to a particular set of people in a single area or occupation. Rather, its presence can be found in religious houses, government offices, courts, political organizations, as well as among the security forces. Recently there were suicide bombings in Lahore and Peshawar in retaliation of army operations against the Taliban in Swat valley. Prior to this, Pakistan faced uncounted terror attacks. While Benazir Bhutto died in such an attack, there were also assassination attempts on Musharraf and Nawaz Sharif. President Zardari and the Prime Minister Yousuf Raza Gilani have also received death threats.

Without local support and patronization, such frequent threats and incidents would not be possible. Tehrik-i-Taliban wants to control the whole of Pakistan. For this, it is soliciting support from fundamentalist religious forces. Its long-term goal is to enforce Shariah law, which at one point was enforced in the Swat Valley in a pact with the Pakistan government before being broken down. Pakistan is passing through a critical juncture. Pakistani leadership is presently facing many challenges, ranging from the activities of the Taliban in Afghanistan to Tehrik-i-Taliban and other terrorist organizations active in Pakistan.

The danger lies not merely in the training camps and weapons of these networks, but in the "love" for the Taliban among the fundamentalists and extremists in Pakistan. The military effort of the Pakistan army, with U.S. backing, may be able to beat back Taliban forces, but until the Taliban ideology has been eradicated, an end to the battle is nowhere in sight. To make any long-term ground, the Pakistan government and army need to find a way to address the virus that has common, white-collared people promoting the interests of the Taliban.

OPIUM AND THE TALIBAN

U.N. drug control officers said the Taliban religious militia has nearly wiped out opium production in Afghanistan - once the world's largest producer - since banning poppy cultivation last summer. A 12-member team from the U.N. Drug Control Program spent two weeks searching most of the nation's largest opium-producing areas and found so few poppies that they do not expect any opium to come out of Afghanistan this year. "We are not just guessing. We have seen the proof in the fields," said Bernard Frahi, regional director for the U.N. program in Afghanistan and Pakistan. He laid out photographs of vast tracts of land cultivated with wheat alongside pictures of the same fields taken a year earlier - a sea of blood-red poppies.

A State Department official said all the information the United States has received so far indicates the poppy crop had decreased, but he did not believe it was eliminated. Afghanistan produced nearly 4,000 tons of opium, about 75 per cent of the world's supply, U.N. officials said. Opium - the milky substance drained from the poppy plant - is converted into heroin and sold in Europe and North America. The 1999 output was a world record for opium production, the United Nations said - more than all other countries combined, including the "Golden Triangle," where the borders of Thailand, Laos and Myanmar meet.

Mullah Mohammed Omar, the Taliban's supreme leader, banned poppy growing before the November planting season and augmented it with a religious edict making it contrary to the tenets of Islam. The Taliban, which has imposed a strict brand of Islam in the 95 per cent of Afghanistan it controls, has set fire to heroin laboratories and jailed farmers until they agreed to destroy their poppy crops. The U.N. surveyors, who completed their search this week, crisscrossed Helmand, Kandahar, Urzgan and Nangarhar provinces and parts of two others - areas responsible for 86 per cent of the opium produced in Afghanistan last year, Frahi said in an interview. They covered 80 per cent of the land in those provinces that last year had been awash in poppies.

They found poppies growing on barely an acre here and there, Frahi said. The rest - about 175,000 acres - was clean. "We have to look at the situation with careful optimism," said Sandro Tucci of the U.N. Office for Drug Control and Crime Prevention in Vienna, Austria. He said indications are that no poppies were planted this season and that, as a result, there hasn't been any production of opium - but that officials would keep checking. The State Department counternarcotics official said the department would make its own estimate of the poppy crop. Information received so far suggests there will be a decrease, but how much is not yet clear, he said, speaking on condition of anonymity.

"We do not think by any stretch of the imagination that poppy cultivation in Afghanistan has been eliminated. But we, like the rest of the world, welcome positive news." The Drug Enforcement Administration declined to comment. No U.S. government official can enter Afghanistan because of security concerns stemming from the presence of suspected terrorist Osama bin Laden. Poppies are harvested in March and April, which is why the survey was done now. Tucci said it would have been impossible for the poppies to have been harvested already.

The areas searched by the U.N. surveyors are the most fertile lands under Taliban control. Other areas, though they are somewhat fertile, have not traditionally been poppy growing areas and farmers are struggling to raise any crops at all because of severe drought. The rest of the land held by the Taliban is mountainous or desert, where poppies could not grow. Karim Rahimi, the U.N. drug control liaison in Jalalabad, capital of Nangarhar province, said farmers were growing wheat or onions in fields where they once grew poppies.

"It is amazing, really, when you see the fields that last year were filled with poppies and this year there is wheat," he said. The Taliban enforced the ban by threatening to arrest village elders and mullahs who allowed poppies to be grown. Taliban soldiers patrolled in trucks armed with rocket-propelled grenade launchers. About 1,000 people in Nangarhar who tried to defy the ban were arrested and jailed until they agreed to destroy their crops.

Signs throughout Nangarhar warn against drug production and use, some calling it an "illicit phenomenon." Another reads: "Be drug free, be happy." Poppies grew on 12,600 acres of land in Nangarhar province. According to the U.N. survey, poppies were planted on only 17 acres there this season and all were destroyed by the Taliban. "The Taliban have done their work very seriously," Frahi said. But the ban has badly hurt farmers in one of the world's poorest countries, shattered by two decades of war and devastated by drought.

Ahmed Rehman, who shares less than three acres in Nangarhar with his three brothers, said the opium he produced last year on part of the land brought him $1,100. This year, he says, he will be lucky to get $300 for the onions and cattle feed he planted on the entire parcel. "Life is very bad for me this year," he said. "Last year I was able to buy meat and wheat and now this year there is nothing."

But Rehman said he never considered defying the ban. "The Taliban were patrolling all the time. Of course I was afraid. I did not want to go to jail and lose my freedom and my dignity," he said, gesturing with dirt-caked hands.

Shams-ul-Haq Sayed, an officer of the Taliban drug control office in Jalalabad, said farmers need international aid. "This year was the most important for us because growing poppies was part of their culture, and the first years are always the most difficult," he said. Tucci said discussions are under way on how to help the farmers. Western diplomats in Pakistan have suggested the Taliban is simply trying to drive up the price of opium they have stockpiled. The State Department official also said Afghanistan could do more by destroying drug stockpiles and heroin labs and arresting producers and traffickers.

Frahi dismissed that as "nonsense" and said it is drug traffickers and shopkeepers who have stockpiles. Two pounds of opium worth $35 last year are now worth as much as $360, he said. Mullah Amir Mohammed Haqqani, the Taliban's top drug official in Nangarhar, said the ban would remain regardless of whether the Taliban received aid or international recognition. "It is our decree that there will be no poppy cultivation. It is banned forever in this country," he said. "Whether we get assistance or not, poppy growing will never be allowed again in our country.

THE CIA, BIN LADEN, AND THE TALIBAN

The U.S. war on Afghanistan is a brutal attack on a country that has already been almost destroyed by more than 20 years of foreign invasion and civil war.' The Soviet occupation, which lasted from 1979 to 1989, left more than a million people dead. Millions still live in refugee camps More than 500,000 orphans are disabled. Ten million land mines still litter the country, killing an average of 90 people per month. At 43 years, life expectancy in Afghanistan is on average 17 years lower than that for people in other developing countries. The countryside is devastated and is currently experiencing a severe drought, with 7.5 million people threatened with starvation.

The death and destruction wrought by the U.S. bombing campaign-and the cut off of food aid deliveries it has caused-have already killed hundreds and produced thousands more refugees scrambling to escape into Pakistan. But not only is Washington attacking one of the poorest countries in the world, past U.S. government actions are in no small part responsible for the current situation in Afghanistan. The Bush administration claims to be targeting Osama bin Laden, who it says masterminded the September 11 terror attacks on the World Trade Center and the Pentagon (even though it has offered no concrete evidence to back up this accusation), and Afghanistan's Taliban government, which is sheltering him.

But as the Economist magazine noted soon after September 11, " [U.S.] policies in Afghanistan a decade and more ago helped to create both Osama bin Laden and the fundamentalist Taliban regime that shelters him." An examination of this history will reveal the extent to which U.S. foreign policy is based on hypocrisy, realpolitik, and the short-term pursuit of narrow interests.

BEFORE THE RUSSIANS INVADED

Modern Afghanistan was created in the nineteenth century as a buffer state between the Russian and British empires as they played their "great game" in the region. This historical circumstance, coupled with the country's forbidding mountainous terrain, not only made it difficult for imperialist countries to conquer Afghanistan (it did not undergo colonial rule), but also resulted in little economic development. The country contains many different ethnic groups. The Pashtuns-from whom Afghanistan's traditional rulers have come-constitute 52 per cent of the population.

The Hazaras are 19 per cent of the population. The Tajiks in the north constitute 21 per cent; Uzbeks, also in the north, 5 per cent. About 85 per cent of Afghans are Sunni Muslims, and about 15 per cent, among the Hazaras, are Shia Muslims. Afghanistan survived as a medieval island in the modern world, characterized by backwardness and extreme poverty. In the postwar period, some changes began to occur as a result of foreign aid from the USSR and, to a lesser extent, the U.S., which were vying for influence during the Cold War. Power shifted toward the state, and an educated middle class began to emerge. But industry still barely existed.

In 1973, following a severe drought, King Zaher's cousin Daud overthrew Zaher's corrupt and repressive regime and declared a republic. But government corruption increased and promised modernization did not take place. Meanwhile, Daud began to collaborate more closely with the Shah of Iran. Lower-level officials and members of the middle class grew increasingly discontented. In April 1978, as Daud attempted to move against his opponents on the left, he was overthrown and killed by army officers sympathetic to the pro-Soviet People's Democratic Party of Afghanistan (PDPA).

Following the coup, a broad ruling coalition was set up, controlled by the Khalq, one of the PDPA's two factions. Nur Mohammad Taraki, a well-known novelist, became president. Within a few months, however, the Khalq pushed Barbrak Karmal and other members of the rival Parcham faction out of the government. Karmal was made ambassador to Prague, and other Parchami were also given diplomatic posts. The new government lacked any social base outside Kabul, and its program of reforms soon provoked a popular backlash. The Kabul regime was completely isolated from the mass of the population in the countryside:

> [They] had neither survey information nor local leaders with knowledge of actual conditions in the countryside. In short, it would have been virtually impossible for them to devise a successful land-reform program. As it was, their reforms were implemented by blundering and often brutal officials from the city who dropped into the countryside by parachute.

Rebellion and resistance started to spread around the country. The resistance was spontaneous, but soon came to be led by an alliance of conservative Islamic groups who referred to themselves as "majahideen" (holy warriors). By the spring of 1979, rebellion had spread to most of the country's 29 provinces. On March 24, a garrison of soldiers in Herat killed a group of Soviet advisers (and their families) who had ordered Afghan troops to fire on antigovernment demonstrators. From this point, the regime was no longer merely isolated from peasants in the countryside, but divided by open hostility from an overwhelming majority of all the people. The regime had no choice now but to crush much of the population.... [Prime Minister Hafizullah] Amin's secret police and a repressive civilian police force went into action across Afghanistan, and army troops were sent into the countryside to subdue "feudal" villagers.

Government repression was severe. "Mass arrests were commonly followed by torture and execution without trial.

Police terror was common in the city as well as the countryside, where virtually all social groups joined in the rebellion." The rebels' tactics were equally brutal. The Washington Post reported that the mujahideen liked to "torture victims by first cutting off their noses, ears, and genitals, then removing one slice of skin after another." As the situation got out of control, the Soviets advised Taraki to dismiss Amin, reunite with Parcham, and adopt a policy of "democratic nationalism."

But Amin got wind of the plan and arrested Taraki in September, assassinating him soon afterward. Amin was now in the position of publicly accusing the Russians of plotting to overthrow the Afghan government while being totally dependent on Soviet military and economic support. In December, hard-liners in Moscow decided that Amin had to go. They believed that he could be removed by a dramatic show of force and quietly replaced by Karmal. On December 27, a force of 5,000 Soviet troops advanced on Kabul, but Amin refused to leave office quietly and fought back.

On December 28, " [a]fter twelve hours of bitter combat with Soviet forces at the presidential palace, Amin was killed, along with 2,000 loyal members of his armed forces." Having killed the man whom they claimed had invited them into the country, the Russians proclaimed Karmal to be president and flew him back from Moscow. Within a few days, the number of Soviet troops in Afghanistan had reached 80,000. The figure later climbed to more than 100,000. What was to be nearly a decade of Russian occupation had begun.

THE CIA'S ANTICOMMUNIST JIHAD

President Jimmy Carter immediately declared that the invasion jeopardized vital U.S. interests, because the Persian Gulf area was "now threatened by Soviet troops in Afghanistan. But the Carter administration's public outrage at Russian intervention in Afghanistan was doubly duplicitous. Not only was it used as an excuse for a program of increased military expenditure that had in fact already begun, but the U.S. had in fact been aiding the mujahideen for at least the previous six months, with precisely the hope of provoking a Soviet response. Former CIA director Robert Gates later admitted in his memoirs that aid to the rebels began in June 1979.

In a candid 1998 interview, Zbigniew Brezinski, Carter's national security adviser, confirmed that U.S. aid to the rebels began before the invasion:

According to the official version of history, CIA aid to the mujahideen began during 1980, that is to say, after the Soviet army invaded Afghanistan [in] December 1979. But the reality, secretly guarded until now, is completely otherwise: indeed, it was July 3, 1979, that President Carter signed the first directive for secret aid to the opponents of the pro-Soviet regime in Kabul. And that very day, I wrote a note to the president in which I explained to him that in my opinion this aid was going to induce a Soviet military intervention.... We didn't push the Russians to intervene, but we knowingly increased the probability that they would....

That secret operation was an excellent idea. It had the effect of drawing the Russians into the Afghan trap.... The day that the Soviets officially crossed the border, I wrote to President Carter: We now have the opportunity of giving to the USSR its Vietnam War." The Carter administration was well aware that in backing the mujahideen it was supporting forces with reactionary social goals, but this was outweighed by its own geopolitical interests. In August 1979, a classified State Department report bluntly asserted that "the United States' larger interest...would be served by the demise of the Taraki-Amin regime, despite whatever setbacks this might mean for future social and economic reforms in Afghanistan."

That same month, in a stunning display of hypocrisy, State Department spokesperson Hodding Carter piously announced that the U.S. "expect[s] the principle of nonintervention to be respected by all parties in the area, including the Soviet Union." The Russian invasion in December was the signal for U.S. support to the Afghan rebels to increase dramatically. Three weeks after Soviet tanks rolled into Kabul, Carter's secretary of defense, Harold Brown, was in Beijing arranging for a weapons transfer from the Chinese to the CIA-backed Afghani troops mustered in Pakistan.

The Chinese, who were generously compensated for the deal, agreed and even consented to send military advisers. Brown worked out a similar arrangement with Egypt to buy $15 million worth of weapons. "The U.S. contacted me," [then-Egyptian president] Anwar Sadat recalled shortly before his assassination [in 1981]. "They told me, 'Please open your stores for us so that we can give the Afghans the armaments they need to fight.' And I gave them the armaments. The transport of arms to the Afghans started from Cairo on U.S. planes." By February 1980, the Washington Post reported that the mujahideen was receiving arms coming from the U.S. government.

The objective of the intervention, as spelled out by Brezinski, was to trap the Soviets in a long and costly war designed to drain their resources, just as Vietnam had bled the United States. The high level of civilian casualties that this would certainly entail was considered but set aside. According to one senior official, "The question here was whether it was morally acceptable that, in order to keep the Soviets off balance, which was the reason for the operation, it was permissible to use other lives for our geopolitical interests." Carter's CIA director Stansfield Turner answered the question: "I decided I could live with that."

According to Representative Charles Wilson, a Texas Democrat, There were 58,000 dead in Vietnam and we owe the Russians one.... I have a slight obsession with it, because of Vietnam. I thought the Soviets ought to get a dose of it.... I've been of the opinion that this money was better spent to hurt our adversaries than other money in the Defense Department budget.

The mujahideen consisted of at least seven factions, who often fought amongst themselves in their battle for territory and control of the opium trade. To hurt the Russians, the U.S. deliberately chose to give the most support to the most extreme groups. A disproportionate share of U.S. arms went to

Gulbuddin Hekmatyar, "a particularly fanatical fundamentalist and woman-hater."' According to journalist Tim Weiner, " [Hekmatyar's] followers first gained attention by throwing acid in the faces of women who refused to wear the veil. CIA and State Department officials I have spoken with call him 'scary,' 'vicious,' 'a fascist,' 'definite dictatorship material."

There was, though, a kind of method in the madness: Brezinski hoped not just to drive the Russians out of Afghanistan, but to ferment unrest within the Soviet Union itself. His plan, says author Dilip Hiro, was "to export a composite ideology of nationalism and Islam to the Muslim-majority Central Asian states and Soviet Republics with a view to destroying the Soviet order." Looking back in 1998, Brezinski had no regrets. "What was more important in the world view of history?... A few stirred-up Muslims or the liberation of Central Europe and the end of the Cold War."

With the support of Pakistan's military dictator, General Zia-ul-Haq, the U.S. began recruiting and training both mujahideen fighters from the 3 million Afghan refugees in Pakistan and large numbers of mercenaries from other Islamic countries. Estimates of how much money the U.S. government channeled to the Afghan rebels over the next decade vary, but most sources put the figure between $3 billion and $6 billion, or more. Whatever the exact amount, this was "the largest covert action program since World War II" - much bigger, for example, than Washington's intervention in Central America at the same time, which received considerably more publicity. According to one report:

The CIA became the grand coordinator: purchasing or arranging the manufacture of Soviet-style weapons from Egypt, China, Poland, Israel and elsewhere, or supplying their own; arranging for military training by Americans, Egyptians, Chinese and Iranians; hitting up Middle-Eastern countries for donations, notably Saudi Arabia which gave many hundreds of millions of dollars in aid each year, totaling probably more than a billion; pressuring and bribing Pakistan-with whom recent American relations had been very poor-to rent out its country as a military staging area and sanctuary; putting the Pakistani Director of Military Operations, Brigadier Mian Mohammad Afzal, onto the CIA payroll to ensure Pakistani cooperation.

When Ronald Reagan became president in 1981, he found the Democratic-controlled Congress eager to increase spending on the Afghan war. A congressional staffer told a reporter, "It was a windfall [for the new administration]. They'd faced so much opposition to covert action in Central America and here comes the Congress helping and throwing money at them, putting money their way and they say, 'Who are we to say no?" Aid to the mujahideen, who Reagan praised as "freedom fighters," increased, but initially Afghanistan was not a priority:

In the first years after the Reagan administration inherited the Carter program, the covert Afghan war "tended to be handled out of [CIA director William] Casey's back pocket," recalled Ronald Spiers, a former U.S. ambassador to Pakistan, the base of the Afghan rebels. Mainly from China's government, the CIA purchased assault rifles, grenade launchers, mines and SA-7 light antiaircraft weapons, and then arranged for shipment to Pakistan.... The amounts were significant-10,000 tons of arms and ammunition in 1983, according to [Pakistani General Mohammed] Yousaf-but a fraction of what they would be in just a few years.

In March 1985, the Reagan administration issued National Security Decision Directive 166,[29] a secret plan to escalate covert action in Afghanistan dramatically:

Abandoning a policy of simple harassment of Soviet occupiers, the Reagan team decided secretly to let loose on the Afghan battlefield an array of U.S. high technology and military expertise in an effort to hit and demoralize Soviet commanders and soldiers....

Beginning in 1985, the CIA supplied mujahideen rebels with extensive satellite reconnaissance data of Soviet targets on the Afghan battlefield, plans for military operations based on the satellite intelligence, intercepts of Soviet communications, secret communications networks for the rebels, delayed timing devices for tons of C-4 plastic explosives for urban sabotage, and sophisticated guerrilla attacks, long-range sniper rifles, a targeting device for mortars that was linked to a U.S. Navy satellite, wire-guided anti-tank missiles, and other equipment.

Between 1986 and 1989, the mujahideen were also provided with more than 1,000 state-of-the-art, shoulder-fired Stinger antiaircraft missiles. By 1987, the annual supply of arms had reached 65,000 tons, and a "ceaseless stream" of CIA and Pentagon officials were visiting Pakistani Inter-Services Intelligence (ISI) headquarters in Rawalpindi and helping to plan mujahideen operations:

At any one time during the Afghan fighting season, as many as 11 ISI teams trained and supplied by the CIA accompanied mujahideen across the border to supervise attacks, according to Yousaf and Western sources. The teams attacked airports, railroads, fuel depots, electricity pylons, bridges and roads....

CIA operations officers helped Pakistani trainers establish schools for the mujahideen in secure communications, guerrilla warfare, urban sabotage and heavy weapons. Although the CIA claimed that the purpose was to attack military targets, mujahideen trained in these techniques, and using chemical and electronic-delay bomb timers supplied by the U.S., carried out numerous car bombings and assassination attacks in Kabul itself.

BIN LADEN AND THE ARAB-AFGHANS

As well as training and recruiting Afghan nationals to fight the Soviets, the CIA permitted its ISI allies to recruit Muslim extremists from around the world. Pakistani journalist Ahmed Rashid reports:

Between 1982 and 1992, some 35,000 Muslim radicals from 43 Islamic countries in the Middle East, North and East Africa, Central Asia and the Far East would pass their baptism under fire with the Afghan mujahideen. Tens of thousands more foreign Muslim radicals came to study in the hundreds of new *madrassas* [religious schools] that Zia's military government began to fund in Pakistan and along the Afghan border. Eventually more than 100,000 Muslim radicals were to have direct contact with Pakistan and Afghanistan and be influenced by the jihad [against the USSR].

In camps near Peshawar and in Afghanistan, these radicals met each other for the first time and studied trained and fought together. It was the first opportunity for most of them to learn about Islamic movements in other countries, and they forged tactical and ideological links that would serve them well in the future. The camps became virtual universities for future Islamic radicalism. One of the first non-Afghan volunteers to join the ranks of the mujahideen was Osama bin Laden, a civil engineer and businessman from a wealthy construction family in Saudi Arabia, with close ties to members of the Saudi royal family.

Bin Laden recruited 4,000 volunteers from his own country and developed close relations with the most radical mujahideen leaders. He also worked closely with the CIA, raising money from private Saudi citizens. By 1984, he was running the Maktab al-Khidamar, an organization set up by the ISI to funnel "money, arms, and fighters from the outside world in the Afghan war."

Since September 11, CIA officials have been claiming they had no direct link to bin Laden. These denials lack credibility. Earlier this year, the trial of defendants accused of the 1998 U.S. embassy bombing in Kenya disclosed that the CIA shipped high-powered sniper rifles directly to bin Laden's operation in 1989. Even the Tennessee-based manufacturer of the rifles confirmed this. According to the Boston Globe, Some military analysts and specialists on the weapons trade say the CIA has spent years covering its tracks on its early ties to the Afghan forces.... Despite the CIA's denials, these experts say it was inevitable that the military training in guerrilla tactics and the vast reservoir of money and arms that the CIA provided in Afghanistan would have ended up helping bin Laden and his forces during the 1980s.

"In 1988, with U.S. knowledge, bin Laden created *Al Qaeda* (The Base): a conglomerate of quasi independent Islamic terrorist cells spread across at least 26 countries," writes Indian journalist Rahul Bhedi. "Washington turned a blind eye to Al-Qaeda, confident that it would not directly impinge on the U.S." After the Soviet withdrawal, however, bin Laden and thousands of other volunteers returned to their own countries:

Their heightened political consciousness made them realize that countries like Saudi Arabia and Egypt were just as much client regimes of the United States as the Najibullah regime [in Afghanistan] has been of Moscow.

In their home countries they built a formidable constituency-popularly known as "Afghanis"-who combined strong ideological convictions with the guerrilla skills they had acquired in Pakistan and Afghanistan under CIA supervision. Over the past 10 years, the "Afghani" network has been linked to terrorist attacks not only on U.S. targets, but also in the Philippines, Pakistan, Saudi Arabia, France, Tajikistan, Azerbaijan, China, Egypt, Algeria, Morocco, and elsewhere. "This is an insane instance of the chickens coming home to roost," one U.S. diplomat in Pakistan told the Los Angeles Times. "You can't plug billions of dollars into an anti-Communist jihad, accept participation from all over the world and ignore the consequences. But we did.

ROMANCING THE TALIBAN

As the Russians withdrew from Afghanistan in early 1989, American policymakers celebrated with champagne, while the country itself collapsed into virtual anarchy. Almost a quarter of the population was living in refugee camps and most of the country was in ruins. Different factions of the mujahideen struggled for power in the countryside, while the government of Muhammed Najibullah, the last Soviet-installed president controlled Kabul.

Eventually, in April 1992, Kabul fell to some of the mujahideen factions and Burhannudin Rabbani was de dared president, but civil war continued unabated. Hekmatyar in particular was dissatisfied with the new distribution of power. With his huge stock of U.S.-supplied weapons, he began an artillery and rocket assault on Kabul that lasted for almost three years, even after he was appointed prime minister in 1993. "The barrage...killed more than 10,000 Afghans [drove] hundreds of thousands into squalid refugee camps, created political chaos, and blocked millions of exiles from returning." The rest of the country disintegrated into isolated fiefdoms dominated by local warlords.

In 1994, a new group, the Taliban (Pashtun for "students"), emerged on the scene. Its members came from *madrassas* set up by the Pakistani government along the border and funded by the U.S., Britain, and the Saudis, where they had received theological indoctrination and military training. Thousands of young men-refugees and orphans from the war in Afghanistan-became the foot soldiers of this movement:

These boys were from a generation who had never seen their country at peace-an Afghanistan not at war with invaders and itself. They had no memories of their tribes, their elders, their neighbors nor the complex ethnic mix of peoples that made up their villages and their homeland. These boys were what the war had thrown up like the sea's surrender on the beach of history.

They were literally the orphans of war, the rootless and restless, the jobless and the economically deprived with little self-knowledge. They admired war because it was the only occupation they could possibly adapt to. Their simple belief in a messianic, puritan Islam which had been drummed into them by simple village mullahs was the only prop they could hold on to and which gave their lives some meaning. Untrained for anything, even the traditional occupations of their forefathers such as farming, herding or the making of handicrafts, they were what Karl Marx would have termed Afghanistan's lumpen proletariat.

With the aid of the Pakistani army, the Taliban swept across most of the exhausted country promising a restoration of order and finally capturing Kabul in September 1996. The

Taliban imposed an ultra-sectarian version of Islam, closely related to Wahhabism, the ruling creed in Saudi Arabia. Women have been denied education, health care, and the right to work. They must cover themselves completely when in public. Minorities have been brutally repressed. Even singing and dancing in public are forbidden. The Taliban's brand of extreme Islam had no historical roots in Afghanistan. The roots of the Taliban's success lay in 20 years of "jihad" against the Russians and further devastation wrought by years of internal fighting between the warlord factions.

Initially, villagers-especially the majority Pashtuns in the south who shared the Taliban's ethnicity-welcomed them as a force that might end the warfare and bring some order and peace to Afghanistan. Their lack of a social base within Afghanistan made them appear untainted by the factional warfare, and their moral purism made them appear above compromise. Before launching their war to conquer power, they first won some public support by appearing as the avenger against the warlords' raping of women and boys. Of course, they could not have risen so far and so fast without the financial and military backing of Pakistan.

The U.S. government was well aware of the Taliban's reactionary program, yet it chose to back their rise to power in the mid-1990s. The creation of the Taliban was "actively encouraged by the ISI and the CIA," according to Selig Harrison, an expert on U.S. relations with Asia. "The United States encouraged Saudi Arabia and Pakistan to support the Taliban, certainly right up to their advance on Kabul," adds respected journalist Ahmed Rashid. When the Taliban took power, State Department spokesperson Glyn Davies said that he saw "nothing objectionable" in the Taliban's plans to impose strict Islamic law, and Senator Hank Brown, chair of the Senate Foreign Relations Subcommittee on the Near East and South Asia, welcomed the new regime: "The good part of what has happened is that one of the factions at last seems capable of developing a new government in Afghanistan."

"The Taliban will probably develop like the Saudis. There

will be Aramco [the consortium of oil companies that controlled Saudi oil], pipelines, an emir, no parliament and lots of Sharia law. We can live with that," said another U.S. diplomat in 1997. The reference to oil and pipelines explains everything. Since the collapse of the USSR at the end of 1991, U.S. oil companies and their friends in the State Department have been salivating at the prospect of gaining access to the huge oil and natural gas reserves in the former Soviet republics bordering the Caspian Sea and in Central Asia. These have been estimated as worth $4 trillion.

The American Petroleum Institute calls the Caspian region "the area of greatest resource potential outside of the Middle East." And while he was still CEO of Halliburton, the world's biggest oil services company, Vice President Dick Cheney told other industry executives, "I can't think of a time when we've had a region emerge as suddenly to become as strategically significant as the Caspian." The struggle to control these stupendous resources has given rise to what Rashid has dubbed the "new Great Game," pitting shifting alliances of governments and oil and gas consortia against one another.

Afghanistan itself has no known oil or gas reserves, but it is an attractive route for pipelines leading to Pakistan, India, and the Arabian Sea. In the mid-1990s, a consortium led by the California-based Unocal Corporation proposed a $4.5 billion oil and gas pipeline from Turkmenistan through Afghanistan to Pakistan. But this would require a stable central government in Afghanistan itself. Thus began several years in which U.S. policy in the region centered on "romancing the Taliban." According to one report, in the months before the Taliban took power, former U.S. assistant secretary of state for South Asia Robin Raphel waged an intense round of shuttle diplomacy between the powers with possible stakes in the [Unocal] project.

"Robin Raphel was the face of the Unocal pipeline," said an official of the former Afghan government who was present at some of de meetings with her.... In addition to tapping new sources of energy, de [project] also suited a major U.S. strategic aim in the region: isolating its nemesis Iran and stifling a frequently mooted rival pipeline project backed by Teheran, experts said.

But Washington's initial enthusiasm for the Taliban's seizure of power provoked a hostile reaction from human rights and women's organizations in the United States. The Clinton administration quickly decided to take a more cautious public approach. Plans to send the U.S. ambassador to Pakistan on a visit to Kabul were canceled, and the State Department decided not to recognize the new regime immediately. Nevertheless, Unocal executive vice president Chris Taggart continued to maintain, "If the Taliban leads to stability and international recognition then it's positive."

Tacit U.S. support for the Taliban continued until 1998, when Washington blamed Osama bin Laden for the bombing of the U.S. embassies in Kenya and Tanzania and retaliated by launching cruise missiles at Bin Laden's alleged training camps in Afghanistan. The Taliban's refusals to extradite Bin Laden-not its atrocious human rights record-led to UN-imposed sanctions on the regime the following year. "Former Secretary of State Madeleine Albright used to say that she cared about the women suffering under the Taliban, but after the Taliban took over the U.S. accepted very few refugees," points out journalist Laura Flanders. "In '96 and '97 no Afghan refugees were admitted to the United States; in '98, only 88, in '99, some 360."

Whatever the U.S. government's current rhetoric about the repressive nature of the Taliban regime, its long history of intervention in the region has been motivated not by concern for democracy or human rights, but by the narrow economic and political interests of the U.S. ruling class. It has been prepared to aid and support the most retrograde elements if it thought a temporary advantage would be the result. Now Washington has launched a war against its former allies based on a strategic calculation that the Taliban can no longer be relied upon to provide a stable, U.S.-friendly government that can serve its strategic interests. No matter what the outcome, the war is certain to lay the grounds for more "blowback" in the future.

9

The United States and the Taliban

Afghanistan is currently undergoing a humanitarian catastrophe of tremendous proportions, to which the international community displays only what appears to be systematic indifference. To understand the crisis in Afghanistan it is particularly important to understand its historical causes. This is because the crisis is a direct result of self-interested American and Russian operations in the region. Afghanistan's coup of 1978 resulted in a new government headed by Nur Muhammad Taraki coming to power in the Afghan capital, Kabul. The coup d'etat that brought Taraki's party - the People's Democratic Party of Afghanistan (PDPA) - to power, had been precipitated by the previous government's arresting of almost the entire leadership of the PDPA.

This was an attempt to annihilate any viable opposition to the existing government, which was led by Muhammad Daud. The leader of the PDPA, Taraki, was then freed in an uprising by the lower ranks of the military, and within a day Daud and his government was overthrown, with Daud being killed in the process. In fact, many of the leaders of the PDPA had studied or received military training in the USSR; moreover, the Soviet Union had pressured the PDPA - which had split into two factions in 1967 - to reunite in 1977. The PDPA had therefore been the principal Soviet-orientated

Communist organisation in Afghanistan; the military coup of 1978 was thus effectively engineered by the USSR, which had significant leverage over the PDPA and its activities. Afghanistan subsequently became exclusively dependent on Soviet aid, unlike previous governments which had attempted to play off the US and USSR against one another, refraining from exclusive alignment with either.

The PDPA did go on to implement certain programmes of social development and reform, like the previous government - although these were primarily related to urban as opposed to rural areas. For example, the previous government under Daud had used foreign aid from both the USSR and the US (primarily the USSR) to build roads, schools and implement other development projects, thereby increasing the mobility of the country's people and products - not that this necessarily eliminated the severe problems faced by masses of the Afghan population. For instance, 5 per cent of Afghanistan's rural landowners still owned more than 45 per cent of arable land. A third of the rural people were landless labourers, sharecroppers or tenants, and debts to the landlords were a regular feature of rural life.

An indebted farmer ended up turning over half his annual crop to the moneylender. Female illiteracy was 96.3 per cent, while rural illiteracy of both sexes was 90.5 per cent. The Communist PDPA government under Taraki had similarly imposed some social programmes like Daud's government: It moved to remove both usury and inequalities in land-ownership and cancelled mortgage debts of agricultural labourers, tenants and small landowners. It established literacy programmes, especially for women, printing textbooks in many languages, training more teachers, building additional schools and kindergartens, and instituting nurseries for orphans. Once more, these policies should be understood in context with the fact that the government was established as the result of a violent military coup without any connection to the wishes of the majority of the Afghan people, and consequently did not engender their participation.

The PDPA's policies served to destroy even the state institutions established over the previous century, having constituted a stage in a revolutionary programme which the government had attempted to impose by force, not by the approval of the population. The new government, like previous governments, was essentially illegitimate, with no substantial representation of the Afghan population. It was, for example, responsible for arresting, torturing and executing both real and suspected enemies, setting off the first major refugee flows to neighbouring Pakistan. Such policies of repression and persecution, resulting in the killing of thousands as well as the forceful imposition of a Communist revolutionary programme that was oblivious to the sentiments of the majority of the Afghan masses, sparked off popular revolts led by local social and religious leaders - usually with no link to national political groups.

These broke out in different parts of the country in response to the government's atrocities. Furthermore, during the Soviet occupation, despite the modest 'modernising' policies that were primarily urban in character, the bifurcation of Afghan society and economy deepened greatly. The PDPA was therefore essentially a Communist dictatorship that was allied with the Soviet Union. This was unlike the previous government of Daud's, that was not exclusively allied to either of the superpowers (neither the US nor the USSR).

However, both the latter superpowers wished Afghanistan to remain within their respective spheres of influence, due to the traditional brand of political, economic and strategic interests. Their wishes resulted in one of the last brutal episodes of the Cold War: the Afghanistan war that began several months after the 1978 Saur coup, and that was a manifestation of the two superpowers' attempts to gain control of a region of very high geostrategic significance.

THE CIVIL WAR AND ITS IMPACT

Although the USSR had been interfering in Afghan affairs long before the US, it is worth noting that contrary to the conventional wisdom, the United States appears to have begun operations in Afghanistan before the full-fledged Soviet invasion. Former National Security Adviser under the Carter Administration, Zbigniew Brzezenski, has admitted that an American operation to infiltrate Afghanistan was launched long before Russia sent in its troops on 27 December 1979. Agence France Press reported that: "Despite formal denials, the United States launched a covert operation to bolster anti-Communist guerrillas in Afghanistan at least six months before the 1979 Soviet invasion of the country, according to a former top US official."

Brzezenski stated that "We actually did provide some support to the Mujahedeen before the invasion." "We did not push the Russians into invading, but we knowingly increased the probability that they would." He also bragged: "That secret operation was an excellent idea. The effect was to draw the Russians into the Afghan trap." In other words, the US appears to have been attempting to foster and manipulate unrest amongst various Afghan factions to destabilise the already unpopular Communist regime and bring the country under US sphere of influence. This included the recruitment of local leaders and warlords to form mercenary rebel groups, who would wage war against the Soviet-backed government, to institute a new regime under American control.

In December 1979, Russia intervened to reinforce its hegemony over Afghanistan, since the PDPA was, according to Brzezenski's testimony, being destabilised by a US operation to infiltrate Afghanistan that had commenced at a much earlier date. The US had therefore evidently also wished to bring this strategic region under its own hegemony. Anticipating this attempt by the US to destabilise the pro-Soviet PDPA and install a new pro-American regime in Afghanistan, Russia undertook a full-fledged invasion to keep the country under its own sphere of influence.

Afghan analyst Dr. Noor Ali observes of the ensuing US policy: "Following the invasion of Afghanistan by the former Soviet Union in late December 1979, hundreds of high ranking Afghan politicians and technocrats as well as army officers including generals entered into Pakistan with the hope of organizing the needed resistance to oppose the invader in order to liberate Afghanistan. Unfortunately and regrettably the US Government in collusion with Pakistan's leaders took abusive advantage of the opportunity so as to exploit it fully and by all manner of means to their own and exclusive illegitimate benefits and objectives, which had been threefold: (i) to rule out the creation of any responsible and independent Afghan organization among Afghans, interacting directly with Washington, to support Afghan resistance, (ii) to repulse the Red Army by using exclusively the blood of Afghans, and (iii) to make of Afghanistan a satellite if not an integrated part of Pakistan in return for Pakistani leaders' services, but in complete disregard to Afghan people's sovereignty and sacrifices."

The overall result was a brutal civil war manipulated by the two superpowers that drove 6 million Afghan people from their homes. By 1991-92, the US and the USSR finally reached an agreement that neither would continue to supply aid to any faction in Afghanistan. However, the numerous militant factions previously funded and armed by the US have been vying for supremacy. One of the armed Afghan factions funded by the CIA during this war was the Taliban, an apparently Islamic movement. With the departure of Soviet troops in 1989, these factions began vying with one another for supremacy, the Taliban eventually arising as the dominant force in Afghanistan. As a coherent politico-military faction or movement, the Taliban did not exist prior to October 1994, but were members of other factions such as Harakat-e Islami and Mohammad Nabi Mohammadi, or operated independently without a centralised command centre.

The ultimate result has been that post-Cold War Afghanistan has remained in a state of anarchical civil war up to this day, with the Taliban having emerged as the most powerful faction in the country by the mid-1990s. One can therefore conclude that as a result of a string of proxy wars, that were the result of manipulation by both the US and the former USSR, Afghanistan has been plunged into a state of perpetual humanitarian catastrophe. Development specialist Dr. J. W. Smith, founder and Director of Research for the California-based Institute for Economic Democracy, summarises the humanitarian catastrophe of Afghanistan, commenting on Brzezinski's admission of the US operation in the country: "Afghanistan was also a US destabilization.

In 1998, Zbigniew Brzezinski, President Carter's National Security Advisor... admitted that covert US intervention began long before the USSR sent in troops... Take note of what was 'an excellent idea': A country rapidly developing and moving towards modernization was politically and economically shattered, almost 2 million Afghans were killed, the most violent and anti-American of the groups supported by the CIA are now the leaders of Afghanistan, these religious fundamentalists set human rights back centuries to the extent they are even an embarrassment to neighboring Muslim fundamentalists, and both Muslim and non-Muslim governments within the region fear destabilization through Taleban fundamentalism."

Smith fails, however, to take into account the illegitimacy of the Soviet puppet regime and its policies of repression. The fact is that both the US and USSR bear responsibility for having attempted to control Afghanistan, thereby shattering the country in the process; if these powers had merely attempted to aid the Afghan people to develop their country, rather than enforce hegemony over the country for their own self-interested strategic designs, there would obviously have been no such humanitarian crisis. Thus, as Barnette Rubin of the Council on Foreign Relations reports: "Despite the end of the proxy war, the massive arms supplies still held by both the Soviet-aided army and the Islamic resistance fighters (backed by the US, with help from Pakistan, Saudi Arabia and others) continue to fuel the fighting."

By August 1992, ongoing rocketing by the forces of Gulbuddin Hekmatyar - a one-time favourite of Pakistan and the US - had driven out half a million civilians from the capital city Kabul and killed over 2,000 people. HRW reports that by the end of the year, "international interest in the conflict had all but vanished and Afghanistan appeared to be on the brink of a humanitarian catastrophe", while the US-Pakistani favourite masterminded the escalation of terror, "carried out with US -and Saudi - financed weaponry". The Economist reported that by summer 1993 about 30,000 people had been killed and 100,000 wounded in the capital. The bombardment of civilian targets has continued ever since, with casuality and refugee figures rising rapidly and steadily.

It is important to note that the Taliban and the forces of Hekmatyar are two separate factions. Moreover, it should also be emphasised that Hekmatyar and his forces are not solely responsible for the deaths of thousands in Kabul and the city's destruction. While Hekmatyar's forces may have killed and destroyed more than other groups, factions under Ahmed Shah Masoud, Burhanuddiin Rabbani, Abdul Rashid Dostum, Abdul Ali Mazari and Abdul Karim Khalili are equally responsible for the violence that raged between 1992 and 1996 in Kabul.

Due to the ravages of such ongoing war, Kabul has been without municipal water and electricity since 1994. This state of affairs has not improved by the time of writing. Trade is frequently blockaded and subjected to extortionate 'taxes' by local power holders. Nearly everywhere a new generation is emerging with minimal education in a land infested with landmines, due to which thousands of civilians continue to be killed or maimed. The UN reports that the socio-economic conditions of the population are amongst the worst in the world. The investment of previous governments into schools, roads and hospitals has been reduced to near insignificance. Literacy rates are at an extreme low, with estimates showing that they have plummeted to as low as 4 per cent for women. Healthcare is rudimentary at best, with many being without access to even the basics.

Every year thousands of children die from malnutrition and respiratory infections, and maternal mortality rates are one of the highest in the world. Irrigation systems and the agricultural sector have been neglected and destroyed. Today's Afghanistan is plagued by a perpetual orgy of destruction, impoverishment and repression. One to two million Afghans have been killed. There remain over 2 million Afghan refugees in Iran and Pakistan, making Afghans the largest single refugee group in the entire world. The Taliban that now dominates Afghanistan has instituted a 'system' in which much of the population is denied their social and human rights; torture, arbitrary detention, mass killings and ongoing warfare are the norm; the masses remain embedded in growing poverty; the rulers falsely legitimise their actions under the guise of Islam.

Poverty is now endemic. According to the UN Office for the Coordination of Humanitarian Affairs: "Millions of Afghans have little or no access to food through commercial markets, just as their access to food through self-production has been severely undermined by drought. The purchasing power of most Afghans has been seriously eroded by the absence of employment. About 85 per cent of Afghanistan's estimated 21.9 million people are directly dependent on agriculture... The agricultural infrastructure has been severely damaged due to war and irrigation facilities are in urgent need of rehabilitation".

Afghanistan also has one of the worst records on education in the world. The UNICEF estimates that only 4-5 per cent of primary aged children receive a broad based schooling - for secondary and higher education, the picture is worse. As Kate Clark reports: "Twenty years of war has meant the collapse of everything. Both sides in the long running civil war prefer to spend money on fighting... However, the desire for schooling runs deep in Afghanistan, even among the uneducated. But the chances of getting a decent education are very slim. A whole generation of children is losing out, prompting questions about where this leaves the future of this devastated country." Indeed, there is no doubt that the Taliban has been ruling Afghanistan with an iron fist. The faction's policies are repressive and involve the perpetration of countless human rights abuses.

However, as the international Muslim newsmagazine *Crescent International* rightly observes, "criticism of the Taliban, whether it comes from non-Muslims or Muslims, is often heavily overlaid with prejudices or political interests." It is therefore important to we ensure that facts are separated from propaganda. Nevertheless, Crescent admits that the Taliban regime is undoubtedly highly repressive, to the extent that therein "the phrase 'Islamic justice' is used as a synonym for tyranny." Numerous reports of "draconian restrictions on women" being enforced falsely in the name of Islam unfortunately reveal harsh realities. "Men responsible for enforcing public decency are said to beat women in the streets who show their faces or ankles. Most women are 'not allowed to work'. They are forbidden to see male doctors, yet there are few female doctors available [to compensate]. Most girls'schools have been closed, and the only religious instruction is for girls who have not reached puberty."

AN ISLAMIC MOVEMENT

A full refutation of the notion that the Taliban is an Islamic movement would require an extensive discussion of Islamic principles based on authoritative scholars and sources, compared to the documented facts of Taliban policy. Unfortunately this important issue falls beyond the scope of this chapter, and so cannot be tackled here with the necessary depth. However, it may still be noted here that the Taliban's status as a genuinely Islamic movement is at the very least highly questionable – there are very few Muslim scholars who would agree that the policies discussed above constitute Islamic policies. As pointed out by former US Congressman Paul Findley – Chairman Emeritus of the Washington-based Council for National Interest and Chairman of the Illinois-based Human Relations Commission - the Taliban "calls itself 'Islamic', but its regulations directly violate some of the most cherished principles of the Islamic faith."

Indeed, most Muslim scholars do not ratify or condone Taliban-like repression or atrocities. For instance, the Pakistani newspaper, the *Daily Star*, reports that "Islamic scholars in neighbouring Pakistan say the Taliban's laws reflect tribal traditions more than Islamic tenets." Abdullahi An-Na'im, a Muslim and US-based legal scholar, challenges the Taliban claims that their edicts come from the Qu'ran. He writes, "Unless Muslims [condemn these policies and practices] from an Islamic point of view as well, the Taliban will get away with their false claim that these heinous crimes against humanity are dictated by Islam as a religion." Indeed, the Associated Press further reports the little known but important fact that while the "Taliban have imposed their harsh brand of Islamic Laws on the 90 per cent of Afghanistan they rule" in actual fact, "Islamic scholars elsewhere say that the Taliban's laws are based more on tribal traditions than the Koran, Islam's holy book."

In a useful study of Taliban policies in comparison with a wide-ranging survey of Islamic thought and culture, American journalist Robin Travis points out that "as to whether the Taliban's practice of Islam is the pure form of Islam, we can see that there is much debate on the interpretation of the Qur'an.... Thus far, we have been able to determine that there are many interpretations of the Qur'an and many definitions of the religious practice of Islam. What we can also see here, is that the majority of those who practice this religion, do not interpret the Qur'an as endorsing oppression and abuse of women." Travis thus concludes from her "research and discussion of the practice of the Islamic faith that the Taliban are practicing an extreme version of Islam, because other forms and practices do not include the oppression of women... The Taliban has clearly manipulated the Qu'ran to serve its own purposes in causing abuse and hardships on women."

The Muslim Women's League concurs with this analysis, observing that the "Taliban's insistence on secluding women from public life is a political maneuver disguised as 'Islamic' law. Before seizing power, Taliban manipulated and used the rights of women as tools to gain control of the country. To secure financial and political support, Taliban emulated authoritarian methods typical of many Middle Eastern countries. The Taliban's stand on the seclusion of women is not derived from Islam, but, rather, from a cultural bias found in suppressive movements throughout the region... The Qur'an and the examples of the first Muslim society give the Muslim Women's League a voice to state that the current manipulation of women to serve geo-political interests, in Afghanistan or elsewhere, is both unIslamic and inhumane."

A representative example of the Taliban's actual contempt for basic Islamic edicts is one of the numerous issues noted by the United Nations Special Rapporteur of the UN Commission on Human Rights, in Afghanistan: "The Special Rapporteur was informed by scholars that it was a religious obligation in Islam to acquire education and that deprivation of education constituted a disobedience of Islamic principles. The view was expressed that the motivations for banning female education on part of the Taliban were neither legal, financial or based on security but were probably politically motivated. One of the most serious consequences of the conflict in Afghanistan was the brain-drain of its educated people."

The authoritative UN report further confirmed: "It should be recalled that the Taliban have a highly idiosyncratic vision of Islam that has been disputed by numerous Sunni Islamic scholars as representing at best a tribal rural code of behaviour applied only in some parts of Afghanistan of which only one aspect is being exploited." Elsewhere, the report points out again that, "The Special Rapporteur heard persistent affirmations from qualified sources that the policies applied by the Taliban in the areas under their control did not constitute a correct interpretation of the Shariah (Islamic law) but were at best a narrow tribal and rural code of conduct in limited parts of Afghanistan." Of course, the repression of women in Afghanistan is not something that was solely introduced by the Taliban, but had existed long before the concrete existence of this faction. Nevertheless, Taliban rule certainly led to the exacerbation of this repression.

MISOGYNISM, GENOCIDE AND ETHNIC CLEANSING

When the Taliban marched into Kabul in 1996, its policies of repression were highlighted. Political opponents were executed without trial. Females were barred from schools and employment; the ban including up to 50,000 war widows who were the sole support of their families. Indeed, there have been endless reports concerning the mass oppression of women in Afghanistan by the Taliban, under the false guise of supposedly 'Islamic' tenets. While an increasing number of women are having to beg to survive and support their families, there have been many reported cases of forced marriages and prostitution; of women being forcefully taken from their homes, or forcefully separated from their husbands and moved to camps; of huge numbers of women throughout the country suffering from clinical depression due to unceasing confinement; and even of sexual assaults.

Radhika Coomaraswamy, the UN Special Rapporteur on Violence Against Women concluded: "Never have I seen a people suffering as much as in Afghanistan... The situation looks very bleak in terms of poverty, in terms of war, in terms of the rights of women." Coomaraswamy has concluded that discrimination against females is official Taliban policy, a veritable war on women which is "widespread, systematic and officially sanctioned." The facts have been documented extensively by numerous independent human rights organisations that have witnessed the impact of the Taliban directly and undertaken meticulous grassroots research.

It is worth quoting copiously from a survey conducted by the Physicians for Human Rights (PHR) to comprehend the scale of the crisis, utilising direct interviews with Afghan citizens and investigations on the ground. PHR reports that "One of the first edicts issued by the regime when it rose to power was to prohibit girls and women from attending school. Humanitarian groups initiated projects to replace through philanthropy what prior governments had afforded as a right to both sexes... On June 16, 1998, the Taliban ordered the closing of more than 100 privately funded schools where thousands of young women and girls were receiving training in skills that would have helped them support their families.

The Taliban issued new rules for nongovernmental organizations providing the schooling: education must be limited to girls up to the age of eight, and restricted to the *Qur'an*... PHR's researcher when visiting Kabul in 1998, saw a city of beggars - women who had once been teachers and nurses now moving in the streets like ghosts... selling every possession and begging so as to feed their children." The Taliban has thus "deliberately created such poverty by arbitrarily depriving half the population under its control of jobs, schooling, mobility, and health care. Such restrictions are literally life threatening to women and to their children. The Taliban's abuses are by no means limited to women.

Thousands of men have been taken prisoner, arbitrarily detained, tortured, and many killed and disappeared. Men are beaten and jailed for wearing beards of insufficient length (that of a clenched fist beneath the chin), are subjected to cruel and degrading conditions in jail... Men are also vulnerable to extortion, arrest, gang rape, and abuse in detention because of their ethnicity or presumed political views." PHR goes on to note that there are "extraordinarily high levels of mental stress and depression" in the country. 81 per cent of participants in the PHR survey "reported a decline in their mental condition. A large percentage of respondents met the diagnostic criteria for posttraumatic stress disorder (PTSD) (42%) (based on the *Diagnostical and Statistical Manual of Mental Disorders, Fourth Edition*) and major depression (97%), and also demonstrated significant symptoms of anxiety (86%) Twenty-one per cent of the participants indicated that they had suicidal thoughts 'extremely often' or 'quite often'.

It is clear from PHR's forty interviews with Afghan women that the general climate of cruelty, abuse, and tyranny that characterizes Taliban rule has had a profound affect on women's mental health. Ninety-five per cent of women interviewed described a decline in their mental condition over the past two years. The denial of education also contributes to Afghan women's deteriorating mental health... The interviews revealed that women attributed the anxiety and depression that affects the vast majority of them to their fear of limited opportunities for their children, specifically denial of education to girl children. Poor and uneducated women spoke with particular urgency of their desire to obtain education for children, and saw health care, schooling, and protection of human rights as a key towards achieving a better future."

PHR notes that the women interviewed "consistently described high levels of poor health, multiple specific symptoms, and a significant decline in women's physical condition since the beginning of the Taliban occupation. Sixty-six per cent of women interviewed described a decline in their physical condition over the past two years. An Afghan physician described declining nutrition in children, an increasing rate of tuberculosis, and a high prevalence of other infectious diseases among women and children." Investigating the Rabia Balkhi Hospital, previously the only facility in Kabul open to women, PHR "found that it lacked basic medical supplies and equipment such as X-ray machines, suction and oxygen, running water, and medications... Yet even these poor facilities are not available to many women who seek treatment for themselves or their children."

A massive 87 per cent of women surveyed by PHR "reported a decrease in their access to health services. The reasons given included: no [male] chaperone available (27%), restrictions on women's mobility (36%), hospital refused to provide care (21%), no female doctor available (48%), do not own a *burqa* (6%), and economics (61%)." A general environment of constant terror has been instituted. "Sixty-eight per cent of women interviewed described incidents in which they were detained and physically abused by Taliban officials... Witnessing executions, fleeing religious police with whips who search for women and girls diverging from dress codes or other edicts, having a family member jailed or beaten; such experiences traumatize and retraumatize Afghan women, who have already experienced the horrors of war, rocketing, ever-present landmines and unexploded ordnance, and the loss of friends and immediate family".

The Taliban's brutal policies were particularly exemplified when its forces captured Mazar-e-Sharif in 1998. Following this military take-over on 8 August, Taliban guards systematically killed 8,000 civilians. The vast majority of those killed were from the Hazara ethnic group, who are mostly Shi'a Muslims, and were killed deliberately in their homes and in the streets, where their bodies were left for several days, or in locations between Mazar-e-Sharif and Hairatan. Victims of these acts of genocide included women, children and the elderly - many of whom were shot trying to flee. Furthermore, 11 Iranian nationals (ten diplomats and one journalist) were killed when Taliban guards entered the Iranian Consulate in Mazar-e-Sharif. According to eyewitnesses, their bodies were left in the consulate for two days, before being buried in a mass grave at the Sultan Razieh girls' school.

Having sealed their military capture of Mazar-e-Sharif, Taliban guards imposed a curfew in the city. In the Uzbek populated areas people were ordered to hand in their weapons, while in the Hazara area people were ordered to stay in their homes. Taliban forces subsequently entered Hazara houses, killing older men and children, and taking away young men without explanation. In some houses they also abducted young women, this time with explanation: they would be married off, whether they liked it or not, to the Taliban militia.

Thousands of detainees were reportedly transferred in military vehicles to detention centres in Mazar-e-Sharif and Shebarghan and interrogated to identify their ethnic identity. Non-Hazaras were released after a few days. Amnesty International reports that former detainees were beaten during their detention, sometimes severely. Moreover, hundreds were reportedly taken by air to Kandahar, while many others were taken during the night to fields in the surrounding areas of Mazar-e-Sharif and Shebarghan to be subsequently executed. Severe restrictions were imposed on the movement of Afghan people in and out of Mazar-e-Sharif - again, for apparently genocidal purposes. Amnesty reports that families who managed to leave the area were stopped at many checkpoints on the way.

At each checkpoint, Taliban guards would ask them whether Hazaras were among them. Anyone whom the guards suspected of being a Hazara was abducted. Hazara men and boys younger than 12 years old were taken to Jalalabad prison while women and girls were sent to Sarshahi camp. Such facts reveal the simple but horrifying fact that the Taliban was implementing a two-pronged programme of ethnic cleansing and genocide. As Amnesty International observes, "A new pattern in Afghanistan's human rights tragedy is the targeting of people on the basis of their group identity". AI confirms that "The Taleban", which is composed of the largest ethnic group in Afghanistan, "is targeting minorities such as Tajiks and Hazaras". By May 1999, brutal treatment of civilians continued as territory around the city of Bamiyam was captured and recaptured by the Taliban and another faction, Hezb-e Wahdat.

While the majority of people fled after the Taliban recaptured the city on 9 May, many civilians who stayed behind were later systematically slaughtered by Taliban guards arriving in the city. In continuation of such policies of terror and repression, in August 1999 tens of thousands of people were violently evicted from their homes by Taliban forces as they attempted to uproot rebels in northern Afghanistan. The Taliban was undertaking a 'scorched earth' policy involving the burning of homes, villages and crops to prevent residents from returning to homes in the Shomali Valley north of Kabul. After the massive expulsion, long lines of men, women and children were reportedly trudging toward Kabul. According to a UN statement from officials in Pakistan, "Families speak of whole villages being burned to the ground and crops set on fire to deter them from moving back to this once-fertile valley."

At this time, Kabul was already hosting a refugee population of 400,000. Thanks to the Taliban-sponsored 'cleansing' of the Shomali Valley, tens of thousands more refugees arrived. Additionally, as many as 150,000 reportedly fled the region towards rebel bases northeast of Kabul. However, it is important to remember that systematic human rights abuses are perpetrated by all major factions in the ongoing conflict in Afghanistan, not just by the Taliban. These have included "the killing of tens of thousands of civilians in deliberate or indiscriminate attacks on residential areas, deliberate and arbitrary killing of thousands of men, women and children by armed guards during raids on their homes, unacknowledged detention of several thousand people after being abducted by the various armed political groups, torture of civilians including rape of women, routine beating and ill-treatment of civilians suspected of belonging to rival political groups or because of their ethnic identity."

More than 25,000 people were killed from 1992 to 1997 in deliberate or indiscriminate attacks against civilian areas, with killings often occurring on a daily basis after severe battles for control of territory. With the war for territory between the Taliban and other factions escalating, civilians increasingly became the victims of indiscriminate attacks. Air raids on residential areas, ongoing fighting, landmines, gunfire, unreported massacres and the uncovering of mass graves, illustrate the extent to which the civil war has pulled the country into a downwards spiral of devastation.

As Human Rights Watch reported at the end of the year 2000 in a succint overview of the tragedy plaguing Afghanistan, "Afghanistan has been at war for more than twenty years. During that time it has lost a third of its population. Some 1.5 million people are estimated to have died as a direct result of the conflict. Another 5 million fled as refugees to Iran and Pakistan; others became exiles elsewhere abroad. A large part of its population is internally displaced... Throughout the war, all of the major factions have been guilty of grave breaches of international humanitarian law. Their warmaking is supported and perpetuated by the involvement of Afghanistan's neighbors and other states in providing weapons, ammunition, fuel, and other logistical support. State and non-state actors across the region and beyond continue to provide new arms and other materiel, as well as training and advisory assistance. The arms provided have been directly implicated in serious violations of international humanitarian law. These include aerial bombardments of civilian targets, indiscriminate bombings, rocketing and other artillery attacks on civilian-populated areas, reprisal killings of civilians, summary executions of prisoners, rape, and torture."

THE WESTERN RESPONSE

Unsurprisingly, calls by human rights organisations for the meaningful intervention of an international body have continued unanswered. This is despite the fact that two key members of the international community, America and Russia, bear primary responsibility for the state of war that has plagued Afghanistan to this day, due to their respective self-interested manipulations of the country. Disregarding their responsibility, these nations refuse to undertake a significant intervention, be it diplomatic or otherwise. Meaningful pressure that could be exerted upon the Taliban to change its policies is not exerted.

As Amnesty notes: "For two decades, the international community has mostly averted its eyes from the human rights catastrophe in Afghanistan... The United States, its West European allies and the former Soviet Union have failed to bring to an end the very human rights crisis that they helped to create." In fact, the systematic, ethnically-motivated killings of thousands of Hazara Afghans has not been enough to elicit other than a rhetorical response from the Western powers, who have thereby clearly illustrated their lack of genuine concern for this tide of genocide. While issuing a statement condemning the killing of Iranian diplomats at Mazar-e-Sharif and calling for investigations into their death, "The UN Security Council... has remained silent about the deaths and arbitrary detention of thousands of 'ordinary' people." As AI emphasises, international pressure combined with condemnation in public "has been shown to be effective in revealing the truth about human rights abuses" and "preventing further massacres".

Yet, the Western powers refuse to impose such pressure. Twenty years of such ongoing refusal and failure have - quite predictably - given effective consent to the Taliban to continue with its policies, in the knowledge that the Western powers are simply unconcerned about a crisis regarding which they *can* undertake significant stops to halt - as AI has made clear. The West has, rather, strangely refrained from implementing even the most simple of such steps, suggesting that there may be other more important interests in allowing the Taliban to rise to power.

The only countries that openly accept the Taliban as Afghanistan's legitimate government are Pakistan, Saudi Arabia and the United Arab Emirates - all of which happen to be Western clients and, in particular, obedient US servants. If the West exerted political or economic pressure on these countries to cease their well documented sponsoring of Taliban terrorism (via arms, for instance), it is highly likely that they would willingly acquiesce, simply because they are virtually absolutely dependent on Western - particularly American - aid. Indeed, while sometimes condemning atrocious Taliban policies in rhetoric, the West turns a blind eye to the actions of its own regional clients, who are actively supporting these same policies, thereby effectively giving a 'green light' to the Taliban to pursue its policies.

Barry Rubin of the CFR reports that the professed US policy of promoting peace in Afghanistan has "suffered from a variety of internal contradictions. US policy toward Iran conflicts with US stated policy toward Afghanistan and is one of the reasons that many in the region believe the US supports the Taliban." Rubin notes: "If the US is in fact supporting the joint Pakistani-Saudi backing of the Taliban in some way, even if not materially, then it has in effect decided to make Afghanistan the victim of yet another proxy war - this time aimed at Iran rather than the USSR." America's professed commitment to supporting the UN as the means of creating peace in Afghanistan is similarly highly flawed: "US support of the UN as the proper vehicle for a negotiated settlement of the Afghan conflict is undermined by congressional refusal to allocate funds for UN dues or the US share of peacekeeping expenses."

Moreover, "The US has not described and criticized in a straightforward manner the specific types of external interference occurring in Afghanistan", from Pakistan and

Saudi Arabia for instance. "Public statements by the State Department condemn such interference but never specify who is undertaking it", effectively annulling the whole purpose of condemnation, thereby strongly suggesting the aforementioned tacit 'green light' to the Taliban's sweep across the region - an issue which we shall be investigating in further detail. Furthermore, expressing the conclusions of the majority of Afghan analysts on current US-UN policy, former Afghan commerce minister (1965-69) Dr. Noor Ali notes other vast internal contradictions in the approach.

Highlighting the UN's claim to have "mediated the withdrawal of foreign (Soviet) forces from Afghanistan", Noor Ali notes that the policy only succeeded in "planting and strengthening the warring factions and factionalism in Afghanistan." "For in connection with this mediation there is a question: mediation between who and who? Normally, logically, and legally, it should be conducted between Afghanistan and the former Soviet Union, and the Geneva Accords should be concluded accordingly. Scandalously and shamefully, the mediation took place among all the interested parties, *but in the sheer exclusion of Afghanistan*. And the accords were signed between the delegate of the Soviet-installed government in Kabul representing the former Soviet Union and that of the Government of Pakistan representing somehow the Government of the United States."

This peculiar form of "mediation", which deliberately excluded Afghanistan, indicates the "US Administration's policy - implemented by the United Nations - to deny Afghanistan its right for a national government representing its people in its relations with foreign nations, letting other powers decide its fate." Furthermore, this state of affairs has continued with all factions in Afghanistan being funded by foreign powers. "There is no doubt that the presaging has been confirmed by the subsequent development: No national Afghan government has yet emerged; the country is fragmented and no longer independent; its fate is in the hands of alien powers; all its social, political, and administrative services are abolished; the warring factions and factionalism -

introduced by the US Administration and maintained by the United Nations - are prevailing."

The Western powers therefore remain content with primarily ignoring Afghanistan's humanitarian catastrophe, refraining from implementing any significant action. One then wonders why the West is so willing to impose massive pressure on a country such as Serbia for its human rights abuses against Kosovans, when it refuses to impose a comparable kind of pressure on the Taliban, although the Taliban follows through with the same brand of mass abuses, yet on a much more brutal and extensive scale. This exposes the selective disparity of alleged Western concern for promoting democracy and protecting human rights. Such Western indifference is probably linked to the fact that, as Ben C. Vidgen remarks: "In Afghanistan and Pakistan fundamentalism could not have bloomed without the CIA's covert assistance - a fact that is apparent when one examines the history of the area".

THE COVERT-US TALIBAN ALLIANCE

Western motives become clearer when one recalls that it was the US that originally trained and armed the faction in Afghanistan - even "long before the USSR sent in troops" - which now constitutes the "leaders of Afghanistan". The record illustrates the existence of an ongoing relationship between the United States and the Taliban. AI reports that even though the "United States has denied any links with the Taleban", according to then US Assistant Secretary of State Robin Raphel Afghanistan was a "crucible of strategic interest" during the Cold War, though she denied any US influence or support of factions in Afghanistan today, dismissing any possible ongoing strategic interests. However, former Department of Defense official Elie Krakowski, who worked on the Afghan issue in the 1980s, points out that Afghanistan remains important to this day because it "is the crossroads between what Halford MacKinder called the world's Heartland and the Indian sub continent.

It owes its importance to its location at the confluence of major routes. A boundary between land power and sea power, it is the meeting point between opposing forces larger than itself. Alexander the Great used it as a path to conquest. So did the Moghuls. An object of competition between the British and Russian empires in the 19th century, Afghanistan became a source of controversy between the American and Soviet superpowers in the 20th. With the collapse of the Soviet Union, it has become an important potential opening to the sea for the landlocked new states of Central Asia. The presence of large oil and gas deposits in that area has attracted countries and multinational corporations. Because Afghanistan is a major strategic pivot what happens there affects the rest of the world."

Raphel's denial of US interests in the region also stands in contradiction to the fact that, as AI reports, "many Afghanistan analysts believe that the United States has had close political links with the Taleban militia. They refer to visits by Taleban representatives to the United States in recent months and several visits by senior US State Department officials to Kandahur including one immediately before the Taleban took over Jalalabad." The AI report refers to a comment by the Guardian: "Senior Taleban leaders attended a conference in Washington in mid-1996 and US diplomats regularly travelled to Taleban headquarters." The Guardian points out that though such "visits can be explained", "the timing raises doubts as does the generally approving line which US officials take towards the Taleban."

Amnesty goes on to confirm that recent "accounts of the *madrasas* (religious schools) which the Taleban attended in Pakistan indicate that these [Western] links [with the Taleban] may have been established at the very inception of the Taleban movement. In an interview broadcast by the BBC World Service on 4 October 1996, Pakistan's then Prime Minister Benazir Bhutto affirmed that the *madrasas* had been set up by Britain, the United States, Saudi Arabia and Pakistan during the *Jihad*, the Islamic resistance against Soviet occupation of Afghanistan." Similarly, former Pakistani Interior Minister,

Major General (Retd) Naseerullah Babar, stated that "[The] CIA itself introduced terrorism in the region and is only shedding crocodiles tears to absolve itself of the responsibility."

In light of Brzezinski's testimony, the establishment of this Western link with the Taliban - as well as other Afghan factions - was initiated even prior to the Soviet invasion. Similarly, Vidgen reports that "the corporate media have... remained silent in regard to America's involvement in the promotion of terrorism. On the issue of right-wing terrorism, little has been reported. On America's intelligence connection to 'Islamic' guerrillas (and their manipulation of Islam), nothing has been said. Yet, the truth is that amongst those who utilise religious faith to justify war, the majority are closer to Langley, Virginia, than they are to Tehran or Tripoli. In a move to recruit soldiers for the Afghanistan civil war, the CIA and Zia encouraged the region's Islamic people to think of the conflict in terms of a jihad (holy war). Thus was fundamentalism promoted."

William O. Beeman, an anthropologist specialising in the Middle East at Brown University who has conducted extensive research into Islamic Central Asia, points out: "It is no secret, especially in the region, that the United States, Pakistan and Saudi Arabia have been supporting the fundamentalist Taliban in their war for control of Afghanistan for some time. The US has never openly acknowledged this connection, but it has been confirmed by both intelligence sources and charitable institutions in Pakistan." Professor Beeman observes that the US-backed Taliban "are a brutal fundamentalist group that has conducted a cultural scorched-earth policy" in Afghanistan. Extensive documentation shows that the Taliban have "committed atrocities against their enemies and their own citizens... So why would the US support them?"

Beeman concludes that the answer to this question "has nothing to do with religion or ethnicity - but only with the economics of oil. To the north of Afghanistan is one of the world's wealthiest oil fields, on the Eastern Shore of the Caspian Sea in republics formed since the breakup of the Soviet

Union." Caspian oil needs to be transhipped out of the landlocked region through a warm water port, for the desired profits to be accumulated. The "simplest and cheapest" pipeline route is through Iran - but Iran is essentially an 'enemy' of the US, due to being overtly independent of the West, as shall be discussed later. As Beeman notes: "The US government has such antipathy to Iran that it is willing to do anything to prevent this." The alternative route is one that passes through Afghanistan and Pakistan, which "would require securing the agreement of the powers-that-be in Afghanistan" - the Taliban. Such an arrangement would also benefit Pakistani elites, "which is why they are willing to defy the Iranians."

Therefore, as far as the US is concerned, the solution is "for the anti-Iranian Taliban to win in Afghanistan and agree to the pipeline through their territory." Apart from the oil stakes, Afghanistan remains a strategic region for the US in another related respect. The establishment of a strong client state in the country would strengthen US influence in this crucial region, partly by strengthening Pakistan - a prime supporter of the Taliban - which is the region's main American base. Of course, this also furthers the cause of establishing the required oil and gas pipelines to the Caspian Sea, while bypassing Russia and opening up the Commonwealth of Independent States (CIS) bordering Russia to the US dominated global market.

Strategic interests therefore seem to have motivated what the Guardian referred to as "the generally approving line that US officials take towards the Taleban." CNN reported that the "United States wants good ties [with the Taliban] but can't openly seek them while women are being repressed" - hence they can be sought covertly. The Intra Press Service (IPS) reports that underscoring "the geopolitical stakes, Afghanistan has appeared prominently in US government and corporate planning about routes for pipelines and roads opening the ex-Soviet republics on Russia's southern border to world markets."

Hence, amid the fighting, "some Western businesses are warming up to the Taliban despite the movement's" institutionalisation of terror, massacres, abductions, and impoverishment. "Leili Helms, a spokeswoman for the Taliban in New York, told IPS that one US company, Union Oil of California (Unocal), helped to arrange the visit last week of the movement's acting information, industry and mines ministers. The three officials met lower-level State Department officials before departing for France, Helms said. Several US and French firms are interested in developing gas lines through central and southern Afghanistan, where the 23 Taliban-controlled states" just happen to be located, as Helms added, to the 'chance' convenience of American and other Western companies.

An article appearing in the prestigious German daily *Frankfurter Rundschau*, in early October 1996, reported that UNOCAL "has been given the go-ahead from the new holders of power in Kabul to build a pipeline from Turkmenstein via Afghanistan to Pakistan. It would lead from Krasnovodsk on the Caspian Sea to Karachi on the Indian Ocean coast." The same article noted that UN diplomats in Geneva believe that the war in Afghanistan is the result of a struggle between Turkey, Iran, Pakistan, Russia and the United States, "to secure access to the rich oil and natural gas of the Caspian Sea." Other than UNOCAL, companies that are jubilantly interested in exploiting Caspian oil, apparently at any human expense, include AMOCO, BP, Chevron, EXXON, and Mobile.

It therefore comes as no surprise to see the *Wall Street Journal* reporting that the main interests of American and other Western elites lie in making Afghanistan "a prime transhipment route for the export of Central Asia's vast oil, gas and other natural resources". "Like them or not," the *Journal* continues without fear of contradiction, "the Taliban are the players most capable of achieving peace in Afghanistan at this moment in history." The *Journal* is referring to the same faction that is responsible for the severe repression of women; massacres of civilians; ethnic cleansing and genocide; arbitrary detention; and the growth of widespread impoverishment and underdevelopment. Despite all this, as the *New York Times* similarly reported, "The Clinton Administration has taken the view that a Taliban victory... would act as a counterweight to Iran... and would offer the possibility of new trade routes that could weaken Russian and Iranian influence in the region."

In a similar vein, the *International Herald Tribunal* reports that in the summer of 1998, "the Clinton administration was talking with the Taleban about potential pipeline routes to carry oil and natural gas out of Turkmenistan to the Indian Ocean by crossing Afghanistan and Pakistan", clarifying why the US would be interested in ensuring that the region is destabilised enough to prevent the population from being able to mobilise domestic resources, or utilise the region's strategic position, for their own benefit. P. Stobdan reports that "Afghanistan figures importantly in the context of American energy security politics. Unocal's project to build oil and gas pipelines from Turkmenistan through Afghanistan for the export of oil and gas to the Indian subcontinent, viewed as the most audacious gambit of the 1990s Central Asian oil rush had generated great euphoria.

The US government fully backed the route as a useful option to free the Central Asian states from Russian clutches and prevent them getting close to Iran. The project was also perceived as the quickest and cheapest way to bring out Turkmen gas to the fast growing energy market in South Asia. To help it canvass for the project, Unocol hired the prominent former diplomat and secretary of state, Henry Kissinger, and a former US ambassador to Pakistan, Robert Oakley, as well as an expert on the Caucasus, John Maresca... The president of Unocol even speculated that the cost of the construction would be reduced by half with the success of the Taliban movement and formation of a single government."

Worse still, this corporate endeavour backed wholeheartedly by the US involved direct military support of the Taliban: "It was reported by the media that the US oil company had even provided covert material support to help push the militia northward against Rabbani's forces." However, as Stobdan also notes, the terrorist antics of Taliban favourite Usama Bin Laden caused a rift in the blossoming US-Taliban relationship, leading the American corporation UNOCAL to indefinitely suspend work on the pipeline in August 1999. It is thus exceedingly hard to see how humanism has played a significant role in defining the policy of the US and the other Western powers toward Afghanistan. On the contrary, strategic and economic interests have evidently far outweighed the West's professed humanitarian benevolence.

It is in this context that Franz Schurmann, Professor Emeritus of History & Sociology at the University of California, comments on "Washington's discreet backing of the Taliban", noting the announcement in May 1996 "by UNOCAL that it was preparing to build a pipeline to transport natural gas from Turkmenistan to Pakistan through Western Afghanistan... UNOCAL's announcement was premised on an imminent Taliban victory." We should therefore take particular note of the authoritative testimony of US Congressman Dana Rohrabacher concerning American policy toward Afghanistan.

Rohrabacher has been involved with Afghanistan since the early 1980s when he worked in the White House as Special Assistant to then US President Ronald Reagan, and he is now a Senior Member of the US House International Relations Committee. Since 1988 he traveled to Afghanistan as a member of the US Congress with mujahideen fighters and participated in the battle of Jalalabhad against the Soviets; he has been involved in US policy toward Afghanistan for twenty years. He has testified as follows: "Having been closely involved in US policy toward Afghanistan for some twenty years, I have called into question whether or not this administration has a covert policy that has empowered the Taliban and enabled this brutal movement to hold on to power.

Even though the President and the Secretary of State have voiced their disgust at the brutal policies of the Taliban, especially their repression of women, the actual implementation of US policy has repeatedly had the opposite effect." After documenting a large number of factors indicating tacit US support of the Taliban, Rohrabacher concludes: "I am making the claim that there is and has been a covert policy by this administration to support the Taliban movement's control of Afghanistan. This amoral or immoral policy is based on the assumption that the Taliban would bring stability to Afghanistan and permit the building of oil pipelines from Central Asia through Afghanistan to Pakistan... I believe the administration has maintained this covert goal and kept the Congress in the dark about its policy of supporting the Taliban, the most anti-Western, anti-female, anti-human rights regime in the world. It doesn't take a genius to understand that this policy would outrage the American people, especially America's women. Perhaps the most glaring evidence of our government's covert policy to favor the Taliban is that the administration is currently engaged in a major effort to obstruct the Congress from determining the details behind this policy.

Last year in August, after several unofficial requests were made of the State Department, I made an official request for all diplomatic documents concerning US policy toward the Taliban, especially those cables and documents from our embassies in Pakistan and Saudi Arabia. As a senior Member of the House International Relations Committee I have oversight responsibility in this area. In November, after months of stonewalling, the Secretary of State herself promised before the International Relations Committee that the documents would be forthcoming. She reconfirmed that promise in February when she testified before our Committee on the State Department budget. The Chairman of the Committee, Ben Gilman, added his voice to the record in support of my document request. To this time, we have received nothing. There can only be two explanations. Either the State Department is totally incompetent, or there is an ongoing cover-up of the State Department's true fundamental policy toward Afghanistan. You probably didn't expect me to praise the State Department at the end of this scathing testimony. But I will. I don't think the State Department is incompetent. They should be held responsible for their policies and the American people should know, through documented proof, what they are doing."

This documentation shows clearly that the US was certainly supportive of the Taliban while they were scoring sweeping victories throughout Afghanistan. As has been noted by Central Asia specialist Ahmed Rashid, the Pakistan, Afghanistan and Central Asia correspondent for the Far Eastern Economic Review and the Daily Telegraph (London), from 1994-96 at least the United States "did support the Taliban, and [the Americans] cannot deny that fact." In an important study of the issue, *Taliban: Militant Islam, Oil and Fundamentalism in Central Asia*, Rashid showed that "between 1994-96 the US supported the Taliban politically through its allies Pakistan and Saudi Arabia, essentially because Washington viewed the Taliban as anti-Iranian, anti-Shia and pro-western. Between 1995-97, US support was driven by the UNOCAL oil/gas pipeline project."

Thus, as Afghan scholar Noor Ali accurately points out, by its covert policy "to make of Afghanistan a satellite or a protectorate of Pakistan, the US Administration ignored the very objectives of Afghans themselves to repulse the invader, to recover their independence, to establish the style of government of their choice, and to live in peace. It disregarded the aspirations of the Afghan masses who bore the actual burden of the war and rendered an unparalleled sacrifice to the cause of freedom." Rather than providing genuine help to the Afghan people by making available to them "the necessary facilities to rebuild an independent Afghan state and to reconstruct Afghan economy, the US Government has shamefully rewarded Pakistan in authorizing it to control Afghanistan as suzerain through the heads of Units - the warring faction's leaders - originated in Pakistan" - evident in America's failure to condemn the policies of its subservient Pakistani client.

"The current warfare in Afghanistan is not a civil war. It is rather an international war among the involved regional states, through their respective proxies - Afghan warring factions - using Afghanistan territory as their battle field... the war is between the interfering foreign powers for their expansionist or protectionist objectives within and beyond the region; the warring factions and their leaders are their surrogates and defacto extension of their state organizations."

Summarising the economic and strategic interests of the US that have motivated the current policy, Dr. Ali remarks that the Great Game in Central Asia is not ending, but rather "going on briskly." Today, however, it is "the United States that is looking North and intended to cross Afghanistan from Pakistan so as to be able (i) to sway Iran; (ii) to expand its power beyond the Amou Daria to control the resources of Central Asia; and (iii) to influence the Federation of Russia from South, and the mainland China from North West, as and when required... The US Government, in complicity with its regional allies, and for want of anything better, is trying to put therein a servile government of its own choice so as to possess the necessary leverage to influence the overall politics and economics of the region in accordance with its imperialistic objectives. Pending the identification and installation of such a government the country has to endure the state of anarchy and instability accordingly."

However, it is extremely unlikely that the US continues to support the Taliban. As indicated above, after the bombings in Africa and Yemen blamed on Afghan warlord Usama Bin Laden, the US relationship with the Taliban soured considerably. Under consequent US pressure, United Nations sanctions preventing Western firms from investing in Afghanistan have been imposed against the Taliban, in light of which it appears that the once blooming US-Taliban relationship is over. One of the reasons for this certainly appears to be the fact that the Taliban is incapable of playing the US-friendly role of a "servile government".

As Ahmed Rashid points out, "The UNOCAL project was based on the premise that the Taliban were going to conquer Afghanistan. This premise was fed to them by various countries like Saudi Arabia, Pakistan and elements within the US administration. Essentially it was a premise that was very wrong, because it was based on conquest, and would therefore make it absolutely certain that not only would they not be able to build the pipeline, but they would never be able to have that kind of security in order to build the pipeline." Once this became absolutely clear to the United States, it also became clear that the Taliban was incapable of providing the security essential to allow the pipeline to go ahead as required. Thus, in other words, by 1998 the US began to see the Taliban as a fundamental obstacle to US interests, and due to this, US policy toward the Taliban took an about-turn.

US POLICY SHIFTS AGAINST THE TALIBAN

The shift in US policy in Afghanistan from pro-Taliban to anti-Taliban, has not brought with it any change in the tragic condition of the Afghan people, primarily because the policy shift is once more rooted in America's own attempt to secure its strategic and economic interests. Since the Taliban no longer plays a suitably subservient role, US policy has grown increasingly hostile to the faction. The shift has also, unfortunately, occurred "without public discussion, without consultation with Congress and without even informing those who are likely to make foreign policy in the next administration." The imposition of sanctions on Afghanistan in the wake of the US embassy blasts in east Africa attributed to Bin Laden, has not only failed to affect the Taliban, but has served primarily to devastate the Afghan population even more. Indeed, "The US engineered a punishing Iraq-style embargo of war-ravaged Afghanistan at a time when many of its 18 million people are starving and homeless," observes the *Toronto Sun*.

The London *Guardian* reports that "When the UN imposed sanctions a year ago on the Taliban because of their refusal to hand over bin Laden, the suffering in Afghanistan increased. The move has not hurt the Taliban. They are well off. It is ordinary Afghans who have suffered. Those in jobs earn a salary of around $4 a month, scarcely enough to live on. The real losers are Afghanistan's women, who have been for bidden by the Taliban from working. Kabul is full of burqa-clad women beggars who congregate every lunchtime outside the city's few functioning restaurants in the hope of getting something to eat." Indeed, the imposition of sanctions amidst the ongoing famine in Afghanistan has quite predictably resulted in the exacerbation of the country's crisis. "The country is in the grip of an unreported humanitarian disaster", notes Luke Harding reporting from Kandahar. "In the south and west, there has been virtually no rain for three years. The road from Herat, near the Iranian border, to Kandahar, the southern desert city, winds through half-abandoned villages and swirlingly empty riverbeds. Some 12 million people have been affected, of whom 3 million are close to starvation."

As Pakistani correspondent Arshad Mahmoud observes that the people, particularly the children, of Afghanistan "are facing the grave consequences of the UN sanctions", in tandem with the continuing drought. Meanwhile, the US desire to eliminate Bin Laden and his likeminded colleagues has led to the formation of a joint US-Russian project to undermine the Taliban to make way for a new more subservient regime. Frederick Starr, Chairman of the Central Asia-Caucasus Institute at Johns Hopkins's Nitze School of Advanced International Studies, reports that "the United States has quietly begun to align itself with those in the Russian government calling for military action against Afghanistan and has toyed with the idea of a new raid to wipe out Osama bin Laden. Until it backed off under local pressure, it went so far as to explore whether a Central Asian country would permit the use of its territory for such a purpose."

Meetings between government American, Russian and Indian government officials took place at the end of 2000 "to discuss what kind of government should replace the Taliban... [T]he United States is now talking about the overthrow of a regime that controls nearly the entire country, in the hope it can be replaced with a hypothetical government that does not exist even on paper." The fact that the US has recently been backing a UN resolution strengthening sanctions against foreign military aid to the Taliban , without including an embargo on the other armed factions in the country, confirms clearly that the shift in policy has no humanitarian basis behind it. The other factions "when they ruled in key areas, showed a brutal disregard for human rights and for other minorities that was comparable to the Taliban at its worst", notes Central Asia specialist Frederick Starr. "Yet the fragment of a government they support limps on and, with US backing, occupies Afghanistan's seat in the United Nations."

HRW criticised the Security Council measures, urging "the adoption of an arms embargo against all combatants, not only the Taliban." Indeed, a joint US-Russia draft resolution ignored the ongoing civil war, responsible for the humanitarian crisis, focusing instead "on the Taliban's harboring of Osama bin Laden... [The resolution] would impose new sanctions only on the Taliban until it gives up bin Laden for extradition and closes camps allegedly used to plan criminal activities overseas. But the draft resolution does not directly address the ongoing civil war in Afghanistan, which has been accompanied by a severe humanitarian crisis." Executive Director of HRW, Kenneth Roth, has pointed out that the international community's failure to "address abuses by the warring parties now because they are an important cause of the continuing humanitarian crisis in Afghanistan", signifies that they are "inexcusably abandoning the Afghan people to suffer atrocities at home while focusing exclusively on the Afghan government's role in attacks on foreigners."

Canadian journalist Eric Margolis reports that "The United States and Russia may soon launch a joint military assault against Islamic militant, Osama Bin Laden, and against the leadership of Taliban, Afghanistan's de facto ruling movement. Such an attack would probably include US Delta Force and Navy Seals, who would join up with Russia's elite Spetsnaz and Alpha commandos in Tajikistan, the Central Asian state where Russian has military bases and 25,000 troops. The combined forces would be lifted by helicopters, and backed by air support, deep into neighboring Afghanistan to attack Bin Laden's fortified base in the Hindu Kush mountains." The plans have little to do with aiding the Afghan people, and more to do with eliminating the current danger to US interests in the region. As the *Guardian* rightly observes, "Another missile attack will merely add to Afghanistan's misery."

We thus see a clear example of how human rights, democracy and egalitarian social development are directly opposed by deliberate Western policies to further the economic interests of Western corporate elites. In this case, a faction whose policies of brutal repression are extensively documented and well known was being covertly supported at the expense of the Afghan people in the name of US strategic and corporate interests. This support only ceased when it became clear that the Taliban was incapable of establishing the sort of conditions necessary for the security of the proposed pipeline.

Evidently, the human rights of the Afghan people are not a very significant factor in the formulation of Western policy toward Afghanistan. AI summarises the crisis aptly: "Civilians are the targets of human rights abuses in a war they have not chosen, by one faction after another... They are pawns in a game of war between armed groups inside Afghanistan backed by different regional powers", with the leading perpetrator of abuses and massacres - the Taliban - having been covertly supported by the United States for several years. "Meanwhile, the world has watched massacres of civilians without making any meaningful effort to protect them."

US POLICY ON TALIBAN

Under the influence of United States oil companies, the government of President George W Bush initially blocked intelligence agencies' investigations on terrorism while it bargained with the Taliban on the delivery of Osama bin Laden in exchange for political recognition and economic aid, two French intelligence analysts claim. In the book *Bin Laden, la verite interdite* (Bin Laden, the forbidden truth), that was released recently, the authors, Jean-Charles Brisard and

Guillaume Dasquie, reveal that the Federal Bureau of Investigation's (FBI) deputy director John O'Neill resigned in July in protest over the obstruction.

The authors claim that O'Neill told them that "the main obstacles to investigate Islamic terrorism were US oil corporate interests and the role played by Saudi Arabia in it". The two claim that the US government's main objective in Afghanistan was to consolidate the position of the Taliban regime to obtain access to the oil and gas reserves in Central Asia. They affirm that until August, the US government saw the Taliban regime "as a source of stability in Central Asia that would enable the construction of an oil pipeline across Central Asia" from the rich oilfields in Turkmenistan, Uzbekistan, and Kazakhstan, through Afghanistan and Pakistan, to the Indian Ocean. Until now, says the book, "the oil and gas reserves of Central Asia have been controlled by Russia. The Bush government wanted to change all that."

But, confronted with Taliban's refusal to accept US conditions, "this rationale of energy security changed into a military one", the authors claim. "At one moment during the negotiations, the US representatives told the Taliban, 'either you accept our offer of a carpet of gold, or we bury you under a carpet of bombs,'" Brisard said in an interview in Paris. According to the book, the Bush administratino began to negotiate with the Taliban immediately after coming into power in February. US and Taliban diplomatic representatives met several times in Washington, Berlin and Islamabad.

To polish their image in the United States, the Taliban even employed a US expert on public relations, Laila Helms. The authors claim that Helms is also an expert in the works of US intelligence organizations, for her uncle, Richard Helms, is a former director of the Central Intelligence Agency (CIA). The last meeting between US and Taliban representatives took place in August, five weeks before the attacks on New York and Washington, the analysts maintain. On that occasion, Christina Rocca, in charge of Central Asian affairs for the US government, met the Taliban ambassador to Pakistan in Islamabad.

Brisard and Dasquie have long experience in intelligence analysis. Brisard was until the late 1990s director of economic analysis and strategy for Vivendi, a French company. He also worked for French secret services, and wrote for them in 1997 a report on the now famous Al-Qaeda network, headed by bin Laden. Dasquie is an investigative journalist and publisher of Intelligence Online, a respected newsletter on diplomacy, economic analysis and strategy, available through the Internet. Brisard and Dasquie draw a portrait of the closest aides to Bush, linking them to the oil business. Bush's family has a strong oil background, as do some of his top aides.

From Vice President Dick Cheney, through the director of the National Security Council Condoleezza Rice, to the ministers of commerce and energy, Donald Evans and Stanley Abraham, all have for long worked for US oil companies. Cheney was until the end of last year president of Halliburton, a company that provides services for oil industry; Rice was between 1991 and 2000 manager for Chevron; Evans and Abraham worked for Tom Brown, another oil giant. Besides the secret negotiations held between Washington and Kabul and the importance of the oil industry, the book takes issue with the role played by Saudi Arabia in fostering Islamic fundamentalism, in the personality of bin Laden, and with the networks that the Saudi dissident built to finance his activities.

Brisard and Dasquie contend that the US government's claim that it had been prosecuting bin Laden since 1998. "Actually," Dasquie says, "the first state to officially prosecute bin Laden was Libya, on the charges of terrorism." "Bin Laden wanted to settle in Libya in the early 1990s, but was hindered by the government of Muammar Gaddafi," Dasquie claims. "Enraged by Libya's refusal, bin Laden organized attacks inside Libya, including assassination attempts against Gaddafi." Dasquie singles out one group, the Islamic Fighting Group (IFG), reputedly the most powerful Libyan dissident organization, based in London, and directly linked with bin Laden. "Gaddafi even demanded Western police institutions, such as Interpol, to pursue the IFG and bin Laden, but never obtained cooperation," Dasquie says. "Until today, members of IFG openly live in London."

The book confirms earlier reports that the US government worked closely with the United Nations during the negotiations with the Taliban. "Several meetings took place this year, under the arbitration of Francesc Vendrell, personal representative of UN Secretary-General Kofi Annan, to discuss the situation in Afghanistan," says the book. "Representatives of the US government and Russia, and the six countries that border with Afghanistan were present at these meetings," it says. "Sometimes, representatives of the Taliban also sat around the table." These meetings, also called Six plus 2, because of the number of states (six neighbors plus the US and Russia) involved, have been confirmed by Naif Naik, former Pakistani minister for foreign affairs.

In a French television news program two weeks ago, Naik said that during a Six plus 2 meeting in Berlin in July, the discussions turned around "the formation of a government of national unity. If the Taliban had accepted this coalition, they would have immediately received international economic aid. And the pipelines from Kazakhstan and Uzbekistan would have come," he added. Naik also claimed that Tom Simons, the US representative at these meetings, openly threatened the Taliban and Pakistan. "Simons said, 'either the Taliban behave as they ought to, or Pakistan convinces them to do so, or we will use another option'. The words Simons used were 'a military operation'," Naik claimed.

GENEVA ACCORDS (1988) AND SOVIET WITHDRAWAL

On April 14, 1988, Gorbachev agreed to a U.N.-brokered accord (the Geneva Accords) requiring it to withdraw. The withdrawal was completed by February 15, 1989, leaving in place the weak Najibullah government. A warming of relations moved the United States and Soviet Union to try for a political settlement to the Afghan conflict, a trend accelerated by the 1991 collapse of the Soviet Union, which reduced Moscow's capacity for supporting communist regimes in the Third World. On September 13, 1991, Moscow and Washington agreed to a joint cutoff of military aid to the Afghan combatants.

The State Department has said that a total of about $3 billion in economic and covert military assistance was provided by the U.S. to the Afghan *mujahedin* from 1980 until the end of the Soviet occupation in 1989. Press reports say the covert aid program grew from about $20 million per year in FY1980 to about $300 million per year during FY1986-FY1990. The Soviet pullout decreased the perceived strategic value of Afghanistan, causing a reduction in subsequent covert funding. U.S. assistance to Afghanistan remained at relatively low levels from the time of the Soviet withdrawal, validating the views of many that the United States largely considered its role in Afghanistan "completed" when Soviets troops left, and there was little support for a major U.S. effort to rebuild the country.

The United States closed its embassy in Kabul in January 1989, as the Soviet Union was completing its pullout, and it remained so until the fall of the Taliban in 2001. With Soviet backing withdrawn, Najibullah rallied the PDPA Army and the party-dominated paramilitary organization called the *Sarandoy*, and successfully beat back the post-Soviet withdrawal *mujahedin* offensives. Although Najibullah defied expectations that his government would immediately collapse after a Soviet withdrawal, military defections continued and his position weakened in subsequent years. On March 18, 1992, Najibullah publicly agreed to step down once an interim government was formed.

That announcement set off a wave of rebellions primarily by Uzbek and Tajik militia commanders in northern Afghanistan-particularly Abdal Rashid Dostam, who joined prominent *mujahedin* commander Ahmad Shah Masud of the Islamic Society, a largely Tajik party headed by Burhannudin Rabbani. Masud had earned a reputation as a brilliant strategist by preventing the Soviets from occupying his power base in the Panjshir Valley of northeastern Afghanistan. Najibullah fell, and the *mujahedin* regime began April 18, 1992.

THE MUJAHEDIN GOVERNMENT AND RISE OF THE TALIBAN

The fall of Najibullah exposed the differences among the *mujahedin* parties. The leader of one of the smaller parties (Afghan National Liberation Front), Islamic scholar Sibghatullah Mojadeddi, was president during April-May 1992. Under an agreement among the major parties, Rabbani became President in June 1992 with agreement that he would serve until December 1994. He refused to step down at that time, saying that political authority would disintegrate without a clear successor. Kabul was subsequently shelled by other *mujahedin* factions particularly that of nominal "Prime Minister" Gulbuddin Hikmatyar, a Pashtun, who accused Rabbani of monopolizing power. Hikmatyar's radical Islamist Hizb-e-Islami (Islamic Party)-Gulbuddin had received a large proportion of the U.S. aid during the anti-Soviet war. (Yunus Khalis led a more moderate faction of Hizb-e-Islami during that war.)

In 1993-1994, Afghan Islamic clerics and students, mostly of rural, Pashtun origin, formed the Taliban movement. Many were former *mujahedin* who had become disillusioned with conflict among *mujahedin* parties and had moved into Pakistan to study in Islamic seminaries ("*madrassas*") mainly of the "Deobandi" school of Islam. Some say this Islam is similar to the "Wahhabism" that is practiced in Saudi Arabia. Taliban practices were also consonant with conservative Pashtun tribal traditions. The Taliban viewed the Rabbani government as corrupt, anti-Pashtun, and responsible for civil war. The four years of civil war (1992-1996) created popular support for the Taliban as a movement that could deliver Afghanistan from the warfare.

With the help of defections, the Taliban seized control of the southeastern city of Qandahar in November 1994; by February 1995, it had reached the gates of Kabul, after which an 18-month stalemate around the capital ensued. In September 1995, the Taliban captured Herat province, bordering Iran, and imprisoned its governor, Ismail Khan, ally of Rabbani and Masud, who later escaped and took refuge in Iran. In September 1996, Taliban victories near Kabul led to the withdrawal of Rabbani and Masud to the Panjshir Valley north of Kabul with most of their heavy weapons; the Taliban took control of Kabul on September 27, 1996. Taliban gunmen subsequently entered a U.N. facility in Kabul to seize Najibullah, his brother, and aides, and then hanged them.

TALIBAN RULE (SEPTEMBER 1996- NOVEMBER 2001)

The Taliban regime was led by Mullah Muhammad Umar, who lost an eye in the anti-Soviet war while fighting under the banner of the Hizb-e-Islami of Yunis Khalis. Umar held the title of Head of State and "Commander of the Faithful," but he remained in the Taliban power base in Qandahar, almost never appearing in public. Umar forged a close bond with bin Laden and refused U.S. demands to extradite him. Like Umar, most of the Taliban were Ghilzai Pashtuns, which predominate in eastern Afghanistan. They are rivals of the Durrani Pashtuns, who are predominant in the south. The Taliban progressively lost international and domestic support as it imposed strict adherence to Islamic customs in areas it controlled and employed harsh punishments, including executions.

The Taliban authorized its "Ministry for the Promotion of Virtue and the Suppression of Vice" to use physical punishments to enforce strict Islamic practices, including bans on television, Western music, and dancing. It prohibited women from attending school or working outside the home, except in health care, and it publicly executed some women for adultery. In what many consider its most extreme action, and which some say was urged by bin Laden, in March 2001 the Taliban blew up two large Buddha statues carved into hills above Bamiyan city, considering them idols.

The Clinton Administration held talks with the Taliban before and after it took power, but was unable to moderate its policies. The United States withheld recognition of Taliban as the legitimate government of Afghanistan, formally recognizing no faction as the government. The United Nations continued to seat representatives of the Rabbani government, not the Taliban. The State Department ordered the Afghan embassy in Washington, DC, closed in August 1997. U.N. Security Council Resolution 1193 (August 28, 1998) and 1214 (December 8, 1998) urged the Taliban to end discrimination against women.

Women's rights groups urged the Clinton Administration not to recognize the Taliban government. In May 1999, the Senate-passed called on the President not to recognize an Afghan government that oppresses women. The Taliban's hosting of Al Qaeda's leadership gradually became the Clinton Administration's overriding agenda item with Afghanistan. In April 1998, then U.S. Ambassador to the United Nations Bill Richardson (along with Asst. Sec. of State Karl Indurfurth and NSC senior official Bruce Riedel) visited Afghanistan but the Taliban refused to hand over bin Laden.

After the August 7, 1998, *Al Qaeda* bombings of U.S. embassies in Kenya and Tanzania, the Clinton Administration progressively pressured the Taliban, imposing U.S. sanctions and achieving adoption of some U.N. sanctions as well. On August 20, 1998, the United States fired cruise missiles at alleged *Al Qaeda* training camps in eastern Afghanistan, but bin Laden was not hit. Some observers assert that the Administration missed several other opportunities to strike him, including following a purported sighting of him by an unarmed Predator drone at his Karnak Farms camp in Afghanistan in mid-2000. Clinton Administration officials say they did not try to oust the Taliban militarily because domestic and international support for doing so was lacking.

THE NORTHERN ALLIANCE CONGEALS

The Taliban's policies caused different Afghan factions to ally with the ousted President Rabbani and Masud and their ally in the Herat area, Ismail Khan-the Tajik core of the anti-Taliban opposition-into a broader "Northern Alliance." In the Alliance were Uzbek, Hazara Shiite, and even some Pashtun Islamist factions. One major faction was the Uzbek militia (the Junbush-Melli, or National Islamic Movement of Afghanistan) of General Abdul Rashid Dostam. Frequently referred to by some Afghans as one of the "warlords" who gained power during the anti-Soviet war, Dostam first joined those seeking to oust Rabbani during his 1992-96 presidency, but later joined Rabbani's Northern Alliance against the Taliban.

Hazara Shiites

Members of Hazara tribes, mostly Shiite Muslims, are prominent in Bamiyan Province (central Afghanistan) and are always wary of repression by Pashtuns and other larger ethnic factions. During the various Afghan wars, the main Hazara Shiite militia was Hizb-e-Wahdat (Unity Party, composed of eight different groups). Hizb-e-Wahdat suffered a major setback in 1995 when its leader Abdul Ali Mazari was captured and killed by the Taliban.

Pashtun Islamists/Sayyaf

Abd-I-Rab Rasul Sayyaf, now a parliament committee chairman, headed a Pashtun-dominated *mujahedin* faction called the Islamic Union for the Liberation of Afghanistan during the anti-Soviet war. Even though his ideology is similar to that of the Taliban, Sayyaf joined the Northern Alliance.

POLICY PRE-SEPTEMBER 11, 2001

Throughout 2001 (but prior to the September 11 attacks), Bush Administration policy differed little from Clinton Administration policy-applying economic and political pressure while retaining dialogue with the Taliban, and refraining from militarily assisting the Northern Alliance. The September 11 Commission report said that, in the months prior to the September 11 attacks, Administration officials leaned toward such a step and that some officials wanted to assist anti- Taliban Pashtun forces. Other covert options were under consideration as well. In a departure from Clinton Administration policy, the Bush Administration stepped up engagement with Pakistan to try to end its support for the Taliban.

In accordance with U.N. Security Council Resolution 1333, in February 2001 the State Department ordered the Taliban representative office in New York closed, although the Taliban representative continued to operate informally. In March 2001, Administration officials received a Taliban envoy to discuss bilateral issues. Fighting with some Iranian, Russian, and Indian financial and military support, the Northern Alliance nonetheless continued to lose ground to the Taliban after it lost Kabul in 1996.

By the time of the September 11 attacks, the Taliban controlled at least 75% of the country, including almost all provincial capitals. The Alliance suffered a major setback on September 9, 2001, two days before the September 11 attacks, when Ahmad Shah Masud was assassinated by alleged *Al Qaeda* suicide bombers posing as journalists. He was succeeded by his intelligence chief, Muhammad Fahim, a veteran figure but who lacked Masud's undisputed authority.

SEPTEMBER 11 ATTACKS AND OPERATION ENDURING FREEDOM

After the September 11 attacks, the Bush Administration decided to militarily overthrow the Taliban when it refused to extradite bin Laden, judging that a friendly regime in Kabul was needed to enable U.S forces to search for *Al Qaeda* activists there. United Nations Security Council Resolution 1368 of September 12, 2001 said that the Security Council: "expresses its readiness to take all necessary steps to respond" (implying force) to the September 11 attacks. This is widely interpreted as a U.N. authorization for military action in response to the attacks, but it did not explicitly authorize Operation Enduring Freedom to oust the Taliban. Nor did the Resolution specifically reference Chapter VII of the U.N. Charter, which allows for responses to threats to international peace and security.

In Congress, S.J.Res. 23 (passed 98-0 in the Senate and with no objections in the House, P.L. 107-40), was somewhat more explicit than the U.N. Resolution, authorizing: all necessary and appropriate force against those nations, organizations, or persons he determines planned, authorized, committed, or aided the terrorist attacks that occurred on September 11, 2001 *or harbored such organizations or persons*. Major combat in Afghanistan (Operation Enduring Freedom, OEF) began on October 7, 2001.

It consisted primarily of U.S. air-strikes on Taliban and *Al Qaeda* forces, facilitated by the cooperation between small numbers (about 1,000) of U.S. special operations forces and the Northern Alliance and Pashtun anti-Taliban forces. Some U.S. ground units (about 1,300 Marines) moved into Afghanistan to pressure the Taliban around Qandahar at the height of the fighting (October-December 2001), but there were few pitched battles between U.S. and Taliban soldiers; most of the ground combat was between Taliban and its Afghan opponents.

Some critics believe that U.S. dependence on local Afghan militia forces in the war strengthened them for the post-war period, setting back post-war democracy building efforts. The Taliban regime unraveled rapidly after it lost Mazar-e-Sharif on November 9, 2001, to forces loyal to Dostam. Other, mainly Tajik, Northern Alliance forces-the commanders of which had initially promised U.S. officials they would not enter Kabul-entered the capital on November 12, 2001, to popular jubilation. The Taliban subsequently lost the south and east to pro-U.S. Pashtun leaders, such as Hamid Karzai.

The end of the Taliban regime is generally dated as December 9, 2001, when the Taliban surrendered Qandahar and Mullah Umar fled the city, leaving it under tribal law administered by Pashtun leaders such as the Noorzai clan. In December 2001, U.S. Special Operations Forces and CIA officers reportedly narrowed Osama bin Laden's location to the Tora Bora mountains in Nangarhar Province (30 miles west of the Khyber Pass), but the Afghan militia fighters who were the bulk of the fighting force did not prevent his escape.

Some U.S. military and intelligence officers (such as Gary Berntsen and "Dalton Fury, who have written books on the battle) have questioned the U.S. decision to rely mainly on Afghan forces in this engagement. Subsequently, U.S. and Afghan forces conducted "Operation Anaconda" in the Shah-i-Kot Valley south of Gardez (Paktia Province) during March 2-19, 2002, against 800 *Al Qaeda* and Taliban fighters. In March 2003, about 1,000 U.S. troops raided suspected Taliban or *Al Qaeda* fighters in villages around Qandahar (Operation Valiant Strike). On May 1, 2003, then Secretary of Defense Rumsfeld announced an end to "major combat."

POST-TALIBAN NATION BUILDING

With Afghanistan devastated after more than 20 years of warfare, the fall of the Taliban paved the way for the success of a long-stalled U.N. effort to form a broad-based Afghan government and for a U.S.-led coalition to begin building legitimate governing institutions. The policy of the Bush Administration was predicated on the assumption that preventing Afghanistan from again becoming a terrorism safe haven required the building of strong governing institutions, functioning democracy, and economic development.

This task has proved more difficult than anticipated because of the effects of the years of war, the low literacy rate of the population, the difficult terrain and geography, and the relative lack of trained government workers. The Obama Administration's "strategic review" of Afghanistan policy-the results of which was announced on March 27, 2009-narrowed official U.S. goals to preventing terrorism safe haven in Afghanistan and Pakistan. However, the strategy, in many ways, tries to enhance nation building by providing more civilian advisers and mentors to expand and reform the Afghan government, security forces, and develop the economy. In an interview with "60 Minutes" on March 22, 2009, President Obama also mentioned the need for an "exit strategy."

POLITICAL TRANSITION

In the formation of the first post-Taliban transition government, the United Nations was viewed as a credible mediator by all sides largely because of its role in ending the Soviet occupation. During the 1990s, proposals from a succession of U.N. mediators incorporated many of former King Zahir Shah's proposals for a government to be selected by a traditional assembly, or *loya jirga*.

However, U.N.-mediated cease-fires between warring factions always broke down. Non- U.N. initiatives made little progress, particularly the "Six Plus Two" multilateral contact group, which began meeting in 1997 (the United States, Russia, and the six states bordering Afghanistan: Iran, China, Pakistan, Turkmenistan, Uzbekistan, and Tajikistan). Other failed efforts included a "Geneva group" (Italy, Germany, Iran, and the United States) formed in 2000; an Organization of Islamic Conference (OIC) contact group; and Afghan exile efforts, including discussion groups launched by Hamid Karzai's clan and Zahir Shah ("Rome process).

BONN AGREEMENT

Immediately after the September 11 attacks, former U.N. mediator Lakhdar Brahimi was brought back (he had resigned in frustration in October 1999). U.N. Security Council Resolution 1378 was adopted on November 14, 2001, calling for a "central" role for the United Nations in establishing a transitional administration and inviting member states to send peacekeeping forces to promote stability and aid delivery. After the fall of Kabul in November 2001, the United Nations invited major Afghan factions, most prominently the Northern Alliance and that of the former King-but not the Taliban-to a conference in Bonn, Germany.

On December 5, 2001, the factions signed the "Bonn Agreement." It was endorsed by U.N. Security Council Resolution 1385 (December 6, 2001). The agreement, reportedly forged with substantial Iranian diplomatic help because of Iran's support for the Northern Alliance faction:

- Formed the interim administration headed by Hamid Karzai.
- Authorized an international peace keeping force to maintain security in Kabul, and Northern Alliance forces were directed to withdraw from the capital. Security Council

Resolution 1386 gave formal Security Council authorization for the international peacekeeping force (International Security Assistance Force, ISAF).

- Referred to the need to cooperate with the international community on counter narcotics, crime, and terrorism. • applied the constitution of 1964 until a permanent constitution could be drafted.

PERMANENT CONSTITUTION

A June 2002 "emergency" *loya jirga* put a representative imprimatur on the transition; it was attended by 1,550 delegates (including about 200 women) from Afghanistan's 364 districts. Subsequently, a 35-member constitutional commission drafted the permanent constitution, and unveiled in November 2003. It was debated by 502 delegates, selected in U.N-run caucuses, at a "*constitutional loya jirga* (CLJ)" during December 13, 2003-January 4, 2004. The CLJ, chaired by Mojadeddi (mentioned above), ended with approval of the constitution with only minor changes.

The Northern Alliance faction failed in its effort to set up a prime minister-ship, but they did achieve a fallback objective of checking presidential powers by assigning major authorities to the elected parliament, such as the power to veto senior official nominees and to impeach a president. The constitution made former King Zahir Shah honorary "Father of the Nation," a title that is not heritable. Zahir Shah died on July 23, 2007. The constitution also set out timetables for presidential, provincial and district elections (by June 2004) and stipulated that, if possible, they should be held simultaneously.

FIRST POST-TALIBAN ELECTIONS

Security conditions precluded the holding of all elections simultaneously. The first election, for president, was held on October 9, 2004, slightly missing a June deadline. Turnout was about 80%. On November 3, 2004, Karzai was declared winner (55.4% of the vote) over his seventeen challengers on the first round, avoiding a runoff. Parliamentary and provincial council elections were intended for April-May 2005 but were delayed until September 18, 2005. Because of the difficulty in confirming voter registration rolls and determining district boundaries, elections for the 364 district councils, each of which will likely have contentious boundaries because they will inevitably separate tribes and clans, have not been held to date.

For the parliamentary election, voting was conducted for individuals running in each province, not as party slates. (There are now 90 registered political parties in Afghanistan, but parties remain unpopular because of their linkages to outside countries during the anti-Soviet war.) When parliament first convened on December 18, 2005, the Northern Alliance bloc achieved selection of one of its own-who was Karzai's main competitor in the presidential election-Yunus Qanooni, for speaker of the all-elected 249 seat lower house. In April 2007, Qanooni and Northern Alliance political leader Rabbani organized this opposition bloc, along with ex-Communists and some royal family members, into a party called the "United Front" (UF) that wants increased parliamentary powers and direct elections for the provincial governors.

The 102-seat upper house (*Meshrano Jirga*, House of Elders), selected by the elected provincial councils and Karzai, consists mainly of older, well known figures, as well as 17 females (half of Karzai's 34 appointments, as provided for in the constitution). The leader of that body is Sibghatullah Mojadeddi, a pro-Karzai former *mujahedin* party leader and elder statesman. With his bloc of 17 non-female slots, Karzai appointed many of his allies, but also some of his perceived political adversaries, to the upper house.

2009 AND 2010 ELECTIONS AND CANDIDATES

The next major political milestone in Afghanistan is the 2009 presidential and provincial elections. On February 3, 2009, Afghanistan's Independent Election Commission (IEC) set August 20, 2009 as the election date - a change from a date mandated by one section of the Constitution (Article 61) as taking place by April 21, 2009, in order to allow at least 30 days before Karzai's term expires on May 22, 2009.

The IEC decision on the latter date cited another article of the Constitution (Article 33) mandating universal accessibility to the voting-and saying that the April 21 date was precluded by difficulties in registering voters, printing ballots, training staff, making the public aware of the elections, and the dependence on international donations to fund the elections, in addition to the security questions. This decision caused the UF bloc to say it would not "recognize" Karzai's presidency after May 22. As expected, the IEC reaffirmed on March 4, 2009 that the election must be held on August 20, 2009.

The official decision did not stop the UF from insisting that Karzai step down on May 22 in favor of a caretaker government, which presumably would be headed by Upper House speaker Sibghatullah Mojadeddi. Karzai argued that the Constitution does not provide for any transfer of power other than in case of election or death of a President. The Afghan Supreme Court backed that decision on March 28, 2009. The Obama Administration publicly backed both the IEC and the Supreme Court rulings, even though, according to U.S. officials, that backing could be interpreted as a U.S. endorsement of Karzai.

Obama Administration Special Representative to Afghanistan and Pakistan Richard Holbrooke says the United States favors no candidate and Ambassador Tim Carney has been appointed to coordinate U.S. support for the elections process - and to ensure U.S. neutrality - from U.S. Embassy Kabul. Despite the political dispute between Karzai and his opponents, enthusiasm among the public appears to be high. Registration (updating of 2005 voter rolls) began in October 2008 and was completed as of the beginning of March 2009.

However, there were also reports of some registration fraud, with some voters registering on behalf of women who do not, by custom, show up at registration sites. U.S./NATO military operations in some areas, including in Helmand in January 2009, were conducted to secure registration centers. The elections are expected to cost about $200 million; on March 31, 2009. At a U.N.-led conference in the Netherlands, the

United States committed $40 million of that amount, which is part of a planned $175 million U.S. funding for elections in FY2009.

OUTLINES OF THE CONTEST

Politically, Karzai has benefitted from the August 2009 date because it gives him more time to restore his popularity and gives more time for the infusion of U.S. troops to secure the Pashtun areas which will be the source of many Karzai votes. With the August date set, candidates registered their candidacies during April 24 - May 8, 2009. In election-related political jockeying, Karzai obtained an initial agreement from Muhammad Fahim, formerly his antagonist and a key member of the ethnic minority dominated United Front (UF), to run as one of his Vice Presidents.

He, Fahim, and incumbent second vice president Karim Khalili (Hazara senior figure) registered their ticket on May 4, 2009, just before Karzai left to visit the United States for the latest round of three way strategic talks (U.S.-Pakistan-Afghanistan). The Fahim choice was criticized by human rights and other groups because of Fahim's long identity as a mujahedin commander/militia faction leader, but the selection, and Fahim's acceptance, was viewed as a major political coup for Karzai by splitting the UF bloc. Karzai is now viewed as the clear favorite for re-election. Anti-Karzai Pashtuns attempted, unsuccessfully, to coalesce around one challenger. In the end, former Finance Minister Ashraf Ghani registered his candidacy, but without explicit endorsement of another strong Pashtun, former Interior Minister Jalali, or strong representation from other ethnicities in his vice presidential slots.

Ghani has criticized Karzai for failing to establish legitimate and successful governance, but he has spent much time in the United States and Europe and might lose support among some average Afghans who might view him as out of touch with day-to-day problems in Afghanistan. Neither was the UF successful in forging a united front to challenge Karzai. Observers in Kabul say the UF had always leaned toward former Foreign Minister Dr. Abdullah Abdullah to its slate, but there were others purportedly challenging Abdullah for the UF mantle.

Dr. Abdullah did register to run, but his running mates are Dr. Cheragh Ali Cheragh, a Hazara who did poorly in the 2004 election, and a little known Pashtun, Homayoun Wasefi. Fahim, as noted above, made a deal with Karzai to join his ticket, thus fracturing the UF's unity. Subsequent to the filing deadlines, it has been reported that Ghani and Dr. Abdullah are in discussions to unify their tickets. That would necessitate one or the other dropping their candidacies for president and endorsing or joining (in a vice presidential slot) the other's slate. In addition, with Karzai now the clear favorite in the race, former U.S. Ambassador to Afghanistan Zalmay Khalilzad declined to run himself or endorse another ticket, and is said to be in talks with Karzai to possibly serve as his chief administrator if Karzai is re-elected.

GOVERNANCE ISSUES

The Obama Administration review strongly emphasizes providing new U.S. and international resources to improve Afghan governance. Since its formation in late 2001, Karzai's government has grown in capabilities and size, although more slowly than expected. At the same time, it has narrowed ethnically, progressively dominated by ethnic Pashtuns, who have traditionally governed Afghanistan. Among the key security bodies, only the Intelligence Directorate continues to be headed by a non-Pashtun (Amrollah Saleh, a Tajik).

Adhering to a tacit consensus, the other security ministries (Defense, Interior) tend to have Pashtun leadership but with non-Pashtuns in key deputy or subordinate positions. One prominent example is the defense ministry, in which the chief of staff is a Tajik (Bismillah Khan), who reports to a Pashtun Defense Minister (Abdul Rahim Wardak). The parliament has emerged, unexpectedly to some, as a relatively vibrant body that creates accountability and has asserted itself politically. Some criticize it for the large presence of *mujahedin* leaders-figures who gained prominence from their anti-Soviet war effort.

In 2007, the parliament compelled Karzai to oust several major conservatives from the Supreme Court in favor of those with more experience in modern jurisprudence. In mid-2007, parliament enacted a law granting amnesty to former *mujahedin* commanders-an attempt to put past schisms to rest in building a new Afghanistan. The law was rewritten to give victims the ability to bring accusations of past abuses; its status is unclear because Karzai did not veto it but he did not sign it either. In May 2007, the UF bloc engineered a vote of no confidence against Foreign Minister Rangeen Spanta for failing to prevent Iran from expelling 50,000 Afghan refugees. Karzai opposed Spanta's dismissal on the grounds that refugee affairs are not his ministry's prime jurisdiction.

The Afghan Supreme Court has sided with Karzai and Spanta remains in position. On the other hand, on some less contentious issues, the executive and the legislature appear to be working well. Since the end of 2007, parliament has passed several laws, including a labor law, a mines law, a law on economic cooperatives, and a convention on tobacco control. The *Wolesi Jirga* also has confirmed Karzai nominees in several cabinet shifts, as well as for the one remaining justice to fill out the Supreme Court. In April 2009, parliament enacted a personal status law for Shiites that caused an outcry in the international community, as discussed below.

EXPANDING AND REFORMING CENTRAL GOVERNMENT/CORRUPTION

With a permanent national government fully assembled, U.S. policy has been to expand governance throughout the country, and this policy will receive increased U.S. financial and advisory resources under the new Obama Administration strategy. The Karzai government is widely estimated by U.S. officials to control about 30% of the country, while the Taliban controls 10%, and tribes and local groups control the remainder.

U.S. commanders and officials assert that Taliban militants are able to infiltrate "un-governed space," contributing to the persistence and in some areas the expansion of the Taliban insurgency. In part because building the central government has gone slowly, there was a U.S. shift during 2008 away from reliance only on strengthening central government, toward promoting local governance. Some argue that doing so is more in synch with Afghan traditions, because Afghans have always sought substantial regional autonomy and resisted strong governance from Kabul.

Marginalization of Regional Strongmen

A key to U.S. strategy, particularly during 2002-2006, was to strengthen the central government by helping Karzai curb key regional strongmen and local militias-whom some refer to as "warlords." These actors have been considered a threat to Afghan stability because of their arbitrary administration of justice, and the popular resentment of their use of their position to enrich themselves and their supporters. However, Karzai has, to some extent, succeeded in marginalizing the largest regional leaders.

- Ismail Khan was removed as Herat governor in September 2004 and later appointed Minister of Water and Energy. On the other hand, Khan was tapped by Karzai to help calm Herat after Sunni-Shiite clashes there in February 2006, and some believe he should be reappointed to curb growing Taliban encroachment into the province.
- In April 2005, Dostam was appointed Karzai's top military advisor, and in April 2005 he "resigned" as head of his Junbush Melli faction. However, in May 2007 his followers in the north conducted large demonstrations in attempting to force out the anti-Dostam governor of Jowzjan Province. In February 2008, Afghan police surrounded Dostam's home in Kabul, but did not arrest him, in connection with the alleged beating of a political opponent by Dostam supporters. Some outside observers have cited Karzai's refusal to order an arrest as a sign of weakness of his leadership. However, in December 2008, Karzai reportedly agreed to drop the charges in exchange for stripping

Dostam of his chief of staff title and his going into exile in Turkey.

- Another key figure, former Defense Minister Fahim (Northern Alliance) has been coopted by Karzai to the extent that he is now his running mate in the August 2009 elections. Fahim was appointed by Karzai to the *Meshrano Jirga,* although he remained in that body only a few months. The appointment was intended to give him a stake in the political process and reduce his potential to activate Northern Alliance militia loyalists. Fahim continues to turn heavy weapons over to U.N. and Afghan forces (including four Scud missiles), although the U.N. Assistance Mission in Afghanistan (UNAMA) says that large quantities of weapons remain in the Panjshir Valley.
- Two other large militia leaders, Hazrat Ali (Jalalabad area) and Khan Mohammad (Qandahar area) were placed in civilian police chief posts in 2005; Hazrat Ali was subsequently elected to the *Wolesi Jirga.*

MILITIA DISARMAMENT: DDR AND DIAG PROGRAMS

A cornerstone of the effort to strengthen the central government was programs to dismantle identified and illegal militias that were empowered by Afghanistan's years of warfare. The main program, run by UNAMA, was called the "DDR" program: Disarmament, Demobilization, and Reintegration" and it formally concluded on June 30, 2006. The program got off to a slow start because the Afghan Defense Ministry did not reduce the percentage of Tajiks in senior positions by a July 1, 2003, target date, dampening Pashtun recruitment. In September 2003, Karzai replaced 22 senior Tajiks in the Defense Ministry officials with Pashtuns, Uzbeks, and Hazaras, enabling DDR to proceed.

The DDR program was initially been expected to demobilize 100,000 fighters, although that figure was later reduced. Figures for accomplishment of the DDR and DIAG programs are contained in the "security indicators table" below. Of those demobilized, 55,800 former fighters have exercised reintegration options provided by the program: starting small businesses, farming, and other options. U.N. officials say at least 25% of these found long-term, sustainable jobs. Some studies criticized the DDR program for failing to prevent a certain amount of rearmament of militiamen or stockpiling of weapons and for the rehiring of some militiamen.

Part of the DDR program was the collection and cantonment of militia weapons, but generally only poor quality weapons were collected. The major donor for the program was Japan, which contributed about $140 million. Figures for collected weapons are contained in the security indicators table, and U.S. spending on the program are in the U.S. aid tables at the end of this chapter. Since June 11, 2005, the disarmament effort has emphasized another program called "DIAG"- Disbandment of Illegal Armed Groups. It is run by the Afghan Disarmament and Reintegration Commission, headed by Vice President Khalili. Under the DIAG, no payments are available to fighters, and the program depends on persuasion rather than use of force against the illegal groups.

DIAG has not been as well funded as was DDR: it has received $11 million in operating funds. As an incentive for compliance, Japan and other donors have made available $35 million for development projects where illegal groups have disbanded. These incentives were intended to accomplish the disarmament of a pool of as many as 150,000 members of 1,800 different "illegal armed groups": militiamen that were not part of recognized local forces (Afghan Military Forces, AMF) and were never on the rolls of the Defense Ministry. These goals were not met by the December 2007 target date in part because armed groups in the south say they need to remain armed against the Taliban, but UNAMA reports that some progress continues to be achieved.

Anti-Corruption Efforts

An accelerating trend in U.S. policy-and emphasized by the Obama Administration's review-is to press Karzai to weed out official corruption. The Administration plans to develop and submit to Congress "metrics" to measure Afghan progress against corruption and overall effectiveness. The widespread corruption has severely tainted Karzai's image in the United States and is widely perceived as a cause of security deterioration as Afghans lose faith in the government and turn to the Taliban as sources of impartial justice and protection. At the highest levels of the Afghan government, it is widely believed that Karzai has tolerated his brothers' use of his position to further their business dealings. (The brothers are discussed in the biography box on Karzai, above.)

However, most allegations of corruption focus on lower level government bureaucrats and Afghan police officers who routinely demand bribes to perform services, or who sell some of the equipment provided to them by international donors. U.S. policy may be starting to yield results. In August 2008, reportedly at U.S. prodding, Karzai formed a "High Office of Oversight for the Implementation of Anti-Corruption Strategy" with wide powers to investigate civilian and security officials. The body is attempting to determine which officials have assets abroad. Karzai attends weekly meetings of the officials of this body.

On March 27, 2009, to set an example for other senior officials, Karzai publicly declared his assets. In October 2008, Karzai shuffled his cabinet, appointing former Communist era official Muhammad Hanif Atmar-avowedly committed to reducing police corruption-as Interior Minister, and placing a widely praised official, Gulam Wardak, as new Education Minister. The Minister of Commerce, Amin Farhang, was voted out of office by the parliament in December 2008 for alleged misfeasance. Karzai told journalists in March 2009 that the government every day arrests officials for alleged corruption.

The U.S. Special Inspector General for Afghanistan Reconstruction (SIGAR) said in his April 2009 report that Karzai has asked the SIGAR to help design additional anti-corruption programs. Partly because of the corruption issue, the Obama Administration has not given Karzai the access and public support that was given by the Bush Administration. A meeting between Vice President-elect Joseph Biden and Karzai in mid-January 2009 reportedly was tense because of Karzai's failure thus far to curb corruption. However, no tension was evident on this issue during Karzai's May 5-8, 2009 visit to the United States.

ENHANCING LOCAL GOVERNANCE

Since the beginning of 2008, there has been a major U.S.-Afghan push to build up local governance, reflecting a shift from the 2001-2007 approach of building only the central government. The approach represents an attempt to rebuild some of the tribal and other local structures, such as *"jirgas"* and *"shuras"*-traditional local councils-that were destroyed in the course of constant warfare over several decades. The leader in this initiative has been the "Independent Directorate of Local Governance" (IDLG), formed in August 2007 and headed by Jelani Popal (a member of Karzai's Popolzai clan). The IDLG reports to Karzai's office, and its establishment was intended to institute a systematic process for selecting capable provincial and district governors by taking the screening function away from the Interior Ministry.

The IDLG is also selecting police chiefs and other local office holders, and in many cases has already begun removing allegedly corrupt local officials. Part of its mission is to empower localities to decide on development projects by forming local "Development Councils" that decide on local development projects and are key to the perceived success of the "National Solidarity Program" discussed later. There are 30,000 such elected positions nationwide. In 2008, with the support of the Bush Administration, the IDLG launched the government's "Social Outreach Program," intended to draw closer connections between tribes and localities to the central government.

The program includes small payments (about $200 per month) to tribal leaders and other participants, in part to persuade them to inform on Taliban insurgent movements. Since its formation, the United States has provided over $100 million to the IDLG for its strategic work plan and its operations and outreach (as of early 2009). Of that, about $8.5 million in FY2009 funds will assist the Social Outreach Program and related "Governor's Performance Fund." The Social Outreach program's security dimensions-primarily the "Afghan Public Protection Force"-are discussed later in this report.

Among the notable successes of the IDLG leadership on gubernatorial appointments is the March 2008 replacement of the ineffective Helmand governor Asadullah Wafa with Gulab Mangal. Mangal is considered a competent administrator, but he is from Laghman province, not Helmand, somewhat to the consternation of Helmand residents. U.N. Office of Drugs and Crime (UNODC) and other officials say Mangal is taking effective action against poppy cultivation in the province. Some observers speculate, however, that Karzai still wants to replace Mangal with a close Karzai ally, the former governor, Sher Muhammad Akunzadeh (governor until 2005, now a Karzai appointee in the upper house of parliament), who purportedly committed numerous human rights abuses in the course of fighting the Taliban in the province and apparently remains powerful informally there.

Karzai maintains Akunzadeh, when he was governor, was highly effective in keeping the Taliban at bay in the province by fielding local tribal forces against the insurgents. The UNODC report on narcotics in August 2008 credits the strong leadership of Ghul Agha Shirzai, Nangarhar's governor, for moving that province into the "poppy free" column in 2008. Atta Mohammad Noor of Balkh province receives similar credit, and Monshi Abdul Majid, governor of Badakkhshan, is cited for achieving significant reduction in cultivation over the past few years.

The governor of Qandahar was changed (to former General Rahmatullah Raufi, replacing Asadullah Khalid) after the August 7, 2008, Taliban assault on the Qandahar prison

(Sarposa) that led to the freeing of several hundred Taliban fighters incarcerated there. However, reflecting continued political infighting over how best to stabilize Qandahar, Raufi was replaced in December 2008 by Afghan-Canadian academic Tooryalai Wesa. Other governors said to be successful in helping stabilize and develop their provinces include former Khost governor Arsala Jamal, and Kabul province governor Hajji Din Mohammad, son of the slain "Jalalabad Shura" leader Hajji Abd al-Qadir.

U.S. EMBASSY/BUDGETARY SUPPORT TO AFGHAN GOVERNMENT

A component of U.S. efforts to strengthen governance has been maintaining a large and active diplomatic presence. Zalmay Khalilzad, an American of Afghan origin discussed above, was ambassador during December 2003-August 2005; he reportedly had significant influence on Afghan government decisions. Lt. Gen. Karl Eikenberry, who served as commander of U.S. forces in Afghanistan during 2004-2005, is now Ambassador. Eikenberry and the rest of the U.S. team will be working closely with new special representative on Afghanistan and Pakistan, Ambassador Richard Holbrooke, who made his second official visit to the region in April 2009.

The U.S. embassy, now in newly constructed buildings, has progressively expanded its personnel and facilities to several hundred. The Embassy will need to accommodate additional civilian hires and Foreign Service officers who will be posted to Afghanistan as mentors and advisers to the Afghan government under the Obama Administration strategy. About $87 million was requested for new construction in a FY2009 supplemental appropriations request, and $1.15 billion in State Department operations and Embassy construction funds are requested for FY2010. Of that latter amount, $60 million is to enhance the air service that takes State Department and USAID people around the country ("PRT Air").

Although the Afghan government has increased its revenue and is covering a growing proportion of its budget,

USAID provides funding to help the Afghan government meet gaps in its budget- both directly and through a U.N.-run multi-donor Afghan Reconstruction Trust Fund (ARTF) account. Those figures are provided in the U.S. aid tables at the end of the paper. As part of an earlier, 2003 U.S. push on reconstruction, the Bush Administration formed a 15- person Afghan Reconstruction Group (ARG), placed within the U.S. Embassy in Kabul, which now focuses on helping Afghanistan attract private investment and develop private industries.

HUMAN RIGHTS AND DEMOCRACY

The Administration and Afghan government claim progress in building a democratic Afghanistan that adheres to international standards of human rights practices and presumably is able to earn the support of the Afghan people. However, the State Department report on human rights practices for 2008 (released February 25, 2009) said that Afghanistan's human rights record remained "poor," noting in particular that the government or its agents commit arbitrary or unlawful killings. Still, virtually all observers agree that Afghans are freer than they were under the Taliban. Some press and other restrictions appear to reflect the government's sensitivity to Afghanistan's conservative nature rather than politically motivated action.

For example, alcohol is increasingly difficult to obtain in restaurants and stores, although the government has not banned alcohol consumption or sales. Afghan political groupings and parties are able to meet and organize freely, but there are also abuses based on ethnicity or political factionalism and arbitrary implementation of justice by local leaders. Since the Taliban era, more than 40 private radio stations, seven television networks, and 350 independent newspapers have opened, but the State Department say that there are growing numbers of arrests or intimidation of journalists who criticize the central government or local leaders.

A press law was adopted in September 2008, requiring media organs to be licensed by the government, and press policy remains highly conservative; in April 2008 the Ministry of Information and Culture banned five Indian-produced soap operas on the grounds that they are too risqué. The ban was later overturned when the broadcasters agreed to also run Islamist-oriented programming from Turkey. That came amid a move by conservative parliamentarians to pass legislation to ban loud music, men and women mingling in public, video games, and other behavior common in the West.

RELIGIOUS FREEDOM

On religious freedom, some note that the government has reimposed some Islamic restrictions that characterized Taliban rule, including the code of criminal punishments stipulated in Islamic law. The death penalty has been re-instituted, reversing a 2004 moratorium declared by Karzai. Fifteen convicts were executed at once on October 7, 2007. In January 2008, Afghanistan's "Islamic council," composed of senior clerics, backed public executions for convicted murderers and urged Karzai to end the activities of organizations that promote Christianity to Afghans. The State Department International Religious Freedom report for 2008 (released September 19, 2008) reported continued discrimination against the Shiite (Hazara) minority and some other minorities such as Sikhs and Hindus, but that "Government and political leaders aspire to a national environment that respects the right to religious freedom."

A *Washington Post* report of January 4, 2009, highlighted the freedom Afghan Shiites now have to celebrate their holy days openly. The Minister of Justice is a Shiite, a development many observers did not expect at any time in Afghanistan. However, in May 2007, a directorate under the Supreme Court declared the Baha'i faith to be a form of blasphemy. In March 2009, the parliament and executive branch attempted to accommodate Shiite demands by passing and signing a new personal status law for members of the sect. However, in April 2009, following an international condemnation of provisions that human rights groups say would legalize the rape of a wife by her husband and restrict the ability of women to go outside the home, Karzai placed the law under review by the Justice Ministry, which drafts government bills.

Karzai said during his May visit to the United States that it would be amended and resubmitted to the parliament. H.Con.Res. 108 and S.Con. Res. 19, expresses the sense of Congress that the law should be repealed; President Obama has called the provisions of the law "abhorrent." On January 25, 2008, in a case that has implications for both religious and journalistic freedom, a young reporter, Sayed Pervez Kambaksh, was sentenced in a quick trial to death for distributing a website report to student peers questioning some precepts of Islam.

On October 21, 2008, a Kabul appeals court reduced his sentence to 20 years, a sentenced reaffirmed by the Afghanistan Supreme Court in March 2009, but he still could obtain a Karzai pardon. A previous religious freedom case earned congressional attention in March 2006. An Afghan man, Abd al-Rahman, who had converted to Christianity 16 years ago while working for a Christian aid group in Pakistan, was imprisoned and faced a potential death penalty trial for apostasy-his refusal to convert back to Islam. Facing international pressure, Karzai prevailed on Kabul court authorities to release him (March 29, 2006). His release came the same day the House passed H.Res. 736 calling on protections for Afghan converts.

HUMAN TRAFFICKING

Afghanistan was again placed in Tier 2 in the State Department report on human trafficking issued in June 2008. The government is assessed as not complying with minimum standards for eliminating trafficking, but making significant efforts to do so. The says that women (reportedly from China and Central Asia) are being trafficked into Afghanistan for sexual exploitation. Other reports say some are brought to work in night clubs purportedly frequented by members of many international NGOs. In an effort to also increase protections for Afghan women, in August 2008 the Interior Ministry announced a crackdown on sexual assault-an effort to publicly air a taboo subject.

The United States has spent $500,000 to eliminate human trafficking in Afghanistan since FY2001. An Afghan Independent Human Rights Commission (AIHRC) was formed in 2002 to monitor government performance and has been credited in State Department reports with successful interventions to curb abuses. Headed by former Women's Affairs minister Sima Samar, it also conducts surveys of how Afghans view governance and reconstruction efforts. The House-passed Afghan Freedom Support Act (AFSA) re-authorization bill (H.R. 2446) would authorize $10 million per year for this Commission until FY2010.

ADVANCEMENT OF WOMEN

According to the State Department human rights report for 2008, the Afghan government is promoting the advancement of women, but numerous abuses, such as denial of educational and employment opportunities continue primarily because of Afghanistan's conservative traditions. A major development in post-Taliban Afghanistan was the formation of a Ministry of Women's Affairs dedicated to improving women's rights, although numerous accounts say the ministry's influence is limited and it is now headed by a male, (the deputy minister is female). It promotes the involvement of women in business ventures, and it plays a key role in referring women victims of domestic abuse to a growing number of women's shelters across Afghanistan.

Many women continue to wear the head-to-toe *burqa* covering, even though wearing it has not been required since the Taliban government was ousted. Three female ministers were in the 2004-2006 cabinet: former presidential candidate Masooda Jalal (Ministry of Women's Affairs), Sediqa Balkhi (Minister for Martyrs and the Disabled), and Amina Afzali (Minister of Youth). However, Karzai nominated only one (Minister of Women's Affairs Soraya Sobhrang) in the 2006 cabinet, and she was voted down by Islamist conservatives in parliament, leaving no women in the cabinet. In March 2005, Karzai appointed a former Minister of Women's Affairs, Habiba Sohrabi, as governor of Bamiyan province, inhabited mostly by Hazaras.

The constitution reserves for women at least 17 of the 102 seats in the upper house and 62 of the 249 seats in the lower house of parliament. There are 68 women in the lower house, meaning six were elected without the quota. There are 23 serving in the upper house, six more than Karzai's mandated bloc of 17 female appointees. There are also 121 women holding seats in the 420 provincial council seats nationwide. However, some NGOs and other groups believe that the women elected by the quota system are not viewed as equally legitimate parliamentarians. More generally, women are performing jobs that were rarely held by women even before the Taliban came to power in 1996, including in the new police force.

There are 67 female judges and 447 female journalists working nationwide. The most senior Afghan woman in the police force was assassinated in Qandahar in September 2008. Press reports say Afghan women are increasingly learning how to drive. Under the new government, the wearing of the full body covering called the *burqa* is no longer obligatory, and fewer women are wearing it than was the case a few years ago. On the other hand, women's advancement has made women a target of attacks by Taliban supporters or highly conservative Afghans. Attacks on girls' schools and athletic facilities have increased in the most restive areas.

On November 12, 2008, suspected Taliban sprayed acid on the faces of several schoolgirls in Qandahar. U.S. officials have had some influence in persuading the government to codify women's rights. After the Karzai government took office, the United States and the new Afghan government set up a U.S.-Afghan Women's Council to coordinate the allocation of resources to Afghan women. According to the State Department, the United States has implemented several hundred projects directly in support of Afghan women, including women's empowerment, maternal and child health and nutrition, funding the Ministry of Women's Affairs, micro-finance projects, and like programs.

The Afghanistan Freedom Support Act of 2002 (AFSA, P.L. 107-327) authorized $15 million per year (FY2003-FY2006) for the Ministry of Women's Affairs. Those monies are donated to the Ministry from Economic Support Funds (ESF) accounts controlled by USAID. S. 229, "Afghan Women Empowerment Act of 2009," introduced in the 111 th Congress, would authorize $45 million per year in FY2010-FY2012 for grants to Afghan women; for the ministry of Women's Affairs ($5 million), and the Afghan Independent Human Rights Commission ($10 million).

OVERALL DEMOCRACY AND GOVERNANCE FUNDING ISSUES

During FY2002 - 2009, USAID has spent $1.9 billion on governance, democracy, and rule of law programs, including: support for elections, civil society programs, political party strengthening, media freedom, and local governance. Funding earmarks for programs benefitting women and girls is contained in the tables at the end of the chapter.

COMBATING NARCOTICS TRAFFICKING

Narcotics trafficking are regarded by some as one of the most significant problems facing Afghanistan, generating what U.S. commanders estimate to be about $100 million per year for the Taliban. Afghanistan is the source of about 93% of the world's illicit opium supply, and according to UNODC, "... leaving aside 19th Century China, no country in the world has ever produced narcotics on such a deadly scale." However, this is one area where there are widespread accounts of progress, although it is not certain whether the progress will be sustained. Ambassador Holbrooke disparaged signs of progress at a meeting in Brussels on March 21, 2009, saying the United States had received "nothing" for its counter-narcotics funding.

The Obama Administration's strategic review focused some additional attention on promoting alternative livelihoods to poppy growing. Some international officials are reporting good results by encouraging the growing of pomegranates and of saffron rice as alternative crops that draw buyers outside

Afghanistan. Encouraging alternative livelihoods is the preferred emphasis of the Afghan government, and the Afghan side maintains that narcotics flourish in areas where there is no security, and not the other way around. In FY 2008, the United States provided $38 million in "Good Performers" funds to provinces that have eliminated poppy cultivation, such as Balkh province. According to Afghan cabinet members, the government also is spending funds on a "social safety net" to help wean landless farmers away from poppy cultivation work. The UNODC report of November 2008 was the most positive such report since at least 2005, saying: "The opium flood waters in Afghanistan have started to recede."

The estimate was based on a drop in area under opium cultivation of 19%, an overall opium production drop of 6%, and a large increase in the number of "poppy free provinces" from 13 in the 2007 report to 18 (out of 34 total provinces) now. A January 2009 UNODC "Afghanistan: Opium Winter Assessment" said the trend in reduction in poppy cultivation is likely to continue in 2009. The report added that all 18 provinces now considered "poppy free" are likely to remain so, and four provinces have the potential to join that category. The report adds that cultivation in Helmand, which produces more than half the poppy crop of all Afghanistan, is likely to fall in 2009.

These reports attribute the progress to strong leadership by some governors, such as those mentioned above in the section on governance. On the other hand, some poppy growers are turning to marijuana cultivation and trafficking, perhaps sensing less pressure on that activity. On June 11, 2008, the U.N. Security Council adopted Resolution 1817, called for greater international cooperation to stop the movement of chemical precursors used to process opium into Afghanistan. In concert with interdiction and building up alternative livelihoods, U.S.-trained Afghanistan counter-narcotics police eradicate poppy fields by cutting down the crop manually on the ground.

During 2007, there was debate between some in the U.S. government, including Ambassador Wood, and Karzai over whether to conduct spraying of fields, particularly by air. President Karzai strongly opposed aerial spraying, arguing that doing so would cause a backlash among Afghan farmers; he appears to have won this argument. Congress has to date sided with Karzai's view; the FY2008 Consolidated Appropriation (P.L. 110-161) prohibited U.S. counter-narcotics funding from being used for aerial spraying on Afghanistan poppy fields without Afghan concurrence. Using U.S. and NATO forces to combat narcotics is another facet under debate. Some NATO contributors, such as Britain, have focused on interdicting traffickers and raiding drug labs.

At a NATO meeting on October 10, 2008, NATO accepted a policy of using force against narcotics traffickers. Under the agreement, each country can choose to keep their forces out of such missions, and press reports say that several NATO nations have done just that, hampering implementation of the October 2008 agreement and causing continued U.S.-NATO frictions over the policy on this tactic. U.S. troops deployed in Helmand have not specifically acted against poppy fields, deliberately to avoid angering the local population on which the success of U.S. counter-insurgency operations depend.

In February 2009, NATO modified its posture somewhat toward viewing some drug traffickers as active participants in the insurgency, and therefore subject to military operations, rather than as a purely criminal/legal issue. The U.S. military, in support of the effort after initial reluctance, is flying Afghan and U.S. counter-narcotics agents (Drug Enforcement Agency, DEA) on missions and identifying targets; it also evacuates casualties from counter-drug operations. The Department of Defense is also playing the major role in training and equipping specialized Afghan counter-narcotics police, in developing an Afghan intelligence fusion cell, and training Afghan border police, as well as assisting an Afghan helicopter squadron to move Afghan counter-narcotics forces around the country.

The Bush Administration took some legal steps against suspected Afghan drug traffickers; in April 2005, a DEA operation successfully caught the alleged leading Afghan narcotics trafficker, Haji Bashir Noorzai, arresting him after a flight to New York. The United States funded a Counternarcotics Justice Center ($8 million) in Kabul to prosecute and incarcerate suspected traffickers.

The Bush Administration repeatedly named Afghanistan as a major illicit drug producer and drug transit country, but did not include Afghanistan on a smaller list of countries that have "failed demonstrably to make substantial efforts" to adhere to international counter-narcotics agreements and take certain counter-narcotics measures set forth in U.S. law. The Bush Administration exercised waiver provisions to a required certification of full Afghan cooperation that was needed to provide more than congressionally stipulated amounts of U.S. economic assistance to Afghanistan.

A similar certification requirement (to provide amounts over $300 million) is contained in the House version of the FY2008 appropriation (P.L. 110-161), and in the FY2009 appropriation, P.L. 111-8 ($200 million ceiling). The latest waiver was issued in May 2008 and another is expected soon. Other provisions, such as cutting U.S. aid to any Afghan province whose officials are determined complicit in drug trafficking, were contained in H.R. 2446 (AFSA reauthorization, 110th Congress), which passed only the House. Narcotics trafficking control was perhaps the one issue on which the Taliban regime satisfied much of the international community; the Taliban enforced a July 2000 ban on poppy cultivation.

POST-WAR SECURITY OPERATIONS AND FORCE CAPACITY BUILDING

One major question among experts is what is the U.S. definition of "winning" the "war" in Afghanistan. While that might be debated, the top security priority of the United States articulated since 2001 has been to prevent the Taliban and its allies from challenging the Afghan government as that government builds capacity to defend itself. The security efforts were part of the "nation- building" priorities discussed in previous sections, intended to weaken popular support for the Taliban by promoting economic and political development, eliminating the sources of funding for the insurgency, and building democracy.

The Obama Administration review, the results of which were announced March 27, 2009, narrowed the official U.S. mission goals to something less ambitious-preventing *Al Qaeda* from re-establishing a base in Afghanistan-although the policy tools announced appear to continue - and in some ways expand - nation-building.

The pillars of U.S. security strategy have been, and largely remain after the Obama Administration review, although with more emphasis on promoting Afghan governance and economic development than previously: (1) continuing combat operations by U.S. forces and a NATO-led International Security Assistance Force (ISAF); (2) U.S. and NATO operation of "provincial reconstruction teams" (PRTs) that promote economic development; (3) the equipping, training, and expansion of an Afghan National Army (ANA) and Afghan National Police (ANP) force; (4) establishing local security organs; and (5) backing Afghan efforts to engage Taliban leaders who might want to end their armed struggle.

Taliban, Al Qaeda, and Related Insurgent Groups [h]

Security is being challenged by a confluence of related armed groups-not only the ousted Taliban still centered around Mullah Umar. Mullah Umar and many of his top advisers from their time in power remain at large, believed in Pakistan in and around the city of Quetta, according to Afghan officials ("Quetta Shura"). One of Umar's top deputies still at large is Mullah Bradar, but others, including Mullah Dadullah, his son Mansoor, and Mullah Usmani, have been killed or captured. Umar reportedly continues to run a so-called "shadow government" from his safehaven, and the Taliban has several official spokespersons, including Qari Yusuf Ahmadi and Zabiullah Mujahid, and it operates a clandestine radio station, "Voice of Shariat," and publishes videos.

The Taliban of Afghanistan are increasingly linked politically to Pakistani Taliban militants such as Beitullah Mehsud and others. The Pakistan Taliban are primarily seeking to challenge the government of Pakistan, but they facilitate the transiting into Afghanistan of Afghan Taliban and support the Afghan Taliban goals of recapturing Afghanistan. Some Pakistani militants are increasingly focused on interrupting U.S. supply lines into Afghanistan that run through Pakistan.

AL QAEDA/BIN LADEN WHEREABOUTS

U.S. commanders say that, with increased freedom of action in Pakistan, *Al Qaeda* militants are increasingly facilitating, through financing and recruiting, militant incursions in Afghanistan. However, only very small numbers of *Al Qaeda* members-including Arabs, Uzbeks, and Chechens-are being captured or killed in battles in Afghanistan itself, according to U.S. commanders. The two most notable *Al Qaeda* leaders at large, and believed in Pakistan, are Osama bin Laden himself and his close ally, Ayman al-Zawahiri. A purported U.S.-led strike reportedly missed Zawahiri by a few hours in the village of Damadola, Pakistan, in January 2006, suggesting that the United States and Pakistan have some intelligence on his movements.

A strike in late January 2008, in an area near Damadola, killed Abu Laith al-Libi, a reported senior *Al Qaeda* figure who purportedly masterminded, among other operations, the bombing at BagramAir Base in February 2007 when Vice President Cheney was visiting. In August 2008, an airstrike was confirmed to have killed *Al Qaeda* chemical weapons expert Abu Khabab al-Masri, and two senior operatives allegedly involved in the 1998 embassy bombings in Africa reportedly were killed by a Predator strike in January 2009.

These strikes have continued under President Obama, indicating the new Administration continues to see the tactic as effective in preventing attacks. There have been no recent public indications that U.S. or allied forces have learned or are close to learning bin Laden's location. In February 2009, some independent U.S. scientists, using geographic mapping and other methodology based on bin Laden's likely needs and lifestyle, speculated that he might be in or near the Pakistani border city of Parachinar-which is across the border from bin Laden's former Afghan stronghold at Tora Bora. Some press reports in April 2009 suggested that Pakistani intelligence believes Zawahiri might be in Quetta, Pakistan, although CRS has no way to corroborate or refute such information.

HIKMATYAR FACTION

Another "high value target" identified by U.S. commanders is the faction of former *mujahedin* party leader Gulbuddin Hikmatyar (Hizb-e-Islami Gulbuddin, HIG) allied with *Al Qaeda* and Taliban insurgents. Hikmatyar's fighters - once instrumental in the U.S.-supported war against the Soviet Union, are operating in Kunar, Nuristan, and Nangarhar provinces, east of Kabul. On February 19, 2003, the U.S. government formally designated Hikmatyar as a "Specially Designated Global Terrorist," under the authority of Executive Order 13224, subjecting it to financial and other U.S. sanctions. (It is not formally designated as a "Foreign Terrorist Organization.")

While U.S. commanders continue to battle Hikmatyar's militia, the Afghan government reportedly is negotiating with his representatives. Hikmatyar has expressed a willingness to discuss a cease-fire with the Karzai government since 2007, but such talks appear to be gaining seriousness and specificity as of May 2009.

HAQQANI FACTION

Yet another militant faction is led by Jalaludin Haqqani and his eldest son, Siraj (or Sirajjudin). Jalaludin Haqqani, who served as Minister of Tribal Affairs in the Taliban regime of 1996-2001, is believed closer to *Al Qaeda* than to the ousted Taliban leadership in part because one of his wives is purportedly Arab. The group is active around Khost Province. Haqqani property inside Pakistan has been repeatedly targeted since September 2008 by U.S. aerial drone strikes. Some reports in May 2009 suggest this faction might also be in talks with the Afghan government.

THE WAR TO DATE: POST-2006 TALIBAN "RESURGENCE" AND CAUSES

In the four years after the fall of the Taliban, U.S. forces and Afghan troops fought relatively low levels of insurgent violence by the Taliban and other groups discussed above. The United States and Afghanistan conducted "Operation Mountain Viper" (August 2003); "Operation Avalanche" (December 2003); "Operation Mountain Storm" against Taliban remnants in and around Uruzgan province, home province of Mullah Umar; "Operation Lightning Freedom" (December 2004-February 2005); and "Operation Pil (Elephant)" in Kunar Province in the east (October 2005). By late 2005, U.S. and partner commanders appeared to believe that the combat, coupled with overall political and economic reconstruction, had virtually ended any insurgency.

An increase in violence beginning in mid-2006 took some U.S. commanders by surprise, by many accounts. Since then, Taliban insurgents have increasingly adapted suicide and roadside bombing characteristic of the Iraq insurgency – such bombings were not characteristic of Afghanistan's past wars. There is no agreement on the causes of the deterioration, but reasons often advanced include some of those discussed above in the sections on governance-Afghan government corruption and the absence of governance or security forces in many rural areas-as well as the safehaven enjoyed by militants in Pakistan; the reticence of some NATO contributors to actively combat insurgents; civilian casualties caused by NATO and U.S. military operations; and the slow pace of economic development that caused Afghans to criticize the international commitment.

The main theater of combat-where many of these factors converge-is southern Afghanistan: particularly, Uruzgan, Helmand, and Qandahar provinces-areas that NATO/ISAF assumed primary responsibility for on July 31, 2006. Along with

Zabol and Nimruz provinces, these provinces constitute "Regional Command South (RC-S)." Suggesting that U.S. and NATO strategy requires more than just military force, NATO counter-offensives in 2006 were only temporary successes, including such operations as Operation Mountain Lion, Operation Mountain Thrust, and Operation Medusa (August-September 2006).

The latter, at the time, was considered a success in ousting Taliban fighters from the Panjwai district near Qandahar, but it proved short lived. In the aftermath of Medusa, British forces-who believe in working more with tribal leaders as part of negotiated local solutions-entered into an agreement with tribal elders in the Musa Qala district of Helmand Province, under which they would secure the main town of the district without an active NATO presence.

That strategy failed when the Taliban took over Musa Qala town in February 2007. A NATO offensive in December 2007 retook it, although there continue to be recriminations between the Britain, on the one side, and the United States and Karzai, on the other, over the wisdom of the original British deal. Taliban fighters reportedly continue to influence or control outskirts of the district.

COALITION RESPONSES TO THE RESURGENCE IN 2007 AND 2008

To address the "resurgence," NATO tried to apply a more integrated strategy involving pre- emptive combat, increased development work, and a more streamlined command structure, in addition to a slow and steady troop buildup. U.S. and partner country troop levels have been increasing significantly since 2006, when NATO/ISAF took over peacekeeping operations nationwide (after October 5, 2006).

Well more than half of the U.S. troops in Afghanistan are under NATO command. The remainder are part of the original post-September 11 anti-terrorism mission Operation Enduring Freedom (OEF). There are also Special Operations Forces in Afghanistan under a separate command.

U.S. COMMAND AND MAY 2009 CHANGES

The NATO/ISAF force has been headed by U.S. Gen. David McKiernan since June 3, 2008. As of September 2008, he also led U.S. troops in OEF and in the training mission for the Afghan security forces as commander of "U.S. Forces Afghanistan"-an attempt to give U.S. commanders greater ability to deploy U.S. forces throughout the war zone. Gen. McKiernan and his successors also report to U.S. Central Command (CENTCOM, headed as of October 31, 2008, Incremental costs of U.S. operations in Afghanistan appear to be running about $2.5 to 3 billion per month.

The FY2008 Defense Authorization Act (P.L. 110-181, Section 1229) requires a quarterly DOD report on the security situation in Afghanistan; the first was submitted in June 2008. Whether under NATO or OEF, most U.S. forces in Afghanistan are in eastern Afghanistan and are under the operational command of Maj. Gen. Jeffrey Schloesser as head of Combined Joint Task Force 101 (CJTF-101, named for the 101 Airborne Division, headquartered at Bagram Air Base north of Kabul).

On May 11, 2009, Secretary of Defense Gates and Joint Chiefs of Staff Chairman Michael Mullen announced that, in concert with the new U.S. strategy announced in March 2009 (discussed below), Gen. McKiernan had been asked to resign and Lt. Gen. Stanley McChrystal, considered an innovative commander as head of U.S. special operations (2003-2008), was named his successor. He is to be assisted by Lt. Gen. David Rodriguez as day-to-day commander of the effort, a move reportedly intended to permit McChrystal (if confirmed) to focus on the combat component of U.S. strategy in Afghanistan.

2008 Deterioration

Continuing to rely heavily on combat operations, in 2007, U.S. and NATO forces, bolstered by the infusion of 3,200 U.S. troops and 3,800 partner forces, pre-empted an anticipated Taliban "spring offensive" with "Operation Achilles" (March 2007) in the Sangin district of northern Helmand Province, around the Kajaki dam. Other operations, including Operation Silicon (May 2007) were conducted in other parts of Helmand. During 2007, the United States also began to experience at least one use (unsuccessful) by the Taliban of surface-to-air missiles (SAM-7, shoulder held) against U.S. C-130 transport aircraft.

The Bush Administration also decided in early 2008 to focus attention and provide additional resources than it had previously. Joint Chiefs Chairman Mullen largely confirmed the perception that the Afghan battlefield was "under-resourced" in December 11, 2007, congressional testimony. Similar findings were emphasized in outside assessments of Afghanistan policy, including a report in November 2007 by the Senlis Council; a January 2008 study by the Atlantic Council ("Saving Afghanistan: An Appeal and Plan for Urgent Action") and a January 30, 2008, study by the Center for the Study of the Presidency ("Afghanistan Study Group Report").

These assessments contributed to a decision by Secretary of Defense Gates, in January 2008, to deploy an additional 3,200 Marines to Helmand Province. Despite the stepped-up coalition military activity, throughout 2008 growing concern took hold within the Bush Administration. This was reflected in such statements as one in September 2008 by Joint Chiefs of Staff chairman Admiral Mike Mullen that "I'm not sure we're winning" in Afghanistan, as well as one by him on October 10, 2008, that "I anticipate next year [2009] would be a tougher year." Similar comments were made in early 2009 by President Obama and top U.S. military officials.

These assessments comport with a reported U.S. intelligence estimate on Afghanistan, according to the *New York Times* (October 9, 2008), that described Afghanistan as in a "downward spiral"-language used also by Commander of U.S. Central Command General David Petraeus (in that position since October 31, 2008). However, there have been some differences of opinion within the command structure on the extent of the security deterioration. Gen. McKiernan acknowledged setbacks but says there are also positive indicators in many parts of Afghanistan and that the conflict is "winnable."

He and others asserted that 70% of the violence in Afghanistan occurs in 10% of Afghanistan's 364 districts, an area including about 6% of the Afghan population, and that militants crossing the border account for about 30% of all attacks in Afghanistan. Some add that the perception of Taliban control over territory is exaggerated. At the same time, Gen. McKiernan said that there was "stalemate" in the south, and that this assessment represented the basis of his request, made during the last year of the Bush Administration, for a total of 30,000 more soldiers in Afghanistan.

The indicators that fed pessimistic assessments include:

1. In 2008 recorded the most U.S. combat casualties, of the war so far (about 150);
2. Numbers of suicide bombings at a post-Taliban high;
3. Number of roadside bombings (2,000 in 2008) at a post-Taliban high;
4. Expanding Taliban operations in provinces where it had not previously been active, including Lowgar, Wardak, and Kapisa, close to Kabul;
5. High profile attacks in Kabul against well defended targets, such as the January 14, 2008, attack on the Serena Hotel in Kabul and the July 7, 2008, suicide bombing at the gates of the Indian Embassy in Kabul, killing more than 50;
6. On April 27, 2008, assassination attempt on Karzai during a military parade celebrating the ouster of the Soviet Union;
7. On June 12, 2008, Sarposa prison break in Qandahar (several hundred Taliban captives were freed, as part of an emptying of the 1,200 inmates there);
8. A reported 40% rise in attacks (over 2007 figures) in the U.S.-led eastern sector;
9. On July 13, 2008, on a U.S. outpost in Nuristan Province that killed nine U.S. soldiers;
10. On August 18, 2008, attack that killed ten French soldiers near Sarobi, 30 miles northeast of Kabul;

11. An attack by militants who broke into the Justice Ministry and other buildings in Kabul on February 11, 2009, killing twenty but being put down by Afghan commandos within four hours; and
12. Figures compiled by NATO/ISAF in April 2009 show continued increases in various categories of insurgent violence, such as a 74% overall increase in insurgent-initiated attacks in early 2009 as compared to that period in 2008.

Contributing to the sense of deterioration have been reports that the Taliban, in some areas under their control, are setting up courts and other "shadow government" structures. Afghan officials say that over half of Helmand Province is under Taliban control, and parts of Qandahar Province are controlled by insurgents as well, although government forces control major population centers.

BUSH AND OBAMA ADMINISTRATION STRATEGY REVIEWS

As the perception of deterioration continued, it was reported in September 2008 that both the U.S. military and NATO were conducting a number of different strategy reviews. The reviews were, in part, intended to prevent an unraveling of the effort from the time of the U.S. election until President-elect Obama takes over. One review was headed by Lt. Gen. Douglas Lute, the Bush Administration's senior adviser on Iraq and Afghanistan (who has been kept on under the Obama Administration); others were conducted by the Department of Defense, by CENTCOM, by NATO, and by the State Department. Almost all of the reviews were completed and briefed to Secretary of Defense Gates prior to the start of the Obama Administration.

OBAMA ADMINISTRATION STRATEGIC REVIEW

The Obama Administration which has stated that Afghanistan needs to be given a higher priority than it was during the Bush Administration- integrated the Bush Administration reviews into an overarching 60-day inter-agency "strategic review." It was chaired by South Asia expert Bruce Riedel, on temporary assignment, and co-chaired by Ambassador Holbrooke and by Undersecretary of Defense for Policy Michele Flournoy. Ambassador Holbrooke invited both Afghanistan and Pakistan to participate in the review.

Several ministers from each country visited Washington, D.C. during February 23-27, 2009, as part of the process, and reached agreement to hold regular trilateral meetings (U.S., Afghanistan, Pakistan). The latest, which included the Presidents of both Afghanistan and Pakistan, took place during May 4-7, 2009. President Obama announced the new "comprehensive" strategy on March 27, 2009, addressing all interlocking factors that have caused security in Afghanistan to deteriorate since 2006. According to the President's statement, and an associated "White Paper" of the inter-agency group that performed the review:

- *Key Goals*- (1) disrupt terrorist networks in Afghanistan and Pakistan to degrade their ability to launch international terrorist attacks; (2) promote a more capable, accountable, and effective government in Afghanistan; (3) develop self-reliant Afghan security forces that can lead the counter-insurgency with reduced U.S. assistance; and (4) involve the international community to actively assist in addressing these objectives. These relatively targeted goals are in line with comments by President Obama in an interview with "60 Minutes," broadcast March 22, 2009, saying that there needs to be an "exit strategy" for Afghanistan so that U.S. policy does not appear to be "perpetual drift."
- *Resources and Troops*- The strategy will provide the resources to the stabilization effort in Afghanistan that U.S. officials say were lacking during the Bush Administration. However, the strategy emphasizes promoting Afghan governance and the growth of its own forces, rather than U.S.-led combat. 17,000 additional combat troops are to be deployed to help secure the restive south and east of Afghanistan -in line with a February 17, 2009 authorization of those deployments by

President Obama-and a long standing requirement for 4,000 U.S. military personnel to train the Afghan National Security Forces (ANSF) would deploy as well.

- *Afghan Forces*- The additional trainers are expected to enable the Afghan National Army to reach its planned goal of 134,000 (from the existing 86,000) by 2011. The strategy left open a future expansion to 250,000 or more ANA and 140,000 ANP, as has been discussed by Afghan officials.
- *Civilian Surge*- To develop Afghan institutions not only in the central government but at the provincial and local levels, there is to be a significant increase (about 430, including 51 direct hires) in U.S. civilian advisors in Afghanistan, both new hires and assignment of existing State Department and other agency personnel. This would more than double the number of civilian experts now in country, of which only 13 serve in the southern sector. Substantial new contributions of personnel from U.S. allies and partners in Afghanistan are expected as well. The FY2009 supplemental request includes $600 million to fund the "civilian surge," including new Embassy construction costs to handle more personnel. According to subsequent testimony and announcements, USAID is to provide 150 of the civilians (45 of which would be in Kabul); U.S. Department of Agriculture is to provide 50 experts; and the remainder would be furnished by the Department of State (Foreign Service officers and civilian hires, of which 50 have been hired). There are reportedly inter-agency discussions about potentially filling some posts temporarily with military reservists.
- *Reconciliation*- The strategy expresses clear support for longstanding Afghan efforts to persuade insurgent commanders and their foot soldiers to lay down their arms and accept the Afghan constitution. However, Mullah Umar and his aides are aligned with the *Al Qaeda* organization and should not be included in any reconciliation deal.
- *Pakistan*- According to Administration officials in briefings for Congressional staff (March 27, 2009), the new

Administration strategy treats Afghanistan and Pakistan as organically linked. Specific points include: (1) institutionalizing stronger mechanisms for bilateral and trilateral cooperation among the United States, Afghanistan, and Pakistan; (2) providing U.S. military assistance to help Pakistani forces conduct counter-insurgency against militants in Pakistan; (3) increasing economic assistance to Pakistan ($1.5 billion per year for the next five years); (4) fostering reform of local governance in areas of Pakistan where militants are operating; and (5) encouraging foreign investment in key sectors of the Pakistani economy, and supporting legislation to create "Reconstruction Opportunity Zones" – areas of Afghan-Pakistan economic cooperation the products of which would enjoy preferential duties for import to the United States.

- *International Dimension-* The Administration will explore new diplomatic mechanisms, including establishing an "Contact Group" consisting of all nations that have a stake in the security of the region-NATO allies and other U.S. partners, as well as the Central Asian states, the Gulf nations and Iran, Russia, India, and China. As explained by Administration officials in briefings to congressional staff on the new strategy (March 27, 2009), NATO and other partners will be asked to contribute whatever they are comfortable contributing- whether that be troops, economic aid, civilian mentors, ANSF trainers-as long as the contribution fills an identified requirement. Some pledges-mostly aid and trainers, rather than combat troops- were made at the NATO summit in France April 3-4, 2009, as discussed further below.
- *Review Process-* The strategy is intended to be reviewed regularly to assess its results. Joint Chiefs Chairman Mullen said on May 18 that the new strategy might reverse the negative security trends within 12-24 months. Secretary Gates said on May 20 that he wants an initial assessment of the strategy's effectiveness by March-April 2010.

U.S. TROOP BUILDUP IN 2009

Even before the new strategy was announced, there was a consensus that U.S. troop levels in Afghanistan needed to increase. In keeping with an announcement in September 2008 by President Bush, about 5,000 more U.S. forces deployed to Afghanistan in January 2009. They deployed to Lowgar and Wardak provinces, south of Kabul, where there has been significant Taliban infiltration since 2008. The additional deployments (17,000 combat troops and 4,000 trainers), which are now starting to flow to Afghanistan, will bring U.S. force levels to about 70,000 by the end of 2009.

The Obama Administration strategy's emphasis on civilian mentorship and development reflected the views of European partners, President Karzai, Defense Secretary Gates, and others who believe that Afghanistan's difficulties are complex and ıequired more innovations than adding forces. The strategy announcement put off decisions on whether to send the remaining 10,000 forces of those requested by Gen. McKiernan in 2008. Secretary of Defense Gates, who has expressed the view that adding too many troops could create among the Afghan people a sense of "occupation" that could prove counter-productive, said in May 2009 that it would be a "hard sell" and it would "take some convincing" for him to agree that additional forces would materially improve security if the current build-up does not.

Those who advocate more troops beyond those approved say that such forces are needed to create permissive security conditions to enable the building of Afghan governance capabilities. Beyond the addition of troops, there is a growing question of equipment. Some experts say that the United States is too reliant on armor in Afghanistan which is not suited for Afghanistan's poor roads and Steep Mountain passes. Others say there should be more emphasis on mobility provided by more helicopters and on greater availability of aerial surveillance assets.

INITIATIVES UNDER WAY BEFORE THE STRATEGY ANNOUNCEMENT

The Obama Administration review supports some of the strategy innovations begun in 2008. One such initiative is a major expansion of the Afghan National Army, which was planned before the strategy announcement and endorsed by it. Others are discussed below.

NEGOTIATIONS WITH THE TALIBAN

During 2008, there was growing U.S. support for new Afghan efforts to bring Taliban fighters off the battlefield and into the political process. President Karzai has consistently advocated talks with Taliban militants who want to consider ending their fight. Noted above is the "Program for Strengthening Peace and Reconciliation" (referred to in Afghanistan by its Pashto acronym "PTS") headed by *Meshrano Jirga* speaker Sibghatullah Mojadeddi and overseen by Karzai's National Security Council. The program is credited with persuading 5,000 Taliban figures and commanders to renounce violence and join the political process. Several Taliban figures, including its foreign minister Wakil Mutawwakil, ran in the parliamentary elections. "Mullah Rocket" a former Taliban commander, are running for president in the August 2009 elections.

The Taliban official who was governor of Bamiyan Province when the Buddha statues there were blown up, Mohammad Islam Mohammedi-and who was later elected to the post-Taliban parliament from Samangan Province-was assassinated in Kabul in January 2007. The issue has gained momentum in recent months. In October 2008, press reports said that Afghan officials (led by Karzai's brother Qayyum) and Taliban members had met each other in Ramadan-related gatherings in Saudi Arabia in September 2008. Another round of talks was held in late January 2009 in Saudi Arabia, and there are reports of ongoing contact in Dubai, UAE. Since the new strategy was announced, the talks have broadened, according to press reports. According to these stories, one track involves negotiations with the Hikmatyar faction.

Other talks reportedly include Afghans close to Mullah Umar. The talks apparently involve Arsala Rahmani, a former Taliban official now in parliament, and the former Taliban Ambassador to Pakistan, Abdul Salam Zaeef, who purportedly is in touch with Umar's inner circle. The Taliban and other militants are still demanding that (1) all foreign troops leave Afghanistan; (2) a new "Islamic" constitution be adopted; and (3) Islamic law is imposed. However, recent press reports say that talks center on lower level confidence building measures, such as removal of the names of Taliban figures from U.N. lists of terrorists, lists established pursuant to Resolution 1390 (January 2002).

Other reports say that the Haqqani faction, reportedly politically close to Al Qaeda, may also be in negotiations with the Karzai government. The Obama Administration strategy has backed negotiations to bring mid and lower level Taliban leaders and their foot soldiers off the battlefield. Even though the recent negotiations involve harder core Taliban figures, U.S. officials have not sought to obstruct these talks, even though President Obama ruled out compromise with Umar in the strategy announcement.

TRAINING TRIBAL MILITIAS/AFGHAN PUBLIC PROTECTION FORCE

Since June 2006, Karzai and international force donors have been considering arming some local tribal militias in eastern Afghanistan, building on established tribal structures, to help in local policing. Until mid-2008, U.S. military commanders opposed assisting local militias anywhere in Afghanistan for fear of creating new rivals to the central government, but the urgent security needs in Afghanistan caused re-consideration. In late 2008, the Bush Administration and Karzai government reached tentative agreement to try the concept.

The militia formation is being conducted as part of the IDLG's Social Outreach Program, which was discussed above, and is intended to strengthen the ability of local communities to keep Taliban infiltrators out. It is being termed the "Afghan Public Protection Force" (APPF) and is funded with DoD (CERP) funds. The program began in Wardak Province in early 2009 and might be expanded to Ghazni, Lowgar, and Kapisa provinces. Participants in the program are given a reported $200 per month. U.S. commanders say that no U.S. weapons are supplied to the militias, but this is an Afghan-led program and some reports say the Afghan government might provide weapons (reportedly Kalashnikov rifles) to the local groups, possibly using U.S. funds.

The Obama Administration review did not repudiate the approach or discontinue it, but did not emphasize or praise it, either. Some elders in Wardak oppose the program, partly due to Taliban intimidation, and have been slow to recommend recruits for it. Ambassador Holbrooke has indicated that the results of the pilot program in Wardak are not yet clear. Karzai has expressed opposition to relying on "tribal militias," although he appears to have acquiesced to the program. U.S. commanders and Afghan officials say they will be able to keep the militias "under control," because they are under the control of the Interior Ministry. As such, they are not *arbokai*, which are private tribal militias.

Some Afghan and U.S. officials fear that the militias could become an additional source of arbitrary administration of justice and of corruption against local populations, and question the apparent deviation from the post-September 11 commitment to building the central government as the only legitimate source of Afghan armed force. As an indication of divisions among Afghan leaders about the concept, the upper house of the Afghan parliament (Meshrano Jirga) passed a resolution in November 2008 opposing the concept.

ADOPTING THE DUTCH APPROACH IN URUZGAN

The Obama Administration strategy appears to, in many ways adopt techniques and policies such as those used in Uruzgan Province, where the Netherlands is the lead force.

The January 2009 DoD report on Afghanistan stability (mandated by P.L. 110-181) notes the substantial success of the Dutch approach in Uruzgan, discussed below. Dutch troops and officials have used an approach that focuses not on combat but on development work and engagement with local leaders to understand their development needs.

In this approach, decisions are made jointly-or at least with extensive consultations-by the commander of the military contingent and the Dutch civilian leader for the province, usually a relatively senior Foreign Ministry diplomat. On March 29, 2009, the Netherlands converted its Provincial Reconstruction Team in Tarin Kowt to civilian leadership rather military leadership. Dutch officials say their projects in Uruzgan encourage the follow-on expansion of governance, and clearly place Afghans in the lead in implementing projects, rather than on delivering projects implemented by foreign donors.

The Netherlands has not added troops to the 1,700+ contingent that took over the peacekeeping in the province in mid-2006. Others say the approach is not unique because the Netherlands relies on an Australian contingent to conduct protective combat. Some say the approach cannot be widely applied because Uruzgan geography is not as hostile as in other provinces, and because the Taliban insurgency is not as strong there. The province does not border Pakistan, an entry point for insurgents.

LIMITING CIVILIAN CASUALTIES/U.S. MILITARY PRESENCE/SOFA

U.S. officials are also attempting to adjust military operations in order to limit civilian casualties. This issue has gained urgency since 2008 as the Taliban have benefitted politically from the backlash caused by Afghan civilian casualties inflicted by U.S. or NATO airstrikes. One such disputed incident occurred near Herat on August 22, 2008, that UNAMA said killed 90 civilians but U.S. investigators say killed only 30 non-combatants. Another incident occurred in early November 2008 in which an alleged 37 Afghan civilians at a wedding party were killed. The latest incident, on May 4, 2009, occurred in a battle in Farah province.

Afghan officials say 140 civilians were killed but the U.S. says far fewer were killed by U.S. strikes and combat. In public statements, Karzai has been increasingly critical of these casualties, and the new Ambassador, Karl Eikenberry, went with Karzai to Farah to apologize and pledge compensation. After the Herat incident, the Afghan cabinet demanded negotiation of a formal "Status of Forces Agreement" (SOFA) that would spell out the combat authorities of non-Afghan forces, and would limit the U.S. of airstrikes, detentions, and house raids.

In late November 2008, at a multi-lateral conference, Karzai called for a timetable for a withdrawal of international forces from Afghanistan, perhaps borrowing from similar nationalistic calls by the government of Iraq in its negotiations with the United States. He has since demanded a larger Afghan role in U.S. operations, and particularly whether or not to use air strikes in selected cases. A purported draft "SOFA"-or "technical agreement" clarifying U.S./coalition authorities in Afghanistan-is reportedly under discussion between the United States and Afghanistan.

U.S. forces currently operate in Afghanistan under a "diplomatic note" between the United States and the interim government of Afghanistan in November 2002; the agreement gives the United States legal jurisdiction over U.S. personnel serving in Afghanistan and stated the Afghan government's acknowledgment that U.S.-led military operations were "ongoing." Even if the Taliban insurgency ends, Afghan leaders say they want the United States to maintain a long-term presence in Afghanistan. On May 8, 2005, Karzai summoned about 1,000 delegates to a consultative *jirga* in Kabul on whether to host permanent U.S. bases.

They supported an indefinite presence of international forces to maintain security but urged Karzai to delay a decision. On May 23, 2005, Karzai and President Bush issued a "joint declaration" providing for U.S. forces to have access to Afghan military facilities, in order to prosecute "the war against international terror and the struggle against violent extremism." The joint statement did not give Karzai enhanced control over facilities used by U.S. forces, over U.S. operations, or over prisoners taken during operations.

THE NATO-LED INTERNATIONAL SECURITY ASSISTANCE FORCE (ISAF)

The strategy announced in March 2009 envisions continued cooperation with partner forces and countries and notes that future contributions might take the form of finances and civilian mentors and advisers, rather than only troops. U.S. cooperation with other donor countries is a major issue, in part because the effectiveness of the NATO alliance in general has come under question as the Afghanistan stabilization effort has not produced quick results. Most U.S. troops in Afghanistan remain under the umbrella of the NATO-led "International Security Assistance Force" (ISAF)-consisting of all 26 NATO members states plus partner countries.

ISAF was created by the Bonn Agreement and U.N. Security Council Resolution 1386, initially limited to Kabul. In October 2003, after Germany agreed to contribute 450 military personnel to expand ISAF into the city of Konduz, ISAF contributors endorsed expanding its presence to several other cities, contingent on formal U.N. approval-which came on October 14, 2003 in U.N. Security Council Resolution 1510.

In August 2003, NATO took over command of ISAF-previously the ISAF command rotated among donor forces including Turkey and Britain. NATO/ISAF's responsibilities broadened significantly in 2004 with NATO/ISAF's assumption of security responsibility for northern and western Afghanistan (Stage 1, Regional Command North, in 2004 and Stage 2, Regional Command West, in 2005, respectively). The transition process continued on July 31, 2006, with the formal handover of the security mission in southern Afghanistan to NATO/ISAF control.

As part of this "Stage 3," a British/Canadian/Dutch-led "Regional Command South" (RC-S) was formed. Britain is the lead force in Helmand; Canada is lead in Qandahar, and the Netherlands is lead in Uruzgan; the three now rotate the command of RC-S. "Stage 4," the assumption of NATO/ISAF command of peacekeeping in fourteen provinces of eastern Afghanistan (and thus all of Afghanistan), was completed on October 5, 2006. As part of the completion of the NATO/ISAF takeover, the United States put about half the U.S. troops operating in Afghanistan under NATO/ISAF in "Regional Command East" (RC-E).

Some accounts say the United States might assume overall command of RC-S in November 2010, after rotations by the Netherlands (2008-2009) and Britain (2009-2010). As of the fall of 2008, a one-star U.S. general, John Nicholson, is deputy commander of RC-S, giving the United States added weight at that headquarters, to which most of the new U.S. forces are flowing. The ISAF mission was most recently renewed (until October 13, 2009) by U.N. Security Council Resolution 1833 (September 22, 2008). It reiterated the previous year's renewal resolution (1776) support for the Operation Enduring Freedom mission. Tables at the end of this report list contributing forces, areas of operations, and their Provincial Reconstruction Teams.

NATO FORCE PLEDGES IN 2008 AND 2009

There have been additional non-U.S. NATO and other troops sent to Afghanistan in 2008 and 2009, although most donor nations are suffering from waning public support for the Afghanistan mission. NATO and other partner forces that are bearing the brunt of combat in southern Afghanistan are Britain, Canada, the Netherlands, Denmark, Romania, and Australia. The need to line up new pledges became acute in February 2008, when Canada said it would extend its 2,500 troop deployment until 2009, but not beyond that, unless other partners contribute 1,000 forces to assist with combat in the Canadian sector (Qandahar province). Canada says its mission in Afghanistan will end in 2011, as does the Netherlands.

At and in conjunction with the NATO summit in Bucharest in early April 2008, twelve countries pledged additional forces. Among the major new contributions in 2008 was the French deployment of about 1,000 additional forces to Kapisa province to block Taliban movements toward northern Kabul. President Sarkozy won a parliamentary vote of support for the mission, in late September 2008, following the killing of ten French soldiers in August 2008.

Britain increased its troop commitment in Afghanistan-mainly in high combat Helmand Province-to about 8,700 in early 2009. Germany repeatedly turned U.S. requests to send forces to the combat- heavy south, but in 2008 it increased its authorized troop ceiling for Afghanistan to 4,500, from 3,500, still in the northern sector. Despite opposition in Germany to the entire Afghanistan mission, Germany's parliament voted by a 453-79 vote margin on October 12, 2007, to maintain German troop levels in Afghanistan.

2009 CONTRIBUTIONS

The Obama Administration strategy review was intended to help build support for new pledges of combat forces, Afghan force trainers, trainers and mentors for Afghan government bureaucrats, and other financial assistance to Afghanistan. Some of those pledges came through at the April 3 - 4, 2009, NATO summit, and since, although some say new troop pledges are less than expected:

- Deployment of 3,000 non-U.S. troops to secure the Afghan elections and 2,000 trainers for the Afghan security forces. Contributing forces for the election period include: Spain (400), Germany (600), Poland (600), and Britain (about 900). For the training missions, a new NATO Training Mission-Afghanistan (NTM-A) is to be set up. France has offered to lead a 300 person European Gendarmerie Force that will help train Afghan forces out in the provinces rather than rely on bringing them to Kabul. Other military trainers-to fill out 70 Operational Mentor and Liaison Teams (OMLTs)-will come from Bulgaria, Estonia, Italy

(200), Greece, Portugal, Turkey, and Slovakia, with Belgium to also send two more F-16 fighters. Italy will also send 100 paramilitary trainers for the NTM-A mission, medical helicopters, and military transport planes.

- $100 million in contributions to an Afghan National Security Forces trust fund were pledged, to help finance expansion of the ANSF. Of this, $57 million was pledged by Germany. Japan, as noted, separately pledged to pay the expenses of the Afghan police for six months.
- $500 million in additional civilian assistance to Afghanistan was pledged at the meeting.
- In subsequent meetings, South Korea announced it would increase its aid contribution to Afghanistan by about $20 million, in part to expand the hospital capabilities at Bagram Air Base. It reportedly is also discussing with the United States returning some combat engineers to Afghanistan for development missions. Some of the pledges address NATO's chronic equipment shortages-particularly helicopters, both for transport and attack-for the Afghanistan mission.

In 2007, to try to compensate for the shortage, NATO chartered about 20 commercial helicopters for extra routine supply flights to the south, freeing up Chinooks and Black Hawks for other missions. Some of the Polish troops deployed in 2008 are operating and maintain eight helicopters. The shortages persist even though several partner nations brought in additional equipment in 2006 in conjunction with the NATO assumption of peacekeeping command. Germany notes that it provides six Tornado combat aircraft to assist with strikes in combat situations in the south. NATO/ISAF also assists the Afghan Ministry of Civil Aviation and Tourism in the operation of Kabul International Airport (where Dutch combat aircraft also are located). In October 2008, Hungary added 60 troops to take over security at the airport.

National "Caveats" on Combat Operations

In an effort to repair divisions within the Afghanistan coalition over each country's respective domestic considerations, Secretary Gates presented, at a NATO meeting in Scotland on December 13, 2007, a "strategic concept paper" that would help coordinate and guide NATO and other partner contributions and missions over the coming three to five years. This was an effort to structure each country's contribution as appropriate to the politics and resources of that contributor. The concept paper, now titled the "Strategic Vision," was endorsed by the NATO summit in Bucharest, Romania in April 2008.

One of the most thorny issues has been the U.S. effort to persuade other NATO countries to adopt flexible rules of engagement that allow all contributing forces to perform combat missions, although perhaps not as aggressively as do U.S. forces. All have agreed that their forces would come to each others' defense in times of emergency anywhere in Afghanistan. At the NATO summit in April 2008, NATO countries pledged to continue to work remove the other so-called "national caveats" on their troops' operations that U.S. commanders say limit operational flexibility. For example, some nations refuse to conduct night-time combat.

Others have refused to carry Afghan personnel on their helicopters. Others do not fight after snowfall. These caveats were troubling to those NATO countries with forces in heavy combat zones, such as Canada, which feel they are bearing the brunt of the fighting.

PROVINCIAL RECONSTRUCTION TEAMS

U.S. and partner officials have generally praised the effectiveness of "provincial reconstruction teams" (PRTs) - enclaves of U.S. or partner forces and civilian officials that provide safe havens for international aid workers to help with reconstruction and to extend the writ of the Kabul government- in accelerating reconstruction and assisting stabilization efforts. The PRTs, announced in December 2002, perform activities ranging from resolving local disputes to coordinating local reconstruction projects, although most U.S.-run PRTs and most PRTs in combat-heavy areas focus mostly on counter-insurgency. (U.S. PRTs in restive regions are "co- located" with "forward operating bases" of 300-400 U.S. combat troops.)

Some aid agencies say they have felt more secure since the PRT program began, fostering reconstruction, and many of the new civilian advisers to be sent to Afghanistan under the new Obama Administration strategy will work out of the PRTs. On the other hand, some relief groups do not want to associate with military forces because doing so might taint their perceived neutrality. Others, such as Oxfam International, argue that the PRTs are delaying the time when the Afghan government has the skills and resources to secure and develop Afghanistan on its own. There are 26 PRTs in operation.

Virtually all the PRTs, including those run by the United States, are now under the ISAF mission, but with varying lead nations. Each PRT operated by the United States is composed of U.S. forces (50-100 U.S. military personnel); Defense Department civil affairs officers; representatives of USAID, State Department, and other agencies; and Afghan government (Interior Ministry) personnel. Most PRTs, including those run by partner forces, have personnel to train Afghan security forces. USAID officers assigned to the PRTs administer PRT reconstruction projects. USAID spending on PRT projects is in the table on USAID spending in Afghanistan at the end of this chapter, and there is a database on development projects completed by each PRT available to CRS.

In the south, most PRTs are heavily focused on security. In August 2005, in preparation for the establishment of RC-S, Canada took over the key U.S.-led PRT in Qandahar. In May 2006, Britain took over the PRT at Lashkar Gah, capital of Helmand Province. The Netherlands took over the PRT at Tarin Kowt, capital of Uruzgan Province. Poland reportedly is considering taking over the U.S. PRT in Ghazni.

Representing evolution of the PRT concept, Turkey opened a PRT, in Wardak Province, on November 25, 2006, to focus on providing health care, education, police training, and agricultural alternatives in that region. There also has been consideration to turn over the lead in the U.S.-run PRTs to civilians rather than military personnel, presumably State Department or USAID officials. That was first attempted in 2006 with the establishment of a civilian-led U.S.-run PRT in the Panjshir Valley. As noted, in March 2009, the Netherlands converted its PRT to civilian lead.

AFGHAN NATIONAL SECURITY FORCES

Capable Afghan National Security Forces (ANSF)-the Afghan National Army (ANA) and Afghan National Policy (ANP)-are the means by which the United States and NATO might wind eventually down their involvement in Afghanistan. The Obama Administration strategy review emphasizes expanding the ANSF and helping it "take the lead" in securing Afghanistan, rather than placing it in a "back seat" to U.S.-led combat-a clear contrast with the 2007 "troop surge" in Iraq. U.S. forces ("Combined Security Transition Command-Afghanistan," CSTC-A), headed as of November 2008 by Maj. Gen. Richard Formica, along with partner countries and contractors, are training the Afghan National Army (ANA) and Afghan National Police (ANP). CSTC-A is under the authority of U.S. Forces-Afghanistan.

The Administration strategy plans to expand the ANA to 134,000 by 2011-essentially a continuation of the Bush Administration expansion plan outlined in September 2008. However, reaching that goal has depended on the availability of additional trainers, and this requirement was met by the Obama Administration strategy announcement of the 4,000 additional U.S. trainers. The funds for the expansion-about $12 billion in that time frame-are expected to come mainly from the United States, possibly defrayed by partner contributions by Japan, Germany, South Korea, or other donors.

The Obama Administration strategy review on Afghanistan did not specifically propose expanding the ANA to about 250,000, which is what Afghan officials and some U.S. military leaders believe will be ultimately needed. However, the expansion to 134,000 is stated to be an interim step, thereby permitting a later decision for further expansion. The Obama

Administration review proposed an initial expansion of the ANP to about 82,000, not much above its current level. A decision to expand the ANP to about 150,000 is put off until later.

AFGHAN NATIONAL ARMY

The Afghan National Army has been built "from scratch" since 2002-it is not a direct continuation of the national army that existed from the 1880s until the Taliban era. That national army all but disintegrated during the 1992-1996 *mujahedin* civil war and the 1996-2001 Taliban period. However, some Afghan military officers who served prior to the Taliban did re-join the new military after the fall of the Taliban. U.S. and allied officers say that the ANA, now about 86,000 trained and assigned (with the total to exceed 90,000 by June 2009) is becoming a major force in stabilizing the country and a national symbol. It now has at least some presence in most of Afghanistan's 34 provinces, working with the PRTs, and it deployed outside Afghanistan to assist relief efforts for victims of the October 2005 Pakistan earthquake.

According to the Department of Defense, the ANA has taken the lead in 30 significant combat and clearing operations to date, and has demonstrated "increasing competence, effectiveness, and professionalism." Then NATO/ISAF commander General McNeill said in April 2008 that it would not be until 2011 that ANA (and ANP) forces would be capable enough to allow for a drawdown of coalition forces. This assessment was corroborated by a June 2008 DoD report on the ANSF. However, recent DoD reports (January 2009) say that 52,000 ANA soldiers are engaged in or leading operations alongside ISAF. The ANA is now leading 75% of the combat operations in the eastern sector, and about 51% of operations overall; it participates in about 90% of all combat operations. The Obama Administration strategy review says that ANA units will be partnered with foreign donor units to enhance effectiveness.

Among specific examples of the ANA taking leadership, in August 2008, the ANA took over security of Kabul city from

Italy, and it took formal control of Kabul Province in early 2009. The commando forces of the ANA, trained by U.S. Special Operations Forces, are considered well- trained and are taking the lead in some operations against high value targets, particularly against HIG elements in Nuristan province. The United States has built five ANA bases: Herat (Corps 207); Gardez (Corps 203); Qandahar (Corps 205); Mazar-e-Sharif (Corps 209); and Kabul.

Other reports cite U.S. officers as observing continuing personnel problems (desertion, absentee), including ill discipline, although some concerns are being addressed. Some accounts say that a typical ANA unit is only at about 50% of its authorized strength at any given time. The GAO study said that there are significant shortages in about 40% of equipment items, although CSTC- A envisions that all ANA brigades are equipped to 85% of requirements as of the end of 2008. ANA battalions, or "Kandaks," are the main unit of the Afghan force. There are 106 Kandaks at this time.

The Kandaks are stiffened by the presence of U.S. and partner embeds, called "Operational Mentor and Liaison Teams" (OMLTs). Each OMLT has about 12-19 personnel, and U.S. commanders say that the ANA will continue to need embeds for the short term, because embeds give the units confidence they will be resupplied, reinforced, and evacuated in the event of wounding. Coalition officers also are conducting heavy weapons training for a heavy brigade as part of the "Kabul Corps," based in Pol-e-Charki, east of Kabul. Among the partner countries contributing OMLTs (all or in part) are Canada, Croatia, Czech Republic, France, Germany, Italy, the Netherlands, Norway, Poland, Slovenia, Spain, Sweden, Britain, and the United States, and additional OMLT contributions were discussed above.

ETHNIC AND FACTIONAL CONSIDERATIONS

At the time the United States first began establishing the ANA, Northern Alliance figures reportedly weighted recruitment for the national army toward its Tajik ethnic base. Many Pashtuns, in reaction, refused recruitment or left the

ANA program. U.S. officials in Afghanistan say this problem has been at least partly alleviated with better pay and more close involvement by U.S. forces, and that the force is ethnically integrated in each unit. The naming of a Pashtun, Abdul Rahim Wardak, as Defense Minister in December 2004 also reduced desertions among Pashtuns (he remains in that position).

The chief of staff is Gen. Bismillah Khan, a Tajik who was a Northern Alliance commander. U.S. officers in Afghanistan add that some recruits take long trips to their home towns to remit funds to their families, and often then return to the ANA after a long absence. Others, according to U.S. observers, often refuse to serve far from their home towns. The FY2005 foreign aid appropriation (P.L. 108-447) required that ANA recruits be vetted for terrorism, human rights violations, and drug trafficking.

AFGHAN AIR FORCE

Equipment, maintenance, and logistical difficulties continue to plague the Afghan Air Force, now called the ANA Air Corps. The force is a carryover from the Afghan Air Force that existed prior to the Soviet invasion, and is expanding gradually after its equipment was virtually eliminated in the 2001-2002 U.S. combat against the Taliban regime. It now has about 400 pilots, as well as 22 helicopters and cargo aircraft. Its goal is to have 61 aircraft by 2011, but Defense Minister Wardak said in September 2008 that it will remain mostly a support force for ground operations rather than a combat-oriented Air Force. Gen. McKiernan, in statements in November 2008, credited the Afghan Air Force with an ability to make ANA units nearly self-sufficient in airlift.

In May 2008, the Afghan Air Force received an additional 25 surplus helicopters from the Czech Republic and the UAE, bought and refurbished with the help of U.S. funds. Afghan pilots are based at Bagram air base. Afghanistan is seeking the return of 26 aircraft, including some MiG-2s that were flown to safety in Pakistan and Uzbekistan during the past conflicts in Afghanistan. U.S. plans do not include supply of fixed-wing combat aircraft such as F-16s, which Afghanistan wants, according to U.S. military officials.

AFGHAN NATIONAL POLICE (ANP)

U.S. and Afghan officials believe that building up a credible and capable national police force is at least as important to combating the Taliban insurgency as building the ANA. There is a widespread consensus that the ANP lags the ANA in its development by about 18 months, although U.S. commanders say that it is increasingly successful in repelling Taliban assaults on villages and that is experiencing fewer casualties from attacks. The major criticism of the ANP is widespread corruption, to the point where many Afghans are more afraid of the police than they are of the Taliban.

To try to advance reform, the U.S. military is conducting reforms to take ANP out of the bureaucracy and onto the streets and it is trying to bring ANP pay on par with the ANA. It has been conducting a re-training program called "focused district development" to concentrate resources on developing individual police forces in districts, which is the basic geographic area of ANP activity. (There are about ten "districts" in each of Afghanistan's 34 provinces.) In this program, a district force is taken out and retrained, its duties temporarily performed by more highly trained police, and then reinserted after the training is complete.

As of April 2009, more than 3,000 ANP officers have undergone this process, which is expected to take five years to complete for the remainder of the country. A similar process is being applied to Afghanistan's border forces. There have been few quick fixes for the chronic shortage of equipment in the ANP. Most police are under-equipped, lacking ammunition and vehicles. In some cases, equipment requisitioned by their commanders is being sold and the funds pocketed. These activities, as well as absenteeism, led to the failure of a 2006 "auxiliary police" effort that attempted to rapidly field large numbers of new ANP officers.

The U.S. police training effort was first led by State

Department/INL, but the Defense Department took over the lead in police training in April 2005. Much of the training is still conducted through contracts with DynCorp. In addition to the U.S. effort, which includes 600 civilian U.S. police trainers (mostly still Dyncorp contractors) in addition to the U.S. military personnel, Germany (originally the lead government in Afghan police training) is providing 41 trainers. The European Union has taken over from Germany as lead and is providing a 190-member "EUPOL" training effort, and 60 other experts to help train the ANP. New training institutions, such as NTM-A and the European Gendarmerie, were discussed above.

CRIMINAL JUSTICE SECTOR

Many experts believe that comprehensive justice sector reform is vital to Afghan governance. Some of the criticisms and allegations of corruption at all levels of the Afghan bureaucracy have been discussed throughout this chapter. Police training now includes instruction in human rights principles and democratic policing concepts, and the State Department human rights report on Afghanistan, referenced above, says the government and outside observers are increasingly monitoring the police force to prevent abuses. However, some governments criticized Karzai for setting back police reform in June 2006 when he approved a new list of senior police commanders that included 11 (out of 86 total) who had failed merit exams. His approval of the 11 was reportedly to satisfy faction leaders and went against the recommendations of a police reform committee.

The ANP work in the communities they come from, often embroiling them in local factional or ethnic disputes. The State Department (INL) has placed 30 U.S. advisors in the Interior Ministry to help it develop the national police force and counter-narcotics capabilities. U.S. trainers are also building Border Police and Highway Patrol forces. U.S. justice sector programs generally focus on building capacity of the judicial system, including police training and court construction; many of these programs are conducted in partnership with Italy, which is technically the "lead" coalition country on judicial reform.

The United States has trained over 750 judges, lawyers, and prosecutors and built at least 40 judicial facilities. USAID also trains court administrators for the Ministry of Justice, the office of the Attorney General, and the Supreme Court. The United States and its partners have, to date, generally refrained from interfering in traditional mechanisms such as village *jirgas* or *shuras* convened to dispense justice. Doing so would likely raise questions among Afghans that the United States is trying to influence traditional Afghan culture and impose Western values on Afghanistan. The traditional mechanisms are still more widely used in Afghan villages, particularly in Pashtun areas, than are the secular judicial mechanisms, in part because of the ease of access of these mechanisms.

U.S. SECURITY FORCES FUNDING/CERP

About half of all U.S. assistance to Afghanistan since 2002 has gone toward building the ANSF. U.S. funds are used to cover ANA salaries as well as to equip and train them. Recent appropriations for the ANA and ANP are contained in the tables at the end of this chapter. In addition to the train and equip funds provided by DOD, the U.S. military in Afghanistan has additional funds to spend on reconstruction projects that build goodwill and presumably reduce the threat to use forces.

These are Commanders Emergency Response Program funds, or CERP. Figures for CERP funds are in the aid tables at the end of this chapter. U.S. funds are supplemented by funds from U.S. partners, although exact numbers are not available. As of FY2005, the security forces funding has been DOD funds, not State Department funds.

REGIONAL CONTEXT

Most of Afghanistan's neighbors believed that the fall of the Taliban would stabilize the region, but the region remains unstable as like-minded militants now threaten the government of Pakistan. Six of Afghanistan's neighbors signed a non-interference pledge (Kabul Declaration) on December 23, 2002. In November 2005, Afghanistan joined the South Asian Association for Regional Cooperation (SAARC), and Afghanistan has observer status in the Shanghai Cooperation Organization, which is discussed below.

PAKISTAN/PAKISTAN-AFGHANISTAN BORDER

The Obama Administration strategy review emphasized the linkage between militants present in Pakistan and the difficulty stabilizing Afghanistan, and the review outlined several new initiatives to strengthen and enhance Pakistan's ability to defeat militants on its territory. The review indicates that new U.S. aid will be provided to Pakistan, but that this aid will be contingent on Pakistan's performance on "benchmarks" to be developed to measure its cooperation.

However, Ambassador Holbrooke and others have said that the security deterioration in western Pakistan in April 2009 has, to some extent, overtaken the Obama Administration Afghanistan-Pakistan strategy and that Pakistan's stability is now a major issue in and of itself. The current U.S. view contrasts with that during 2001-2006, when the Bush Administration praised then President Pervez Musharraf for Pakistani accomplishments against Al Qaeda, including the arrest of over 700 *Al Qaeda* figures since the September 11 attacks. After the attacks, Pakistan provided the United States with access to Pakistani airspace, some ports, and some airfields for OEF.

Others say Musharraf acted against *Al Qaeda* only when it threatened him directly; for example, after the December 2003 assassination attempts against him. Musharraf resigned in August 2008, and the civilian government is led by the party of the late Pakistani secular leader Benazir Bhutto. The President is her widower, Asif Ali Zardari. Pakistan's policy in Afghanistan is heavily colored by fears of historic rival, India. Pakistan viewed the Taliban regime as providing Pakistan strategic depth against rival India, and Pakistan apparently remains wary that the current Afghan government may come under the sway of India.

Numerous militant groups, such as Laskhar-e-Tayyba (Army of the Righteous) were formed in Pakistan to challenge India's control of part of the disputed territories of Jammu and Kashmir. Some observers believe Pakistan wants to retain the ability to stoke these militants against India, even though some of these militants are connected to and maybe assisting Islamist groups that are now challenging the stability of Pakistan. Pakistan says India is using its Embassy and four consulates in Afghanistan to train and recruit anti-Pakistan insurgents, and is using its reconstruction funds to build influence there. Afghan officials have said they have evidence that, to counter that influence, ISI agents were involved in the July 7, 2008, suicide bombing of India's embassy in Kabul.

In connection with that act, U.S. officials, in July 2008, confronted Pakistani officials with evidence that Pakistan's Inter-Services Intelligence agency (ISI) is actively helping Afghanistan militants, particularly the Haqqani faction. Some Afghan leaders still resent Pakistan as the most public defender of the Taliban movement when it was in power and they suspect it wants to have the option to restore a Taliban-like regime. (Pakistan was one of only three countries to formally recognize it as the legitimate government: Saudi Arabia and the United Arab Emirates are the others.) Pakistan ended its public support for the Taliban after the September 11, 2001, attacks, but Pakistan-Afghanistan relations began deteriorating after the March 2006 Afghan accusation that Pakistan was allowing Taliban remnants, including Mullah Umar, to operating there. Pakistan's unwillingness to confront militants on its soil led the Bush Administration, in 2007, to criticize Pakistan even during Musharraf's rule. That shift accelerated following a *New York Times* report (February 19, 2007) that *Al Qaeda* had re-established some small *Al Qaeda* terrorist training camps in Pakistan, near the Afghan border.

This possibly was an outgrowth of a September 5, 2006, compromise between Pakistan and tribal elders in this region. In April 2008, the new government dominated by Bhutto's party, which prevailed in February 2008 parliamentary elections, negotiated a similar "understanding" with members of the Mehsud tribe, among which is Tehrik-e-Taliban (Pakistan Taliban) leader Baitullah Mehsud. U.S. commanders in Afghanistan blamed the Pakistani compromises for an increase in militant infiltration across the border. A February 2009 Pakistani truce with militants in Swat Valley, and militant advances to areas as close as 60 miles from Islamabad, stimulated renewed U.S. concerns, even though Swat is not near the Afghanistan border, particularly about the willingness of the Pakistani government to confront militants threatening its own survival.

The deterioration in Pakistan is a setback from late 2008, when U.S. officials said they saw improved Pakistani cooperation with U.S. efforts in Afghanistan. In June 2008, Pakistan ended a six month suspension in attendance at meetings of the Tripartite Commission" under which NATO, Afghan, and Pakistani military leaders meet regularly on both sides of the border. In April 2008, in an extension of the Tripartite Commission's work, the three agreed to set up five "border coordination centers"-which will include networks of radar nodes to give liaison officers a common view of the border area.

These centers build on an agreement in May 2007 to share intelligence on extremists' movements. Only one has been established to date-near the Torkham Gate at the Khyber Pass. Even though Pakistan's internal security has deteriorated, there has been a dramatic improvement in Afghanistan-Pakistan relations since the Musharraf era ended Karzai attended the September 9, 2008, inauguration of President Asif Ali Zardari, the widower of Benazir Bhutto.

The "peace jirga" process-a series of meetings of notables on each side of the border, which was agreed at a September 28, 2006, dinner hosted by President Bush for Karzai and Musharraf, has resumed. The first *jirga*, in which 700 Pakistani and Afghan tribal elders participated, was held in Kabul August 9-10, 2007. Another was held in the improving climate of Afghanistan-Pakistan relations during October 27-28, 2008; the Afghan side was headed by former Foreign Minister Dr. Abdullah.

It resulted in a declaration to endorse efforts to try to engage militants in both Afghanistan and Pakistan to bring them into the political process and abandon violence. Zardari and Karzai held bilateral meetings in Turkey on December 6, 2008, and, in the clearest sign of closer ties, Zardari visited Kabul and met with Karzai on January 9, 2009, where the two signed a joint declaration against terrorism that affects both countries. Additional progress was made during the visit of Afghan and Pakistani ministers to Washington, D.C. during February 23-27, 2009, to participate in the Obama Administration strategic review. As noted above, Karzai and Zardari visit Washington, D.C. in May 2009 to continue the strategic dialogue.

INCREASED DIRECT U.S. ACTION

The Obama Administration has continued to combat militants in Pakistan without directly violating Pakistan's restrictions on the U.S. ability to operate "on the ground" in Pakistan. Pakistani political leaders across the spectrum publicly oppose any presence of U.S. combat forces in Pakistan, although the *New York Times* reported on February 23, 2009, that there are about 70 U.S. military advisers in Pakistan to help train Pakistani forces to battle *Al Qaeda* and Taliban militants. U.S. cross-border raids still appear to be "off limits"-on September 3, 2008, a U.S. helicopter borne force reportedly crossed the border to raid a suspected militant encampment, drawing criticism and possibly some weapons fire from Pakistani forces. U.S. forces in Afghanistan acknowledge that they shell purported Taliban positions on the Pakistani side of the border, and do some "hot pursuit" a few kilometers over the border into Pakistan.

The Obama Administration has continued to use Predator and Reaper unmanned aircraft to strike militant targets in Pakistan, often incurring Pakistani official protestations. Press reports say there is increasing focus on striking the Haqqani network and on Pakistani militant Beitullah Mehsud. A major issue for the Obama Administration is whether Pakistan will tacitly permit such UAV attacks on the core of the Afghan Taliban leadership that is believed based in Quetta, the capital of Baluchistan province of Pakistan. To date, Pakistan has not cooperated with the United States to pressure Taliban leaders in this area.

Regarding the long-term relationship, Pakistan wants the government of Afghanistan to pledge to abide by the "Durand Line," a border agreement reached between Britain (signed by Sir Henry Mortimer Durand) and then Afghan leader Amir Abdul Rahman Khan in 1893, separating Afghanistan from what was then British-controlled India (later Pakistan after the 1947 partition). It is recognized by the United Nations, but Afghanistan continues to indicate that the border was drawn unfairly to separate Pashtun tribes and should be re-negotiated. As of October 2002, about 1.75 million Afghan refugees have returned from Pakistan since the Taliban fell, but as many as 3 million might still remain in Pakistan, and Pakistan says it plans to expel them back into Afghanistan in the near future.

IRAN

As it attempts to stabilize Afghanistan, nearly eight years after the United States helped Afghan militias overthrow the Taliban, the Obama Administration sees Iran as potentially helpful to its new strategy for Afghanistan, announced March 27, 2009. The U.S. special representative for Afghanistan and Pakistan, Ambassador Richard Holbrooke, has advocated a "regional" component of the strategy, which focuses primarily on Pakistan but also envisions cooperation with Iran to help keep Afghanistan calm. Still, Iran and U.S. interests in Afghanistan, while in many ways coincident, are not identical. Iran perceives its key national interests in Afghanistan as exerting its traditional influence over western Afghanistan, which Iran borders and was once part of the Persian empire, and to protect Afghanistan's Shiite minority.

Iran's assistance to Afghanistan has totaled about $1.164 billion since the fall of the Taliban, mainly to build roads and schools and provide electricity and shops to Afghan cities and villages near the Iranian border. This makes Iran among the top financial donors to Afghanistan and is in many ways supportive of the U.S. policy of attempting to pacify Afghanistan in part through economic development. In public statements, in part because of the economic development work done by Iranian firms, President Hamid Karzai has, at times, called Iran a "friend" of Afghanistan. Karzai received Iranian President Mahmoud Ahmadinejad in Kabul in August 2007, and he is expected to visit Tehran at the end of May 2009 as part of a new tripartite diplomatic process between Iran, Pakistan, and Afghanistan.

During his visit to the United States in May 2009, Karzai said he had told both the United States and Iran that Afghanistan must not become an arena for the broader competition and disputes between the United States and Iran. In discussing conflict between Iran and the United States in Afghanistan, Karzai was referring to the reports that Iran has sporadically offered support for Taliban and other militants in Afghanistan. The State Department report on international terrorism for 2008, released April 30, 2009, said Iran continues to provide some training to and ships arms to "selected Taliban members" in Afghanistan.

Weapons provided, according to the State Department report, include mortars, 107mm rockets, rocket-propelled grenades, and plastic explosives. Several shipments of such weapons were captured by the U.S. military in Afghanistan in 2007. Secretary of Defense Gates testified before the Senate Armed Services Committee in late January 2009 that the Defense Department had seen a slight increase in Iranian shipments of arms into Afghanistan in the few preceding months.

Iran has opposed the U.S. use of the Shindand air base, which Iran fears the United States might use to attack or conduct surveillance against Iran. Iranian aid to Taliban fighters puzzle some experts since these shipments would appear to conflict with Iran's support for the government of Karzai-which Iran actively helped put together, in cooperation with the United States-at the December 2001 "Bonn Conference." In addition, Iran has traditionally supported

Persian-speaking non-Pashtun factions in Afghanistan, who would presumably be suppressed and marginalized by any new Taliban-led regime in Afghanistan. Iran saw the Taliban regime, which ruled during 1996-2001, as a threat to its interests in Afghanistan, especially after Taliban forces captured Herat (the western province that borders Iran) in September 1995.

Iran subsequently drew even closer to the ethnic minority-dominated Northern Alliance than previously, providing its groups with fuel, funds, and ammunition. In September 1998, Iranian and Taliban forces nearly came into direct conflict when Iran discovered that nine of its diplomats were killed in the course of the Taliban's offensive in northern Afghanistan. Iran massed forces at the border and threatened military action, but the crisis cooled without a major clash, possibly out of fear that Pakistan would intervene on behalf of the Taliban.

Iran offered search and rescue assistance in Afghanistan during the U.S.-led war to topple the Taliban, and it also allowed U.S. humanitarian aid to the Afghan people to transit Iran. In attempting to explain the continuing shipments, some experts believe Iran's policy might be shifting somewhat to gain leverage against the United States by causing U.S. combat deaths, or by demonstrating that Iran is in position to cause U.S. combat deaths in Afghanistan. Others see Iran as a marginal player in Afghanistan, because it is identified primarily with non- Pashtuns and its links to Taliban fighters are tenuous and sporadic.

Those who take this view question whether U.S. engagement with Iran would contribute much to solving the core problems plaguing the U.S. mission there. Still others believe that talks with Iran on Afghanistan could lead to broader U.S.-Iran talks, or potentially even open up the possibility of using Iran as a supply line for non-U.S. NATO forces in Afghanistan. Secretary of State Clinton made a point of announcing that Iran would be invited to the U.N.-led meeting on Afghanistan at the Hague on March 31, 2009.

At the meeting, Special Representative Holbrooke briefly met the Iranian leader of his delegation to the meeting, and handing him a letter on several outstanding human rights cases involving Iranian-Americans. At the meeting, Iran pledged cooperation on combating Afghan narcotics and in helping economic development in Afghanistan-both policies Iran is already pursuing to a large degree. After the fall of the Taliban in late 2001, President Bush warned Iran against meddling in Afghanistan.

Partly in response to the U.S. criticism, in February 2002 Iran expelled Karzai opponent Gulbuddin Hikmatyar, but it did not arrest him. At other times, Afghanistan and Iran the two countries have had disputes over Iran's efforts to expel Afghan refugees. About 1.2 million remain, mostly integrated into Iranian society, and a crisis erupted in May 2007 when Iran expelled about 50,000 into Afghanistan. About 300,000 Afghan refugees have returned from Iran since the Taliban fell.

INDIA

The interests and activities of India in Afghanistan are almost the exact reverse of those of Pakistan. India's goal is to deny Pakistan "strategic depth" in Afghanistan, and India supported the Northern Alliance against the Taliban in the mid-1990s. Tajikistan allows India to use one of its air bases; Tajikistan supports the mostly Tajik Northern Alliance. Many of the families of Afghan leaders have lived in India at one time or another and, as noted above, Karzai studied there. India saw the Taliban's hosting of *Al Qaeda* as a major threat to India itself because of Al Qaeda's association with radical Islamic organizations in Pakistan dedicated to ending Indian control of parts of Jammu and Kashmir.

Some of these groups have committed major acts of terrorism in India, and there might be connections to the militants who carried out the terrorist attacks in Mumbai in November 2008. Pakistan accuses India of using its four consulates in Afghanistan (Pakistan says there are nine such consulates) to spread Indian influence in Afghanistan. However, many U.S. observers believe India's role in Afghanistan is constructive, and some would support an Indian decision to deploy more security forces in Afghanistan to protect its construction workers, diplomats, and installations.

India reportedly decided in August 2008 to improve security for its officials and workers in Afghanistan, but not to send actual troops there. India is the fifth largest single country donor to Afghan reconstruction, funding projects worth about $1.2 billion. India, along with the Asian Development Bank, financed a $300 million project, mentioned above, to bring electricity from Central Asia to Afghanistan.

It has also renovated the well known Habibia High School in Kabul and committed to a $25 million renovation of Darulaman Palace as the permanent house for Afghanistan's parliament. India financed the construction of a road to the Iranian border in remote Nimruz province. India is also helping the IDLG with its efforts to build local governance organizations, and it provides 1,000 scholarships per year for Afghans to undergo higher education in India.

RUSSIA, CENTRAL ASIAN STATES, AND CHINA

Some neighboring and nearby states take an active interest not only in Afghan stability, but in the U.S. military posture that supports U.S. operations in Afghanistan. The region to the north of Afghanistan is a growing factor in U.S. efforts to secure new supply lines to Afghanistan. Some of these alternative lines have begun to open, at least to non-lethal supplies.

Russia

Russia wants to re-emerge as a great power and to contain U.S. power in Central Asia, including Afghanistan. However, it supports U.S. efforts to combat militants in the region who have sometimes posed a threat to Russia itself. In an effort to try to cooperate more with NATO at least in Afghanistan, in conjunction with the April 2008 NATO summit, Russia agreed to allow NATO to ship non-lethal supplies to coalition forces in Afghanistan by land over Russian territory. That pledge was put into doubt following the August 2008 crisis over Georgia, an outcome of which has been suspension of Russian military cooperation with NATO; Russia says this land route cooperation constitutes military coordination covered under that suspension announcement.

However, in February 2009, Russia said it would again allow the United States to ship non-lethal equipment into Afghanistan through Russia, and, as noted, some of these shipments began in February 2009. Russia provides some humanitarian aid to Afghanistan, although it keeps a low profile in Afghanistan because it still feels humiliated by its withdrawal from Afghanistan in 1989 and senses Afghan resentment of the Soviet occupation. During the 1990s, Russia supported the Northern Alliance against the Taliban with some military equipment and technical assistance in order to blunt Islamic militancy emanating from Afghanistan.

Although Russia supported the U.S. effort against the Taliban and *Al Qaeda* in Afghanistan out of fear of Islamic (mainly Chechen) radicals, Russia continues to seek to reduce the U.S. military presence in Central Asia. Russian fears of Islamic activism emanating from Afghanistan may have ebbed since 2002 when Russia killed a Chechen of Arab origin known as "Hattab" (full name is Ibn al-Khattab), who led a militant pro-*Al Qaeda* Chechen faction. The Taliban government was the only one in the world to recognize Chechnya's independence, and some Chechen fighters fighting alongside Taliban/*Al Qaeda* forces have been captured or killed.

Central Asian States

These states are becoming increasingly crucial to U.S. strategy in Afghanistan. Uzbekistan, Turkmenistan, and Tajikistan are pivotal actors in U.S. efforts to secure alternate supply routes into Afghanistan. These states are increasingly important in light of Kyrgyzstan's decision in February 2009 to end U.S. use of Manas airbase, although that decision might be reversed. During Taliban rule, Russian and Central Asian leaders grew increasingly alarmed that radical Islamic movements were receiving safe haven in Afghanistan.

Uzbekistan, in particular, has long asserted that the group Islamic Movement of Uzbekistan (IMU), allegedly responsible for four simultaneous February 1999 bombings in Tashkent that nearly killed President Islam Karimov, is linked to Al Qaeda. One of its leaders, Juma Namangani, reportedly was killed while commanding Taliban/*Al Qaeda* forces in Konduz in November 2001. Kazakhstan and Kyrgyzstan do not directly border Afghanistan, but IMU guerrillas transited Kyrgyzstan during incursions into Uzbekistan in the late 1990s.

During Taliban rule, Uzbekistan supported Uzbek leader Abdul Rashid Dostam, who was part of that Alliance. It allowed use of Karshi-Khanabad air base by OEF forces from October 2001 until a rift emerged in May 2005 over Uzbekistan's crackdown against riots in Andijon, and U.S.- Uzbek relations remained largely frozen. Uzbekistan's March 2008 agreement with Germany for it to use Karshi-Khanabad air base temporarily, for the first time since the rift in U.S.-Uzbek relations developed in 2005, suggests that U.S.-Uzbek cooperation on Afghanistan and other issues might be rebuilt.

Stepped up U.S. discussions with Uzbekistan, in light of Kyrgyzstan's denial of the U.S. use of Manas air base, have apparently borne some fruit with the Uzbek decision in February 2009 to allow the use of Navoi airfield for shipment of U.S./ NATO goods into Afghanistan. At the April 2008 NATO summit in Bucharest, Uzbekistan proposed to revive the "6 + 2" process of neighbors of Afghanistan to help its stability, but Karzai reportedly opposes this idea as unwanted Central Asian interference in its affairs. In 1996, several of the Central Asian states banded together with Russia and China into a regional grouping called the Shanghai Cooperation Organization to discuss the Taliban threat. It includes China, Russia, Uzbekistan, Tajikistan, Kazakhstan, and Kyrgyzstan.

Reflecting Russian and Chinese efforts to limit U.S. influence in the region, the group has issued statements, most recently in August 2007, that security should be handled by the countries in the Central Asia region. Despite the Shanghai Cooperation Organization statements, Tajikistan allows access primarily to

French combat aircraft, and Kazakhstan allows use of facilities in case of emergency. A meeting of the Shanghai Cooperation Organization to discuss Afghanistan was held in Moscow on March 25, 2009, and was observed by a U.S. official, as well as by Iran.

Of the Central Asian states that border Afghanistan, only Turkmenistan chose to seek close relations with the Taliban leadership when it was in power, possibly viewing engagement as a more effective means of preventing spillover of radical Islamic activity from Afghanistan. It saw Taliban control as facilitating construction of a natural gas pipeline from Turkmenistan through Afghanistan. The September 11 events stoked Turkmenistan's fears of the Taliban and its *Al Qaeda* guests and the country publicly supported the U.S.-led war. No U.S. forces have been based in Turkmenistan.

China

A major organizer of the Shanghai Cooperation Organization, China has a small border with a sliver of Afghanistan known as the "Wakhan corridor." China had become increasingly concerned about the potential for *Al Qaeda* to promote Islamic fundamentalism among Muslims in China. In December 2000, sensing China's increasing concern about Taliban policies, a Chinese official delegation met with Mullah Umar.

China did not enthusiastically support U.S. military action against the Taliban, possibly because China was wary of a U.S. military buildup nearby. In addition, China has been allied to Pakistan in part to pressure India, a rival of China. Still, Chinese delegations continue to assess the potential for new investments in such sectors as mining and energy, and a deal was signed in November 2007 for China Metallurgical Group to develop the Aynak copper mine south of Kabul, and build related infrastructure.

PERSIAN GULF STATES: SAUDI ARABIA AND UAE

Saudi Arabia is playing a growing role in hosting negotiations between the Karzai government and "moderate"

Taliban figures for a negotiated settlement. Saudi Arabia has leverage because, during the Soviet occupation, Saudi Arabia channeled hundreds of millions of dollars to the Afghan resistance, primarily Hikmatyar and Sayyaf. Saudi Arabia, a majority of whose citizens practice the strict Wahhabi brand of Islam similar to that of the Taliban, was one of three countries to formally recognize the Taliban government.

The Taliban initially served Saudi Arabia as a potential counter to Iran, but Iranian-Saudi relations improved after 1997 and balancing Iranian power ebbed as a factor in Saudi policy toward Afghanistan. Drawing on its reputed intelligence ties to Afghanistan during that era, Saudi Arabia worked with Taliban leaders to persuade them to suppress anti-Saudi activities by Al Qaeda. Some press reports indicate that, in late 1998, Saudi and Taliban leaders discussed, but did not agree on, a plan for a panel of Saudi and Afghan Islamic scholars to decide bins Laden's fate. According to U.S. officials, Saudi Arabia cooperated extensively, if not publicly, with OEF.

It broke diplomatic relations with the Taliban in late September 2001 and quietly permitted the United States to use a Saudi base for command of U.S. air operations over Afghanistan, but it did not permit U.S. airstrikes from it. As noted above, it has hosted talks between the Karzai government and moderate Taliban leaders to pursue potential reconciliation. The United Arab Emirates, the third country that recognized the Taliban regime, is emerging as another major donor to Afghanistan. Its troop contribution was discussed under OEF, above.

At a donors conference for Afghanistan in June 2008, UAE pledged an additional $250 million for Afghan development, double the $118 million pledged by Saudi Arabia. That brought the UAE contribution to Afghanistan to over $400 million since the fall of the Taliban. Projects funded include housing in Qandahar, roads in Kabul, a hospital in Zabol province, and a university in Khost. There are several daily flights between Kabul and Dubai emirate.

U.S. AND INTERNATIONAL AID TO AFGHANISTAN AND DEVELOPMENT ISSUES

Many experts have long believed that accelerating economic development would do more to improve the security situation-and to eliminate narcotics trafficking-than intensified anti- Taliban combat. This belief appears to underpin the Obama Administration strategy. Afghanistan's economy and society are still fragile after decades of warfare that left about 2 million dead, 700,000 widows and orphans, and about 1 million Afghan children who were born and raised in refugee camps outside Afghanistan.

More than 3.5 million Afghan refugees have since returned, although a comparable number remain outside Afghanistan. The U.N. High Commission for Refugees (UNHCR) supervises Afghan repatriation and Afghan refugee camps in Pakistan. The literacy rate is very low and Afghanistan lacks the skilled labor pool needed to build a large modern economy.

U.S. ASSISTANCE TO AFGHANISTAN

During the 1990s, the United States became the largest single provider of assistance to the Afghan people. During Taliban rule, no U.S. aid went directly to that government; monies were provided through relief organizations. Between 1985 and 1994, the United States had a cross-border aid program for Afghanistan, implemented by USAID personnel based in Pakistan. Citing the difficulty of administering this program, there was no USAID mission for Afghanistan from the end of FY1994 until the reopening of the U.S. Embassy in Afghanistan in late 2001.

Since FY2002 and including funds already appropriated for FY2009, the United States has provided over $32 billion in reconstruction assistance, including military "train and equip" for the ANA and ANP and counter-narcotics-related assistance (which is about $15 billion during that time period). This does not include funds requested in a FY2009 supplemental appropriation request. The Obama Administration budget for

FY2010 says that reconstruction aid to Afghanistan would "increase" in FY2010, but figures are not available to date. The figures in the tables do not include costs for U.S. combat operations, which are discussed in CRS Report RL33110, *The Cost of Iraq, Afghanistan, and Other Global War on Terror Operations Since 9/11*, by Amy Belasco.

AID OVERSIGHT

Still heavily dependent on donors, Karzai has sought to reassure the international donor community by establishing a transparent budget and planning process. Some in Congress want to increase independent oversight of U.S. aid to Afghanistan; the conference report on the FY2008 defense authorization bill (P.L. 110-181) established a "special inspector general" for Afghanistan reconstruction, (SIGAR) modeled on a similar outside auditor for Iraq ("Special Inspector General for Iraq Reconstruction," SIGIR).

On May 30, 2008, Maj. Gen. Arnold Fields (Marine, ret.) was named to the position. He has filed three reports on Afghan reconstruction, most recently on April 30, 2009, which include discussions of SIGAR staffing levels and activities, and lays out the auditing plan of specific projects.

AID AUTHORIZATION: AFGHANISTAN FREEDOM SUPPORT ACT

A key post-Taliban aid authorization bill, S. 2712, the Afghanistan Freedom Support Act (AFSA) of 2002 (P.L. 107-327, December 4, 2002), as amended, authorized about $3.7 billion in U.S. civilian aid for FY2003-FY2006. For the most part, the humanitarian, counter-narcotics, and governance assistance targets authorized by the act were met or exceeded by appropriations. However, no Enterprise Funds have been appropriated, and ISAF expansion ($1 billion in U.S. funds were authorized in the Act) was funded by the contributing partner forces. The act authorized the following:

- $60 million in total counter-narcotics assistance ($15 million per year for FY2003-FY2006); .

- $30 million in assistance for political development, including national, regional, and local elections ($10 million per year for FY2003-FY2005);
- • $80 million total to benefit women and for Afghan human rights oversight ($15 million per year for FY2003-FY2006 for the Afghan Ministry of Women's Affairs, and $5 million per year for FY2003-FY2006 to the Human Rights Commission of Afghanistan);
- $1.7 billion in humanitarian and development aid ($425 million per year for FY2003-FY2006);
- $300 million for an Enterprise Fund;
- $550 million in draw-downs cf defense articles and services for Afghanistan and regional militaries. (The original law provided for $300 million in drawdowns.

That was increased by subsequent appropriations laws. A subsequent law (P.L. 108-458, December 17, 2004), implementing the recommendations of the 9/11 Commission, contained "The Afghanistan Freedom Support Act Amendments of 2004." The subtitle mandates the appointment of a U.S. coordinator of policy on Afghanistan and requires additional Administration reports to Congress, including (1) on long-term U.S. strategy and progress of reconstruction, an amendment to the report required in the original law; (2) on how U.S. assistance is being used; (3) on U.S. efforts to persuade other countries to participate in Afghan peacekeeping; and (4) a joint State and Defense Department report on U.S. counter- narcotics efforts in Afghanistan. An overarching annual report on U.S. strategy in Afghanistan is required until 2010, the other reporting requirements expired.

AFGHAN FREEDOM SUPPORT ACT RE-AUTHORIZATION

In the 110th Congress, H.R. 2446, passed by the House on June 6, 2007 (406-10), would reauthorize AFSA through FY2010. A version (S. 3531), with fewer provisions than the House bill, was not taken up by the full Senate. Some observers say that versions of AFSA re- authorization are expected to be reintroduced in the 111th Congress. The following are the major provisions of H.R. 2446:

- A total of about $1.7 billion in U.S. economic aid and $320 in military aid (including draw-downs of equipment) per fiscal year would be authorized.
- A pilot program of crop substitution to encourage legitimate alternatives to poppy cultivation is authorized. Afghan officials support this provision as furthering their goal of combating narcotics by promoting alternative livelihoods.
- Enhanced anti-corruption and legal reform programs.
- U.S. aid would be cut off to any Afghan province in which the Administration reports that the leadership of the province is complicit in narcotics trafficking. This provision has drew criticism from observers who say that the most needy in Afghanistan might be deprived of aid based on allegations.
- $45 million per year for the Ministry of Women's Affairs, the Afghan Independent Human Rights Commission, and programs for women and girls.
- $75 million per year for enhanced power generation, a key need in Afghanistan.
- A coordinator for U.S. assistance to Afghanistan.
- Military drawdowns for the ANA and ANP valued at $300 million per year (un- reimbursed) are authorized (versus the aggregate $550 million allowed currently).
- Appointment of a special envoy to promote greater Afghanistan-Pakistan cooperation.
- Reauthorizes "Radio Free Afghanistan."
- Establishes a U.S. policy to encourage Pakistan to permit shipments by India of equipment and material to Afghanistan.

INTERNATIONAL RECONSTRUCTION PLEDGES/ NATIONAL DEVELOPMENT STRATEGY

International (non-U.S.) donors have provided over another $25 billion since the fall of the Taliban, as of 2009. When combined with U.S. aid, this by far exceeds the $27.5 billion for reconstruction identified as required for 2002-2010. The major donors, and their aggregate pledges to date, are listed below. These amounts were pledged, in part, at the following donor conferences: (Tokyo), Berlin (April 2004), Kabul (April 2005), the London conference (February 2006), and the June 12, 2008 conference in Paris, discussed below.

The Afghanistan Compact leaned toward the view of Afghan leaders that a higher proportion of the aid be channeled through the Afghan government rather than directly by the donor community. Only about 20% of the funds disbursed are channeled through the Afghan government. In the Afghanistan Compact, the Afghan government promised greater financial transparency and international (United Nations) oversight to ensure that international contributions are used wisely and effectively. At the June 12, 2008, conference in Paris, Afghanistan formally presented its Afghan National Development Strategy, asking for $50.1 billion during 2009-2014 from international donors.

Of that, $14 billion was requested to improve infrastructure, including airports and to construct a railway. Another $14 billion would be to build the ANSF, and about $4.5 billion would be for agriculture and rural development. However, citing in part a relative lack of transparency in Afghan governance, donors pledged about $21 billion, but that included $10.2 billion already committed by the United States.

Of the other major pledges, the Asian Development bank pledged $1.3 billion, the World Bank pledged $1.1 billion, Britain pledged $1.2 billion; France pledged $165 million over two years; Japan pledged $550 million; Germany offered $600 million over two years, and the European Union pledged $770 million. Among multilateral lending institutions, in May 2002, the World Bank reopened its office in Afghanistan after 20 years. Its projects have been concentrated in the telecommunications and road and sewage sectors.

The Asian Development Bank (ADB) has also been playing a major role in Afghanistan. One of its projects in Afghanistan was funding the paving of a road from Qandahar to the border with Pakistan, and as noted above, it is contributing to a project to bring electricity from Central Asia to Afghanistan. Efforts to build the legitimate economy are showing some results, by accounts of senior U.S. officials, including expansion of roads and education and health facilities constructed.

KEY SECTORS

The following are some key sectors and what has been accomplished with U.S. and international donor funds:

- Roads: Road building is considered a U.S. priority and has been USAID's largest project category there, taking up about 25% of USAID spending since the fall of the Taliban. Roads are considered key to enabling Afghan farmers to bring legitimate produce to market in a timely fashion and former commander of U.S. forces in Afghanistan Gen. Eikenberry (now Ambassador) said "where the roads end, the Taliban begin." The major road, the Ring Road, is 73% re-paved, according to the Defense Department January 2009 report on Afghan stability. Among other major projects completed are: a road from Qandahar to Tarin Kowt, built by U.S. military personnel, inaugurated in 2005; and a road linking the Panjshir Valley to Kabul. In several provinces, U.S. funds (sometimes CERP funds) are being used to build roads connecting remote areas to regional district centers in several provinces in the eastern sector. A key priority is building a Khost-Gardez road, under way currently.
- Education: Despite the success in enrolling Afghan children in school since the Taliban era, setbacks have occurred because of Taliban attacks on schools, causing some to close.
- Health: The health care sector, as noted by Afghan observers, has made considerable gains in reducing infant mortality and improving Afghans' access to health professionals. In addition to U.S. assistance to develop the health sector's capacity, Egypt operates a 65-person field hospital at Bagram Air Base that instructs Afghan physicians. Jordan operates a similar facility in Mazar-e-Sharif.
- Agriculture: USAID has spent about 5% of its Afghanistan funds on agriculture, and this has helped Afghanistan

double its agricultural output over the past five years. Afghan officials say agricultural assistance and development should be a top U.S. priority as part of a strategy of encouraging legitimate alternatives to poppy cultivation. (Another 10% of USAID funds is spent on "alternative livelihoods" to poppy growing, mostly in aid to farmers.) One emerging "success story" is growing Afghan exports of high quality pomegranate juice called Anar. Other crops now substituting for poppy include wheat and saffron. To help Afghanistan develop this sector, the U.S. National Guard is deploying "Agribusiness Development Teams" in several provinces to help Afghan farmers with water management, soil enhancement, crop cultivation, and improving the development and marketing of their goods.

- Electricity: About 10% of USAID spending in Afghanistan is on power projects. The Afghanistan Compact states that the goal is for electricity to reach 65% of households in urban areas and 25% in rural areas by 2010. There have been severe power shortages in Kabul, partly because the city population has swelled to about 3 million, up from half a million when the Taliban was in power, but power to the capital is growing. The Afghan government, with help from international donors, has been importing electricity from Central Asian and other neighbors.
- A major power project is the Kajaki Dam, located in unstable Helmand Province. USAID has allocated about $500 million to restore the three electricity- generating turbines (two are operating) of the dam which, when functional, will provide electricity for 1.7 million Afghans and about 4,000 jobs in the reconstruction. In an operation involving 4,000 NATO troops (Operation Ogap Tsuka), components of the third and final turbine was successfully delivered to the dam in September 2008 and it is expected to be operational in mid-late 2009.

NATIONAL SOLIDARITY PROGRAM

The United States and the Afghan government are also trying to promote local decision making on development. The

"National Solidarity Program" (NSD) largely funded by U.S. and other international donors - but implemented by Afghanistan's Ministry of Rural Rehabilitation and Development-seeks to create and empower local governing councils to prioritize local reconstruction projects, and it is widely hailed as a success.

The assistance, channeled through donors, provides block grants of about $60,000 per project to the councils to implement agreed projects, most of which are water projects. Elections to the nearly 30,000 local councils- discussed above in the discussion on the IDLG-have been held in several provinces, and almost 40% of those elected have been women. The U.S. aid to the program is part of the Afghanistan Reconstruction Trust Fund (ARTF) account. The FY2009 supplemental request asks about $85 million for the ARTF account, of which much of those funds would be used to fill a $140 million shortfall in the NSP program. H.R. 2346, the House version, earmarks $70 million to defray the shortfall.

TRADE INITIATIVES/RECONSTRUCTION OPPORTUNITY ZONES

The United States is trying to build on Afghanistan's post-war economic rebound with trade initiatives. In September 2004, the United States and Afghanistan signed a bilateral trade and investment framework agreement (TIFA). These agreements are generally seen as a prelude to a broader and more complex bilateral free trade agreement, but negotiations on an FTA have not yet begun. On December 13, 2004, the 148 countries of the World Trade Organization voted to start membership talks with Afghanistan. Another initiative supported by the United States is the establishment of joint Afghan-Pakistani "Reconstruction Opportunity Zones" (ROZ's) which would be modeled after "Qualified Industrial Zones" run by Israel and Jordan in which goods produced in the zones receive duty free treatment for import into the United States.

For FY2008, $5 million in supplemental funding was requested to support the zones, but P.L. 110-252 did not specifically mention the zones. Bills in the 110th Congress, S. 2776 and H.R. 6387, would authorize the President to proclaim duty-free treatment for imports from ROZ's to be designated by the President. In the 111th Congress, a version of these bills was introduced. President Obama specifically endorsed passage of these bills in his strategy review announcement.

MAJOR PRIVATE SECTOR INITIATIVES

Some international investors are implementing projects, and there is substantial new construction, such as the Serena luxury hotel that opened in November 2005 (long considered a priority Taliban target, the hotel was attacked by militants on January 14, 2008, killing six) and a $25 million new Coca Cola bottling factory that opened in Kabul on September 11, 2006. Several Afghan companies are growing as well, including Roshan and Afghan Wireless (cell phone service), and Tolo Television. A Gold's Gym has opened in Kabul as well.

The 52-year-old national airline, Ariana, is said to be in significant financial trouble due to corruption that has affected its safety ratings and left it unable to service a heavy debt load, but there are new privately run airlines, such as Pamir Air, Safi Air, and Kam Air. Some Afghan leaders complain that not enough has been done to revive such potentially lucrative industries as minerals mining, such as of copper and lapis lazuli (a stone used in jewelry). In November 2007, the Afghan government signed a deal with China Metallurgical Group for the company to invest $2.8 billion to develop Afghanistan's Aynak copper field in Lowgar Province; the agreement includes construction of a coal-fired electric power plant and a freight railway. Work has begun on the mine.

Afghanistan's prospects also appeared to brighten by the announcement in March 2006 of an estimated 3.6 billion barrels of oil and 36.5 trillion cubic feet of gas reserves. Experts believe these amounts, if proved, could make Afghanistan relatively self-sufficient in energy and able to export energy to its neighbors. USAID is funding a test project to develop gas resources in northern Afghanistan. Afghan officials are said to be optimistic about increased trade with Central Asia now that a new bridge has opened (October 2007) over the Panj River, connecting Afghanistan and Tajikistan. The bridge was built with $33 million in (FY2005) U.S. assistance.

The bridge will further assist what press reports say is robust reconstruction and economic development in the relatively peaceful and ethnically homogenous province of Panjshir, the political base of the Northern Alliance. Another major energy project remains under consideration. During 1996-1998, the Clinton Administration supported proposed natural gas and oil pipelines through western Afghanistan as an incentive for the warring factions to cooperate.

A consortium led by Los Angeles-based Unocal Corporation proposed a $2.5 billion Central Asia Gas Pipeline, estimated to cost $3.7 billion to construct, that would originate in southern Turkmenistan and pass through Afghanistan to Pakistan, with possible extensions into India. The deterioration in U.S.-Taliban relations after 1998 largely ended hopes for the pipeline projects. Prospects for the project have improved in the post-Taliban period. In a summit meeting in late May 2002 between the leaders of Turkmenistan, Afghanistan, and Pakistan, the three countries agreed to revive the project. Sponsors held an inaugural meeting on July 9, 2002 in Turkmenistan, signing a series of preliminary agreements.

Turkmenistan's leadership (President Gurbanguly Berdimukhamedov, succeeding the late Saparmurad Niyazov) favors the project as well. Some U.S. officials view this project as a superior alternative to a proposed gas pipeline from Iran to India, transiting Pakistan. Some of the more stable provinces, such as Bamiyan, are complaining that international aid is flowing mostly to the restive provinces in an effort to quiet them, and ignoring the needs of poor Afghans in peaceful areas.

RESIDUAL ISSUES FROM PAST CONFLICTS

A few issues remain unresolved from Afghanistan's many years of conflict, such as Stinger retrieval and mine eradication.

STINGER RETRIEVAL

Beginning in late 1985 following internal debate, the Reagan Administration provided about 2,000 man-portable "Stinger" anti-aircraft missiles to the *mujahedin* for use against Soviet aircraft. Prior to the U.S.-led ouster of the Taliban, common estimates suggested that 200-300 Stingers remained at large, although more recent estimates put the number below 100. The Stinger issue resurfaced in conjunction with 2001 U.S. war effort, when U.S. pilots reported that the Taliban fired some Stingers at U.S. aircraft during the war.

No hits were reported. Any Stingers that survived the anti-Taliban war are likely controlled by Afghans now allied to the United States and presumably pose less of a threat, in part because of the deterioration of the weapons' batteries and other internal components. In 1992, after the fall of the Russian-backed government of Najibullah, the United States reportedly spent about $10 million to buy the Stingers back, at a premium, from individual *mujahedin* commanders.

The *New York Times* reported on July 24, 1993, that the buy back effort failed because the United States was competing with other buyers, including Iran and North Korea, and that the CIA would spend about $55 million in FY1994 in a renewed buy-back effort. On March 7, 1994, the *Washington Post* reported that the CIA had recovered only a fraction (maybe 50 or 100) of the at-large Stingers. In February 2002, the Afghan government found and returned to the United States "dozens" of Stingers. 53 In late January 2005, Afghan intelligence began a push to buy remaining Stingers back, at a reported cost of $150,000 each.

The danger of these weapons has become apparent on several occasions, although U.S. commanders have not reported any recent active firings of these devices. Iran bought 16 of the missiles in 1987 and fired one against U.S. helicopters; some reportedly were transferred to Lebanese Hizballah. India claimed that it was a Stinger, supplied to Islamic rebels in Kashmir probably by sympathizers in Afghanistan, that shot down an Indian helicopter over Kashmir in May 1999. It was a Soviet-made SA-7 "Strella" man-portable launchers that were fired, allegedly by Al Qaeda, against a U.S. military aircraft in Saudi Arabia in June 2002 and against an Israeli passenger aircraft in Kenya on November 30, 2002. Both missed their targets. SA-7s were discovered in Afghanistan by U.S. forces in December 2002.

MINE ERADICATION

Land mines laid during the Soviet occupation constitute one of the principal dangers to the Afghan people. The United Nations estimates that 5 -7 million mines remain scattered throughout the country, although some estimates are lower. U.N. teams have destroyed one million mines and are now focusing on de-mining priority-use, residential and commercial property, including lands around Kabul.

The U.S. aid for FY1999-FY2002 and for the U.S. de-mining program was to provide about $3 million per year for Afghanistan, and the amount increased to about $7 million in the post-Taliban period. Most of the funds have gone to HALO Trust, a British organization, and the U.N. Mine Action Program for Afghanistan. The Afghanistan Compact adopted in London in February 2006 states that by 2010, the goal should be to reduce the land area of Afghanistan contaminated by mines by 70%.

10

Afghan Women under the Taliban

Thirty thousand men and boys poured into the dilapidated Olympic sports stadium in Kabul, capital of Afghanistan. Street hawkers peddled nuts, biscuits and tea to the waiting crowd. The scheduled entertainment? They were there to see a young woman, Sohaila, receive 100 lashes, and to watch two thieves have their right hands amputated. Sohaila had been arrested walking with a man who was not a relative, a sufficient crime for her to be found guilty of adultery. Since she was single, it was punishable by flogging; had she been married, she would have been publicly stoned to death.

As Sohaila, completely covered in the shroud like burqa veil, was forced to kneel and then flogged, Taliban "cheerleaders" had the stadium ringing with the chants of onlookers. Among those present there were just three women: the young Afghan, and two female relatives who had accompanied her. The crowd fell silent only when the luckless thieves were driven into the arena and pushed to the ground.

Physicians using surgical scalpels promptly carried out the amputations. Holding the severed hands aloft by the index fingers, a grinning Taliban fighter warned the huge crowd, "These are the chopped off hands of thieves, the punishment for any of you caught stealing." Then, to restore the party atmosphere, the thieves were driven in a jeep once around the stadium, a flourish that brought the crowd to their feet, as was intended.

These Friday circuses, at which Rome's Caligula would doubtless have felt at home, are to become weekly fixtures for the entertainment starved male residents of Kabul. Now that "weak officials" have been purged from key ministries, says the city's governor, Manan Niazi, who like many of the regime's officials is also a mullah, the way has been cleared for such displays.

"We have a lot of such unpunished cases, but the previous civil servants didn't have the courage to do what we are doing. These people have now been replaced, and these events will continue." In fact, the next scheduled program, as announced, would be one stoning to death and three amputations.

Earlier that same week, three men accused of "buggery" had been sentenced to death by being partially buried in the ground and then having a wall pushed over on them by a bulldozer, a bizarre and labor intensive form of execution dreamed up by the supreme leader of the Taliban, the 36 year old Mullah Mohammad Omar. After another man, a saboteur, was hanged, his corpse was driven around the city, swinging from a crane. Clearly, there is nothing covert about the regime's punitive measures.

In fact, the Taliban insure they are as widely publicized as possible. Last March, for example, the regime's radio station, the only one permitted to operate, broadcast to the nation that a young woman caught trying to flee Afghanistan with a man who was not her relative had been stoned to death. On another occasion, it was announced over the airwaves that 225 women had been rounded up and sentenced to a lashing for violating the dress code.

One woman had the top of her thumb amputated for the crime of wearing nail polish. And when the Taliban castrated and then hanged the former communist president and his brother in 1996, they left their bloodied bodies dangling from lampposts in busy downtown Kabul for three days. Photographs of the corpses appeared in news magazines and newspapers around the world.

The Taliban now control between 65 and 85 per cent of Afghanistan, a country where statistics are anyone's guess. (Even the population size of Afghanistan is uncertain: possibly 15, maybe 22 million. The U.S. Department of State's figure on war fatalities1.5 million has not changed since 1985, although the armed conflict there is now in its 19th year.) For the last two years, the Taliban have been trying to win both a seat at the United Nations and international recognition. Thus far, only three countries have recognized the regime: Pakistan, the United Arab Emirates, and Saudi Arabia. And even Pakistan is becoming embarrassed by its neighbor.

Until the Taliban came to power, Saudi Arabia was the most oppressive country on earth for women, and many of the Taliban's restrictions are rooted in that hardline Gulf state's gender apartheid. Saudi Arabia has also been financially supportive of the Taliban and the religious schools in which they are indoctrinated. "We have long regarded the Saudi kingdom as our right hand," says the head of the Taliban governing council.

The Taliban regime claim they are restoring Afghanistan to the "purity of Islam," and the Western press invariably parrots them. But authorities in a number of Muslim countries insist that few of the regime's dictates have a basis in Islam. And just as the U.N. has denied the Taliban a seat in the General Assembly, so too, the Organization of Islamic Conference, a 55 country body, has withheld both a seat and recognition from the regime. "The Taliban is not the image the Islamic world wants to project," says one Muslim diplomat. And with good reason.

Now in its fourth year of existence, the pariah regime has expunged all leisure activities. Their list of what is illegal grows daily: music, movies and television, picnics, wedding parties, New Year celebrations, any kind of mixed sex gathering. They've also banned children's toys, including dolls and kites; card and board games; cameras; photographs and paintings of people and animals; pet parakeets; cigarettes and alcohol; magazines and newspapers, and most books. They've even forbidden applause a moot point, since there's nothing left to applaud.

"Whatever we are doing in our country, it is not in order for the world to be happy with us," Sher Abbas Stanakzai, who until recently was the Taliban's 36 year old deputy Minister of Foreign Affairs. told me during my visit. Explaining why his regime has banned virtually all forms of entertainment, he says, "Time should be spent serving the country and praying to God. Nothing else. Everything else is a waste of time, and people are not allowed to waste their time."

For women, the restrictions are even harsher. Female education, from kindergarten through graduate school, banned. Employment for women, banned. It's now illegal to wear makeup, nail polish, jewelry, pluck your eyebrows, cut your hair short, wear colorful or stylish clothes, sheer stockings, white socks and shoes, high heel shoes, walk loudly, talk loudly or laugh in public. In fact, the government doesn't believe women should go out at all: "Women, you should not step outside your residence" reads one of the Taliban dictates.

If women do venture out, it must be for an essential, government sanctioned purpose, and they must wear the all enveloping burqa. Even then they risk their lives. Not so long ago, a young mother, Torpeka, was shot repeatedly by the Taliban while rushing her seriously ill toddler to a doctor. Veiled as the law requires, she was spotted by a teenage Taliban guard, who tried to stop her because she shouldn't have left her home.

Afraid her child might die if she were delayed, Torpeka kept going. The guard aimed his Kalashnikov machine gun and fired several rounds directly at her. She was hit, but didn't die on the spot, as she could have. Instead, Afghans watching the incident in the crowded marketplace intervened, and Torpeka and her child received prompt medical attention. When her family later complained to the Taliban authorities, they were informed that it was the injured woman's fault. She had no right being out in public in the first place.

The burqa is a garment that covers women from head to toe, the heavy gauze patch across the eyes makes it hard to see, and completely blocks peripheral vision. Since enforced veiling, a growing number of women have been hit by vehicles because the burqa leaves them unable to walk fast, or see where they are going. Recently in Kabul, a Taliban tank rolled right over a veiled woman. Fortunately, she fell between the tracks. Instead of being crushed to death, she was not seriously hurt, but was severely traumatized.

To insure women are effaced as effectively as if they never existed, the government ordered all exterior windows of homes to be painted black. The only public transport permitted women are special buses, which are rarely available, and have all windows, except the driver's, covered with thick blankets. It is now illegal for women to talk to any men except close relatives, which precludes them from visiting male physicians, no matter how sick. At the time of my recent visit, the evening curfew began at 7:30 p.m., after which no one, except government troops, was allowed out, even for medical emergencies. Even women in labor and needing hospital care must remain at home until morning.

It would probably be quicker to list what the Taliban haven't banned. The regime has even outlawed paper bags. Like many of their edicts, this would be laughable if the penalties for infractions weren't so severe. Break the Taliban's law and you risk imprisonment, flogging, or worse. And to insure their dictates are followed, religious police, part of the "Department for the Propagation of Virtue and the Suppression of Vice," constantly roam the streets. Often teenage boys armed with automatic weapons, they also carry broken off car aerials or electrical cabling to whip women they decide are not properly observing the regulations.

Despite its disastrous and very public record on human rights, when the Taliban was petitioning the United Nations for a seat in the General Assembly last May, its then New York representative, Abdul Hakeem Mujahid, claimed his government was "protecting human rights and liberties in

Afghanistan." He also stated that, having put a stop to the "miserable living conditions under which our women were living," they had "restored women's safety, dignity and freedom."

He then went on to justify the Taliban's ban on women's education: Afghanistan lacks the resources to educate them, he said, adding that the Taliban also do not trust the values that became part of the education system under previous governments. Those reservations, however, only apply to women, since the regime continues to educate boys. Mujahid omitted to mention a personal detail how he circumvents the ban for his own daughter by sending her to an English language school in Pakistan. But this kind of hypocrisy is common in Afghanistan today.

Under the regime, cigarette smoking is severely punished, yet in every Taliban office I entered in Kabul even that of the head of the department of Virtue and Vice, Mullah Qalam ad Din, from whom most of the restrictions originate, used ashtrays were always in evidence. While touting to the U.N. the Taliban's "improved" living conditions for women, Mujahid didn't mention the regime's banning of women's employment, or any of their myriad other restrictions, which have so constrained women's lives that half the population of the country is now effectively confined to house arrest. Amnesty International calls Afghanistan under the Taliban "a human rights catastrophe." Afghan women, struggling to survive in what has become a police state claiming to be a theocracy, describe themselves as the "living dead."

It is hardly surprising, then, that the U.N. has not seated the Taliban delegation; or, indeed, that the credentials committee has refused even to meet with the regime's representative in New York, and most officials prefer to duck his phone calls. But the U.N. has seated the representatives of some pretty brutal regimes in the past, and the ostracism is unlikely to last forever especially with lobbyists for American oil concerns entering the picture.

Unocal, a California based global energy company, heads up one of two consortiums engaged in fierce competition to build gas and oil pipelines from landlocked Turkmenistan to Pakistan through war torn Afghanistan. In testimony to the U.S. Congress this February, John Maresca, vice president in charge of Unocal's international relations, referred to the $4.5 billion, some 790 mile project as the "new Silk Road...a commercial corridor that can link Central Asia supply with the demand, once again making Central Asia the crossroads between Europe and Asia."

Iran offers an alternative pipeline route, but because of U.S. sanctions legislation, American companies would not be able to participate in its construction or, as a result, gain any benefit from what are considered the largest untapped oil and gas reserves outside the Middle East.

And while Unocal says it cannot sign any deal with the Taliban until they are formally recognized, this hasn't stopped them from wining and dining Taliban officials, and arranging shopping trips for them to purchase luxury items on their visits to the oil company in the U.S. Unocal already has a $900,000 training program underway, in collaboration with the University of Nebraska at Omaha, for pipeline construction personnel, a program limited to Afghan males. Additionally, the duo has established two technician training centers in Afghanistan, also benefitting men only.

Unocal's main partner in the consortium is Delta Oil Co., a Saudi owned company, in whose behalf former White House legislative assistant Paul Behrends and Delta's American vice president Charles Santos, a recent U.N. peace negotiator in Afghanistan, are busy lobbying in Washington.

The pipeline would bring the Taliban some $100 million annually in transit fees, in addition to providing thousands of jobs and improving infrastructure building roads, supplying electricity, telephones, etc. in the war devastated country. The Clinton administration reportedly supports the Afghan pipeline, which would free the new nations of Central Asia from dependence on Russia, avoid the Iranian route, and bring needed energy to the Indian subcontinent.

Competing with Unocal to build the pipeline is Bridas International of Argentina, whose managing director, Mario Lopez Olacireegui, has gone on record saying he is not concerned about the Taliban's human rights violations. "We are just an oil and gas company," he says. "We are not bothered by human rights or politics."

The Taliban, for their part, say they will award the pipeline contract to the consortium that is first able to start construction. Unocal's deadline to begin is this coming December. A number of American women's organizations, headed by the Feminist Majority and the National Organization for Women, have mobilized to prevent the Clinton administration from recognizing the Taliban government unless it radically changes its treatment of women.

They are also campaigning for Unocal to include women in their training programs. As we went to press, sources within Unocal admitted this campaign is beginning to have an effect. A split has occurred within the oil company those who want to press ahead, and those who do not want a politically embarrassing "rogue operation." As the U.S. women's campaign gains momentum, Unocal is also finding foreign investors suddenly unenthusiastic about being affiliated with a regime with such a disastrous public relations record.

None of which has affected the Taliban, however, who have since clamped down harder on women, this time ordering that all foreign Muslim women working with the U.N. or NGOs be accompanied by male chaperones, which in effect will halt their employment in Afghanistan. While it may be some time before Taliban coffers are swollen by petrodollars, one of the mainstays of the regime's economy is heroin production, which they use in part to supply their war machine.

Afghanistan now produces more of the narcotic than any other country and much of it ends up on the streets of the U.S. Despite promises by the Taliban to eradicate the industry, according to a report released last February by the U.N. International Narcotics Control Board, the harvest of opium poppy, from which heroin is derived, increased by 25 per cent in Afghanistan during 1997. The Taliban control 96 per cent of Afghanistan's total opium output, this country's only real remaining cash crop.

Though it was always impoverished, before the Soviet invasion Afghanistan was able to feed its people. Today, after almost 20 years of war, this is no longer true. Afghan women, in the rural areas, have always worked alongside men in the fields. In the capital, until the Taliban took over, they often wore Western dress, served in parliament, and worked in a variety of professions, including medicine, engineering, architecture, the media and law. During the long years of fighting, as men were killed, went missing, or became disabled, the survival of many families came to depend on women's income.

Before the Taliban ban on female employment, 70 per cent of the teachers in Kabul were women, as were 50 per cent of the civil servants and university students, and 40 per cent of the doctors. Why does the regime insist that women be confined at home?

Reducing women to mere objects, the minister of education says, "It's like having a flower, or a rose. You water it and keep it at home for yourself, to look at it and smell it. It [a woman] is not supposed to be taken out of the house to be smelled." Another Taliban leader is less poetic: "There are only two places for Afghan women in her husband's house, and in the graveyard."

Legions of women and children reduced to beggary, the result of the Taliban's ban on women's employment. Many families, having sold all their household items, even blankets, are surviving on bread and sugarless tea.

Supplementary feeding centers, funded by foreign agencies, are dotted across the capital. Here, malnourished children four year olds weighing 16 pounds, 18 month old toddlers weighing 9 pounds are fed. Their mothers are not, even though they, too, are malnourished. Women often eat once every two or three days, preferring instead to give whatever food they have to their children. According to new U.N. figures, some 40 per cent of the Kabul population now exists on food handouts, either from humanitarian agencies or from begging.

The legally mandated burqa has also become a severe financial hardship. The veil now costs the equivalent of five months salary if any women were still receiving one. Most cannot afford to buy the garment, and whole neighborhoods must share one. It can take several days for a woman's turn to come round; even if she has money to shop for food, she can't go out until then.

In Kabul, the number of street children has risen from an estimated 28,000 to 60,000 in the last year. This city, once a symbol of modernity for Afghanistan, is now in ruins the most bomb damaged capital in the world. It is also the most land mined. Mines maim and/or kill an average of 25 people a day in Afghanistan. Two thirds of them are children. It is predominantly children who herd animals, or search for fuel or for scrap metal to sell to help support their families. Scrap metal merchants will only purchase unexploded bombs or shells if the children disarm them first. Kids doing this highly risky work earn on average enough to buy just two or three pieces of bread per day.

Despite the terrible toll mines are taking, the Taliban have interfered with programs to teach women and children how to locate and stay clear of mines. Board games used by foreign humanitarian agencies to instruct a mostly illiterate population in mine awareness have been disallowed because they use now banned pictures of humans or animals coming too close to a mine; an alternative, flash cards, has also been outlawed as gambling.

Conditions are so deplorable for women under the Taliban that many are now severely depressed. Without the resources to leave the country, an increasing number are now choosing suicide, once rare there, as a means of escape. A European physician working in the city told me, "Doctors are seeing a lot of esophageal burns. Women are swallowing battery acid, or poisonous household cleansers, because they are easy to find. But it's a very painful way to die."

Spoghmai, a 24 year old former teacher, refers to herself as being "buried alive." The young woman lost her right arm up to the shoulder, and her right leg to the thigh, in a shelling attack three years ago. After her injury, when she spent weeks in a poorly equipped hospital, Spoghmai was, not surprisingly, so depressed she wanted to die.

A lifesaver, literally, was a job she found with a Western relief agency that enabled her to work with the disabled. But four months later, when the Taliban took Kabul in September 1996, she was forced to stop working. Today, she wears a badly fitted, and painful, prosthesis because, in Afghanistan now, false limbs come in only three sizes. Disabled as she is, walking is difficult, and is impossible if she is wearing a burqa veil. Since she cannot go out without one, she hasn't left the house in two years. "There are so many days when I am too depressed to get out of bed. Why should I? There is nothing for me to do. So many times I ask, Why didn't I die when I was injured?" She refused. "I am afraid. It is too dangerous, for you and me. Afghans are not allowed to be with foreigners, or talk with journalists. If we are caught, the Taliban will beat us, maybe worse. And anyway, to go out briefly would be too painful. It will remind me of what I have lost. One day of freedom will make this prison so much worse."

INTERNATIONAL COMPLICITY

A major concern today is how most of the international community operating in Afghanistan is going along with the Taliban's restrictions on women out of fear of having their agencies forced to close. Complicating this issue is the fact that a number of U.N. officials posted there in senior positions are from developing countries where women are traditionally second class. Consequently, they consider the Taliban's restrictions on women unimportant, or choose to look the other way. One such head of a U.N. agency in Kabul has often told colleagues, "the gender issue is too dangerous, I don't plan to risk my career over it."

The director of a major American humanitarian agency in Kabul, who asked that his name not be used for security reasons, admitted he found it "personally abhorrent," but felt he had no choice when he had to tell his female employees first to wear the burqa, and then to stay home. "I felt awful that I was forcing them to veil. When you only see women in burqas, you realize the power of covering a woman like that. You don't treat them like people anymore, just bits of cloth moving down the street. But on a pragmatic level, that's what had to happen to keep everybody safe, and to keep our program moving.

"When the Taliban started threatening and then beating our guards and drivers, we had no choice. When I realized that no one, no authority, was going to stop the Taliban from beating women if they worked, it became an issue of protecting the staff. I know that is a rationalization, but they have demonstrated what the consequences are of not complying with their edicts. And so you compromise."

He admits that there is an "incredible drift in the international community here with regard to the gender issue. Women are told: 'Stay home, suffer your fate, it's easier for everyone.' It's a slippery slope we're on."

One agency in Kabul, Oxfam, which is headed by a retired American professor, Nancy Smith, chose to make a stand against the regime, and closed down her multimillion dollar program until such time as the Taliban remove the restrictions on women. With her agency charged with restoring 40 per cent of the water supply system to Kabul, a project that would also benefit the Taliban, Smith, a wiry 65 year old, told the regime her agency's mandate was to relieve poverty, distress and suffering, and that included women's. "We concluded that our core principles are not negotiable," she says. "Oxfam will work with women in Kabul, or not at all."

Afghan women also defy the Taliban. I visited several underground schools that women were running for girls out of their homes. Operating one room school houses accommodating students aged 6 to 24, these dedicated women were breaking the Taliban law on a number of counts, including the one forbidding gatherings of unrelated people. In a city where paper and pencils are now hard to acquire, the teaching aids were handmade from scraps of whatever they could find, including stones and twigs.

While these women risk their safety to keep teaching, much of the regime that threatens them are either illiterate or nearly so. Even the Taliban's Ministers of Education and Higher Education have little schooling. Most Talibs (the name means religious student) are young zealots, graduates of the regime's *madrassas*, so called religious schools that are based, for the most part, in Pakistan, and funded in part by the Saudis.

In these cloister like environments, boys grow up totally segregated from any women, including those in their own families. The highest honor they can earn there is that of qari, a Muslim honorific given to those who memorize and can recite the entire Koran, and a number do. Sadly, however, they learn to do so in Arabic, a language they do not understand, and is not taught to them. Consequently, they have no idea of the rights given to women in Islam.

"Islam dictates that education is mandatory for both males and females," says Zieba Shorish Shamley, Ph.D., chair of the Women's Alliance for Peace and Human Rights in Afghanistan, based in Washington, D.C. Hassan Hathout, M.D., Ph.D., the director of the outreach program at the Islamic Center of Southern California, agrees: "At the time of the Prophet, Muslim women attained such scholarship they became teachers to prominent men."

They also worked. In fact, the Prophet met his first wife because she was his employer. "The medical corps of the Prophet's army was an all woman corps, and in some battles, women took up swords and joined active combat. Women participated in public affairs, were involved in negotiating treaties, were even judges. Islam declared gender equality through the Prophet's words, 'Women are the siblings of men.'"

Islamic scriptures are very clear on the veil: Only the prophet's wives were required to cover their faces. In fact, when women undertake the Islamic pilgrimage to Mecca, the Hajj, they are required to do so with their faces uncovered. They also mingle with men not related to them. "Obviously, the Taliban's military prowess far exceeds their knowledge of Islam," says Dr. Hathout. Perhaps the regime's most important oversight is the Prophet Mohammad's teaching: "There is no compulsion in Islam."

The Taliban is sheltering Saudi terrorist Osama bin Laden. In turn, bin Laden is providing substantial support to the Taliban as reported by *The Guardian* on September 5, 2001. Arab fighters funded by bin Laden have become increasingly influential with the Taliban and are building a foreign alliance to expand the Taliban's extremist version of Islam, according to aid workers and political analysts. Arab mercenaries have already participated in civilian massacres against minority Shia Muslims in central Afghanistan earlier this year, and Islamic aid agencies, at least one of which is believed to be funded by bin Laden, have recently set up offices in Kabul.

U.S. CORPORATE INTERESTS AND THE TALIBAN

International oil interests are in fierce competition to build pipelines through Afghanistan to link Caspian Sea oil and gas reserves to Central and South Asia. California-based UNOCAL, a US energy company, led the CentGas consortium that planned to build an oil and gas pipeline through Afghanistan. The Taliban stood to gain over $100 million a year from this pipeline.

UNOCAL announced it was suspending the project at the end of 1998, citing in part, pressure from feminist organizations protesting the company's involvement with the Taliban. Other US and international corporate interests are vying for business in the country. Recently, Telephone Systems International (TSI), a New Jersey-based telecommunications firm, reached an agreement with the Taliban to install a satellite-based system throughout Afghanistan. Corporate investment under current conditions could mean billions of dollars to shore up the Taliban regime without regard for women's rights.

THE HUMANITARIAN CRISIS

Millions of people in Afghanistan are in the most desperate poverty imaginable. Added to the Taliban's barbaric rule, the region is suffering under the most severe drought in decades and military incursions continue to displace hundreds of thousands of Afghans. As the U.N. asks for humanitarian assistance from the nations around the world, the Taliban puts impossible restrictions on the international organizations that are trying to deliver food and medicine to desperate Afghans.

Workers for international aid organizations are continually harassed, subjected to unreasonable restrictions, and even arrested, by the Taliban. Afghan refugees, who comprise the largest refugee population in the world today, are facing insurmountable odds. Both Iran and Pakistan are forcing Afghan refugees to return to Afghanistan to almost certain death. A ship with hundreds of Afghan refugees rescued by the crew of a Norwegian ship became an international pariah as the government of Australia refused assistance while the ship, crowded with many ill and starving refugees, sat within view of residents of Australia's Christmas Island.

THE CAMPAIGN TO HELP

Eleanor Smeal, President of the Feminist Majority Foundation, announced the launching of a new campaign, chaired by Mavis Leno and supported by many women's organizations, leaders and celebrities to help Afghan women and girls and to ensure they will not be forgotten. Over 500 college students from 38 states and 145 colleges were briefed during the weekend of March 20th by Dr. Samar on the disastrous current conditions of women and girls. Hundreds of girls' schools have been destroyed.

Teachers have been murdered – some right in front of their students. Girls are being attacked with acid being thrown in their faces on their way to or from school. One 75 year-old woman was nailed to a tree and killed for "collaborating" with the government and the US; another woman was beheaded. Those terrorizing the girls and women are Taliban or well-known human rights violators.

In 1997, The Feminist Majority launched the Campaign to Stop Gender Apartheid in Afghanistan to urge the US government and the U.N. to do everything in their power to restore the human rights of Afghan women and girls. Chaired by Mavis Leno, the Feminist Majority Foundation's campaign has brought together more than 200 leading human rights and women's organizations to condemn the Taliban's human rights abuses against women and girls and to put pressure on the US and UN to end gender apartheid in Afghanistan.

The Campaign was successful in increasing public awareness about the plight of women and girls in Afghanistan, preventing US and UN recognition of the Taliban, increasing the admission of Afghan women and girls as refugees, increasing humanitarian aid to the region and pressuring UNOCAL, a California oil company to abandon its plans for an Afghan oil and gas pipeline which would have produced over $100 million in royalties for the Taliban.

With the fall of the Taliban regime, the Feminist Majority Foundation is now working to convey to the world that women are an essential part of the solution for the future of Afghanistan. In 2002, the Feminist Majority Foundation has intensified its nationwide public education campaign - renaming it the Campaign to Help Afghan Women and Girls- to win the full and permanent restoration of women's rights, promote the leadership of women in the planning and governing of post-Taliban Afghanistan, increase and monitor the provision of emergency and reconstruction assistance to women and girls, urge the expansion of peace-keeping forces, and support the Afghan Ministry for Women's Affairs and Afghan women-led non-governmental organizations (NGOs).

Afghanistan is a country of approximately 23 million which, after three years of severe drought, 23 years of war and devastation and five years under the Taliban authorities, has been left as one of the poorest countries in the world. Afghanistan has the second highest maternal mortality rate in the world.

Even before the Taliban came to power, Afghanistan had high maternal and child mortality rates and a very low literacy rate for women. But women participated economically, socially and politically in the life of their societies. Women helped to draft the 1964 Constitution. In the 1970s, there were at least three women legislators in the Parliament. Up to the early 1990s, women were teachers, government workers and medical doctors. They worked as professors, lawyers, judges, journalists, writers and poets.

After the Taliban's rise to power, women and girls were systematically discriminated against and marginalized, and their human rights were violated. This resulted in the deteriorating economic and social conditions of women and girls in all areas of the country, in particular in areas under Taliban control. Women and girls continued to be severely restricted in their access to education, health care facilities and employment.

During the Taliban's rule, only about 3 per cent of girls received some form of primary education. The ban on women's employment also affected boys' education, as the majority of teachers had been women. Poor health conditions and malnutrition made pregnancy and childbirth exceptionally dangerous for Afghan women. The Taliban's policies also severely limited women's freedom of movement. Women could travel only when accompanied by a male relative, which put a particular strain on female-headed households and widows.

In May 2001, a decree was issued by the Taliban, banning women from driving cars, which further limited their activities. The resulting seclusion of women to the home constituted a form of solitary confinement and also created obstacles to women meeting with each other. Women were harassed and beaten by the Taliban if their public appearance was perceived to be in contradiction with Taliban edicts.

Women's removal from the public space also meant that women could not play any role in the political process and were excluded from all forms of formal or informal governance. Afghan women suffered domestic and other types of violence for the past 25 years, not just under the Taliban regime. Prior to September 2001, the United Nations Resident/ Humanitarian Coordinator, with the UN agencies on the ground and UN senior staff within the UN Special Mission to Afghanistan (UNSMA) continued to address issues related to the discrimination against women and girls.

They made numerous efforts to negotiate the withdrawal of various discriminatory decrees, including those banning women's employment, which nevertheless remained in effect. The Afghanistan 2001 consolidated inter-agency appeal emphasized that the assistance community would collectively aim to expand access for Afghan women to education, health services and employment and income-generating activities.

Despite many years of concern about the situation of Afghan women, it is only now, under conditions of extreme tragedy, political violence and destruction, that the situation has propelled Afghanistan and the plight of its women and girls firmly back into the global spotlight. For the first time outside of the setting of the United Nations and of the international community, there is a groundswell of concern, from Parliaments to First Ladies, from entertainers and media stars to non-governmental organizations, all calling for the full recognition of the rights of women and girls in Afghanistan.

ACTIONS BY THE INTERNATIONAL COMMUNITY

- The United Nations Charter proclaims the equal rights of men and women. Two years ago, the groundbreaking United Nations Security Council resolution 1325 (2000) called for an end to impunity for war crimes committed against women and girls, but also recognized the need to increase women's role in peace negotiations and in peace-building. The United Nations has urged the Afghan parties to bring women into every stage of the political process; and the UN is recruiting Afghan women as quickly as it can to help to provide humanitarian assistance.

The United Nations and its family of organizations have had a long interest in Afghanistan. UNICEF set up its first office there 52 years ago. The situation of Afghanistan, in general, and the situation of women and girls in particular, have remained under intense scrutiny by several United Nations bodies, including the Security Council, the General Assembly, and several of the Economic and Social Council's functional commissions and expert bodies, in particular the Commission on Human Rights, the Sub-Commission on the Promotion and Protection of Human Rights, and the Commission on the Status of Women.

In November 1997, Angela E.V. King, the Special Adviser to the Secretary-General on Gender Issues and Advancement of Women, led an inter-agency gender mission in Afghanistan, to specifically address issues related to discrimination against women and girls under the Taliban. The mission made a set of recommendations aiming to improve the gender situation within Afghanistan and in the United Nations system, so as to better serve the needs of Afghan women.

One such recommendation was the appointment of a senior UN adviser on gender in Afghanistan. After September 2001, the Special Adviser on Gender Issues and Advancement of Women continued to address the situation of women's rights in Afghanistan in meetings with the Special Representative of the Secretary-General and other senior officials within the United Nations system, in inter-agency consultations and in meetings with representatives of non-governmental organizations.

She also facilitated contacts between Afghan women and women's organizations and the UN system and supported the organization of the Afghan Women's Summit in Brussels, and follow-up meetings with the Secretary-General and members of the Security Council in an Arria Formula meeting. She also called on Afghan women to return to their country and former jobs, including in the civil service and elsewhere.

The first Integrated Mission Task Force, which was established at UN Headquarters to advise the Special Representative of the Secretary-General for Afghanistan, Lakhdar Brahimi, included a gender specialist from the Division for the Advancement of Women. Three Executive Committees, reporting to the Secretary-General, on Peace and Security, Humanitarian Affairs and the United Nations Development Group (UNDG), have been meeting regularly and have drawn up strategic recovery plans on the political process, humanitarian assistance and reconstruction of Afghanistan, including gender perspectives.

In addition, the UNDG and Executive Committee on Humanitarian Affairs formed a Sub-Group on Gender in Afghanistan, to monitor developments on the ground in order to devise strategies to ensure that a gender perspective was mainstreamed in the peace negotiations and the reconstruction process. On 14 November 2001, in its resolution 1378, the Security Council expressed its strong support for the efforts of the Afghan people to establish a new and transitional administration leading to the formation of a government, which would be broad-based, multi-ethnic and fully representative of all the Afghan people, and should respect human rights regardless of gender, ethnicity or religion.

Most recently, on 30 January 2002, the 26th session of the Committee on the Elimination of Discrimination against Women issued a statement of solidarity and support for Afghan women, which stated, among other things, that "The participation of Afghan women as full and equal partners with men is essential for the reconstruction and development of their country."

The Committee also called upon all parties concerned to respect internationally recognized principles, norms and standards of human rights, particularly the human rights of women, in all their actions and activities, which the Committee considered essential to achieve peace and stability in Afghanistan.

Today, as the reconstruction and rehabilitation of Afghanistan continues, a number of United Nations entities continue to be actively involved in improving the situation of women and girls in Afghanistan. Some examples of this work includes:

- During the Taliban's rule of Afghanistan, bakeries sponsored by the World Food Programme (WFP) represented one of the few job opportunities open to women; WFP bakery projects employed 300 women in Kabul and 100 women in Mazar-I-Sharif before September 2001. Today, WFP is currently assisting about six million people in Afghanistan. Beginning in April 2002, the focus will shift from relief to recovery, with particular emphasis on school feeding for education.
- The United Nations Children's Fund (UNICEF) managed to implement a massive polio eradication campaign, which reached over 10 million children under five years of age, and delivered life-saving humanitarian assistance, including nutrition, water and environmental sanitation, emergency obstetric care and provision of non-food items.
- The UN has launched a large-scale drive to immunize Afghan children against measles - a major, yet preventable, killer disease among the young. Measles is responsible for an estimated 40 per cent of all vaccine-preventable childhood deaths in Afghanistan, killing about 35,000 Afghan children each year. The $8 million effort, which is being organized by WHO and UNICEF, aims to vaccinate up to 9 million Afghan children.
- In mid-November 2001, women national staff members of the Office of Humanitarian Affairs, UNICEF, WFP and other agencies returned to work in Kabul and were expected to resume their posts in other urban areas as well.
- In December 2001, WFP conducted a major survey on food needs in Kabul. Of 3,612 surveyors employed, some 2,400

were women, the first boost to women's employment since the fall of the Taliban.

- The World Health Organization (WHO) and UNICEF shipped emergency health kits into Afghanistan in October 2001 to serve more than a million people for three months.
- In late September 2001, responding to the grave health emergency facing Afghan women, the United Nations Population Fund (UNFPA) mounted its largest-ever humanitarian operation. Thousands of pregnant women were among the Afghan civilians who fled their homes and massed along the country's borders. The lack of shelter, food and medical care, and unsanitary conditions posed a serious risk to these women and their infant children. To provide displaced Afghan women with lifesaving reproductive health care services, UNFPA prepared to pre-position emergency relief supplies in the countries bordering Afghanistan. UNFPA, supported by non-governmental organizations, continues to provide its essential obstetric care services through a network of about 130 clinics.

  The Office of the UN High Commissioner for Refugees (UNHCR) focused on assistance to internally displaced persons inside Afghanistan and on the needs of refugees in neighbouring countries, including the voluntary return of refugees.
- The Mine Action Programme initiated the clearing of an estimated 25,000 unexploded cluster bomblet units.
- In December 2001, the Office of the UN High Commissioner for Human Rights (UNHCHR) deployed a needs-assessment mission in Pakistan and Afghanistan to assess the human rights situation, which paid particular attention to the systematic discrimination against women and girls.
- Under the leadership of the World Bank, the Asian Development Bank (ADB) and the United Nations Development Programme (UNDP), a number of meetings were held to prepare and coordinate the efforts of the

assistance community and donors in the reconstruction and rehabilitation process in Afghanistan.

- The World Bank, ADB and UNDP submitted a joint assessment, entitled "Afghanistan: preliminary needs assessment for recovery and reconstruction", to the International Conference on Reconstruction Assistance to Afghanistan (Tokyo, 21 and 22 January 2002). The assessment addressed gender equality as an important element for the overall reconstruction and development agenda.
- The United Nations system, in consultation with the Interim Authority and international and national organizations and non-governmental organizations, prepared a transitional assistance programme, which was presented to the donor community following the Tokyo Ministerial Meeting.

WOMEN'S ROLE IN THE REHABILITATION AND RECONSTRUCTION

Since September 2001, Afghan women have begun to increase their activities. Numerous events were organized during the last few months by and with Afghan women's organizations inside and outside Afghanistan, such as panel discussions, conferences and international meetings, in order to ensure that the experiences and needs of Afghan women would receive the needed attention in all efforts directed at the post-Taliban Afghanistan.

For the first time in many years, new opportunities have been presented for women to reclaim their rights as active participants in the governance, as well as in the rehabilitation and reconstruction of Afghanistan. Schools for girls are being reopened, and young women are enrolling in universities. Women are seeking to return to their former jobs as teachers, doctors and civil servants. Radio and television broadcasts in Kabul once again feature woman commentators.

The United Nations Talks on a transitional government for Afghanistan began in Bonn on 27 November under the leadership of the Special Representative of the Secretary-General Lakhdar Brahimi. Representatives of four Afghan groups participated, representing the Rome process, linked to the former King; the United Front (also known as the Northern Alliance); the Cyprus Group and the Peshawar Group.

All political groups had been encouraged by the UN to include women in their delegations and Afghan women's organizations were asked to contact the four groups for participation in the Talks. Two women, Sima Wali and Rona Mansuri, participated as full delegates of the Rome process; Amena Afzali participated as a full delegate of the United Front; Seddiqa Balkhi participated as adviser to the Cyprus Group; and Fatana Gilani participated as adviser to the Peshawar Group.

The Agreement on Provisional Arrangements in Afghanistan pending the re-establishment of permanent government institutions was signed in Bonn on 5 December 2001. In response to requests from Afghan women, a number of non-governmental organizations convened the Afghan Women's Summit for Democracy in Brussels, from 4 to 5 December 2001, in collaboration with the Office of the Special Adviser on Gender Issues and Advancement of Women and the United Nations Development Fund for Women (UNIFEM).

About 40 Afghan women leaders from different ethnic, linguistic and religious backgrounds participated, including three who had also attended the UN negotiations in Bonn. The Summit concluded with the adoption of the Brussels Proclamation, which included concrete demands for the recovery of Afghan society in the areas of education, media and culture; health; human rights and the constitution; and refugees and internally displaced women.

Participants of the Summit met with members of the European Parliament, members of the U.S. Congress, members of the Security Council in the Arria Formula meeting, and women ambassadors to the United Nations. In their talks, the Afghan women called for measures to increase security in

Afghanistan and facilitate the disarmament of all warring factions. UNIFEM organized a roundtable in Brussels from 10 to 11 December 2001 in cooperation with the Government of Belgium on "Building Women's Leadership in Afghanistan".

The roundtable brought together Afghan women and UN agencies, the World Bank and donors, and issued an Action Plan calling for mechanisms to support the role and leadership of women in shaping the future of their country. On 19 December 2001, the Special Adviser on Gender Issues and Advancement of Women organized a breakfast meeting between Afghan women non-governmental organizations and women ambassadors from the permanent missions to the UN, allowing Afghan women to share their vision and priorities for Afghan women.

In addition, these Afghan women met with the Secretary-General to share such vision and their views about their role in the reconstruction of Afghanistan. In January 2002, Hamid Karzai, the head of the Interim Administration, demonstrated his support for women's rights by signing the "Declaration of the Essential Rights of Afghan Women", which affirmed the right to equality between men and women. The Declaration had been adopted by a meeting of Afghans in Dushanbe, Tajikistan, in 2000.

When the Secretary-General visited Kabul on 25 January 2002, he made a symbolic visit to a girls school, which is assisted by UNICEF. Girls from six through 16 were preparing to resume their education after a Taliban-imposed break of five years. Women are at the helm of two Ministries which are part of the new Interim Administration headed by Hamid Karzai.

The Ministry of Women's Affairs, which had never existed before, is headed by Sima Samar, a physician and founder of the Shuhada Organization network of clinics, hospitals and schools in Pakistan and central Afghanistan. Ms. Samar is also one of the five Vice-Presidents of the Interim Administration. Suhaila Siddiq, a surgeon who continued to practice in Kabul throughout the Taliban regime, heads the Ministry of Public Health.

INTERNATIONAL WOMEN'S DAY: 8 MARCH 2002

The observance of International Women's Day (8 March 2002) at United Nations Headquarters, under the theme "Afghan Women Today: Realities and Opportunities", is being organized by the Special Adviser on Gender Issues and Advancement of Women and the UN Department of Public Information, in cooperation the Inter-Agency Network on Women and Gender Equality and UNIFEM.

The special event will focus on the recent developments in Afghanistan, which have created new opportunities for women to claim their rightful roles as full participants in Afghan society. The event will also underscore the international community's support for and solidarity with the women and girls of Afghanistan in the face of the long-term challenges that remain.

11

The Taliban and the Reconstruction of Afghanistan

It was exactly two years ago today. In the first major battle of Operation Enduring Freedom, the Taliban were driven from the town Mazar-e-Sharif, a strategic crossroads dating back to the days of Alexander the Great. Mazar's fall represented the start of a major acceleration of the war to end the Taliban's terrible rule over Afghanistan. Before the fall of Mazar, pundits were warning of many, many months of fierce fighting before the end of the Taliban's control. Yet only three days after the fall of Mazar, Kabul fell, then Kandahar fell, and then the remnants of the Taliban fled to the mountains. By the end of November, the international community was meeting in Washington to discuss our plans for economic reconstruction.

Now is the time to start another major acceleration, but this time on the economic reconstruction front. As in the case of the battle for Mazar, much has been done to prepare the way. The Afghan Transitional Authority under President Karzai is in control of the economic functions of government. Finance Minister Ghani has embarked on an impressive program to increase revenue. A new currency, the afghani, has been successfully introduced. A law creating an independent central bank has been passed. New commercial banking laws now allow foreign banks to open in Kabul. An Afghan Investment Support Agency has been created to reduce the red tape that entrepreneurs have had to endure when they start up or expand their business.

Afghanistan is also working to improve regional trade and transit with its neighbors. Construction of roads, bridges, airports and tunnels is underway. Schools have been reopened, refurbished, or built from scratch; and millions of girls and boys are back in school. The United States has fully supported this reconstruction effort. And so have many other donors following that initial upbeat meeting in Washington two years ago. The World Bank, the Asian Development Bank, the International Monetary Fund, and the UN agencies have played an important role.

Measurement systems are being put in place to measure the results of reconstruction assistance with set timelines, so that financial aid is used effectively. For example, the timeline for paving the U.S.-funded road construction from Kabul to Kandahar is December 31. The same date applies to the road construction from Kandahar to Spin Boldek funded by the Asian Development Bank. In sum, the stage has been set. A surge in our reconstruction effort can now yield big payoffs both economically and politically. Afghanistan is an extremely poor country.

Without strong economic growth, it will stay poor for a long time. An acceleration of the economic reconstruction effort now will help stimulate that economic growth. It will also help to lock-in politically the important gains that have been achieved thus far. When the Afghan people go to the polls next June, how will they view the improvements in their own lives? Will they feel that the transitional government and the international community have met their commitments to help reconstruct Afghanistan? Will they feel that the progress lives up to their expectations? We want the answer to be "Yes."

To help make this acceleration effort a reality, last week the U.S. Congress passed, and the President signed, a supplemental appropriations bill with an additional $1.2 billion for Afghanistan. We have also re-programmed funding from the regular budget to bring the total acceleration to over $1.6 billion. Our goal is to use these funds to generate visible, measurable, on-the-ground results. Timelines for achieving measurable results are needed if our assistance is to be effective. Timelines are especially needed if you what to accelerate assistance; timelines measure the extent of the acceleration. We plan to finish this accelerated effort by June 2004. So, for each sector, we have set specific interim and final goals through June 2004.

A major part of our accelerated assistance will go towards improved security, which is needed for an improved investment climate and for raising economic growth. About $700 million will go for police, army training and counter narcotics. Our stated goal is for over 19,000 police to be trained by June. About $900 million will go to economic assistance, including roads, schools, health clinics, power generation, and private sector initiatives. We plan for 1,000 kilometers of secondary roads to be completed. To further stimulate private sector economic activity, we have a goal of building 100 market centers and 5 new industrial parks. And to help establish the rule of law we are planning on 16 new provincial courthouses.

This acceleration plan will not work if other donors do not also accelerate their assistance. Even with the increased U.S. funding, there are still many areas in urgent need. These include irrigation projects, rebuilding major sections of the city of Kabul, and the National Solidarity Program, which provides block grants for community projects throughout Afghanistan. To be successful the acceleration by other donors requires both speeding up disbursements of existing pledges and making new pledges to be disbursed during this crucial period. This, indeed, is what the United States is doing.

For this reason, the government of Afghanistan is urging other donors to accelerate their assistance by moving forward commitments and by pledging additional funds this month. We, along with the government of Afghanistan, are also asking donors to set measurable results and timelines to meet those results. The reconstruction of Afghanistan is a collaborative effort and it is imperative that donors work together closely.

We are pleased that the European Community has already come forward with an additional pledge. Japan has also committed to accelerating a portion of its assistance. We urge others to join in. The United States is committed. We will continue to work with the international community. We look to Afghan government's continued leadership role. Our ultimate goal is nothing short of security, freedom, and prosperity for the Afghan people. With this timely acceleration, the Afghan people will be given the chance to achieve that goal.

DILEMMAS OF HUMANITARIAN ASSISTANCE IN AFGHANISTAN

The world of humanitarian aid has changed significantly since its heyday in the 1980s: more questions are now asked of international non-governmental organisations (INGOs) by both institutional donors and their national public. INGOs have also become more critical of themselves and of one another. Humanitarian aid is no longer accepted without question as a universal right and a good thing. Instead its positive value is dependant upon its outcomes and whether it does no harm.

The complex emergencies of the 1990s served to test the idea of neutral, apolitical humanitarianism. As the distinctions between combatants and non-combatants were blurred it became increasingly difficult for INGOs to remain neutral. At the same time as the ground rules of neutrality and impartiality are being questioned and the benefits of aid increasingly scrutinised INGOs are also faced with growing levels of insecurity.

Humanitarian aid workers are no longer seen as 'respected and protected neutral healers', instead they are increasingly becoming targets, hostages and victims 'of an anarchy they cannot control'. Recent research by the Humanitarian Policy Group of ODI found that from 1997-2005 politically motivated incidents involving aid workers had increased by 208%. The study found that most aid worker victims were 'deliberately targeted, for political and/or economic purposes, rather than being randomly exposed to violence'. This change in the security environment is impacting on INGOs and the way in which they deliver aid.

GLOBAL POLITICAL CLIMATE AND CHANGING DONOR FUNDING

The global political climate is also impacting on donors. The global war on terror has rejuvenated cold war attitudes of aid provision being influenced by geo-political interest. Many of the gains made in changing donor and government mindsets are being undermined by an increasingly close association between security and aid budgets. The rhetoric of 'opposing terrorism' has edged its way into the criteria for allocating aid.

Aid policy is increasingly being linked to diplomatic and military interventions as donors' interest in 'failed and fragile states' increases due to the possible implications for the security of northern states. This arguably reduces the degree of focus upon the poor, as aid once again becomes a mechanism for leveraging political support and achieving political aims. Changing motivations for the allocation of aid are clearly illustrated by aid to Afghanistan and Iraq.

Both the UK and the US have increased their total aid allocations since 2001, resulting in almost $22 billion in new aid resources. However more than $7 billion of this was disbursed to Afghanistan and Iraq. Since 2001, $27 billion's worth of new aid resources has been made available by all donors, but again more than one third of this has gone to Afghanistan and Iraq. This change in focus comes at a cost as resources allocated to low and medium income countries are cut back.

In the future such significant allocations of aid to Iraq and Afghanistan will not be sustainable unless funding is cut from existing budgets and money intended for the Millennium Development Goals (MDGs). Donors are releasing more funds for INGOs willing to work in areas of high insecurity as they focus on 'low-income countries under stress', 'difficult partnerships' and 'fragile states'.

Donors' acknowledgement of the increased risks to INGO personnel comes in the form of programme budget allocations to cover an increasingly security dominated climate. For example, ECHO acknowledge in their security manual a worsening of the security situations for INGO staff and recommend that donors 'subsidise a variety of models for field-based security training for humanitarian organisations' in order to maintain the quality of programming and ensure that it achieves its goals.

USAID also acknowledged in 2001 that 'the neutrality that once sheltered humanitarian workers is no longer sufficient protection', in response to which OFDA agreed to fund the equipment needed by NGOs to meet increased technical security requirements (radios, satellite phones, guards, increased employee benefits as well as increased insurance premiums and secure housing). However, not enough consideration has been given to the impact on INGO staff and on programming methods of working in such insecure environments.

THE EXPERIENCES OF AID WORKERS

This briefing chapter is based largely on qualitative data collected through professional life history interviews with 16 humanitarian aid workers working with a range of British INGOs. Whilst the research focused on the experience of individuals it is possible to draw some general lessons. Although this sample size is small the interviews aimed for depth and a richness of data which is often absent in larger quantitative samples.

Although there is a great deal of both academic and NGO sector literature about the changing security environment, very little research has been done to look at the situation from the perspective of aid workers. The aid workers revealed a number of ways in which, personally and organisationally, they were forced to change their ways of working as a result of the growing insecurity in many field sites. The research highlighted that higher levels of incidents amongst NGO staff was having an impact upon humanitarian aid and the way it was delivered, and that this would continue unless agencies made a focused effort to review their practice.

According to the aid workers organisational change in response to the worsening security environment is not happening systematically but locally as a means of coping with evolving field contexts. Those interviewed had worked both in Asia and in Africa and in some cases had been functioning in the field for many years. The aid workers, unlike claims made in the academic literature, commented that there was a growing reduction of security in conflict and post-conflict environments.

The reality on the ground was that security had been gradually deteriorating for some time and was now far worse than they had previously experienced. Whilst the literature tends to focus on one cause of this change, the context, the aid workers' responses were often multi-causal. The workers confirmed theories about the emergence of a 'new' and radicalised Islamic context which had often made the security situation worse.

However, they held this in tension with the idea that there are similar security threats and vulnerabilities across all contexts and that they affect different groups of people in different ways. Most of the aid workers interviewed believed that good systems and procedures within INGOs and the right equipment and training for staff could make a difference. They acknowledged that INGOs were starting to reform and review their security measures especially in the high risk contexts but they felt that the necessary changes were happening too slowly.

The worsening security context seems to be impacting humanitarian ways of working on a number of levels. One cross cutting impact was particularly significant: aid workers felt that they were becoming increasingly distant from their beneficiaries which they felt was problematic on a number of fronts. As aid work becomes more pressured, more hectic and more confined by security guidelines, it seems that not only are aid workers living in high security, high walled and guarded compounds but that their time with beneficiaries is often curtailed by the insecure environment: 'We often received advice from local administration, police and military not to travel or not to go anywhere.

So often our movements were restricted not just of us but of the whole community'. (Chris) Aid workers are increasingly pressed for time by their agencies and donors. Therefore, time spent trying to really understand the needs or issues facing the community they work with has been substantially reduced. Fred, for example, describes the process of talking with communities where they work in Afghanistan.

His experience is not uncommon: 'The manner in which we talk is very much, we come, we talk with you, we ask you questions and we go away and we do our job...we're a bit too quick with all our...sort of modern ideas and all our training to decide what's best for people and then get on and do it. And that's a problem, it's a problem of funding, it's a problem of you know, pressure from everybody to get things done.' Several aid workers provided examples of the ways in which increasing insecurity limited their ability to operate, or made their work more resource intensive.

The distancing effects seen as a result of increased security measures and less integration with the local communities were considered to have negative impact not only upon the level of participatory programming but also upon the organisational security. INGOs can no longer rely upon 'acceptance' in insecure environments, one of the three key areas for safeguarding the security of their staff, as aid workers contact with the people and place they are there to serve has become increasingly restricted.

As a result security planning relied more heavily on protection and deterrence which often resulted in further distancing of INGO staff from local communities. Tighter security controls are already having negative consequences on the poor, whose humanitarian and developmental needs are being ignored. Unless this progression is stemmed or new ways of working are developed humanitarian aid risks becoming less and less about those it seeks to serve.

This shift of focus away from beneficiaries makes aid more vulnerable to serving political or other elite purposes and susceptible to doing more harm than good. The names of the aid workers interviewed have been changed to protect their confidentiality. Not only did those interviewed reveal that ways of working were changing but they also felt that worsening security in some field sites was having an impact upon how some INGOs were staffing their programmes.

Stoddard et al's (2006) research on the increased risk to aid workers highlights the fact that vulnerability to security incidents is different for national staff and expatriates. The interviewees confirmed this and also pointed out that when the security context worsened INGOs would tend to be more reliant upon national or regional staff. Some even suggested that there was increased risk-taking with non-western staff members due to the relative lack of international media interest.

This is alarming if true and further complicated by the fact that for southern aid workers motivations may be primarily financial. The recruitment of increasing numbers of aid workers from the south will inevitably impact upon programming and security. The aid workers interviewed felt that mixed; particularly north/south expatriate teams worked differently and networked less, and this affected the INGO's security.

It was not just ethnicity and nationality that were raised as having an impact upon the security of INGO staff. Interviewees argued that an individual's age and gender were important, as were their personality, religious beliefs, attitudes, values and experience. Obviously due to employment law some of these factors are difficult to take into account in the recruitment of aid workers. However, a person's attitude, values and experience should perhaps be given more attention in both the recruitment and training of aid workers for insecure environments.

The introduction of psychometric testing at interview would be one way of doing this. It may also be worth considering whether security training needs to be more carefully tailored to individuals; particularly for those who are 'experienced', as the research identified a blasé attitude as another potential problem in insecure environments. Whilst there has been a complete loss of naiveté amongst aid workers since the 1980s, the interviews suggest growing levels of cynicism.

New contexts, high levels of risk and donor pressure are increasingly trying to undermine the neutrality and impartiality of humanitarian aid. As a result, aid workers struggle to deal not only with the realities on the ground but often with many conflicting messages. They know that they have become in the current climate, political actors, often without choice, but they are also aware of high levels of criticism about the sector from different quarters, both national and international.

Yet in most cases they continue to hold the high aspirations of humanitarian concern for everybody. Clearly there are no easy answers to the apparent contradictions in aid work today, but it is important to continue to ask questions about the rapidly changing environment of work and its impact on both aid workers and the communities where they work. More support from donors and governments engaged in various conflicts, particularly in the war against terrorism, and much more open debate is needed among INGOs and with aid workers to ensure that conscious decisions are made in the field rather than slippages towards politicisation.

Aid workers who are reflexive and questioning are vital for good humanitarian aid, but their views need to be valued and the environment in which they work supportive to reflective practice. If new ways of working are needed for what is definitely a new context INGOs need to be managing change in their organisation to ensure that, despite insecurity, their programming continues to fulfil their objective to serve the world's poorest and most vulnerable.

THE CHALLENGE OF THE TALIBAN

The current crisis of militancy gripping Pakistan is the most serious threat to the integrity of the State since the loss of East Pakistan in the war of 1971. Pakistan today is surrounded by hostile neighbours, is crippled economically and is slowly being crushed under the weight of world public opinion that it is a terrorist State, which is being generated by its supposed ally America.

With Balouchistan already rumbling with a separatist insurgency which has not yet thankfully gained popular traction, the armed conflict which is being fought with Taliban forces in Swat, Buner and Dir is threatening to roll back the writ of the Pakistani State to just the provinces of Sindh and Punjab. A solution must urgently be found to prevent further bloodshed on both sides of this conflict. The problem however requires a detailed analysis and also a solution that provides a lasting fix and not just another short term truce or treaty that will be broken.

The roots of the current conflict between the Pakistani armed forces and Taliban fighters can be traced back to the American invasion and occupation of Afghanistan. This conflict is a direct spill over from the fighting in Afghanistan against the Americans and a reaction against the support of the Pakistani State for America's war and its actions of bombing and killing its own Pakistani citizens at America's behest. The opponents of the Pakistani armed forces, the Taliban, are not a coherent or unified group.

Made up of various factions known collectively as the Taliban you have the CIA Taliban, Afghan Taliban, KGB Taliban, Punjabi Taliban, ISI Taliban, Tehrek-e-Taliban and others. These numerous factions have varying agendas, with some being armed resistance to US occupation, some being armed resistance to Pakistani attacks, others still being those who are funded and equipped by foreign intelligence agencies to create unrest and strife in Pakistan.

Varyingly, apart from those foreign sponsored groups using the following reasons as cover, these groups are demanding an end to the bombing of Pakistani territory by American and Pakistani armed forces and an end of Pakistani support for the American occupation in Afghanistan. Some groups, failing this, want an end to interference from a Pakistani State which has proven itself incapable of looking after both the needs and security of its people.

In origin the demands of the Taliban do not constitute a military threat to Pakistan. These groups are not foreign invaders seeking to control land/territory as part of some imperial adventure as America is in the Muslim world. The principle grievances of these groups are political in origin. The challenge to the Pakistani State therefore is from Pakistanis, civilians who have taken up arms against the nature and policies of the State.

This problem is further being driven by America in collusion with the Zardari government of using force to wipe out any resistance to the American occupation of Afghanistan, as it has lost the battle for hearts and minds a long time ago. It is interesting to note that this is actually a complete continuation of the policies of the Musharraf era, and that the popular change which people were expecting with the departure of the military dictator has not materialised.

America and the Zardari government are actually instrumental in creating and perpetuating this crisis in order to turn Pakistani public opinion in favour of America's imperial campaign in Afghanistan and the wider Muslim world by repackaging this conflict from being America's war to Pakistan's war, as the people have rejected the colonial ambitions of the US and its 'War on Terror'. This was one of the key sound bites issued by Zardari as he came to power, which was a pledge for Pakistan to adopt America's 'War on Terror' as Pakistan's own war.

The fact of the matter is that this is America's war, not Pakistan's. Pakistan is being pushed in to a conflict with its own people and neighbours. Pakistan is being directed towards civil unrest and ultimately breaking point, and this is in accordance with the American plan for Pakistan. Lt Col (ret) Ralph Peters, in his article Blood borders: How a better Middle East would look for the US Armed Forces Journal, proposed a new map of the Middle East which showed the breakup of country, with only Sindh and Punjab remaining as Pakistan. It is now well established that the both America and the UK are trying to fragment or Balkanise Pakistan for four principle objectives.

- To take control of Balochistan for its immense resources.
- To use the port of Gwadar in Balochistan to establish an economically viable energy corridor from the Caspian Sea through Afghanistan and away from the influence of Russia.
- To remove a strong Pakistan as an obstacle for India so it may act as a true counterweight to China.
- To break up Pakistan to remove the potential of an Islamic ideological threat from Pakistan which it brands as the 'Islamist threat'.

With this being the true reality of the problem which is manifesting itself as the conflict with the Taliban, tribal areas and Balochi insurgency, how is the Pakistani State equipped to respond to such crises? It is clear for all to see that the current government is insincere, incapable and lead by corrupt politicians. The country is now almost openly being run by America.

When you have a situation where the military head of a foreign power, Admiral Mike Mullen, is paying regular visits to Pakistan and the fact that the Pakistani armed forces are deployed to Dir when Hillary Clinton criticises the Pakistani government for "basically abdicating to the Taliban and the extremists" in the wake of the Swat deal, it is a no brainer that Pakistan is no longer a sovereign state.

This is aside from the regular bombings and killings of Pakistani territory and civilians by US Predator drones. Such a situation is leading to instability in the country as Pakistan participates in America's colonial war. As the Pakistan follows a foreign agenda, people are beginning to challenge the legitimacy of the State, questioning its purpose and the use it provides to the people. If the Pakistani State is going to kill its own citizens on the orders of a foreign power, it is clearly not serving its people by any stretch of the imagination. What then is the nature of this Pakistani state? If it will not look after its people, what is the source of its strength, and where does it derive its authority from?

The Pakistani State is the manifestation of the contradiction embodied by the political classes and a product of external agendas as defined by foreign powers. The Pakistani State has no organic authority from the people; hence it is constantly challenged by the people. These challenges in the past have manifested themselves in various forms over the course of history, with military coups and the break up in 1971 being some examples. The current problem of militancy is the latest incarnation of this challenge to the authority and legitimacy of the Pakistani State.

Currently there is one strata of society ruling Pakistan and implementing a system which the people do not respect. Politically the system has no value as many of the politicians are known to be corrupt, inept or both. Ideologically, the system has little support from the people as it is simply an imported British product and a relic of the colonial era based upon secularism.

As democracy loses its façade of providing a mechanism for electing and accounting rulers and reveals itself simply to be a tool for the rich and powerful to change laws as they see fit, the people are shunning the system and apathy is rampant in society. The ideal of Pakistani nationalism, which the system is supposed to represent and protect, has shown itself to be incredibly weak at binding the various peoples in Pakistan together.

Pakistani nationalism is founded upon a contradiction, namely that the State of Pakistan was created in response to a popular movement to live according to Islam by the Muslims of India yet what was yielded was secularism. As this Islamic ideal was left by the wayside, the only situation in which the people within the borders of Pakistan would come together and bond as Pakistanis would be when faced with an external threat like India. As such the State, lacking internal domestic support, is propped up by foreign powers that manipulate it for their own ends.

The ruling class therefore willingly follows the diktats of those it relies upon to stay in power, namely the colonial nations such as America and the UK. If we look at the response of the Pakistani State to the current Taliban militancy crisis, we can see that it has been one of almost colonial ruler to a conquered people rather than a State dealing with its citizens. General Ashfaq Kayani declared that "The army will not allow the militants to dictate terms to the government or impose their way of life on the civil society of Pakistan".

Interior Minister Rehman Malik before the latest operation said that "Enough is enough" adding that "a handful of militants cannot challenge the writ of the government". For the sake of argument, if General Kayani is given the benefit of the doubt for thinking as a military man responding to the threat of violence no such excuse can be made for the Rehman Malik. As the civilian authority and representative of the State Malik's response epitomises the response of a State that is out of ideas as to how to deal with a population dissatisfied with its performance. By using physical means to put down an uprising which is political in origin is to stoke the flames of internal unrest and civil war.

If the stick of the government is leading to violence, then the carrot being deployed is leading to the voluntary amputation of the State itself. Nizam-e-Adl, the government bill being implemented in Swat as part of a peace deal with the Taliban where Sharia law will allegedly be implemented, is a non-starter as a method of conflict resolution. The fact that the implementation of a few social rules makes a mockery out of Sharia law and a farce of Islamic ruling is only part of the issue at hand.

If one goes along with the ridiculous assertion that Sharia law is indeed being implemented in Swat, then what you have is a recipe for disaster as effectively within the borders of one

State there are two legal codes in operation. This will serve only to entrench separation and division between a group of people and the State as you begin to have two sets of laws running in parallel, which is impractical and inconceivable for any successful and progressive State.

All this is despite the fact that if Sharia law was to be sincerely applied it would not be in the form of a neutered 'Bill' but as the source of all laws in a State which then defines the economic policies, judicial system, foreign policy, social system etc. Clearly then this is at best a foolish attempt to remedy a deeper ideological problem or at worst an insincere attempt to show the application of Sharia law.

Both of these responses show a State which is at a loss for ideas as to how to deal with a population which neither respects its authority nor recognises its legitimacy. These actions of the Pakistani State are leading to a tremendous loss of life and civil unrest, whilst revealing the nature of the State and its relationship with the people. It is being driven by foreign instructions and threats by America and is attacking the local population, the very people it should be defending. What is then the way out of this quagmire that Pakistan finds itself sinking in?

The solution is not to deploy an increasing amount of armed forces to the region, let alone allow a foreign colonial power to help with an armed operation. The solution is to strengthen the authority and legitimacy of the State in the eyes of the people. The State must regain the initiative by establishing a sovereign authority which derives its support from the people and not from external forces; otherwise the State shall always be weak, externally dependent, subject to manipulation by foreign forces and fire fighting insurgencies constantly.

The core problem that Pakistan faces is that the people are disenfranchised and disillusioned with the State and do not identify with it. The interests of the State now clearly diverge from the interests of the people. Such a situation is not tenable and will sooner rather than later lead to either massive bloodshed or the breakup of the Pakistani State, or both, as was the case in the war of 1971. This is clearly in the interests of the foreign powers like America and part of their plans which are out in the open. The interests of the State must urgently be defined so that the people can be united around these. Nationalism has failed to define the interests and could never succeed in origin.

Pakistani nationalism neither has the depth of history to which all the disparate ethnic and tribal groups in Pakistan can lay claim to as being common heritage nor does it have the necessary political depth which can be used to define specific interests. At best it will result in Pakistani colonialism, as it offers nothing to the people except shallow loyalty to a centralised administration, which is what the people in provinces outside of Punjab are feeling. There must be one basis upon which the interests and all laws of the State are based upon. This basis must be the casus belli of the State and the idea for which the State exists to protect, implement and propagate. This basis must serve as the source of all values and ideals in the society which bind people together.

This basis must not be confused with opinion, as even if a basis is agreed there could be multiple opinions as to how best to implement this basis. This is not an issue, rather this is healthy. For example, in the UK you have the Conservative, Labour, Liberal Democrats, UKIP and Green Parties whilst in America you have the Republicans and the Democrats. The key is for a State to adopt one coherent and consistent basis. In the UK and America this is Capitalism and secularism applied in tandem within the Democratic ruling system. So whilst all of these parties may differ in their opinions on policy and indeed engage in heated or bitter debates on specific issues at times, no one contends the basis of the State.

The discussion only centres on how best to adhere to this basis and which rules will result in the best application of this basis. The result of this is that regardless of what party comes to power, the nature of the State never changes and the people will obey the laws of the new government, even if they do not agree with all the new laws or policies of the new government. The problem in Pakistan is that there is no coherent basis upon which the State is built. People may form parties and groups and come to power on ideas as varied as secularism, socialism or Islam. In effect,Pakistan has no basis for existence.

Laws, regulations and even the constitution change according to the whims and wishes of every new ruler. The identity of the Pakistani citizen is undefined. Indeed,Pakistan and what it stands for is not defined. As of now, the State of Pakistan stands for nothing. It is clear then that the basis for the State must urgently be established and it should be something which the people identify with and trust. There is only one idea that has the ability to bring together the various ethnicities and tribes in Pakistan as one and at the same time has the political depth to define very clearly both the interests of the individual and the State in perfect unity. This is Islam.

Islam is the ideology which has a natural resonance with the people and has a track record of success when applied correctly in its entirety and in its true State form. Once Islam is adopted as the coherent and consistent basis, an ideologically strong State shall emerge as this State will naturally derive its authority from the people. This State shall have a clear direction as defined by the Sharia and the legitimacy to tackle both external threats and internal rebels who seek to implement their own views upon the people. The State will then be seen to represent the people and not foreign interests.

The current State apparatus is not equipped to support the implementation of Islam. It does not posses the appropriate departmental bodies, courts, ruling structure or economy. The State will thus need to be revamped and re-established in the form of a Khilafah. Only the Khilafah State would posses the structure needed to implement Islam as a State ideology. This is not an administrative issue where one can swap or rename a few departments in the current Pakistani State and implement a few Sharia rulings on theft or adultery and be declared Islamic.

The new Khilafah structure is needed to reflect the transference of sovereignty away from Parliament to the Sharia and the investment of authority in an elected Khaleefah, not a President, Prime Minister or military dictator. If one attempts to implement Islam and Sharia in the current State structure, then you will produce a circus show of the like that is currently going on with Nizam-e-Adl. Once this new State structure is set up on a clearly defined and coherent basis with support from the people, the issue then will be to assess the claims of any restless groups such as the Taliban via a due process of law through the appropriate organs of the state (councils,courts etc) and then issue a verdict which shall have universal legitimacy.

The State will also be able to lead the people the Taliban currently rule to progression. For instance, education for girls will be enforced; Taliban like groups can have no objection to such rulings as the curriculum would teach values which are consistent with Islam and the verdict would be handed down by a legitimate Islamic authority. Issues will not be disputed as the Khaleefah will adopt public laws which everyone must follow. Anything not adopted will be the right of individuals to decide upon, no compulsion. As with any other ideological State, differences of opinions will be allowed and if people want to lobby the Khaleefah for a change in opinion then appropriate channels shall exist.

Indeed it shall be the responsibility of the Islamic civil society, such as political parties, to account the Khaleefah to ensure that the Sharia is being followed at all times. The current system does not provide this. It is the lack of such a legal framework which causes frustration amongst the various Islamic groups as there is no official mechanism to address their concerns or consider their opinions. This legal process would be the correct method for not only dealing with the Taliban but also any other movement which seeks to be separate from the State or establish an alternative order.

By establishing the Khilafah State the impracticalities of the Pakistani State shall be swept away and the people shall be united on a shared intellectual basis rather than a shallow idea of nationalism,which is a colonial construct in origin anyway which serves to divide rather than unite people. The Khilafah

State shall not only solve the problem of unity and address any issues of militancy within society,but it shall give direction to the whole of society. As the national interests are defined according to Islam, many of the current problems shall be solved. The foreign policy of the State shall be in line with the wishes of the people as the State shall refuse to take part in any colonial adventure with nations such as America.

The security and property of its citizens shall be protected, as the State shall exist to serve the people, not the other way around as it is currently.Separatist movements shall lose legitimacy as the basis for the State shall not be divisive nationalism but an inclusive ideology. The economy shall be revived as inflation is brought under control with investment in industry and production, a gold standard backed currency, capital flows freed up as interest is removed and the taxation system simplified. Industrialisation shall occur, leading to a rise in education standards and employment as the State seeks to provide for the people and project the ideological strength and power of Islam globally.

A variety of topics have been addressed briefly in the closing paragraphs, with each topic warranting a lengthy explanation in its own right. However for the current issue at hand the challenge presented to Pakistan by the internal dissenters and foreign powers is one of challenging the ideological soul of the State, and this has been addressed. This challenge must be met with a barrage of ideas,not bullets or missiles. Islam is capable of meeting this challenge and providing a resounding answer. It is then up to the people of influence in civil society, politics and the military to adopt this call and save the people of Pakistan before it is too late.

12

Afghanistan on the Brink of Ethnic and Tribal Disintegration

Wedged between the comparatively larger countries of Iran and Pakistan, lies the landlocked, war-torn yet resilient little nation of Afghanistan. Afghanistan s population seems to be a veritable hodge-podge of ethnically, religiously, and linguistically distinct groups. One would be hard-pressed to say whether the little land belongs more in Central Asia (India) or in the Middle East. Historically, Afghanistan has had fairly strong ties with Iran and Central Asia by virtue of the fact that the country lies astride the ancient trade route between Europe and China.

This chapter will address questions regarding whether Afghanistan is just some backwater, fundamentalist Islamic state, or if there is more than meets the eye at work in the development of the country s Islamic religion. Rick Wood begins his article on Afghanistan in the December 2001 issue of Mission Frontiers, by stating, The history of Afghanistan is a long and brutal one: more brutal than the rugged and desolate terrain that characterizes this land. The majority of Afghani history can largely be reduced to times of either internal strife or external invasion. If the country wasn t in the midst of civil, ethnic, or political unrest, it was being overrun by the Mongols, the British, or the Soviet Union.

Wood goes on to explain the outcomes of these various

invasions. He says, In 1221 Ghengis Khan and the Mongols brutally invaded Afghanistan , setting many of the Afghani cities aflame, as well as demolishing its irrigation system. The result was the permanent desertification of much fertile land. The Mongols ruled the land for about 100 years. Then, in 1747, Ahmad Shah Durani established the first united Afghan state. Afghanistan, in which Islam had entered in 652 AD as the consequence of Arab-Muslim conquests, became a great Muslim empire during his reign.

The British, wishing to expand their own empire, hostilely took over the nation in 1838, commencing the first of three Anglo-Afghan wars. It wasn t until 1919 that Afghanistan finally won its independence from Britain. After the assassination of his father in 1933, Zahir Shah inherited the Afghan throne, and in 1934, the US formally recognized the country. Wood states that a period of relative stability and, along with it, economic and political prosperity ensued. The king [Zahir Shah] changed Afghanistan to a constitutional monarchy in 1964 with freedom of the press and permission for political parties.

The Soviet Union saw this as a perfect opportunity to induce subterfuge and undermine King Zahir Shah s rule, and in 1973, his cousin, Prince Daoud Khan ousted him, while he was away from the country. Khan ruled until the Soviets, being displeased with his independence , decided to overthrow him (in 1978) and set up a Marxist regime, the first in Afghanistan. This was followed by an invasion of Soviet troops in 1979, and after a 10-year war with the Mujahadeen, a loose alliance of Islamic rebel groups supported by the US, the Soviet Union withdrew from Afghanistan and the US withdrew its support of the Mujahadeen.

The withdrawal of the US led to a resentment of the Afghanis as well as opening the door for more radical groups to enter the still-reeling country. In 1992 the Mujahadeen overthrew the Soviet government and an Islamic state was established. Soon, however, the different factions of the Mujahadeen turned their guns inward, and embittered infighting ensued. The year 1994 brought forth a previously unknown group of Taliban militias, and they rapidly advanced against the government. In September of 1996, the Taliban (being supported by Pakistan) overtook the capital city of Kabul. Soon thereafter, in October of the same year, various opposition groups from the pre-Taliban government came together to form the Northern Alliance to oppose Taliban rule.

Now, the US-backed Northern Alliance and the Taliban are in the midst of a bitter struggle to free the people from the other s rule. Islam, for the Afghanis, is (and has been) as much a means of self-identification as a religion. Peter Marsden states, Belief in Islam has & been important for the population, not only in providing spiritual fulfillment but also in giving a sense of identity to the people. Just as in other parts of the world, popular belief in Afghanistan arose from a mixture of various origins: superstition, spiritualism, saint worship, mysticism, and organized religion, to name a few origins.

Out of necessity, Islam in Afghanistan has therefore found itself to be exceptionally sensitive to influences around the country. The two major religious stimuli from peoples outside the country have been Hinduism and Buddhism, and as Islam has spread eastward, scholars have had to decide whether or not they were going to adapt Islam to the surrounding religious cultures or keep Islam pure by purging the other two religions from Islam itself. In the introduction to his book, Fundamentalism Reborn: Afghanistan and the Taliban, William Maley cites several religious and cultural problems the nation of Afghanistan faces: [Afghanistan] population has never been fully counted by census, but at present [in 1998] probably stands between 15 and 20 million people.

The overwhelming majority of its people are Muslims, although a significant minority between 10 and 20 per cent adhere to the heterodox Shiite rather than the orthodox Sunni confession. However, prior to the twentieth century, the Afghan population considered itself to be part of the Sunni Muslim society, sandwiched between both the British and Russian empires and the Shi a empire of Iran. Maley also speaks of the linguistic multiplicity one finds in the population; this linguistic diversity tends to reinforce some manifestations of ethnic identification, as also do group norms and practices which socialization within the household or family tends to replicate across generations.

Mission Frontiers provides several tribal expressions of Islam within the confines of Afghanistan: the Pushtun (the largest tribe, consisting of about half the population), Uzbek and Turkmen, Tajlk, the Hazara, the Kuchi nomads, the Aimaq, Baluch, Brahui, Nuristani tribes, and the Sikh, Hindu, and Parsee minorities. Islam has & been mixed with pre-Islamic beliefs and with tribal codes such as the Pushtunwali. It is this tribalism that the religious authorities of Afghanistan, the Ulema (men of religious learning who interpret Shari a law), seem to be attacking. However, they are interested in the keeping and promotion of Pushtunwali.

Marsden says it is this group that seems to be seek to move away from the more inward-looking tribalism towards a transcendence over tribal, ethnic, and national allegiances. Pushtunwali is the code of conduct whereby the Pushtun tribe lives. It is this code that has influenced the Taliban in their setting of laws on the conduct of both men and women. There are areas of variance between Pushtunwali and Shari a law; areas also exist where Pushtunwali contradicts what a Sura says.

For example, where the Shari a requires the testimony of four witnesses to prove guilt, in matters of adultery, in Pushtunwali, only hearsay evidence is adequate to condemn an individual. Since the honor of the family, and not the morality of the issue is at stake, only hearsay is sufficient. Pushtunwali places a strong emphasis on hospitality, bravery, chivalry, and the defense of honor, particularly in women. Because of its variance with and occasional contradiction to the code of conduct set out in the Qur an, Pushtunwali has historically run loggerheads with traditional Islam.

The question of where a group like the Taliban got its power and why it s still a very influential organization arises from the whole situation. Maley describes the origins of the name Taliban as the Persianized, pluralized name for religious students. The Taliban is comprised of Sunni Muslims, the majority of the populace in regards to Islamic beliefs. As stated before, the Taliban overran the capital city of Kabul in September of 1996. The group originated in the Pushtun heartland of Southern Afghanistan; therefore it is reasonably tempting to suppose it received much of its philosophy from the old tribal code of Pushtunwali. This is, however, not so much the case as there are times where, Marsden says, the Ulema called upon men to disregard the tribal code in favor of the Shari a in order to engage in a jihad against a common enemy.

He concludes a chapter with one can see a range of influences in the creed of the Taliban, drawn from Islamic movements in the Middle East, Iran, the Indian subcontinent and Afghanistan. However, the dominant influence appears to be that of the Afghan Ulema. The fact that Afghanistan is such a battered country may be the very reason the tiny nation is a veritable breeding-ground for the domination of extremist factions of Islam, like the Taliban. Political influence on the Afghanis, however, has not always come from within the borders. A School of Islamic Studies was initiated at Deoband, near Delhi, India, in 1867.

Several generations of Afghan Ulema attended this school; because they had trained in the Qur an, the Hadith, and Islamic law, these Ulema were in a position to advise on behavior consistent with Islam. They met in councils to dispense justice, as well as to discuss matters important to Afghan Islamism. During the 1930s and 1940s the power of the Ulema was at its peak; they were advisors to both the legislative and executive branches of the Afghan government on religious issues. In the early 1930s the Ulema had quite a bit of influence over the new king, Nadir Shah, who reigned for only a few years before being assassinated.

The Ulema created a structure through which all laws and regulations, having been scrutinized by a body of Ulema in order to assure compliance with Shari a law, were passed. The Ulema also held sway over the courts, the schools, and both public and private morality. They seemed to be the dominant, ruling group in Afghanistan; Marsden tells us, The Ulema [at the height of their power] were distinct from the mullahs [the traditional prayer leaders], who had received a basic training in the main elements of Islam, sufficient to enable them to lead prayers at the local mosque and to provide some guidance on Islamic observance. Ulema tended to be dismissive of practices such as the worship of saints, whereas the mullahs would normally participate fully in them.

In his article, "Has Islamism a Future in Afghanistan" Olivier Roy states, Although it had its own momentum, Afghan Islamism has always been closely dependent on other Islamist movements. The ideology of the Afghan Islamists has been entirely borrowed from the two biggest mainstream Islamist organizations, namely Muslim Brotherhood and the Pakistani Jamaat-e Islami. Moreover, the Afghan movement has sometimes been seen as just an offspring of these organizations. Roy argues that the long-term dependence of Afghan Islamism on other Islamic movements, and the consequent hostility to Shiism, Sufism, and western culture which these links either injected into or accentuated in [the country] is a big reason why he doesn't think Islamism has much of a future in Afghanistan.

The allegiances of Afghani people seem to be mostly tribal expanding to national, while there are traces of some trans-national adherences interspersed among them, as we have seen in the fact that much (if not all) of the Afghan Islamic ideology is taken from the Islamic ideologies of surrounding countries. Marsden reiterates this point by stating that many Afghan religious leaders, during the time shortly after King Nadir Shah s reign, had the influence of a Pakistani Islamic theorist named Abdul Ala Maududi. This man advocated that change was to come from within the government, while the Muslim Brotherhood promoted change beginning from the bottom of society.

Bernt Glatzer begins his article, Is Afghanistan on the

Brink of Ethnic and Tribal Disintegration? with the statement: Afghan society is usually labeled as tribal , a notion which is not the same as simple or primitive. He goes on to discuss how, in actuality, Afghan society is complex and that there are practically countless different ethnic groups inhabiting the confines the little nation. Obviously, this could lead to a multitude of varying interpretations of how Islam should be practiced, although not always. Glatzer states, Every Afghan belongs to an ethnic group; thus a quarrel between two Afghans who by chance do not belong to the same ethnic group may easily be misinterpreted as ethnically motivated.

As we have seen, the number of factors surrounding Afghanistan s Islamic heritage and maintenance are vast and numerous; many factors are religious, yet there are many more that are social and/or political. Although much of the population is of Sunni persuasion, tiny pockets of Shiism and Sufism are intermingled with the rest. The Ulema are the religious leaders of this linguistically and ethnically diverse people, guiding them in the Straight Path of the Islamic religion.

THE ETHNIC SYSTEM

When it comes to the meaning of ethnicity concerning the current Afghan War different opinions collide. On one hand, there are numerous journalists and researchers as well as policy-makers such as Colin Powell or Joschka Fischer who categorise the Afghan conflict as an ethnic one. On the other hand, the majority of Afghan politicians - in spite or just because of their different ethnic backgrounds - deny the importance of ethnicity in public.

Against this background I intend to discuss in this chapter the perception of ethnic groups by the Afghan people as well as the significance of ethnic groups regarding the design of a future government in Afghanistan. Deriving from the perception that ethnicity is the predominant argument in the Afghan War, the peace process that was initiated at the Petersberg Conference near Bonn end of November 2001 is based on an ethnic representative government. Thus in consequence it is nowadays nearly impossible to fade out the ethnic affiliation of any political actors.

In full contrast to this approach I highly suggest that the rebuilding of political institutions should endeavour to diminish the influence of ethnicity in the political sphere. The implementation of an ethno- federalism as well as the introduction of an ethnic quota system would rather intensify the highly fragile conflict situation rather than contribute to a stable peace. Ethnic groups can not be considered as the predominant references of solidarity in Afghanistan. It has to be kept in mind that an ethnicization of the Afghan War occurred, but an ethnicization of the masses failed. The still not domineering importance that ethnicity has among the Afghan populace should be harnessed for political reconstruction, rather than being enforced by an 'ethnical solution'.

THE CHIMERA OF ETHNIC GROUPS

The dilemma with including ethnicity into a peace approach begins with the question of what constitutes an ethnic group. Already the controversy about the definition of 'ethnicity' and 'ethnic groups' in the academic world is extremely intense. Regarding Afghanistan most researchers have the view that ethnic groups have existed since time immemorial. They assume that ethnic groups are solid cultural units which are divided by obvious boundaries and have engaged in conflict for hundreds of years. Set against this opinion, this chapter argues that most of those ethnic groups in Afghanistan were shaped or even 'created' in the course of the 20th century and are still not the main references of identity in Afghanistan itself.

FUZZINESS OF ETHNIC GROUPS

Reviewing the literature and reports of British agents, soldiers and explorers it is worth noting that the term 'ethnic group' was completely unknown in the 19th century and many authors used different categories and references in their endeavours to describe and define the population of Afghanistan. A good example of this fuzziness is Henry B ELLEW'S report "The races of Afghanistan; being a brief account of the principal nations inhabiting the country". Already in the title B ELLEW equated 'races' and 'nations'. Moreover he divided the inhabitants of Afghanistan into eight major groups, the Pathans [Pashtuns], Yusufzai, Afridi, Khattak, Daticae, Ghilji, Tajik and Hazara; most of these categories are today subsumed under the label of "Pashtuns".

Not until the mid-20th century did foreign academics and the government start to divide Afghan society systematically into ethnic categories by differences in language, sectarianism, culture etc. The French anthropologist D OLLOT was the first researcher, who used the term groupe ethnique for Afghanistan and categorized the Afghan people in several ethnic units. W ILBER introduced the ethnic taxonomy of the Afghan people into the Anglophone literature in the mid-50s. Driven by the academic intention to eliminate the hybrid transition between once established ethnic groups by the creation of new groups according to cultural customs, anthropologists invented an entire series of ethnic groups: Nuristani, Pashai, Aimaq, Tajik, Mountain-Tajik or Farsiwan.

Probably, the best example for the construction of these so-called ethnic groups is the creation of the Tajiks. The term Tajik, which was used in social interactions only in a negative sense for somebody who did not belong to any other social category (e.g. not a Pashtun, not a Hazara), implied an anti-ethnic notion in general. The ethnic category Tajiks applied to the residual group of all Sunnite Persian-speaking villagers or urban dwellers without tribal background, which meant to all those without a genealogical knowledge, and finally without a shared history. The lack of a belief in a shared past turned out to be the major obstacle concerning political attempts to establish a consciousness of being a Tajik and to create a real ethnic group of "Tajiks" again and again.

Against this background the main difficulties of fixing ethnic groups in Afghanistan are still:

- The segments of the populace for whom ethnic categories were invented are often even today not even familiar with such ethnic labels, much less aware of any common identity. Ismail Khan, one of the most important regional leaders, is sometimes considered to be a Tajik, a Pashtun or a Farsiwan. He himself steadily refuses to be assigned to a certain ethnic group.
- The criteria, which have been set by anthropologists, do not correspond with the reality of social behavior. For example, those who maintain that Pashtuns speak Pashtu and are Sunni Muslims are in serious error, since there are also Shiite Pashtuns in the Qandahar region and Pashtuns from Kabul who often do not speak a word of Pashtu. A good example of the aforementioned is the former king Zahir Shah.
- The difficulties with differentiating are being aggravated by the fact that many Afghans - if they are mastering the cultural patterns - in different situations claim to be of different ethnicity.

The former Afghan president Babrak Karmal used to emphasize his Pashtun origin, whereas many Afghans considered him to be a Tajik or an immigrated Kashmiri. Against this background it is impossible to calculate how many ethnic groups exist in Afghanistan and how large they are. Also it has to considered that the different scientific approaches of researchers result in different ways of ethnic categorizing. A German survey concludes there are about 54 ethnic groups, while a Soviet study claims there to be 200. Therefore the crucial problem emerges of which ethnic groups and to which scale are to be taken into consideration in an 'ethnical solution', as promoted by the United Nations.

INSTRUMENTALIZATION OF ETHNICITY

The question comes to mind as to why ethnic groups rose to political relevance in Afghanistan. To answer this question one has to look back into history. The Afghan state was created by the rival colonial powers British India and Russia at the end of the 19th century. The ruling family of the Pashtuns, enthroned by British India, favored Pashtun elements in their concept of the nation-state. That is the reason why 'Afghan' is the Persian synonym for Pashtun, Pashtu was always the Afghan national language and the Afghan history was written from a Pashtun point of view. The politics of the ruling family employed the ethnic patterns which came into existence in order to regulate access to public goods and offices. Pashtuns were privileged in all areas and dominated the military.

Tajiks were left with the economic sector and the educational institutions, whereas the Hazaras were marginalized in general. The different treatment of the people went along with the forming of ethnic stereotypes: Pashtuns were considered 'bellicose', Tajiks were said to be 'thrifty', Uzbeks were known as 'brutal' and the Hazaras as 'illiterate' and 'poor'. Even though the politics of the nation-state thus created an ethnic hierarchy, there were surprisingly few ethnic conflicts. The main reason for this lack of conflicts was the enormous contrast between the rural and urban areas.

Politics in the capital Kabul was of little interest for the people in rural Afghanistan. Thus the ethnic groups remained blurred concepts for the Afghan population and were not respected as frameworks for collective actions. Accordingly the ordinary Afghans did not articulate a political will to overcome the ethnic hierarchy stipulated by the state. Furthermore Afghans recognized the nation-state as a hostile factor which intervened by force into their social life and not as a key to the access to resources (such as offices or land rights) which they should take control of.

Ethnicity became a political-military force to reckon with when the Afghan war broke out in 1979. Even though the war was dominated by the antagonism of communism versus Islam regarding the paradigms of the Cold War, the belligerent parties increasingly enhanced the ethnic momentum to strengthen their positions. The communist rulers hoped to tie certain ethnic groups closer to them by raising them to the status of nationalities. Even more important was the creation of militias that relied on ethnic affiliation; well-known is the

Uzbek militia of Rashid Dostum. Also Pakistan and Iran used the ethnic potential for conflicts.

On the grounds of Shiite loyalties Iran established the Hizb-i wahdat, which was strong amongst the Shiite Hazaras. During the 1980s the Jamiat-i islami, the oldest resistance movement, developed into a representation for the Tajiks. Pakistan supported the Taliban which followed a radical Islam but this was also Pashtun-dominated. All four warring factions, which dominated the military and political actions in the last decade, were more or less supported by members of one of the four major ethnic groups. The political movements used ethnicity as main argument for the legitimacy of their political existence, because all other ideologies – Islamic as well as communistic or royalist one – lost ground as a basis for the mobilization of the masses and as instrument of political demands.

The leaders of the warring factions made their supporters aware of their social and economic deprivation on the basis of their ethnic belonging in past and present. They claimed at least that the survival of the 'own ethnic group' was endangered through the aggressive behavior of 'other ethnic groups'. Nevertheless, by means of the ethnic moment the warring factions stirred up a collective anxiety as well as hate and jealousy. Also, the parties demanded economic and political resources of the state and society in the name of their ethnic groups.

Furthermore all warring factions justified their political demands referring to the size of their ethnic group and their territorial roots. In these efforts they frequently lost their sense of reality. Also all warring factions used ethnicity in their military actions. Ethnic cleansing and ethnocides occurred frequently in Kabul between 1992 and 1994, in the Shomali plains between 1996 and 2001, in the Hazarajat between 1998 and 2001 and in Northern Afghanistan, especially Mazar-i Sharif, since 1997.

LIMITATION OF ETHNIC PROPAGANDA

However the ethnicization of the conflict was restricted with regard to one important aspect: The ethnic card was never played openly, but remained covert. Thus one can find very little proof of ethnocentrism among any of the political movements involved. No single political movement is linked to a certain ethnic group by its self-description. The published speeches of leaders such as Ahmad Shah Masud, Burhanuddin Rabbani or Mullah Omar, have been imbued with an Islamic rhetoric, but all of them vehemently denied any ethnic dimension of the war.

All politicians never tire of declaring their respective parties as being multi-ethnic. The underlying reason is that Afghans refrain from picking ethnicity out as a central theme. Therefore it should be taken into consideration that ethnicity as a potential source of mobilization has been strictly limited. All warring parties used the ethnic moment rather in an undercover and strategic way. The reason is that there are serious barriers for a public emphasis of ethnicity:

- First of all, a major value in Islam is the idea that all believers are part of a united community (ummah). The fragmentation of society along ethnic lines contrasts with the concept of ummah. That is why ethnocentric slogans are avoided in public and many Afghans consider the accentuation of ethnicity as un-Islamic. Especially the parties which are rooted in the mujahidin movement of the 1970s/1980s strongly rejected any ethnic tensions in public.
- Secondly, due to the resistance against the communist regime and the exile of many Afghans the identification of the Afghans with their country increased in the 1980s. The majority of Afghans support the continuance of the Afghan nation state. Against that, the fragmentation of Afghanistan implies an uncertain future. Through this fact the warring parties avoid questioning the integrity of the Afghan state. This means that their appeal for ethnicity is strategically very limited. There is a wide-ranging consensus amongst Afghans, that to bring forward arguments along ethnic lines will threaten the continued existence of the Afghan nation-state. Whoever claims rights in the name of an ethnic group is quickly considered a traitor.

- Thirdly, the ethnic groups, which are involved in the Afghan struggle for power, are represented in the neighboring countries as well, with the exception of the Hazaras. If the Jamiat-i islami and the Jombish-i milli stress ethnicity, they will run the risk that their separation from Tajikistan and Uzbekistan becomes blurred. Also, these parties are not interested in the unification with these countries, because this could mean a limitation of their political freedom and their access to economic and social resources. The Taliban faced a different situation: Due to the influence of Pakistan on the Taliban, this movement was not able to turn to an obvious Pashtun ethno-nationalism.
- Fourth and last, as long as the parties strive for central power, they had to demonstrate their ability to rule a multi-ethnic Afghanistan. I have tried to demonstrate that all parties, which have been influential in the last decade, are using ethnicity regarding a specific political demand. But the certain political and cultural situation in Afghanistan regulates and strictly limits the utilization of ethnicity as an instrument for political claims and military mobilization.

THE DOMINANCE OF CLIENTELISM AND THE ABSENCE OF A CIVIL SOCIETY

Taking the limited importance of ethnicity into consideration the question arises as to what are the dominant frameworks of identity and action in Afghan society. In general it can be noted that Afghan society is based on small-scale communities and is characterized by a series of overlapping obligations of solidarity. This means that groups are formed less along interests but more along family and kinship networks.

However we have to be aware that the social structures of communities in Afghanistan are extremely heterogeneous, thus social systems are changing from place to place: Village or valley communities, clans, tribes and religiously defined communities (e.g. Sufi orders) form the most important reference points of political identity and action and today constitute the basis for modern forms of clientelism. Because of the dominance of clientelism one of the most crucial problems of the political reconstruction process is that Afghanistan lacks a viable civil society and political parties that can address, in a credible way, matters which concern Afghan people the most. Today, collective action seems to be short-lived without a long-term orientation.

The permanent conditions of war as well as the heightened insecurity emphasized the need to stick together in small communities that can best be described as clientelistic organized 'survival networks'. The necessity for such 'survival networks' grew stronger as the war began to polarize Afghans due to ideological, sectarian and ethnic based recruitment by the political movements and warlords. Distrust grew to an extent that clientelism spread into almost every sphere of Afghan society: politics, economy, education, and even the formation of so-called civil society organizations as NGOs, social and cultural associations and interest groups. This is why ministries, NGOs or political organizations are today usually occupied by one clientelistic group only.

A good example is that the Afghan government is not dominated by the ethnic groups of Tajiks, but by the clientelistic network of the Panjshiris. It is true that this government also has included many non- Panjshiris. But on looking more carefully many of these officials are in one or the other way related by marriage or patronage to the leading Panjshiri network. For example the Pashtun Taj Mohammad Wardak, the Interior Minister until January 2003, is married to a niece of the Panjshiri leader Yunus Qanuni, and the Minister for Culture and Information Sayyed Makhdom Rahin, an Arab by descent, is married to a woman from the Panjshir valley.

THE ETHNIC TRAP

Regarding their endeavor to develop a peace arrangement for Afghanistan, in my opinion, the United Nations are caught in the 'ethnic trap'. The media and the policy-makers, who have been confronted abruptly with the confusing political and military situation in Afghanistan since September 11, identified the Afghan conflict as an ethnic one and highlighted ethnicity as the most important template to analyze the conflict.

Although, the ethnicity turned out to be one of the major guiding lines of the Afghan conflict, the narrowing of the conflict on its ethnic dimension only, excludes the fact that there are several other dimensions to the conflict:

- Firstly, the relevance of ethnicity as a factor of military and political cohesion remained limited in the Afghan war: countless combat units and commanders such as Haji Qadir or Abdul Haq changed their allegiance several times out of political opportunism and economic incentive – independent of their ethnic affiliation.
- Secondly, the mistake commonly made by policy-makers is to understand ethnic groups as uniform, constant bodies acting in accord, and to equate the ethnic group with the political movements, who claim to represent a certain ethnic group. What is ignored in the present debate is the fact that, despite the ethnicization of the war, the ethnicization of the Afghan masses failed.
- Thirdly, policy-makers ignore the abovementioned limitation of utilization of ethnicity in the Afghan context. Ethnicity is rather a hidden driving force of the Afghan conflict, which is only used to a certain extent, than a general argument used in public speeches. The crucial misunderstandings of the peace process as initiated by the United Nations at the Petersberg Conference were
  - That the predominance of clientelism was explained with ethnicity and both terms were equated and;
  - That an conflict labeled as an 'ethnic' one can be brought to an end by an 'ethnic solution'.

There is a broad consensus amongst policy-makers that the Afghan government should not only be multi-ethnic. Moreover, it should reflect the ethnic composition of the Afghan society accurately. The power-sharing arrangement compiled at the Petersberg Conference was based on the following quota of ministers: 11 Pashtuns, 8 Tajiks, 5 Hazaras, 3 Uzbeks and 3 not appointed.

Although an 'ethnic solution' sounds appropriate in recognizing the interests of the various ethnic groups, it offers tremendous obstacles such as which ethnic groups and to what extend should be included. Another risk is that this ethnic solution produces frustrations if the ethnic quota is not recognized accurately. Also this approach ignores the constructive character of ethnicity and assumes that a government in which all ethnic groups are represented would supposedly suffice to reflect all facets of the Afghan population. A good example for this misunderstanding is Hamid Karzai.

While the Pashtun affiliation was one of the strongest arguments to appoint Hamid Karzai as the president of the transition government, it has to consider that the elite and political leaders of the Pashtuns did not recognize Karzai as their representative. Thus Karzai obtains no stronghold within the Pashtun population.

SUGGESTIONS FOR THE DESIGN OF A FUTURE GOVERNMENT

The following suggestions for the design of a future Afghan government strongly reject the politicization of ethnicity in general. While it is, of course, not to promote the idea that a future Afghan government should be mono-ethnic, the crucial problem derives from the fact to impose ethnicity to the fundament of political legitimacy. Thus the raising of ethnic representation will have dire consequences. Afghans will reach political and administrative positions regarding their ethnicity and not their qualifications, and this diametrically opposes the concepts of a civil, democratic society as propagated by the West.

Furthermore ethnicity could not be neglected in the political context and would turn into the bedrock of all political action. This will not only stabilize an ethnic suspicion but avert that any political actor will enter the political arena refusing the meaning of ethnicity. Thus I will demonstrate in which way it seems appropriate to cope with ethnicity and what are alternative strategies to design new political institutions.

To follow my argument to diminish the influence of ethnicity on the political sphere it is important that a new Afghan constitution, which will be elaborated on this year, should likewise keep clear of ethnic or cultural factors as much as possible. It would be devastating to establish Sunni Islam as the state religion, for that would shut the Shiites, Hindus and Sikhs out. As to language policy, Farsi – Afghanistan's lingua franca – and Pashtu should be given coequal status, while such languages such as Uzbeki, Turkmeni or Baluchi could be granted the status of additional provinces' languages.

The goal to ensure the right of individual self- expression (sectarian, language etc.) should be aspired to. If everybody in Afghanistan has the right to express him/herself in cultural terms, the need for an ethnicization of politics will decrease. Of course, it would be a major failure to suppress the question of ethnicity completely. But the politicization of ethnicity will not surmount ethnic tensions in Afghanistan. I plead for an open discussion within the Afghan community about ethnic prejudices and stereotypes. It has to be revealed that ethnicity is created by those in power and is not the basis for dividing the populace in Afghanistan seriously.

This discussion should be part of a reconciliation process. It should be enforced to disenchant the myths of ethnic hatred and of ethnic stereotypes. It has to be demonstrated that members of different ethnic groups have lived together peacefully in the past. Also it has made clear that there is nothing wrong in identifying with an ethnic group: It is legitimate to identify oneself as a Pashtun, a Tajik etc. Thus an ethnic reconciliation should not try to diminish or destroy ethnic identities.

TERRITORIALIZATION OF POWER

The question of how to position the new state on the axis between centralization and decentralization is also of the greatest relevance. The actual fragmentation of Afghanistan in myriads of fiefdoms ruled by various warlords or local leaders makes clear that today's Afghanistan is far from establishing a strong central government. Thus the transitional government can be characterized as the 'city council of Kabul'. It's authority hardly exceeds the boundaries of the capital. Against this background, even if the establishment of a strong central government could be envisaged, it would not only take generations to achieve this goal, but would immediately lead into another round of violent conflicts and might lure the country into endemic chaos.

Also it has to be kept in mind that centrifugal forces have always stood in the way of centralizing state-building processes. Even more it can hardly be assumed that a strong central government could cope in a contenting way with the political, social and cultural diversity of the country and that one single homogeneous political and legal system can cover whole Afghanistan. There has been much discussion of establishing an ethnic federalism as a way of doing justice to ethnic demands. But that approach could prove counterproductive, since no province in Afghanistan is ethnically homogenous and the various population groups are very difficult to site geographically.

Often enough there are villages and valleys in which members of different ethnic groups reside. The introduction of an ethno-federalism entails often enough that on the level of the constituent states, the practice of ethnocratic intolerance by representatives of titular ethnic groups quickly becomes rooted. Ideas of ethnic homogenization could easily be projected onto the territory as highlighted by the example of Bosnia-Herzegovina and 'ethnic cleansing' will occur as a political practice.

The expulsion and arbitrary atrocities against Pashtuns in Northern Afghanistan since Winter 2001/2 are alarming signs of an ethnic cleansing process. Another consequence is that for minority elites, either shifting provincial boundaries or founding a new province of their own becomes more attractive. Political instability becomes endemic. Against this background the suggestion to separate Afghanistan into a northern, Tajik-Uzbek zone and a southern Pashtun one or to breakup Afghanistan and to include its regions into the neighboring countries does not only seem naïve but highly dangerous.

Furthermore it has to consider that the introduction of ethno-federalism would entail a new gerrymandering of the constituent states. Here with established identities, which could be used for the political reconstruction process would be destroyed. For the ordinary population the provinces, which were established in 1964, have been raised to major references of identity within the last few years. In Kabul 1997 it was usual to identify one's personal origin by stating the name of the province and not by stating the ethnic or tribal origin. Instead of ethno-federalism, discussions concerning the creation of a federal state in Afghanistan, in which the exceptionally strong tradition of local autonomy and self- government can proceed, are very promising.

The Indian or Swiss model, where the federal entities are not exclusively or primarily defined in ethnic terms, and where they enjoy strong provincial or local autonomy, might serve as a model. Regarding the case of Afghanistan the once established provinces and districts should remain the territorial basis of the administration of this federal system. Certain of these administrative units could receive autonomy in legal, lingual, religious or cultural spheres. For example local, customary law plays an important role in many parts of the country, as do religious notables in the judiciary process.

It would certainly be alienating for large sections of the population if judicial reform were to impose a unified code for the entire country and block access to justice through non-state channels such as religious courts. It is therefore certainly sensible to allow for a certain degree of legal pluralism, perhaps comparable to the practice that has developed in Indonesia. However, it would seriously undermine the project of modern statehood and the establishment of basic principles of equality and protection from arbitrary violence if courts of appeal were not organised on the basis of one and the same legal corpus in the entire country, a corpus that was compatible with sharia on the one hand and fundamental human rights on the other hand.

However, any form of federalism in the Afghan context may imply the perpetuation of the rule of regional warlords, who are amongst the very few in the current debate about the future Afghan state who advocate a decentralised mode of government. And indeed, capture of regional state structures by warlords and other regional bosses represents a danger for an integrated Afghan state. On the other hand, there is no reason to believe that warlords cannot be transformed into provincial governors, as was the case in other regions of the world, including Europe, in comparable phases of state-building processes.

ADMINISTRATION

The introduction of a system of ethnic representation, in which fixed quotas determine how many representatives each ethnic group will have at the center of power, could have negative consequences for Afghanistan. Research indicates that such regimes mainly work in a sustainable fashion in highly developed states with a strong capacity for redistribution, as well as an established political culture of compromise. An ethno-religious quota system of the sort that many have in mind at the moment would tend rather to increase conflict than to reduce it.

Against that background the setting of ethnic quotas for government posts harbors the danger of permanently fixing the importance of ethnicity, thus setting the stage for a juggling of numbers at the filling of every official position. A study recently undertaken by a Pashtun NGO (Wak Foundation for Afghanistan 1999) summarized that 62,63% are Pashtuns. In contrast Abdullah Abdullah, who was appointed as foreign minister of the transition government at the Bonn talks, countered that Pastuns are only 38% of the Afghan people.

The road into a war of numbers is prognosticated. Thus, if a government is based on ethnicity, then criteria on how these ethnic groups in Afghanistan should be shaped, must be fixed. In a second step a census must be carried out to fix the size of the ethnic groups. Afghans who ignore ethnicity are encouraged to affiliate with one of the official recognized ethnic groups. Regarding the fact that often enough the ethnic identity, individuals are choosing, depends on the social context, this quota will be turn out to be unstable. Furthermore this census will face the problem of how to cope with Afghans who belong to non-recognized ethnic groups.

Ethnicity will emerge as an insurmountable criterion in Afghan politics. Furthermore ethnic leaders claim not only a certain share of ministers in the transition government in the name of a certain ethnic group, but also specific core positions. That the core ministries of foreign affairs, interior affairs and defense were all delivered to the Panjshiris on the Petersberg Agreement fostered suspicions. Rashid Dostum claims one of these ministries for the Uzbeks, while many Afghans support the idea that each of the core ministries should be hold by a politician from a certain ethnic group. To balance these ethnic claims seems quite impossible.

Lastly, a problem arises from the existence of the bunch of minor ethnic groups. The Aimaq, Qizilbash, Baluchs, Nuristani, Turkmen, Pashai, Sikhs or Hindus are significant ethnic groups in Afghanistan, which while not numerous, are politically and economically influential. In an 'ethnic solution' they will claim a political representation in the central as well as in the provincial governments sooner or later. How should these ethnic demands be satisfied? In full contrast to the 'ethnic solution' that the qualification for a position in the Afghan government should be determined by professional competence and not by ethnic affiliation.

Of course it is impossible to exclude ethnicity from the compilation of the government at all. But the significant question is, should ethnicity be installed as the basis of the government or as a criteria of subordinated importance, as favored in this approach? The solution is not a rigid ethnic quota system, but care must be taken to insure ethnic balance in staffing the government at all levels in an informal way.

DEMOCRACY

The establishing of a multi-party system on civil and not on ethnic basis is the most important aim in ensuring an enduring peace in Afghanistan. However the political and social-structural preconditions for democratic development in Afghanistan are rather unfavorable. Democratization in conditions of weak civil societies and weak institutional capacity for conflict resolution can lead to a sharpening and escalation of conflict. As already mentioned, Afghanistan has no civil society tradition and hardly any experience of democratic control of government. If the center of political power in Kabul is now acquiring importance thanks to international legitimacy and support of it, control of this center will assume existential significance.

Elections produce losers and may lead to their permanent exclusion from power if institutional mechanisms for distributing and dissolving power are not established at the same time. The struggle for success at the ballot box becomes a struggle for political and material survival, and means of winning are chosen accordingly. The fact that democratic government is carried out 'in the name of the people' also has the effect of politicizing ethnic differences.

Defining the boundaries and character of 'the people' becomes increasingly significant, so that the struggle for power is frequently perceived as a conflict between ethno-religiously defined groups, whose leaders are now presenting themselves as the representatives of 'their people' in order to seize the greatest possible share of power at the center. The ethnicization of politics may lead to constellations of conflict that are difficult to resolve through negotiation and compromise. Now we can already consider that political actors such as Burhanuddin Rabbani and Abdurlrab Rasul Sayyaf, who have been sidelined in the last two rounds of government formation and who represent extreme political opinions, are the most effective and successful ones in establishing political parties.

In this context it is to suggest that elections in 18 months are too early for establishing a stable democratic system. A democracy can only release the potential for political integration following successful political stabilization and institutional consolidation. To this end, it should proceed within institutional frameworks that are capable of countering the danger of ethno-religious conflicts over distributional issues. In the medium term, more realistic than holding democratic elections would be the institutionalization of the traditional system of consensus-building between notables, bureaucrats and tribal leaders combined with the careful democratization of its principles of recruitment.

In this respect the loya jirga represents a suitable body, provided that actual power relations are sufficiently taken into account - that is, provided the dominant clientelistic groups are adequately represented, at least in the period of transition. The emergency loya jirga that convened in June 2002 endeavored to include elected representatives as well as the ruling clientelistic groups and warlords. Although many Afghans have been disappointed by the proceedings and the results of the loya jirga, it at least helped to stabilize the fragile political situation. Thus for Afghanistan, democracy represents a long-term project. As with other processes of political modernization, here too the pulse of the time must be measured in generations, not years.

In Afghanistan, the international community is once again faced with the challenge of dealing with a conflict that is interpreted as an ethnic one. The architects of a future Afghanistan would be well advised to work against the ethnic polarization of the country. In this chapter I have tried to demonstrate that ethnicity is neither the cause of Afghan conflict nor a natural constant of human being: Ethnic groups have been created or furnished with cultural substance mainly by Western anthropologists. While ethnicity was not a domineering political factor in pre-war Afghanistan it emerged as a main source of political and military mobilization especially since 1992.

Hence acceding to ethnic demands will only strengthen those who - as has happened before on the Balkans - use ethnicity as an instrument for promoting their own interests, but will not contribute toward the resolving of the Afghan conflict. Hence I suggest that the international power brokers in Afghanistan should consider ethnicity merely in an informal way in power-sharing arrangements, and should not stress ethnicity as the fundament of political decision-making processes. The major challenge of a suitable and sound peace process in Afghanistan is the question how to cope with the dominance of clientelistic networks.

13

The UN in Afghanistan

Afghanistan has long suffered from great power rivalry and foreign military intervention, including the bitter Anglo-Afghan wars of the nineteenth century. Beginning in 1979, the country again descended into a prolonged period of devastating conflict. A Soviet military intervention (1979-1988) took a heavy toll, as US-backed Islamic militants fought a bitter conflict against the Soviet occupiers. There followed a period of civil war and warlordism 1988-mid1990s, then rule by a government organized by the Islamic Taliban, and finally in 2001 a military intervention by the United States followed by further violence, instability and civil war.

In late 2001, the Security Council authorized the United States to overthrow the Taliban government, as an offensive against the terrorist al-Qaeda organization, said to be based in the country. The Council also authorized the US and its NATO allies to set up the International Security Assistance Force (ISAF) to provide military support for a newly-established pro-Western government (the United States also continued to run a separate anti-terrorist military operation). In March 2002 the Council established the United Nations Assistance Mission for Afghanistan (UNAMA) to manage all UN humanitarian, relief, recovery and reconstruction activities.

Despite (or perhaps because of) these military-centered initiatives, Afghanistan has remained a "failed state." The authority of President Hamid Karzai, victor in the presidential election of October 2004, barely extends beyond Kabul's suburbs, warlords have gained back control of most of the country, and opium is now the principal agricultural crop. The Taliban has enjoyed an upsurge of military success in 2007-2008 and several NATO countries have expressed concern about the political viability of the operation.

Public support for deployments to Afghanistan in countries such as Germany and Canada has evaporated. The media have reported on US-UK air bombardment of innocent civilians as well as bold Taliban attacks against US and NATO forces, suggesting that the intervention is failing to produce the promised security, democracy and prosperity. The UN's role in the country includes an election operation that is working with Afghan authorities to register voters and organize elections for 2009 and 2010.

Other efforts include promoting of good governance and the rule of law, training of police, and the like. But in a land torn by violence, warlordism, drug production and intense suspicion of foreigners, these programs seem unreal and very unlikely to succeed. Until Afghanistan achieves a lasting and stable peace designed and supported by Afghanis, there can be no prospect of progress, electoral or otherwise.

The Afghan nation began to emerge in the late eighteenth century. It was ruled, with brief interruptions, by a succession of monarchs whose consolidation of power was constantly undermined by civil wars and foreign invasions. The current borders of Afghanistan were delineated in the nineteenth century, as a result of the "great game" rivalry between Russia and Britain. Britain exerted some influence over Afghan foreign policy from the late nineteenth century until the Third Anglo-Afghan War in 1919. Afghanistan joined the UN in 1946. In 1973, King Zahir Shah was overthrown in a coup by his cousin and former Prime Minister, Muhammad Daud. Daud declared Afghanistan a republic, with himself as president, and the King went into exile in Italy.

Daud's government, however, was opposed by both the

leftist People's Democratic Party of Afghanistan (PDPA) and traditional ethnic leaders. In April 1978, leftist military officers overthrew and killed Daud and PDPA leader Noor Muhammad Taraki became President. Late in 1978, Islamic traditionalists and ethnic leaders began an armed revolt, and by the summer of 1979 they controlled much of Afghanistan's rural areas. In September, Taraki was deposed and later killed. He was replaced by his deputy, Hafizullah Amin, but Amin also failed to suppress the rebellion, and the government's position weakened. On 25 December 1979, Soviet forces entered Afghanistan, and took control of Kabul. Babrak Karmal, leader of a less hard-line faction of the PDPA, became President. Karmal adopted more open policies towards religion and ethnicity. However, the rebellion intensified.

THE 1980s

Early in 1980, the Security Council met to consider a response to the Soviet intervention, but a draft resolution condemning it was not passed, due to the negative vote of the USSR. The matter was then taken up in the General Assembly, which held an Emergency Special Session on Afghanistan over five days, from 10 to 14 January 1980. The Assembly adopted the first of a series of 'Situation in Afghanistan' resolutions (resolution ES-6/2), in which it deplored the armed intervention in Afghanistan, called for the withdrawal of all foreign forces, asked States to contribute humanitarian assistance, and asked the Secretary-General to keep it informed of developments.

Various approaches to the parties were made with a view to finding a means to end the conflict, but war continued. Its effects were devastating. During the next few years about 3 million refugees fled to Pakistan and 1.5 million to Iran. Many people were also driven from the countryside to Kabul, and in total more than half of the population was displaced. Estimates of combat fatalities range between 700,000 and 1.3 million people. With the school system largely destroyed, industrialization severely restricted and large irrigation projects badly damaged, the economy of the country was crippled. The Assembly maintained its focus on Afghanistan throughout the 1980s, adopting a series of resolutions which called for an end to the conflict, withdrawal of foreign troops, UN assistance to find a political settlement and international help for refugees and others affected by the conflict.

In 1985, the General Assembly also began a separate consideration of the human rights situation in Afghanistan. This followed receipt of the first report from a newly appointed Special Rapporteur on human rights in that country. The first in what was to become an annual resolution on human rights and fundamental freedoms in Afghanistan was adopted on 13 December (resolution 40/137). In it, the Assembly expressed its profound concern about widespread disregard for human rights and large-scale violations. It also expressed concern at the severe consequences for the civilian population of indiscriminate bombardments and military operations aimed primarily at villages and the agricultural structure.

In May 1986, Karmal was replaced as PDPA leader by Mohammad Najibullah, who subsequently became President in November 1987. Following the exercise of the UN Secretary-General's good offices, Afghanistan, Pakistan, the USSR and the United States signed Agreements on the Settlement of the Situation Relating to Afghanistan under United Nations auspices on 14 April 1988. These provided for an end to foreign intervention in Afghanistan, and the USSR began withdrawing its forces.

With the Security Council's agreement on 25 April 1988 (and subsequently authorized in resolution 622 of 31 October 1988), Secretary-General Javier Perez de Cuellar set up a mission to monitor the withdrawal of foreign forces - the United Nations Good Offices Mission in Afghanistan and Pakistan (UNGOMAP) - and made plans to support the anticipated repatriation of refugees. The Soviet withdrawal was completed in February 1989.The rebels, however, who had not signed the agreements, maintained their fight against Najibullah's government and the civil war continued."

Following the May 1987 agreement, the UN had begun strenuous efforts to coordinate humanitarian assistance. Afghanistan had long been designated by the UN as one of the world's least developed countries and war only made it more difficult to respond to the challenge of reconstruction and development. The United Nations Food and Agriculture Organization (FAO) estimated that the area under agricultural cultivation in Afghanistan fell by 40 per cent between 1979 and 1991. In 1989, under the guidance of the Secretary-General's newly-appointed Coordinator for United Nations Humanitarian and Economic Assistance Programmes, a plan of action was developed jointly by United Nations agencies and programmes, including the UN Children's Fund (UNICEF), the UN Development Programme (UNDP), the UN High Commissioner for Refugees (UNHCR) and the World Food Programme (WFP).

THE 1990S

In 1991, responsibility for Operation Salam - the UN's emergency relief programme for Afghanistan - was taken over by the Secretary-General's Personal Representative at the time, Benon Sevan. In that year, WFP provided 60,000 metric tons of food to needy Afghans, while FAO provided 6,800 tons of seed and more than half a million fruit and poplar saplings. Agricultural assistance, food aid, public and maternal health services and economic recovery programmes were initiated with resources provided to the United Nations by the international community. But other programmes that had been planned - to repair infrastructure, provide shelter and discourage narcotics production - had to be shelved because of insufficient funds.

As civil war between various factions continued following the Soviet withdrawal, the number of civilians fleeing the country increased steadily, making Afghanistan the world's worst refugee crisis. By 1990, there were 6.3 million civilians in exile -3.3 million in Pakistan and 3 million in Iran. In addition to setting up a voluntary repatriation project, UNHCR established more than 300 villages in Pakistan for the mainly ethnic Pashtun refugees. In Iran, the mostly ethnic Tajiks, Uzbeks and Hazaras lived and found work in local communities. In 1992, fighting intensified, making the aid effort more difficult. Rebel forces closed in on Kabul and the Najibullah government fell. On 24 April 1992, leaders of the mujaheddin (guerilla) forces except one (Gulbuddin Hekmatyar) agreed to form a government under Sigbatullah Mojaddedi.

According to the agreement, Mojaddedi would head a Transitional Council for two months. He would then be replaced by a Leadership Council - to last four months - that would be headed by Burhannudin Rabbani. Rabbani was declared President of the Islamic State in Afghanistan in July 1992. According to the agreement (called the Peshawar Accord) he should have relinquished power in October, but didn't. By that time, Massoud, Rabbani's Defence Minister, and Hekmatyar were engaged in armed confrontation in Kabul-which had largely been spared during the Soviet occupation.

The General Assembly's annual assessment of the situation - summarized in a resolution on emergency international assistance for the reconstruction of Afghanistan (resolution 47/119 of 18 December) - noted that establishment of the Islamic State provided a new opportunity for reconstruction, welcomed the Secretary-General's efforts to draw attention to mobilizing assistance for rehabilitation and reconstruction, and sought funds for an emergency trust fund to support that rehabilitation. In 1993, two peace accords were negotiated between President Rabbani and eight other Afghan leaders- in Islamabad on 7 March and in Jalalabad on 18 May. In these accords, the leaders agreed to form a government for 18 months, to set in motion an electoral process, to formulate a constitution, and to establish a defence council to set up a national army.

In his annual report issued in September, the Secretary-General observed that although the accords were encouraging, they had neither resolved the problems of the government nor removed the threat of renewed fighting around Kabul. In

December 1993, at the request of the General Assembly, the Secretary-General established the United Nations Special Mission to Afghanistan (UNSMA) to canvass a broad spectrum of Afghan leaders and solicit their views on how the UN could best help with national reconciliation and reconstruction. Meanwhile, the movement of civilians mirrored the ebb and flow of battlefield realities, with many refugees returning to peaceful parts of the country. In 1992, more than 1.2 million returned home from Pakistan.

However, despite all these positive developments, Kabul was soon besieged again: first by various mujaheddin factions, and then by the Taliban - a movement with its foundations in Kandahar. The Taliban were mostly sons and orphans of mujaheddin, who had been raised in refugee camps in Pakistan and were opposed to what they saw as the corruption of the mujaheddin. This round of fighting led once more to the displacement of populations, with some 350,000 people fleeing the Kabul region for camps near Jalalabad, bringing the total of internally displaced people dependent on the UN for food and sustenance to 800,000. By 1994, there were an additional 700,000 Afghan refugees, living mostly in camps in Pakistan and Iran.

In 1994, the first of a series of annual consolidated appeals to aid Afghanistan was launched. The appeals detailed the emergency needs of Afghan people and asked for funds to enable non-governmental and UN agencies to address those needs. This first appeal had some success, with donors supplying 75 per cent of the funds requested. Rehabilitation projects focussed on human development and poverty alleviation in rural communities. High quality seed was distributed to farmers - yielding some 80,000 tons of grain - while some 125,000 hectares of land were irrigated and over 8,000 hectares of orchards rehabilitated. From 1995, however, the annual consolidated appeals were less successful in raising the necessary funds. The 1995-1996 appeal, for example, raised only 50 per cent of the amount deemed urgent - of which practically nothing was available for crucial infrastructure repairs.

However, the absence of conflict in some parts of the country made it possible to reopen some roads, allowing greater aid distribution by the United Nations and aid agencies. From January to June 1995, WFP distributed more than 53,000 tons of food aid, while the UN Centre for Human Settlements helped some 10,000 families rebuild their homes. During a health campaign in 1995, nearly 2.4 million children under five years of age were immunized against polio and more than 80,000 under two years old were inoculated against measles.

THE TALIBAN TAKES KABUL

Meanwhile, the Taliban rebellion was growing in strength. In late 1994 and early 1995, the rebels took control of much of southern and western Afghanistan, including Kandahar and Herat. In a presidential statement on 15 February 1996, the Security Council expressed concern about intensified hostilities around the capital city of Kabul, which prevented deliveries of humanitarian aid. It was also deeply concerned that the continuing conflict provided fertile ground for terrorism, arms transfers and drug trafficking, which destabilized the whole region and beyond.

In September, the Taliban took Kabul. Rabbani joined an opposition alliance, the United Islamic Front for the Salvation of Afghanistan (the United Front or the Northern Alliance). The Taliban soon controlled much of Afghanistan, with the Alliance holding territory only in the north. On 22 October, the Security Council adopted resolution 1076 (1996), calling on all Afghan parties to end hostilities and engage in a political dialogue aimed at achieving national reconciliation. It repeated its deep concern that the conflict provided fertile ground for terrorism and drug trafficking and called on the parties to halt such activities.

The General Assembly, along with the Council, condemned the abduction from United Nations premises in Kabul of former President Najibullah and his brother on 26 September, and their subsequent brutal execution by the

Taliban (Assembly resolution 51/108, Council statement S/PRST/1996/40). Najibullah had taken refuge there four years earlier, but repeated calls by the Secretary-General to allow his safe departure from the country had been ignored.

Fighting continued between the Taliban and Northern Alliance groups between 1997 and 2000, but military positions changed little. In July of 1997, the Secretary-General appointed Lakhdar Brahimi, the former Foreign Minister of Algeria, as his Special Envoy for Afghanistan, to consult with interested and relevant countries and parties and make recommendations on UN peacemaking activities there. He visited Afghanistan as part of a 13-nation tour and in October, with the Under-Secretary-General for Political Affairs, convened a series of informal meetings with what became known as the "Six plus Two" group - composed of the six States bordering Afghanistan (China, Iran, Pakistan, Tajikistan, Turkmenistan and Uzbekistan) plus the United States and Russia.

In April 1998, through a presidential statement, the Security Council noted the increasingly ethnic nature of the conflict, and reports of ethnicity-based persecution. It also deplored the continued supply of war-making materials to the factions from foreign sources, warning that a resumption of large-scale fighting would seriously undermine efforts towards a political solution. In July, the Council raised concerns at reports of harassment of humanitarian organizations and at a decision by the Taliban to insist on the relocation of all humanitarian organizations' offices to a single location in Kabul. It also expressed deep concern at continuing discrimination against girls and women.

Following the 7 August terrorist bomb attacks on United States embassies in Nairobi, Kenya, and Dar-es-Salaam, Tanzania, which claimed hundreds of lives, the Council adopted resolution 1193 (1998) on 28 August, which repeated its concern at the continuing presence of terrorists in the territory of Afghanistan. It condemned attacks on UN personnel in Taliban-held areas, including the killing of two Afghan staff members of the World Food Programme and the

UN High Commissioner for Refugees in Jalalabad, and of the Military Adviser to UNSMA in Kabul. It also condemned the capture of the Consulate-General of Iran in Mazar-e-Sharif. On 8 December, by resolution 1214 (1998), the Council demanded that the Taliban stop providing sanctuary and training for international terrorists and their organizations and that all Afghan factions cooperate in bringing indicted terrorists to justice.

On 15 October 1999, citing the failure of the Taliban authorities to respond to this demand, the Council applied broad sanctions under the enforcement provisions of the UN Charter. In resolution 1267 (1999), it noted that Usama bin Laden had been indicted by the United States for the August 1998 embassy bombings and demanded that the Taliban faction - never recognized as Afghanistan's legitimate government - turn him over to the appropriate authorities to be brought to justice. The sanctions, imposed on 14 November following non-compliance, included the freezing by States of all funds and other financial resources owned or controlled by the Taliban.

In a statement on 22 October, the Security Council also expressed deep distress over reports of involvement in the fighting, on the Taliban side, of thousands of non-Afghan nationals, some of whom were below the age of 14. It expressed grave concern at the seriously deteriorating humanitarian situation and deplored the worsening human rights situation - including forced displacements of civilian populations, summary executions, abuse and arbitrary detention of civilians, violence against women and girls, and indiscriminate bombing. The capture of Iran's Consulate-General in Mazar-e-Sharif was described as a flagrant violation of international law, along with the murder there of Iranian diplomats and a journalist.

Deeply disturbed by a significant increase in the cultivation, production and trafficking of drugs, especially in Taliban-controlled areas, it demanded that such illegal activities be halted. By the late 1990s, Afghanistan had become notorious as the source of nearly 80 per cent of the world's illicit opium, with nearly 1 per cent of its total arable land - some 640 square kilometres - devoted to poppy growing. In response, the UN Drug Control Programme (UNDCP) established a poppy crop reduction project, as part of which it introduced alternative crops, rehabilitated irrigation systems and improved roads. It worked with the Taliban with some success, and in December 2000 noted that the Taliban had banned opium production, although the Security Council sanctions made it difficult to support alternate crop development projects.

2000 AND BEYOND

The conflict in Afghanistan continued unabated until the end of 2001. Throughout this period, the international aid community, including the United Nations, tried with varying levels of success to ensure that the victims of the war and turmoil - ordinary Afghans trying to live their lives - received at least the minimum needed for survival. Political and security problems, in the absence of an effective government, caused frequent interruptions in the flow of humanitarian assistance, and various crises required the temporary departure of UN and non-governmental aid workers.

In the late 1990s, the people of Afghanistan, already suffering the devastating effects of civil war, also faced a series of natural disasters - starting with earthquakes in February and May 1998 that killed more than 7,000 and adversely affected the livelihoods and shelter of a further 165,000. In June, some 6,000 people were killed in severe flooding. Since then, a severe and protracted drought - the worst in living memory - has brought further suffering to some 2.5 million people already living on the edge of survival. In the face of such a daunting situation, the UN redoubled its efforts, delivering more than 94,000 tons of food aid to 1.13 million people in 2000 alone, while vaccinating some 5.3 million children against polio and providing support for non-discriminatory education to more than 300,000 children - including home schooling projects for girls.

Nevertheless, one quarter of all children born in Afghanistan were dying of preventable diseases before the age of five. Afghan women were nearly five times more likely to die in childbirth than in other developing countries. Typhoid and cholera epidemics were rampant and pneumonia and malaria had re-emerged as public health threats. The condition of women had deteriorated markedly, and only one in 20 girls received any kind of education. Between 1988 and 2000, more than 4.6 million Afghan refugees returned to their homes with UNHCR assistance, but as the fighting continued they were soon replaced by new refugees; themselves in need of clothing and housing from UNHCR and their host countries.

All told, by the end of 2001 UNHCR had spent at least $1.2 billion for refugee operations in Pakistan, $352 million in Iran, and $72 million inside Afghanistan. As the year ended, some 2 million refugees remained in Pakistan and 1.5 million in Iran. To compound the problem, refugees were returning to what the UN Mine Clearance Programme has called the most heavily mined country in the world, with a staggering 9.7 million landmines. As part of its efforts, the Programme cleared some 68 square kilometres of previously infested areas, but much remains to be done.

In 2000, as in previous years, the vast majority of funding for the UN-coordinated appeals for Afghanistan was earmarked by donors for emergency relief - notably food aid by WFP. Funds to promote Afghan self-sufficiency remained in short supply, with only $6 million being received for projects to increase access to sustainable livelihoods. Programmes to promote agricultural development - a particularly acute area of need given the drought - were almost non-existent.

On 4 September 2001, the UN and its partners issued a report entitled "The Deepening Crisis", which highlighted the desperate and worsening humanitarian situation faced by Afghans across the country. The report contained a plan of action to support critically vulnerable Afghans during the upcoming winter period and beyond, identifying the needs of 5 million people severely affected by three years of drought and many years of fighting. The plan envisaged providing food aid, shelter for internally displaced people, and support to help people remain in their own homes instead of adding to the numbers of those displaced.

POST 11 SEPTEMBER

In the escalation of the conflict in Afghanistan following the 11 September terrorist attack on the United States by the Afghan-based *Al Qaeda* group, the Security Council expressed support for the efforts of the Afghan people to replace the Taliban regime, once again condemned for allowing Afghanistan to be used as a base for the export of terrorism and for providing safe haven to Usama bin Laden. On 1 October, in his address to a special week-long session of the General Assembly on terrorism, Secretary-General Kofi Annan said, "As we summon the will and the resources needed to succeed in the struggle against terrorism, we must also care for all the victims of terrorism, whether they are the direct targets or other populations who will be affected by our common effort. That is why I have launched an alert to donors about the potential need for much more generous humanitarian assistance to the people of Afghanistan."

That new alert called on the international community to provide $584 million to meet the humanitarian needs of some 7.5 million Afghan civilians over the following six months, with particular concern to ensure adequate food supplies ahead of winter setting in. Unfortunately, increasing conflict in Afghanistan, including the military response to the terrorist attacks on the US, compelled UN agencies to withdraw international staff from the country, and the flow of food and other essentials into the country was slowed or halted. As the situation unfolded, the UN continued its role in promoting dialogue among Afghan parties, aimed at establishing a broad-based, inclusive government. On 3 October, the Secretary-General reappointed Lakhdar Brahimi, who had resigned two years earlier, as his Special Envoy for Afghanistan.

On 12 November, the "Six plus Two" group met in New York under the chairmanship of the Secretary-General, agreeing on the need for a broad-based and freely chosen Afghan government and pledging continued support for UN humanitarian efforts in Afghanistan, as well as in refugee camps in neighbouring States. On 27 November, a conference on Afghanistan's reconstruction sponsored by UNDP, the World Bank and the Asian Development Bank, opened in Islamabad. Over 300 participants attended, including many from Afghanistan. Issues discussed included the role of women, the importance of education and the creation of a comprehensive health system.

A further donor conference - focusing on the immediate and longer-term needs of the country - was held in Berlin in early December. Meanwhile, the Northern Alliance had entered Mazar-e-Sharif, Herat and then Kabul - a decisive event in the defeat of the Taliban. The United Nations organized a meeting of Afghan political leaders in Bonn in late November. When it concluded on 5 December, the four groups represented, including the Northern Alliance, signed an agreement on a provisional arrangement pending re-establishment of permanent government institutions in Afghanistan.

As a first step, the Afghan Interim Authority was established. On 20 December, the Security Council, by resolution 1386 (2001), authorized the establishment of an International Security Assistance Force (ISAF) to help the Authority maintain security in Kabul and its surrounding areas. On 22 December, in Kabul, the internationally recognized administration of President Rabbani handed power to the new Interim Afghan Administration, established in Bonn and headed by Chairman Hamid Karzai. Special Representative Brahimi moved to Kabul to commence his activities in support of the new Afghan Administration. At the same time, the first of the ISAF troops were deployed, under British control.

With the easing of hostilities, WFP was able to deliver a record 114,000 metric tonnes of food aid in December - enough to feed 6 million people for two months. Still, by 20 December, only some $358 million of the nearly $662 million being sought for UN relief work in Afghanistan had been received, and the needs of only one agency - the UN Population Fund (UNFPA) - had been fully covered. And while the WFP had achieved 81 per cent of its funding requirements, UNHCR had secured only 59 per cent. As in the past, funds were mostly being donated for emergency relief, with very little for reconstruction and rehabilitation.

To maintain the momentum for international assistance to Afghanistan generated by the political process an International Conference on Reconstruction Assistance on Afghanistan was held in Tokyo on 21 and 22 January 2002. Addressing the Conference, Secretary-General Kofi Annan said such assistance would require $10 billion over a 10-year period, including $1.3 billion to cover immediate needs for 2002. That latter covers recurrent costs of the Interim Authority, as yet unfunded humanitarian assistance, and $376 million for quick impact and recovery projects "that are ready to go." "Two months from today, some 1.5 million Afghan girls and boys will return to school, to start a new school year in a new Afghanistan," he said.

"For many girls of primary school age, it will be the first time in their lives that they have been allowed to attend school. Supplies and safe learning spaces are needed. Teachers will need to be deployed and paid. If we want to help the next generation of Afghans improve upon the country's recent history, surely this is one place where our efforts must begin." "Our challenge is to help the Afghans help themselves," Mr. Annan added, describing the country's reconstruction needs as immense. They include the reintegration of former combatants; revival of economic activity; a fairer justice system, democratic institutions and mechanisms to protect human rights; such basic serves as clean water, sanitation, schools, health care and roads; ensuring the country is no longer a haven for terrorists or drug traffickers; ending violence against women; protecting childrens' rights; and ensuring security throughout the country.

A preliminary needs assessment prepared by the World Bank, UNDP and Asian Development Bank identified possible high-priority areas. These include: mine action; a basic health-services package to reduce child and maternal mortality; an education programme to enrol over a million girls and boys in school; rapid increase in food production through irrigation and other programmes; increased access to safe water; shelter to facilitate resettlement and development of a national urban management capacity; emergency energy supply while restoring the existing power system; urban and rural employment generation; supporting local-level reconstruction; and creating a conducive socio-economic environment for returning refugees.

The Tokyo Conference resulted in pledges of over $4.5 billion, which the Secretary-General described as "remarkably successful." He also praised its Interim Administration Chairman Hamid Karzai for welcoming international auditors to ensure that the money will be well spent. Secretary-General Kofi Annan visited Kabul on 25 January to offer moral support to the new Interim Administration and to thank members of the United Nations staff in Afghanistan for their sustained effort to provide humanitarian assistance to the Afghan people.

The first milestone of the Bonn Agreement was achieved with the announcement that same day of the composition of the Special Independent Commission for the Convening of the Emergency Loya Jirga (pashto for grand council - a traditional forum in which tribal elders can come together and settle affairs). The Commission is composed of 21 members. It has the final authority for determining the procedures for and the number of people who will participate in the Emergency Loya Jirga, which will elect a Head of State for the Transitional Administration and will approve proposals for the structure and key personnel of the Transitional Administration. The Bonn Agreement sets out that free and fair elections must be held within two years of the establishment of the Loya Jirga.

UN MEDIATION IN AFGHANISTAN

Condemning the spiral of violence and destruction in Afghanistan, Secretary-General Kofi Annan urged the Organization of the Islamic Conference on 9 December to renew efforts to help end the fighting in the region. Stressing the need for a complete ceasefire and an effective arms embargo, he charged that the conflict was fuelled by the unabated military and financial support of the warring factions by foreign Powers, which undermined United Nations attempts to mediate a lasting peace.

In view of the deteriorating safety conditions in Mazar-i-Sharif, the Head of the United Nations Special Mission in Afghanistan (UNSMA), Norbert Holl, urgently appealed to the warring factions on 10 October to facilitate the evacuation of international personnel from the city. Humanitarian conditions worsened due to the fighting. On 18 November, mass graves containing the remains of thousands of Taliban soldiers were found in northern Afghanistan. The number of internally displaced persons increased by 200,000 this year, exacerbating the already dire refugee situation.

The crisis was intensified by landmines. The Secretary-General reported on 17 September that nearly 777 square kilometers were contaminated by mines. Of this, 322 square kilometers were classified as "high priority", requiring urgent removal. In his emergency assistance report on Afghanistan of 28 October, the Secretary-General pointed out that a large number of families headed by women were unable to support themselves because of the interdiction of women's employment, while, at the same time, women and girls could no longer receive education.

"In response to discriminatory practices imposed by the Taliban, almost all United Nations education projects were suspended or were not implemented", Mr. Annan reported. "United Nations agencies and NGOs faced constraints in undertaking needs assessment, humanitarian programmes and monitoring without the benefit of contributions provided by female national staff." On 26 November, the World Food

Programme (WFP) announced that it was planning to airdrop urgent food supplies to the Bamyan region in north-central Afghanistan, blockaded since 4 May.

The WFP warned that, with winter fast approaching, the situation was "becoming critical", with 1.2 million inhabitants suffering from lack of adequate food and about 160,000 of them facing starvation "unless aid arrived immediately". According to a survey conducted by the United Nations International Drug Control Programme, released on 11 September, Afghanistan's opium poppy production rose to 2,800 metric tons in 1997, an estimated 25 per cent increase over the previous year.

It also found that 96.4 per cent of the estimated 58,400 hectares under opium cultivation, generating over $60 million in annual income for approximately 200,000 farmers, originated in provinces controlled by the Taliban. However, according to the interim report of 16 October by the Special Rapporteur of the Commission on Human Rights, the Taliban authorities were reported to have taken measures to ban the cultivation, sale and use of illegal drugs. The Special Rapporteur welcomed that the Taliban authorities had voiced their readiness to cooperate with the international community in eradicating drugs.

14

The Future of Afghanistan

Since the fall of the Taliban in November of 2001, the insurgency in Afghanistan has undergone a metamorphosis. Once written off as defeated, the Taliban are staging a comeback. Aided to a large degree by the sanctuary provided by refuges in the Federally Administered Tribal Areas in Pakistan, the Taliban have survived the initial onslaught of Coalition forces and begun a re-emergence as a viable political and military opposition to the democratically elected Karzai government in Kabul. This re-birth is the result of both a political and military vacuum throughout the country, and exploitation of Pashtun tribal fissures, particularly in the south, by the Taliban.

Additionally, the Taliban have implemented a revised military strategy which, although unique to Afghanistan, has adopted some of the more successful tactics of Iraqi insurgents. The purpose of this chapter is to examine these recent developments and forecast trends to determine the potential implications on future Coalition military and political strategy.

THE CHANGING NATURE OF THE INSURGENCY

The speed at which the Taliban regime collapsed in the fall of 2001 was indicative of the lack of support for the fundamentalist Islamic government outside of their traditional tribal homelands in the south. Indeed, for most Afghans, the initial embrace of the Taliban in the mid- 1990s was made not out of deeply held agreement and commitment to the Taliban's beliefs and ideals, but out of a sense of desperation. The population was eager for any group who provided an alternative to the chaos and lawlessness that followed the withdrawal of Soviet forces in 1989, the collapse of the Najibullah regime in 1992 and the subsequent years of civil war.

On the surface, the Taliban seemed to offer the security and stability that most people thought was missing from their daily lives. The Taliban promised to bring a halt to the seemingly endless rounds of factional fighting, and to restore the rule of law and order. It was not until after they had come to power that most Afghans realized they had sacrificed both their personal and political freedom to win the peace that they so desperately sought. The pre-9/11 Taliban conquest of most of Afghanistan followed a similar pattern. The Taliban would apply steady military pressure to an area until local warlords/ tribal chiefs either submitted or fled in defeat.

Once in power, the Taliban appointed a local/regional governor chosen from among the trusted Pashtun ranks, and immediately imposed their interpretation of Sharia law on the local population. The case of Herat provides an illustrative example. Following the defeat of local warlord Ismael Khan in September 1995, the Taliban appointed an administration comprised almost entirely of Durrani Pashtuns and implemented their strict form of Sharia law. The implementation of the law included bans on what they considered to be 'un- Islamic' social contact between men and women, and enforcement of strict dress codes.

Additionally, the Taliban immediately closed down every girl's school in the city and even proscribed that women were forbidden from studying at home. Needless to say, to the more cosmopolitan populations of Afghanistan such as those found in Herat, Kabul, Mazar-e-Sharif, and other large urban centers these restrictions were unwelcome limitations to the personal freedoms that they had enjoyed for decades, if not centuries. Additionally, the domination of local politics by Pashtuns appointed by the central government to rule over non-Pashtun areas bred resentment and conflict. Most of these leaders were poorly educated and demonstrated more concern for imposing strict adherence to Taliban rule then they did for the welfare of the local population.

In areas where the Taliban met resistance, their response was both harsh and indiscriminate. In Bamian Province, Taliban commanders used a combination of starvation of the indigenous population and military operations to ruthlessly suppress the native Hazara Shia populace. In Mazar-e-Sharif, the massacre of Taliban forces in 1997 was followed by what can only be described as a reprisal massacre (allegedly authorized by Mullah Omar) in August of 1998 that included the targeting of the city's Tajik and Hazara Shia civilian population and left an estimated 6000 to 8000 dead. However, it was not just the denial of personal freedoms, Pashtun hegemony of the central government, and usually brutal suppression of opposition that led to their widespread unpopularity.

In time, most Afghans were also to realize that the Taliban offered little to nothing in the way of economic development and recovery. Following their dramatic victories in Herat, Kabul, Bamian, and across the Northern provinces during the period 1995-1998, the Taliban were often dependent on the international community to provide the basic necessities of life for the local populations. However, as time passed the Taliban proved ineffective at organizing a government that was capable of providing the most rudimentary of services. At the same time, through threats and intimidation, they had succeeded in alienating the United Nations and the various Non-Governmental Organizations that they relied on to provide the basic necessities that they themselves could not.

The end result was a worsening humanitarian crisis within the country created by the gradual diminishing of external support and the inability, and unwillingness, of the Taliban to take the steps needed to assume the responsibility for themselves. Additionally, the Taliban showed no signs of conforming to international standards of behavior that might bring it additional support. In fact, throughout the period the Taliban had become increasingly isolated on the international stage. Their fundamentalist ideology, perceived disregard for human rights as demonstrated by the harsh imposition of Sharia law, poor treatment of women, and sometimes brutal conduct of its military forces had alienated the regime from most of the outside world.

While the Taliban had come to power in part to due to the substantial military aid it received from Pakistan, and to a lesser extent from the financial backing of Saudi Arabia and other wealthy patrons in the Gulf, that aid would in no way be sufficient to facilitate a recovery from 20 years of war. The aid from Pakistan was largely military in nature and had taken the form of money, equipment and training, and perhaps most importantly, military manpower. (The Government of Pakistan supported the flow of tens of thousands of *madrassa* students from Pakistan into Afghanistan that had swelled the ranks of the Taliban at critical times during their advance northward).

While this aid was instrumental in facilitating a Taliban military victory, it did not provide for the day-to-day operation of a civilian government. As a result of their harsh rule and inept handling of the government and the economy, by late 2001 the Taliban had worn out their welcome throughout most of Afghanistan. Although in many cases they had brought the peace and stability that was wanted, they offered little hope for the future. When Northern Alliance forces swept Afghanistan in November and December 2001, the Taliban were forced to flee into remote areas of their native provinces in the south or across the border into Pakistan.

Given their lack of domestic support outside their home towns and villages as evidenced by their quick collapse, and the manner in which Coalition Forces were greeted upon their arrival, how is it possible that they have proven to be so resilient? What appeal could the Taliban possibly have other than to those committed to the cause for radical religious reasons or to those closely associated to the inner circle of Taliban leadership who benefited from their domination?

CHANGES TO THE TALIBAN STRATEGY

It were obvious by their words and deeds that the Taliban had adjusted both their strategy and tactics in 2005-2006. Having survived the initial onslaught of Coalition Forces in 2001-2004, the Taliban are attempting to seize the initiative by making the transition from strategic defensive to the strategic offensive. In statements to the press, senior Taliban leadership, including Taliban leader Mullah Omar, senior Taliban commander Mullah Dadullah Lang, and others, have broadly outlined their strategy and intentions.

Although they have not provided any insight into their decision making process, an analysis of the factors affecting the political and military environment in Afghanistan today, and an examination of how they have adapted their tactics provides clues into the evolution of their strategic vision. It also provides a baseline for an analysis of how the insurgency is likely to continue to adapt in the coming years as the Taliban leadership continues to pursue its goal of returning to national power.

FACTORS AFFECTING THE ENVIRONMENT POPULAR SUPPORT

Unlike the Iraq insurgency, insurgents in Afghanistan do not enjoy widespread popular support. This is due primarily to three reasons. The first is the perception of US/Coalition Forces as a stabilizing (and transitional) force as opposed to an occupying power. The majority of Afghans accept the legitimacy of the US/ISAF as an international military presence sent to aid in reconstruction and recovery. Although I would stop short of saying that we are loved by most Afghans, we are tolerated. Given the British experience with a hostile Afghan population in the 19th century and a similar experience by the Russians in the 20th century, the benefits of that toleration should not be underestimated. 7 The second reason why the insurgency is not widely popular is the collective memory of the Afghan population of their experience with the Taliban when they were in power from 1996- 2001.

Without question, the Hazara, Tajik, Uzbek, and other minority populations have no illusions about what Taliban domination would bring, or perhaps more appropriately, bring back. Additionally, while Taliban support is mainly derived from Pashtun areas, the Pashtun community is itself divided. Pashtuns do not view the Taliban as a Pashtun nationalist movement or representative of all the tribes but instead see them for what they are– a relatively small political entity with an active military wing and an ultra-conservative religious ideology. As a result, the Taliban also do not enjoy widespread support even among their core consituency.

The third reason has to do with both war-weariness and the potential for recovery. Most Afghans recognize the significance of the opportunity provided by the commitment of the international community to reconstruction. From experience, they doubt the Taliban's ability to govern effectively, and their ability, or even willingness, to sustain the same level of external support. To them the international community is the safer bet because they bring with them the required resources and technical expertise to get the job done. This lack of public support has had a substantial impact on Taliban strategy, tactics and the way they conduct their public diplomacy. Unlike Iraq where many insurgent groups have fueled sectarian violence by deliberately attacking non-combatant civilian populations, the Afghan insurgency, with a few notable exceptions, has been much more careful to avoid collateral civilian deaths.

The Taliban appear to be deeply concerned with the potential backlash that would likely result from attacks on civilian populations. The Taliban are sensitive to this lack of public support because of the tribal ties that most Taliban leaders still have with their communities and their collective experience during the Soviet occupation and subsequent years of civil war. Additionally, a reduced presence of religiously motivated radical foreign fighters (as compared to Iraq) with no ties to the community or concern with civilian deaths has had a moderating influence on the Taliban's decision making.

Because they wish to portray themselves as the true representatives of the people of Afghanistan in order to maintain or perhaps increase their public appeal, they must demonstrate some sensitivity to the suffering that the Afghan people have endured over the past 25 years. That sensitivity has taken the form of minimizing the potential for civilian non-combatant collateral damage.

TRIBAL DYNAMICS

In Afghanistan, as is the case everywhere else, all politics are local. The Afghan Presidential Election in October 2004, and the National Assembly and Provincial Council Elections in September 2005 are all important milestones for the re-establishment of a national government and government bureaucracy. The emergence of a weak government at the national and provincial levels has been mirrored by the establishment of local governments at the district level.

As this government has coalesced, what has emerged is not a western-style representative democracy but one whose members, particularly at the local level in rural areas, continue to identify more with their tribal/ethnic group than they do with the geographically area they were elected to represent. This has created situations where whole tribal groupings feel unable to defend themselves from the Taliban, alienated from the political process, or worse, victimized by a rival tribe that holds government office. In many ways it is naïve to assume that all locally elected Afghan officials will put aside their tribal and ethnic biases and act in accordance with the collective good.

All politicians have constituencies, those in western democracies included, that forms the basis of their popular support and keeps them in office. The Afghans are no different. But the politics of exclusion in Afghanistan have far more serious consequences than in the West. For example, being a registered Democrat or Republican in the United States does not mean that you lose your livelihood, access to the judicial system to settle disputes, or your sense of physical security if your party is not elected to office.

Life continues pretty much as normal with all of the basic necessities of life either provided or readily available. The same cannot be said in Afghanistan. Being excluded from the political process there can pose a threat to your very survival. It can mean less access to recovery and reconstruction aid and projects, and the reduced presence of security forces. Even worse, in some cases involving longstanding disputes between tribes, it may involve the use of security forces by one side to settle those disputes. In a country that has not had a functioning judicial system in over 25 years, exclusion from the political process can mean you may have no legal recourse to settle grievances.

Finally, the use of political power or security forces to support criminal activity targeting rival individuals or tribes is widespread. The Taliban, particularly in southern Afghanistan, are keenly aware of the current shortfalls in the political and judicial systems, particularly at the local level. They are becoming masters of exploiting tribal fissures and grievances that are serious to those parties involved and somewhat invisible to Coalition authorities and the central government in Kabul. As a result, the apparent growth in support for the Taliban in the south is less about a renewed commitment to their ultra-conservative Islamic ideology than it is about the appeal of the Taliban as a viable political alternative, which in some cases is the only alternative, to the emerging and sometimes flawed Afghan government structure.

PAKISTAN

The Afghan insurgency could not survive but for the sanctuary provided it in the Federally Administrated Tribal Areas in Pakistan. Despite significant Pakistani efforts to combat extremism to include the capture of several high profile *Al Qaeda* and Taliban leaders and major military operations aimed at expanding Islamabad's sovereignty in the FATA, Pakistan remains a safe haven for Afghan insurgents. According to senior Coalition and Afghan officials, there is strong evidence that Pakistan provides not only a refuge for the insurgent senior leadership, but also serves as a recruiting and training ground for insurgent fighters.

The problems in the FATA and northern Balochistan stem from historically weak central government control, a sympathetic Pashtun population with close ties to the tribes in Afghanistan, endemic poverty, and a 2400-kilometer border that to a large extent is neither patrolled or even recognized by the local population. While significant progress has been made between the US, Pakistan and Afghanistan on combined border security operations, the shear size of the border and difficulty of terrain make sealing it a near impossible task. Additionally, while there has been some discussion between the three parties on creation of a border barrier, such as a fence, it has met with fierce local resistance and skepticism as to both cost and feasibility.

THE ILLEGAL NARCOTICS INDUSTRY

In 2005, the size of the illegal narcotics industry in Afghanistan was about 51% of the size of the legal economy, and generated approximately $2.7 billion in revenues for growers and traffickers. There are no reliable estimates of illegal narcotics related crime, but associated corruption permeates every level of Afghan society. From the local farmers who break the law in the hope of providing a slightly better than sustenance level of existence for their families, to the government officials who protect the lab owners and traffickers (or who often control the local industry) in order to profit themselves, large segments of the Afghan populace are involved in the trade. Beyond the threat to public health, the illegal drug industry undermines the nascent rule of law by turning ordinary farmers into criminals and local government officials into willing participants whose first priority is to protect the trade as opposed to serving the people.

From an Information Operations perspective, the Taliban have been quick to exploit alleged linkages between the illegal narcotics industry and the Afghan government. After the insurgency, the illegal narcotics industry poses the greatest threat to the long-term peace and stability of the country.

Despite their ideological objections to poppy cultivation, the Taliban fully understand that the illegal narcotics industry is part of the operating environment of Afghanistan. When pressed, the Taliban can be very pragmatic when it comes to dealing with the business. Although many remember Mullah Omar's initial ban on poppy cultivation once the Taliban came to power in Kabul, few recall that that the Taliban had a history of cooperation with the industry when their interests were served.

For, example, in 1994 they built an alliance with lesser drug lords to wrestle control of Helmand Province away from Ghaffar Akhunzadeh, the de facto ruler of Helmand and local king of the opium trade. Only after they had secured control of most of the country did they turn on the drug lords. Now out of power, the Taliban have resumed a more pragmatic view of the trade. They see it as both a source of funding, and a means with which to drive a wedge between local populations and the central government. Funding usually takes the form of protection money paid by traffickers to local Taliban commanders to prevent attacks on their fields or workers.

A form of extortion, it is nonetheless successful as a fundraising tool. Additionally, some Taliban commanders have been involved in more active measures, such as providing convoy security to drug shipments, in exchange for payment. The benefits of this system to local commanders are significant when you consider that the alternative to raising funds locally is to have the money hand couriered to remote locations from sanctuaries in Pakistan and elsewhere. Probably the most effective use of the illegal narcotics industry by the Taliban has been as a mechanism to divide the people from the Karzai government. Nowhere has this been more effective than in Kandahar and the Helmand River Valley in Helmand and Uruzgan Provinces. In March and April 2006, the Afghan government launched an aggressive poppy eradication operation in the area to destroy local poppy crops.

The Taliban responded by offering local tribes and farmers protection in the form of men and material from the Afghan government forces. Because the operation focused more on eradication than it did on promoting alternative crops to the poor farmers, the Taliban were often viewed as defenders of the local population from an indifferent government. Though the tangible impact of the Taliban assistance was likely minimal, it provided them with a needed psychological victory. To the local subsistence farmer, only the Taliban appeared sympathetic to their plight.

NATO/ISAF EXPANSION

The transition of responsibility for military operations in Afghanistan from a US led international coalition to the NATO led International Security Assistance Force (ISAF) began in 2004 with the transfer of responsibility for operations in the eight northern provinces that comprise Regional Command (RC) North. That transition was followed in 2005 with the transfer to ISAF of the four provinces in RC West. However, it was not until 2006 that NATO, and more importantly NATO conventional forces, took over responsibility for a Regional Command with an active and large insurgent presence that would require continuous combat operations to address – that is, RC South. Until 2006, the US had provided the bulk of conventional ground forces in RC South.

However, starting in early 2006, significant numbers of Canadian and British forces began to arrive in Kandahar and Helmand Provinces in preparation for the eventual transition to ISAF control that occurred on 1 August. These forces were followed by the arrival of Dutch troops into Uruzgan Province later in the summer. From a US perspective, the introduction of these forces symbolized, and enhanced, the depth of the international community's commitment to Afghanistan's recovery. From the Taliban's perspective the arrival of these forces meant something different. To them, the Coalition was substantially increasing the number of conventional forces in RC South and introducing large numbers of Coalition Forces into places where neither the Coalition nor Afghan National Security Forces had been present before.

The largest increase in troop presence occurred in Helmand Province with the introduction of a British Battle Group of 3500 soldiers where before only 150 American troops had been stationed. For the Taliban, this troop introduction was viewed as a direct challenge within areas that they had considered either relatively safe or at least neutral due to the lack of Coalition Force presence. At the strategic level, ISAF expansion introduced foreign troops into contested areas of Afghanistan that were viewed perhaps as less committed and less capable as compared to US forces. Although not particularly sophisticated in their understanding of world affairs, the Taliban do understand the nature of coalitions and alliances. In this way, the presence of additional Coalition combat forces was viewed as both a threat and an opportunity if the Taliban could apply enough pressure on those nations involved to cause them to withdraw.

CONFLICT IN IRAQ

The conflict in Iraq has aided the Taliban in two ways. First, it has fueled continued resentment among Muslims against the United States by bringing into question American intentions in the Middle East specifically and towards the Islamic community as a whole. In its press releases, the Taliban have linked the conflict in Iraq with the insurgency in Afghanistan in an effort to feed the perception that the US is involved in a religious war against Islam. While the extent to which this message has helped the Taliban is unknown, it undoubtedly resonates within the extremist community and among their sympathizers, and has most likely boosted recruiting and fundraising efforts. The second way the conflict in Iraq has assisted the Taliban is by providing a proving ground for insurgent tactics, techniques, and procedures.

Without question, the use of suicide bombers by Iraqi insurgents had an impact on the Taliban leadership's decision to employ similar tactics in Afghanistan beginning in 2005. While the linkage between the two insurgencies remains limited and the speed with which the migration of technical advances in weapons development (such as advanced IED manufacture) remains slow, the Taliban are keenly aware that events in Iraq are relevant to their struggle in Afghanistan.

Continued Availability of Weapons and Ammunition Despite Coalition attempts to reduce the availability of arms and ammunition among the general public, supplies remain plentiful and relatively cheap in both Afghanistan and within the Federally Administered Tribal Areas in Pakistan. In Afghanistan, Coalition forces continue to collect, either from deliberate turn-ins or discoveries, illegal weapons caches from around the country. Numerous caches are found each week. They range in size from a few simple assault rifles with accompanying ammunition to huge stockpiles that include shoulder-fired man- portable air defense missiles, large numbers of 107-mm rockets, crew served automatic weapons, plastic explosives, and, occasionally, armored vehicles.

There are no records of exactly what was shipped into Afghanistan during the Soviet occupation or during the period of the civil war from 1989-2001, so there is no record of who maintains these caches. Some are held for personal use by individuals that still have little faith in the growing Afghan National Security Forces or judiciary.

Others are maintained by tribes and warlords at the collective level but for the same reason as the average Afghan. For all, the retention of weapons caches is both a way of hedging bets on the likely success of the current Afghan government and a potential source of funds if they choose to sell them on the black market. In addition to caches in Afghanistan, a thriving black market for arms and munitions exists just across the border in the FATA. This market includes stockpiles of weapons that remain from the Soviet occupation and civil war periods, and towns whose economies are based in part on a thriving industry of local metal smiths who can produce functional copies of most modern automatic weapons.

The result is a plentiful and relatively cheap supply of weapons in an area in which the Pakistani government exerts nominal control. "A 2003 survey by SPADO found there were 1,200 shops selling guns in Darra Adam Khel alone. These were supplied by nearly 1,500 small workshops and more than 50 medium-scale manufacturing units employing over 6,000 gunsmiths." Foreign Funding To a large extent, the Afghan insurgency relies on foreign donors for the funding it needs to sustain operations. In considering the sources of these funds, the US should keep in mind that the Taliban has had 25 years to develop close ties to potential backers in Pakistan and in the Gulf States.

In all likelihood, Taliban funding efforts are also being fueled by the increased animosity toward the United States over events in Iraq, as well as high oil prices which undoubtedly creates additional disposable income for wealthy individuals in the Gulf. It is safe to assume that since 2004, the Taliban have been successful in raising money to support an insurgency that does not require a very high capital investment to begin with. The readily available stores of weapons and ammunition, coupled with an economy that supports an average monthly wage of less than $212/month means that there are ample supplies of men and materiel available at cheap prices.

Tactics Since 2004, the Taliban have conducted their own assessment of the political and military situation inside Afghanistan and have adjusted their tactics accordingly. The changes have taken the shape of an increased reliance on the use of suicide bombers, the selective targeting of discreet target sets, and the incorporation of what can best be described as local militias into their operations in RC South. These changes are intended to support a strategy that is focused on attacking the growing power of the central government throughout southern and eastern Afghanistan with the intent of de-legitimizing the government in the eyes of the people. Suicide Bombings Suicide bombings are a new phenomenon to Afghan culture.

There was no history of suicide operations in Afghanistan during even the most tumultuous periods of the 19th and 20th centuries. Even today, there is a stubborn reluctance on the part of Afghan government and military officials to admit that

Afghans are participating in these attacks. In private, most are quick to tell you that the bombers are actually Pakistanis recruited and brainwashed in the FATA before being sent into Afghanistan to conduct an attack. Yet they usually offer no proof to support their claims and in time you are left with the very strong impression that what they are telling you is derived from their deeply held belief that Afghans could not do such things as opposed to the facts of the incident. In other words, they are in denial. Perhaps the exact truth will never be known.

Positive identification of the attackers is often limited by the lack of identifiable remains (there is often little left of the bomber after one of these attacks) and/or the lack of an identification database. However, one statistic is indisputable – the number of suicide attacks is clearly on the rise. In 2001, there was only one suicide attack in Afghanistan. In 2002, there were none, and in 2003, there were four. In 2006, there were 140 suicide attacks, targeting mostly Coalition Forces and Afghan government officials. In 2006 there were over 200 civilian casualties associated with the bombings; almost all of these casualties have been the result of collateral damage caused during an attack.

While the Taliban have learned from insurgent experiences in Iraq and have been quick to employ suicide bombings tactics, their targeting strategy remains vastly different. For the Taliban, the suicide bomber is the most efficient means of inflicting casualties and undermining confidence in the new government. It is perhaps the most effective way for an insurgency that does not enjoy widespread popular support and is still essentially rural to employ limited resources in a manner that provides for the possibility of maximum effect and media coverage. It is important to point out that the Taliban have not made any attempt to incite the kind of sectarian violence seen in Iraq.

Given Afghanistan's diverse ethnic and religious (Sunni 80%, Shi'a 19%, other 1%) mix, the creation of ethnic strife through the deliberate targeting of civilian ethnic populations is a viable course of action open to the Taliban if they do not believe they can succeed in de-legitimizing the government through other means. The fact that they have yet to employ this strategy is an indication of their concern over the popular backlash against them it would create if such a strategy were to be adopted. Unlike Iraq where Coalition Forces are largely viewed as an occupying power, in Afghanistan both Coalition Forces and the Afghan government enjoy much broader support. The Taliban understand that they are in competition with the government for the hearts and minds of the Afghan people with the government enjoying broad acceptance, if not always popularity.

SELECTIVE TARGETING

In many respects, the targeting strategy of the Afghan insurgency follows a predictable pattern. Insurgents attack both military and government targets in an effort to undermine the existing government and extend their own span of control. However, the nature of the Afghan insurgency with its own unique cultural, religious and historic elements has had a significant impact on the Taliban's decision making process of what is, and what is not, targeted. Below is a list of the target sets that currently represent the focus of Taliban targeting efforts. Coalition Military Forces Coalition military forces have been and will continue to be a primary target for Afghan insurgents.

The insurgents have attempted to portray Coalition troops as an occupying force. As part of their Information Operations strategy, they try to paint the conflict in terms of a religious struggle between the Christian West and the Islamic world. As noted earlier, the introduction of ISAF forces into Afghanistan has added a new dimension to their targeting strategy as they now face Coalition conventional forces from countries other than the US. Afghan Government Officials Afghan government officials have also been a prime target for insurgents.

The major difference between the period of 2005-2006 and the preceding years is the growth of the Afghan government within the districts in each province. This has created both an increased threat to the insurgents at the local level and a more target rich environment. Although better protected than their counterparts at the district level and below, both senior national and provincial level officials continue to be the target for spectacular attacks, particularly suicide bombings.

AFGHAN NATIONAL SECURITY FORCES (ANSF)

Generally viewed as less capable than Coalition forces, and not as well armored or equipped, ANSF are also a focus for Afghan insurgent attacks. As in the case of increasing numbers of Afghan government officials, the growing ranks of ANSF present a direct threat to the insurgents at the local level and a more target rich environment. As would be expected, isolated and poorly manned outposts are the prime targets. Pro-Government Clergy In a departure from more traditional insurgent targeting strategies, in 2004 the Taliban began a campaign to intentionally target Afghan clergymen who it felt were supporting the government.

Despite the risk of public backlash, the Taliban began this campaign because they perceived it as a direct threat to their religious legitimacy, and because the pro-government clergy were an effective means of communicating the government's message to the average Afghan. In a country where the typical citizen does not enjoy easy access to mass media, news is often spread by word of mouth. The clergy were proving an effective way for the government to reach the people because they enjoyed regular access and carried legitimacy.

EDUCATION INFRASTRUCTURE

In another departure from traditional insurgent strategies, in 2004 the Taliban began a campaign of deliberately targeting education infrastructure focusing on facilities, teachers, and administrators. Because there is a conservative religious influence throughout the country and due to the lack of security force presence in many rural areas, not all attacks against education infrastructure can be attributed to insurgents. However, in the Pashtun south and east, the

Taliban have initiated a campaign to target any educational institution that it believes is not conforming to its ultra-conservative Islamic views, particularly on the co-education of men and women.

In its early phases the Taliban uses 'night letters' posted anonymously throughout a town or village to warn residents that a school has become a possible target for attack. When the attack occurs it typically takes place in the middle of the night and involves an assault on the physical structure of the school with an incendiary device (e.g. Molotov cocktail) often in combination with an explosive (old artillery shell). However, much more brutal and callous attacks involving the execution of teachers and administrators have also taken place.

RECONSTRUCTION WORKERS

Afghan reconstruction workers, to include Coalition military forces directly involved in reconstruction work, are frequently targeted. Although insurgent commander's decisions to attack reconstruction workers are often weighed against the perceived reaction of the local community that would be affected by the consequences of the action, there have been several high profile attacks against contractors working on the Ring Road that runs in a large semi-circle within Afghanistan around the foothills of the Hindu Kush Mountains.

While these attacks have not halted repairs or improvements to the road, they have slowed progress by forcing some donor nations to temporarily withdraw there workers, and have significantly increased the cost of security thereby making the actual completion costs much higher than what was actually budgeted. What is Not Targeted Interestingly, Afghan insurgents do not generally target civilian infrastructure. Unlike Iraq, where oil pipelines and electrical infrastructure are routinely attacked, Afghan insurgents tend to avoid these types of attacks. One reason could be the relative lack of infrastructure throughout the country and therefore the lack of targets to attack.

However, a more likely explanation is again tied to the Taliban's perception of weak popular support and the repercussions such attacks would likely have among a population that has suffered incredible hardship during 25 years of war. Massing of Forces for Attacks A third and final change in insurgent tactics that has occurred largely in the past 18 months, is tied to the Taliban's ability to mass relatively large numbers (100-400) of fighters for attacks in the south. However, this change in tactics is more notable for its implications concerning growing popular support at the local level than it is for its success on the battlefield.

In June of 2005, the Taliban massed 100-125 fighters in the Miana Shin District of Kandahar Province for an attack against the District Government Headquarters. Although the insurgents were at least temporarily successful in accomplishing their objectives, the end result was a tactical disaster. Coalition and Afghan Forces responded to the attack with ground forces supported by close air support. In the end, the insurgents were forced to flee, suffering casualties perhaps as high as 75% or greater. After the battle was over, many senior Coalition and Afghan officers had assumed that the Taliban had learned a painful lesson and would not attempt such massing of forces for attacks again for the foreseeable future. But events in Kandahar and Helmand Provinces in 2006 would prove them wrong.

Throughout 2006, the Taliban proved both capable and willing to mass forces despite the painful lesson of Miana Shin. Although these tactics often resulted in high casualties and rarely achieved any long-term military purpose, they often succeeded in severely shaking the confidence of district and provincial level government and military officials. They were also significant in that they demonstrated the Taliban's ability to generate significant numbers of armed recruits from among the local population.

It is the use of these recruits in mass that represents the change in tactics, and also, a change in capability. But what is behind this change? What is motivating these people to fight?

The introduction of ISAF conventional forces (British) into Helmand Province and Afghan government poppy eradication operations in the Helmand River Valley coupled with skillful Taliban manipulation of tribal fissures and public opinion are most likely to blame.

WHAT THE FUTURE HOLDS FOR THE INSURGENCY

In many respects, the surge in Taliban activity over the past 18 months is less the result of the growing strength of the insurgency and more about the expanding influence of the Afghan government and the presence of Coalition Forces. The results of the September 2005 National Assembly and Provincial Council Elections along with increased numbers of Afghan National Security Forces are both contributing to an increase in resistance in areas that the Taliban had previously considered benign.

Additionally, in Regional Command South in the Helmand River Valley in Spring 2006 ISAF recently introduced the equivalent of a British Brigade where before there had only been a US company and Special Forces teams. However, the Taliban undoubtedly feel they have enjoyed some measure of success with their strategy over the last 18 months. In all likelihood, 2007 will see the Taliban attempting to expand their presence to other Provinces and Districts in the south and east using the same methods that they perceive have been successful. From their perspective the situation does not call for a radical change in tactics. Therefore, barring any wildcards, such as the death or replacement of Mullah Omar as Taliban leader, 2007 will be a repeat of 2006.

IMPLICATIONS FOR US POLICY

The illegal narcotics industries in Afghanistan possess perhaps the greatest long-term challenge for the Coalition. A failure to curb poppy cultivation and heroin production will undermine the continued development of the Afghan government, and to a lesser extent provide a needed source of revenue for local Taliban commanders. At the same time, overly aggressive poppy eradication operations have the potential to push large segments of the population into the hands of the insurgents. The best course of action is to proceed cautiously with eradication while taking an aggressive approach to counter-trafficking efforts. The three principles to apply to eradication operations are:

- They must be planned and led by Afghans.
- They must be tied to a robust alternative livelihoods program.
- They must be executed equitably to minimize any perceptions of bias in execution.

To realistically have a chance to accomplish the above, the Coalition will be required to provide the supporting technical expertise and oversight of all aspects of both planning and execution. The Coalition will also have to take the lead in developing the supporting alternative livelihoods programs, although actual execution should be done by the Afghans. As a rule, no eradication operation should take place without a supporting alternative livelihoods program. Otherwise, the local populace will be pushed into the arms of the Taliban.

Execution of eradication operations must also be closely monitored to prevent abuse. Eradication operations that are perceived to be biased for or against a particular tribe will only deepen the fissures that already exist and further undermine the authority of the Provincial and District governments. No single event could change the strategic direction of US and international strategy in the region more than the fall of the current GOP either by assassination, coup, or popular uprising. It would deal a severe blow not only to international efforts in Afghanistan, but also to the GWOT as a whole. Worse yet, if the GOP were to be replaced by an Islamist regime, it would have strategic implications for US and world security in the areas of both terrorism and nuclear weapons proliferation.

While the elimination of insurgent sanctuaries is critical to success, the US must be mindful of the potential domestic Pakistani political implications of US and Pakistani actions taken in the FATA or Baluchistan. In addressing the issue of insurgent sanctuaries in Pakistan, the US should continue to allow the Pakistanis to take the lead in all actions. However, to date Pakistani attempts to address the problem have run hot and cold. Periods of aggressive military action supporting Islamabad's attempts to assert sovereignty have been followed by 'truces' between the GOP and local tribes that have provided Afghan insurgents needed respites during which to regroup.

While the Pakistanis are accurate in asserting that the solution to the problems of the FATA and Baluchistan lies in economic development, the lack of that development does not preclude action against senior Afghan insurgent leadership targets in Pakistan. Given that the best tool for such selective targeting is a national law enforcement or intelligence agency, as opposed to the Pakistani military, the job falls on the Inter-Services Intelligence Directorate (ISID). It is against the ISID with which the US needs to apply pressure on the GOP.

The purpose of this pressure is, first and foremost, to weed out those elements within the agency that are sympathetic to the Taliban and other insurgent groups and who may be providing covert support. Secondly, this pressure must result in the aggressive recruiting of human intelligence sources that can locate and identify Afghan insurgent leadership nodes in their country. It is important to point out that as the ISID forms an integral part of the GOP's security apparatus, such a reform carries some risk. However, as the US will not make progress targeting senior insurgent and *Al Qaeda* leadership unless this happens, the risk is unavoidable.

IMPROVING GOVERNANCE AND SECURITY AT THE LOCAL LEVEL

According to the International Crisis Group, an independent, non-profit, non-governmental organization, "Internal reform is equally essential to end nearly five years of misrule by predatory leaders and a culture of impunity... This state of affairs has particular implications in the south, where many of the worst provincial and district leaders have close links to the central administration. As a result, the disillusioned, the disenfranchised, and the economically desperate are responding again to the call of extremists in a region radicalized through decades of conflict."

Therefore, nothing will go further to undermine Taliban gains in the south and east more than improving the quality of governance and security at the Provincial and District level. In terms of Coalition action, this translates into more funding for local reconstruction initiatives and better trained and paid security forces, particularly the Afghan National Police. For the Afghan government, it means putting legislative emphasis on issues related to governance and accountability such as development of the judiciary and anti-corruption laws. It also means calling for improved accountability of local officials to ensure that they are not behaving in ways that will incite or exacerbate inter-tribal rivalry.

EXPLOITING POPULAR SUPPORT

In Afghanistan, Coalition Forces are perceived in a positive light by the local population who support reconstruction efforts and welcome the security that these forces bring. Here, the Coalition should seek to maintain the momentum we have had since 2001 by a continued campaign highlighting reconstruction efforts, and by undertaking a more aggressive campaign targeting the Taliban's motives and methods. Because we are looked upon favorably, and because the Taliban enjoys little popular support, the population may be much more receptive to Coalition and Afghan government Information Operations.

In Afghanistan, the real question is how we maintain the momentum that we started with. Information Operations in Afghanistan should follow a two track approach. First, they should seek to foster the goodwill we have enjoyed since 2001 through a continued IO campaign highlighting reconstruction efforts and the growth of the Afghan government and security forces. This campaign should continue to be closely linked to visible progress on the ground. Secondly, the Coalition should adopt a much more aggressive campaign targeting the Afghan/Pakistani publics' perceptions of the Taliban.

The Coalition should develop and employ negative IO messages highlighting Taliban attacks on the clergy, education infrastructure and reconstruction workers, and the collateral civilian casualties of suicide attacks as evidence of the Taliban's lack of concern for the average Afghan. The purpose of these messages is to maintain the negative perception most Afghans have for the insurgents. Clamping Down on the Supply of Weapons. Given the vast quantities of arms and ammunition still in circulation in Afghanistan, the problem of a cheap and plentiful supply of weapons and munitions for insurgents, warlords and criminals is unlikely to go away anytime in the next decade.

However, as Coalition Forces continue to make incremental progress in addressing the problem inside the country, little is being done on the Pakistani side of the border – thus ensuring that overall no progress is made. To have any real hope for success, the GOP must act to shut down the arms bazaars in the FATA. It is a task best suited to Pakistani military forces and is likely to illicit a negative local response as closing these markets will have an immediate and negative impact on the livelihoods of those involved. Like actively targeting insurgent leaders, it is a task that cannot wait. The situation in Afghanistan today is more about Taliban efforts to counter the growing expansion of central government authority than it is about the increased popularity of the Taliban.

The Afghan government and Coalition Forces still maintain the initiative and enjoy popular support. The appeal of the ideology of the insurgents is still largely limited to hard-line religious conservatives who represent a minority of the population in the mostly Pashtun south and east. The fact that the Taliban have been able to exploit tribal fissures, poor governance, and the desperate economic conditions to their advantage should be cause for concern but not interpreted as evidence of the impending collapse of the democratically-elected Afghan government.

What the recent surge in insurgent activity represents is a growing challenge to continued progress, which if successful could derail the entire effort. To meet this challenge, the Coalition and the Afghan government need to continue to place emphasis on developing the country's weak national institutions, and increase their efforts to expand the government's authority at the local level. In many respects, such an approach represents the next logical step in the reconstruction of the country. We have put in place a central government, created the basis for a disciplined Afghan National Army, and started the process of forming a professional police force.

All of our efforts in Afghanistan will be fruitless if we do not leave behind strong national institutions, but we will never bring peace or prosperity if we do not improve governance and security at the local level, and succeed in instituting the rule of law for the average Afghan. The Afghan government and Coalition also need to take steps to combat the illegal narcotics industry to deny insurgents both a source of funding and eliminate an issue with which the insurgents can drive a wedge between the people and the government.

Even without an insurgency, Afghanistan will never achieve the security and stability it seeks if half of its economy is tied to the production of illegal drugs. This problem primarily requires an economic solution that provides alternative livelihoods to Afghan farmers. Poppy eradication operations should support the overall campaign and not be the focus of the Government's efforts. To do otherwise would be to push the people into the arms of the insurgents. Additionally, Pakistan must do more to both deny senior Afghan insurgent leaders sanctuary and to curb the flow of illegal weapons and munitions across the border.

The targeting of insurgent leaders would best be performed through selective methods that would avoid inciting a popular backlash in the FATA and Baluchistan, and thus reduce the risk to President Musharraf. This task cannot be accomplished without the active participation of a willing and committed ISID. To curb the flow of illegal arms will require the intervention of Pakistani military forces in those areas, such as Darra Adam Khel, where there is a thriving industry. As in dealing with the illegal narcotics industry in Afghanistan, a program emphasizing alternative livelihoods for the craftsmen involved in the industry is needed if it is to stand a chance for success.

Finally, in support of all the above, the Coalition and Afghan Government should re-double their efforts within the context of a broader information operations campaign. After all, it is perhaps in the court of public opinion where the Coalition enjoys its most significant advantage. Such a campaign should be designed to re-enforce positive national perceptions of the Coalition and Afghan Government, and attack Taliban methods in areas in dispute.

Bibliography

Ahmed Rashid. *TALIBAN: Militant Islam, Oil and Fundamentalism in Central Asia*, Yale, 2001.

Antonio Giustozzi. *War, Politics and Society in Afghanistan, 1978-1992*, Georgetown University Press, 2000.

Arthur Bonner. *Among the Afghans*, Duke University Press, 1987.

Abu Khalil, As'ad. *Bin Laden, Islam, and America's New 'War on Terrorism'*. Open Media Pamphlet Series. New York: Seven Stories Press, 2002.

Abraham, A. J. *Islamic Fundamentalism and the Doctrine of Jihad*. Lima, OH: Wyndham Hall Press, 2002.

Brigitte L. Nacos.*Terrorism & the Media: From the Iran Hostage Crisis to the World Trade Center Bombing*, Columbia University Press, 1994 .

Bar, Shmuel. *Warrant for Terror: Fatwas of Radical Islam and the Duty of Jihad*. Hoover Studies in Politics, Economics, and Society. Lanham, MD: Rowman & Littlefield, 2006.

Catholic Institute for International Relations, *Guatemala, Never Again*. Maryknoll, NY: Orbis Books, 1999.

David B. Edwards. *Heroes of the Age: Moral Fault Lines on the Afghan Frontier*, University of California Press, 1996 .

Davies, Barry. *Terrorism: Inside a World Phenomenon*. London: Virgin Books, 2003.

Eric S. Margolis. *War at the Top of the World: The Struggle for Afghanistan, Kashmir, and Tibet*, Routledge, 2001.

Esposito, John L. *Islam: The Straight Path.* 3rd edition. New York: Oxford University Press, 1998.

Esposito, John L. *The Islamic Threat: Myth or Reality?* New York: Oxford University Press, 1992.

Hasan Kakar. Afghanistan: *The Soviet Invasion and the Afghan Response, 1979-1982,* University of California Press, 1995.

Henry S. Bradsher. *Afghan Communism and Soviet Intervention,* Oxford University Press, 1999 .

Huband, Mark. *Warriors of the Prophet: the Struggle for Islam.* Boulder, CO: Westview Press, 1999.

Ian O. Lesser, Bruce Hoffman, John Arquilla, David F. Ronfeldt, Michele Zanini, Brian Michael Jenkins. *Countering,* RAND, 1999.

Jason Elliot. *An Unexpected Light: Travels in Afghanistan,* St.Martin's, 2001.

Jeffrey D. Simon. *Terrorist Trap,* Indiana University Press, 2001.

Jessica Stern. *The Ultimate Terrorists,* Harvard, 2000.

John Arquilla and David Ronfeldt. *Networks and Netwars: The Future of Terror, Crime and Militancy,* RAND, 2001.

Kamal Matinuddin.*The Taliban Phenomenon, Afghanistan 1994-1997,* Oxford University Press. 2000.

Larry P. Goodson. *Afghanistan's Endless War: State Failure, Regional Politics, and the Rise of the Taliban,* University of Washington Press, 2001.

M.J. Gohari.*Taliban: Ascent to Power,* Oxford University Press, 2001.

Marc Miller and Jason File.*Terrorism Factbook: Our Nation at War,* White Wolf Publishing Inc. 2001.

Mark Juergensmeyer. *Terror in the Mind of God: The Global Rise of Religious Violence,* University of California, 2001.

Martha Crenshaw.*Terrorism in Context,* Penn State

University Press, 1995 .

Omar Malik. *Enough of the Definition of Terrorism*, Brookings Institution Press, 2001.

O'Ballance, Edgar. *Islamic Fundamentalist Terrorism: 1979-95*. Basingstoke: Macmillan, 1997.

Ojeda, Auriana. *Islamic Fundamentalism*. San Diego, CA: Greenhaven Press, 2003.

Paul R. Pillar.*Terrorism and U.S. Foreign Policy*, Brookings Institution Press, 2001.

Philip B. Heymann. *Terrorism and America: A Commonsense Strategy for a Democratic Society*, MIT Press, 1998.

Sarah E. Mendelson. *Changing Course: Ideas, Politics, and the Soviet Withdrawal from Afghanistan*, Princeton University Press, 1998.

Walter Laquer.*The New Terrorism: Fanaticism and the Arms of Mass Destruction*, Oxford University Press, 1999 .

William Maley. *Fundamentalism Reborn? Afghanistan and the Taliban*, New York University Press, 1998.

Yossef Bodansky. Bin Laden: *The Man who Declared War on America*: Prima, 2001.

Index